World War I

World War I

S.L.A. Marshall

With an introduction by
David M. Kennedy

A MARINER BOOK
HOUGHTON MIFFLIN COMPANY
BOSTON • NEW YORK

First Mariner Books edition 2001

Introduction copyright © 2001 by David Kennedy
Copyright © 1964 and copyright © renewed 1992 by American
Heritage Inc.

Visit our Web site: www.houghtonmifflinbooks.com.

An American Heritage Book

Library of Congress Cataloging-in-Publication Data
Marshall, S.L.A. (Samuel Lyman Atwood), 1900–1977.
World War I
Includes index.
1. World War, 1914–1918. I. Title
D521.M412 1985   940.3   85-3968
ISBN 0-618-05686-6 (pbk.)

Printed in the United States of America

DOC   10

Contents

Introduction

"Two rounds from one pistol and the world rocked." With characteristic thrift and punch, S.L.A. Marshall opens his account of the events that triggered World War I. On June 28, 1914, the shots from a Serbian assassin's side arm in Sarajevo brought swift death to the Austrian archduke Francis Ferdinand and his wife, Sophie. They also heralded a protracted struggle whose astonishing gore and complexity pose daunting challenges to the historian. Few writers have risen to those challenges more artfully than S.L.A. Marshall.

World War I was a peculiarly modern affair. It was the first major contest of arms fought by large, centrally organized nation-states since the dawn of the Industrial Revolution. Germany, Austria-Hungary, and Italy were all creations of the mid-nineteenth century. (So, in a sense, was the United States, which had secured its national integrity only in the Civil War of 1861–1865.) In all of Europe, indeed in all the world, industrialization—the mechanized production of goods in enormous quantities, accompanied by an accelerating pace of technological innovation—was scarcely a century old in 1914. The nineteenth century had considered burgeoning nationhood and the galloping Industrial Revolution to be benign developments, reassuring emblems of history's progress. But the violence that erupted in the wake of those shots at Sarajevo unveiled the monstrous implications of nationalism and industrialism alike. To many who endured it, the war also made a cruel mockery of the idea of progress.

The sheer scale of the conflict proclaimed its historical uniqueness. The fighting engulfed all the principal states of the European continent as well as Britain, Turkey, and Japan; spread to the British, French, and German imperial domains in Africa, Asia, and the Pacific islands; raged on the high seas; sucked in colonial peoples from Australia and Indochina to India and Canada; and eventually obliged even the distant and isolationist United States to shoulder arms. Vast conscript armies took the field: 12 million Russians, 11 million Germans, nearly 8 million

Austro-Hungarians, more than 8 million Frenchmen and a like number of Britons, 5 million Italians, almost 3 million Turks, and 4 million Americans.

Yet to a degree that set it apart from all preceding conflicts, World War I did not turn only on the mustering and deployment of armed forces in the field. This was the first "total war," and its totality was perhaps the most important marker of its modernity. This war's novel logic blurred the distinction between civilians and combatants. The character of economies on the home-front—a revealing neologism that bespoke the enveloping dimensions of twentieth-century warfare—counted as much as the courage of troops of the line in determining the war's outcome.

The wages of modernity were apparent even in the war's opening days, as sophisticated transportation systems, of a sort unknown just a few decades earlier, moved enormous forces and their elaborate impedimenta with startling speed. In scarcely more than two weeks in August 1914, Marshall relates, the French railway system embarked 3,781,000 military personnel. German trains wheeled 2 million lavishly equipped men into the line in even less time. As Europe's industrial economies mobilized, modern factories poured forth munitions of war in stupefying quantities. Modern technology put unprecedentedly lethal arsenals at the military's disposal: artillery that could lob explosives from distances up to seventy-five miles, poison gas, airplanes, dreadnoughts, and submarines.

Most murderously efficient of all World War I weaponry was the machine gun, the emblematic military innovation of the age. A tool for industrial-strength killing, aptly described as "concentrated essence of infantry," the machine gun hugely amplified the firepower of stationary forces and thereby conferred nearly insuperable advantages on the defense. Its withering fire consumed attacking troops wholesale, forcing the fighting on the Western Front into a grisly deadlock. In the face of such awesome implements of slaughter, 10 million men perished; another 20 million were maimed. In time the machine-gun-bred stalemate of trench warfare compelled fundamental changes in both strategic and tactical doctrines, notably the advent of deep-penetration aerial bombing and of mechanized warfare organized around another invention spawned by World War I, the tank.

War, said the nineteenth-century Prussian general Karl von

Clausewitz, is "a political instrument, a continuation of political relations, a carrying out of the same by other means." World War I both confirmed and confounded Clausewitz's famous dictum. The scope of the conflict, and the speed with which it overwhelmed Europe in the weeks after the fateful fusillade in Sarajevo, owed much to the peculiar constellation of political tensions and alliances in 1914. But when the fighting endured beyond anyone's anticipation, it threatened to stand Clausewitz's formula on its head, as politics appeared to be turning into war by other means. The war came to seem no longer the instrument of statesmen but their implacable master. In the end it destroyed many of them, even while ushering new political forces, and new political personalities, onto history's stage. By 1918 the Russian czar had abdicated, replaced by a Bolshevik regime that confidently awaited the worldwide outbreak of Communist insurgencies among peoples made ripe for revolution by the war's apparently endless agonies. The new states of Poland, Czechoslovakia, and Yugoslavia tentatively emerged from the shattered Austro-Hungarian Empire. The German kaiser fled to Holland as a fragile republic struggled to arise from the wreckage of the Hohenzollern monarchy. Among the most impassioned antagonists of that fledgling republic, embittered beyond endurance by Germany's surrender, thirsting to avenge the fatherland's defeat, was a twice-decorated German soldier, Lance Corporal Adolf Hitler. Meanwhile, the swaggering firebrand Benito Mussolini was scheming to exploit Italy's seething postwar chaos and would soon introduce a new term into the world's political lexicon: fascism.

Small wonder that the conflict of 1914–1918 was also known, until overshadowed by the even broader conflagration that Hitler ignited just three decades later, as the Great War. If measured in terms of impact and consequences, World War I might in fact be judged to weigh even more heavily in the scales of history than World War II. For despite the greater bloodshed and destruction that it wrought, the second war did not so fearsomely demonstrate the bankruptcy of entrenched political institutions and ideas, nor so thoroughly discredit regnant cultural attitudes, nor — with the conspicuous exception of the atomic bombs — generate as much fundamental military innovation as did the first. The earlier war served in many significant ways as a rehearsal and prelude for what followed. The inconclusive peace treaty signed at Versailles was a compound disaster. It failed to lay to rest the issues that had caused the war, even while sowing the seeds for renewed conflict. For those reasons, some historians have suggested that the period from 1914 to 1945 might best be understood as the twentieth century's own Thirty Years' War, a thirty-one-year period, to be precise, in which the Great War forms but the first dramatic chapter.

The epic range and moment of World War I have drawn the attention of some remarkably gifted historians, from Winston Churchill and Basil H. Liddell Hart to A.J.P. Taylor and John Keegan. S.L.A. Marshall can take his rightful place in that distinguished company. Indeed, he brought some special assets of his own to the enterprise of making historical sense out of the Great War, and his account is unlike any other. Like Churchill and Liddell Hart, he had felt the war's fury himself, having seen action with the American Expeditionary Forces at Ypres, Soissons, Saint-Mihiel, and the Meuse-Argonne. Like Taylor and Keegan, he wrote with a cool, sometimes almost jaded, scholarly detachment. Unlike all those other authors, each of them British, he was an American—perhaps the only American who both served in World War I and undertook to compose a comprehensive history of it.

Some forty years elapsed between Marshall's participation in World War I and his decision to write about it. Those years afforded him time to season his memories, to absorb the rich body of literature about the war that had appeared in the interim, to form mature judgments and balanced historical perspectives, and to perfect his own writerly craft.

To that last pursuit he devoted himself with special ardor. Leaving the army in 1919 with a lieutenant's commission, a year shy of his twentieth birthday, Marshall spurned a college education and went to work for a newspaper in his boyhood hometown of El Paso, Texas. In 1927 he moved to Michigan to join the *Detroit News*. There he gained a national reputation, reporting, improbably enough, on polo matches as well as on Latin American military affairs. He covered the Spanish Civil War in 1936–37, and then in 1940 published his first book, *Blitzkrieg*, a timely and prophetic analysis of the tactics with which Hitler's *Wehrmacht* was then intimidating all Europe.

Blitzkrieg's success led to a fresh military commission, and when World War II began, Lieutenant Colonel Marshall found himself posted to the Pacific theater and charged with compiling reliable histories of the American campaigns against Japan in the Marshall and Gilbert Islands. There he developed the investigative technique that became his hallmark: the post-action interview with ordinary GIs, both individually and in groups. It was a method that reflected his experience as a journalist and his affinity, also born of personal experience, for the perspective of the frontline trooper. Transferred to the European theater in time for the Normandy landings in June 1944, Marshall continued to gather interviews. On the basis of that evidence he wrote *Men Against Fire* (1947), probably his most renowned and controversial book, which advanced the decidedly unsettling (and later disputed) claim that in a typical World War II firefight, more than seventy-five percent of American infantrymen never fired their weapons. *Men Against Fire* contributed heavily to a new approach in the writing of military history, one that supplemented the usual emphasis on high politics, strategy, logistics, and the recondite arts of generalship with an appreciation for the role of the common soldier. (It was an approach that John Keegan was to bring to a brilliant consummation some three decades later in *The Face of Battle*.) Marshall was called up again in the Korean War and used his trademark approach to produce several notable books, including *Pork Chop Hill*, which Hollywood adapted for film.

Marshall's own exposure to combat and his reportorial training deeply informed his writing of *World War I*. So did another product of his lengthy career as a military observer: his frequently acerbic appraisal of mankind's capacity for folly, martial folly in particular. The result is a grand magisterial history, leavened by the veteran newsman's instincts for telling detail, vivid characterization, and summary anecdote and a relish for unvarnished, frequently irreverent verdicts. Of the British field marshal Douglas Haig, "of the whiskey-making Haigs," he writes: "What is to be marked of his earlier career is that the rate of rise was in disproportion to the brilliance." Austrian foreign minister Count Leopold von Berchtold is "the deep-dyed villain of the 1914 summer's tragedy." As for Winston Churchill's histrionic pilgrimage to the front in 1915: "Rifle bullets were never afforded a better opportunity to thwart history." Even America's own beloved John J. Pershing is not exempt: "almost nothing has been handed down concerning him," Marshall writes, "that reflects deep military wisdom." Yet he also judges Pershing to have possessed "fundamental qualities that went far in the shaping of an army — patience, sobriety, emotional balance, and an unshakable fortitude." Balance indeed.

Marshall neglects no part of the war's tangled story. He is above all a military historian, but readers of *World War I* will find probing, cogent discussions of imperial courts, parliamentary politics, diplomacy, and economics, as well as strategy, tactics, and weapons. His opening chapter on the complex political geometry of prewar Europe is a small masterpiece of concision and clarity, as well as a searching rumination on the capacity of inertial momentum in bureaucratic systems to swamp individual human judgment. His discussion of the industrial capacities of the various belligerents deftly foreshadows their respective fates on the battlefield. His dissection of master plans such as those devised by Schlieffen, Hindenburg, Ludendorff, Falkenhayn, Joffre, Foch, Kitchener, Haig, and Pershing is consistently trenchant. He speaks with incomparable authority about the performance characteristics of the French 75-mm. gun, various German howitzers, and the fabled "Austrian 88," the supreme achievement of the Czech Skoda armament factories. And he brings his narrative to a rounded conclusion with a brief but thoughtful analysis of the peace negotiations at Paris, Woodrow Wilson's failed effort to secure the Senate's ratification of the Versailles Treaty in 1919, and the birth of the Nazi Party. Throughout, his impressive command of narrative technique gives the reader a clear understanding of the simultaneity, and hence the connectedness, of events ranging from the killing-grounds of Gallipoli, Passchendaele, Verdun, and Tannenberg to the chancelleries of Berlin, Vienna, Paris, London, and St. Petersburg.

But Marshall's distinctive strength as a historian is his deep understanding of small-unit action and particularly the combat role of the citizen at arms, the common man swept up in the great maelstrom and struggling to do his duty and stay alive. Few writers about this or any other war have conveyed a better feel for the importance of terrain, the way that the peculiar geography of each combat encounter shaped its evolution and its outcome. Marshall sets his battle scenes with panoramic overviews, replete with detail on commanders, geography, strategy, and political context, then cinematographically pans to the ground-level view of the tommy, the poilu, or the doughboy—especially the doughboy.

Most British and European writers about World War I respectfully (or ruefully) acknowledge the American contribution to the eventual Allied victory but display no substantial interest in the details. Virtually alone among general histories of the war, Marshall's *World War I* gives generous coverage to the American engagements—not only the battles he himself had seen, but the full range of action, including Château-Thierry and Belleau Wood. The result is a history that is especially instructive to American readers about the implications for their country of those two shots that rocked the world in the summer of 1914.

DAVID M. KENNEDY
Stanford, California
December 2000

World War I

I
When the Lights Went Out

Archduke Francis Ferdinand and his wife
Sophie (far right) were photographed in
Sarajevo just before their assassination,
which sparked four years of world war.

In the Bosnian town of Sarajevo on the morning of June 28, 1914, a chauffeur misunderstood his instructions, made the wrong turn, tried too late to correct his blunder, and so doing delivered his passengers to a point where a waiting assassin did not have to take aim to gun them down.

Two rounds from one pistol and the world rocked. The crime was the small stone that, loosened, brings the avalanche. There followed four years of universal violence. Millions met untimely death. Many mistaken instructions, wrong turnings, and belated tries to redress error went into the making of World War I. The ambush of an Austrian couple was the precipitating incident.

This book is about that crime and what came from it. It tells why the killers killed and how it happened that the tragedy did not end there. The players and the performance at Sarajevo are the beginning of the tale to be unfolded. Intrigue, violence, and death color the scene. They also mark the larger story to the finish. But for murder at Sarajevo there might never have been a war. Men can speculate to the contrary. They cannot know.

So to begin. Seven young Serbian nationalists formed the murder mob. They were a carpenter, a printer, a teacher, and four students. Five were under twenty; the elder of the other two was twenty-seven. This was their first and only venture together in crime.

Their arrangements were so haphazard, their skill with weapons so little, that the plot should have failed. They were armed with Belgian pistols, crude hand bombs, and cyanide capsules, the last for suicide. Under a burning sun in midmorning they parted, walked through flag-bedecked streets and holiday crowds, and took up separate positions along a street called the Appel Quay, flanking the Miljačka River. It was a gala morning, for Sarajevo was celebrating the Feast of Saint Vitus, the symbol of Serbian resurrection and victory over the Turks. To the seven young conspirators, it was the right day for a good deed.

So they awaited their target, the Archduke Francis Ferdinand. Their motives in seeking the death of the heir apparent of Austria-Hungary were as bizarre, contradictory, and rooted in personal emotion as were his reasons for affording them the opportunity. The Archduke was not personally an oppressor of their people, the southern Slavs, and had actually tried to play their friend.

The Serbs and Croats in Austria's southern provinces of Bosnia and Herzegovina were not abused and maltreated under the empire. By the standards of the day, they lived well.

The seven assassins were not bent on bringing down Austria-Hungary's Dual Monarchy, which, with its many faults, still afforded Central Europe a better life than its various peoples had ever known separately. They went gunning for the Archduke because they wanted a bigger place in the sun for Serbia, and he kept the rendezvous because he wanted a bigger place in the sun for his wife.

June 28 was a special day for the Archduke and his wife: their fourteenth wedding anniversary. She had been Countess Sophie Chotek, child of a noble but obscure Czech family, lady in waiting to the Archduke's cousin, Isabella. Old Emperor Francis Joseph was so offended by his nephew's choice of a mate beneath his station that the two wrangled about the marriage for one year. When at last the Emperor consented, Francis Ferdinand got only half of what he wanted. He was compelled to renounce the rights of succession and rank for his children, taking Sophie as a morganatic wife. The marriage proved to be a great love affair, blessed by three children. But the humiliation and bitterness lasted, the more so because the court in Vienna snubbed Sophie and did what it could to cut her dignity. She could not ride in the royal carriage with her husband or sit in the royal box at the theatre. At court balls, where he led the procession, she was placed behind the last princess of royal blood.

Gradually the old Emperor softened toward Sophie, but Francis Ferdinand could never forgive the court. Such sentiment was not in him. Swollen with pride, dangerously thin-skinned, a misanthrope, religious bigot, and miser, he was the loneliest man in Vienna, loved only by his wife and children. There was no moderation in him; his humors and rages were those of a spoiled child. No worthwhile subordinate could abide him for very long. His career was littered with broken friendships, ruined by his venomous temper and petty spite. Not addicted to small vices, he showed his love of excess in more lordly ways. By the age of thirty-three he had shot his thousandth stag; by forty-six he had bagged five thousand. In Sarajevo, at the age of fifty-one, the hunter became the hunted.

Francis Ferdinand's love for Sophie and his desire that she should have special honor on her wedding anniversary took him to Sarajevo. Two corps of the Austrian Army, regularly stationed in Bosnia, were holding their annual maneuvers next to the border with Serbia, Austria's tiny neighbor. The Archduke was the Inspector General of the Army and it was his duty to go. But he prearranged the meeting with Sophie in Sarajevo because in that company on that day she would have to be treated with royal honors.

There were political overtones to the visit transcending these personal considerations. Prewar Austria-Hungary was a loose linking of two empires run by strong races, the Germans and the Magyars. There were large, submerged Slav minorities in both countries, the Czechs and Slovaks in the north, the Serbs and Croats in the south. The Hapsburgs, who were the feudal German overlords of this weird amalgam of mutually distrustful peoples, had their greatest difficulties with the largest and proudest of the blocs, the Hungarians. They therefore inclined to favor certain of their Slav subjects in order to offset the power and influence of their strongest vassal. Francis Ferdinand was an extreme champion of this policy. Further, he nursed the false conceit that since he had married a northern Slav he was viewed with extra grace by the southern Slavs.

The people of Serbia viewed Francis Ferdinand as a threat to all they coveted, simply because he advocated "Trialism," or triple reorganization of the empire in place of the existing "Dualism." He was credited with believing that giving the Slavs an equal voice with Germans and Magyars was the way to regenerate the empire. Right or wrong, the suspicion in the Serbian mind doomed him at the Serbian hand. Should he rule and have his way, there could never rise a Greater Serbia. So Serbian nationalists had to cast him as the blackest of villains.

Bosnia and the sister province of Herzegovina were at the core of this scheming and striving. Although their populations were mainly Serb and Croat, Vienna had administered them since 1878, when the Turks had been expelled. But juridically the two provinces had remained Turkish until 1908, when they were annexed to the Dual Monarchy. While the Great Powers took this high-handed act quite calmly, it outraged the Serbians. The southern provinces became a hotbed of subversion, and anti-Hapsburg propaganda flowed out of Belgrade, Serbia's capital.

Vienna kept looking for ways to soothe and placate its southern subjects. That was one of the objects when the Archduke and his wife went riding in Sarajevo on June 28.

A cleaner pack of assassins than the seven young men staked out along their route could hardly be imagined. Only one had a police record, and that for striking his teacher. All were temperate: several had never touched liquor. There was not a gambler among them and all were free of personal debts. They had one other thing in common: all were ill with tuberculosis. Fever does color the view, and in their case it probably made them more ready to die early, and, as they thought, heroically.

There were four cars in the procession that rolled through the unguarded streets. Francis Ferdinand and Sophie rode in the second car. Although there were thousands of troops in the vicinity, and they might have been used to secure the route, by the Archduke's order Sarajevo had been put off limits to them for one day.

At the Čumuria Bridge the motorcade passed the first conspirator, Mohammed Mehmedbašić. He froze and later offered the excuse that he didn't use his bomb because a policeman got in the way. Standing a few paces from Mehmedbašić was the second conspirator, Nedjelko Čabrinović. He took careful aim at the green feathers on Francis Ferdinand's military helmet and heaved his bomb.

In that instant the royal car acccelerated. The bomb passed behind Sophie's back. Raising his arm to protect his wife, the Archduke with that motion deflected the bomb into the street. A flying splinter hit Sophie in the face. Other splinters wounded Count Boos-Waldeck, who rode in the third car, as well as Colonel Erik von Merizzi and Countess Lanjus, Sophie's attendant. A dozen or so spectators were hit. The Archduke kept silent, lest he frighten Sophie more. Čabrinović swallowed his capsule of cyanide and dived into the Miljačka. The cyanide merely made him retch and the river was only a few inches deep.

The first two cars sped on toward the City Hall, shooting past three more of the assassins, Vasco Čubrilović, Cvijetko Popović, and Danilo Ilić, who did nothing. In the lead vehicle rode the Sarajevo burgomaster, Fehim Effendi Curcić. He had missed the explosion in the roar of the crowd, and his mind stayed on his speech of welcome.

On dismounting, Francis Ferdinand was livid with rage. He

grabbed Curcić's arm and shouted: "One comes here for a visit and is received with bombs. Mr. Mayor, what do you say? It's outrageous. All right, now you may speak."

Curcić still didn't understand. So he began reading: "Our hearts are filled with happiness—" Nothing that followed indicated that his heart also had room for regret over the bomb or joy over the escape. Now in control of himself, Francis Ferdinand responded like a prince, smiling as he closed with the words "I assure you of my unchanged regard and favor." Next, he got off a wire to the Emperor, assuring him that he was unhurt. There was a discussion about whether to continue with the day's program. General Oskar Potiorek, the Military Governor, favored it, speculating that another attack was unlikely. The Archduke overruled him on a point of duty: he must go to the hospital to see how the bomb victims were faring.

But he begged Sophie not to share the risk. She replied: "No, I must go with you." At the Imperial Bridge, just beyond the City Hall, the motorcade passed directly by Trifko Grabež, the sixth assassin. He did not make a move. The Archduke's chauffeur simply followed the mayor's car. At the next intersection, where both cars should have taken the Appel Quay to the hospital, they made a right turn into Francis Joseph Street. Potiorek, who was riding with the Archduke, cried: "What's this? We've taken the wrong way!"

The driver braked and stopped, preparatory to turning. That move put the party at a standstill within five feet of Gavrilo Princip, the seventh and most resolute of the assassins. He drew and fired instantly and the pistol snapped twice, with as little noise as if it had fired blanks.

One bullet struck Francis Ferdinand in the neck. The other hit Sophie in the abdomen. Potiorek looked at them and judged that they were both unhurt. They sat upright, looking calmly ahead. So Potiorek directed the chauffeur to return the way they had come.

As the car picked up speed a stream of blood shot from the Archduke's mouth. Sophie cried: "For heaven's sake, what's happened to you?" then crumpled in a heap. Thinking only that she had fainted from shock, Potiorek tried to lift her. Some instinct told her dying husband that the truth was more dreadful. He cried: "Sophie dear, Sophie dear, don't die! Stay alive for our children!" He then sagged, and when asked if he was suffering, whispered: "*Es ist nichts*"(It is nothing), several times. Those were his last words. Sophie was dead before they could get her from the car. Francis Ferdinand soon followed her. By 11:00 A.M. the drama of Sarajevo was over.

Princip tried to turn his pistol on himself. It was knocked down by a spectator. Then the crowd closed in and roughed him. Still he managed to swallow the cyanide capsule, which merely made him vomit. In this way, the pistol and poison failed both the killer and the world. Had Princip and Čabrinović died, they couldn't have talked, the conspirators might not have been rounded up, and Vienna might not have made a halfway case against Serbia, which served mainly to stir world sympathy for that country. All things conspired to mock mankind by making mountainous the deed that the dying Archduke had called nothing.

Emperor Francis Joseph received the news that night in Ischl, where he was on vacation. His chief aide, General Count Paar, told him. For some ninutes the old man sat silent and motionless with his eyes closed, as if he were stricken. Then he said to Paar: "Terrible! The Almighty cannot be provoked!" A pause followed while Paar wondered about the ambiguity. Then the Emperor said: "A Higher Power has restored that order which unfortunately I was unable to maintain."

That was the first view—thanks to the assassins, something had been gained by the House of Hapsburg. There was no feeling of outrage against the killers, no outcry against Serbia, no premonition that the Dual Monarchy faced great peril. It was a local incident, a family problem to be solved by a double funeral. The Emperor could not imagine the major nations of Europe would shortly be destroying their wealth and their manhood because of the carelessness of his own nephew in getting shot.

Kaiser Wilhelm II of Germany was yachting at Kiel. A launch sped toward the royal yacht. Aboard it, an admiral held high a piece of paper, folded it into a cigarette case, and tossed it toward the royal party. Opening the case and reading the paper, Wilhelm got his first news of the double murder. According to onlookers, he turned pale, but did not foresee that the crime would convulse Europe.

At first, that was how it went everywhere. Although the crime was sensationally shocking, those who read and talked of it did

12

not tremble for themselves. As to what it signified or portended, kings were no wiser than peasants. None of the Great Powers wanted a European war to the finish. Their rulers and ministers knew it would be calamitous. Their peoples were not yearning for an oportunity to kill and be killed. Nevertheless, the war came. The unthinkable happened because in each of the great states, leaders did certain things that inflamed the crisis, or failed to do things that might have eased it. All shared in some degree the responsibility for the general failure.

But it was not a case of the great figures of the time, in Vienna, Berlin, Paris, London, or Saint Petersburg, suddenly veering from the high road into wasteland and thereby betraying their peoples. Europe had long been spoiling for what came to it. Its governments and races did not hate one another. They merely ranged emotionally in different orbits and they did not strive sufficiently to guard against the likelihood of collision.

No treatment of World War I is ever complete. Least of all is it possible to fix precisely the blame for the disaster. To get a European war in motion required millions of people ready to fight. Part of the story can be told in black and white. Austria was more responsible for the war's outbreak than any other Great Power. There can be no such positiveness about the underlying causes that through the years had been moving Europe to the brink. To know more about how governments and men were carried over it, we must look at Europe's explosive situation prior to the crime, we must regard how the crime was investigated, and we must see how crowned heads, statesmen, and soldiers fumbled and blundered before and after Sarajevo, thereby infinitely compounding what should have been a small family tragedy.

Seeds of Conflict

Historians analyzing the causes of World War I generally choose the year 1870 as a conveniently limiting starting point. In that year, the Germans humiliated the French Army in a lightning campaign, took Emperor Napoleon III prisoner, and crushed France's Second Empire. Out of a welter of blood were born the German Empire and the French Third Republic.

Having provoked the 1870 war, France deserved ignoble defeat. She got it. The Germans were remorseless. Besides a huge in-

Central Europe in 1914 was dominated by the empires of Germany and Austria-Hungary, which, together with Bulgaria and Turkey, formed the Central Powers (black) of World War I. Allied

ESTONIA
LIVONIA
KURLAND
LITHUANIA

*ALTIC
SEA*

EAST
PRUSSIA

POLAND

**PREWAR
EUROPE**

RUSSIA

N

UKRAINE

—HUNGARY

RUMANIA

SERBIA

BULGARIA

BLACK SEA

—GRO—

—BANIA—

TURKEY

GREECE

Cyprus

cale

200   300 Miles   Crete

and associated countries, banded together against the Central
Powers, are shown in white; neutrals, in dark gray.

demnity, they wrested from France the northeast provinces of Alsace and Lorraine. Over the strong objection of Prince Bismarck, the Chancellor, the German military compelled the annexation. Bismarck was fearful that the French would never forgive it. The soldiers who made the demand were willing to take that chance. Said Field Marshal Helmuth von Moltke, who commanded the army: "What our sword has won in half a year our sword must guard for half a century." He was right—but German arms were not given quite that much time.

Germany's seizure at gunpoint of the two French provinces need not have been fatal to the peace of Europe. Before and since, territory more extensive and valuable than Alsace-Lorraine has changed hands in war without the losing state feeling intolerably affronted. In this instance, other factors aggravated the injury. European industry was expanding phenomenally, intensifying trade competition and the fight for markets abroad. In France, the birth rate was falling, in Germany it kept rising. Already outnumbered, France was bound to feel alarm.

Bismarck used the 1870 war and the victory to consolidate Germany. On January 18, 1871, Wilhelm I of Prussia was proclaimed Emperor of Germany in the Hall of Mirrors at Versailles. What had been a loose grouping of provincially minded states rapidly coalesced as the most powerful nation in Europe, dominated by warlike Prussia. Bismarck said to some of his friends: "I am bored. The great things are done. The German Reich is made."

France came out of the war demoralized, bankrupt, and seemingly ruined. Yet her recovery was prodigiously swift. Well ahead of schedule, the reparations bill was paid. By mid-1873 the last German soldier had been withdrawn from occupation duty. French industry boomed and trade flourished as if energized by hitherto untapped sources of national vigor. When Paris staged an international exposition in 1878, visitors saw a France that was again materially and spiritually robust.

Having escaped the blast of criticism following the 1870 debacle, the French Army wasted no time in self-recrimination. Defeated generals are prone to blame their failures on the parsimony and meddling of the politicians; this is fair enough, since beaten monarchs and ministers do not voluntarily make scapegoats of themselves. As it happened in France, the politicians were cast out and most of the generals stayed. Their new civilian superiors knew too little about their sins to discredit them.

The army got its share of the new prosperity. Officer pay was increasing for the first time in a century. Sweeping military reforms were voted and financed by the government. But the initiative came from the army, which was determined to overtake Germany's lead in fighting power.

By 1885 France had adjusted itself, though somewhat uneasily, to the system of republican government that would serve Frenchmen until the surrender to Germany in 1940. The army in that relatively brief span had become truly formidable. Many storms would beat around it in the years immediately ahead; it would lose public favor and prestige, due mainly to its own intrigues, carelessness, and the arrogance of its high command. But the plateau of strength once gained was thereafter held. That happened because the nation was more fearful of German might than of French militarism. The army's mission and the volatile nature of French politics both kept it sacrosanct. During the first eighteen years, while the army reformed and expanded, nineteen governments rose and fell and sixteen war ministers came and went. Ministerial instability prevented effective opposition to army programs.

In its military reforms France copied Germany. As the first step, the National Assembly in July, 1872, passed a law embodying the principle of universal service. Initially, the conscript was required to serve a full five years; the enlistment term was later cut to three, which most soldiers agree is the more practical figure. To raise the intellectual level of the officer corps, the Ecole Supérieure de Guerre, or staff college, was created in 1875. This was the true beginning of a French General Staff based on the Prussian model. Spaces were established for three hundred General Staff officers. Finally, the Etat-Major de l'Armée was formed to regulate training during peace and to plan mobilization. In war, it would take the field, becoming the high command over groups of armies. Such was the beginning of the Grand Quartier Général, or G.Q.G., an innovation that the world would little note until it became famous in 1914 as the entourage around General Joseph Jacques Césaire Joffre.

Weapons changes followed these army reforms of structure. The first model Lebel rifle was adopted; French soldiers carried the same piece, somewhat modified, in 1914. A superior explosive, lyddite, replaced black powder as a filling for shells. Artillery organization was greatly improved, the General Staff specifying what gun calibers and numbers would be needed to beat Germany.

Noting how France was rearming, Germany began to worry. Bismarck had a saying: "A generation that has taken a beating is always followed by a generation that deals one." While the words are more trite than true, he must have believed them. So for a time he toyed with the idea of waging a preventive war to stop France before Germany could be hurt. But there was no good cause, and Bismarck himself had mellowed with the years.

THE ALLIANCES

The division of Europe into two armed camps took place by slow stages over a period of nearly forty years. It started with the 1879 alliance between Germany and Austria-Hungary, a partnership that, regularly renewed, remained in force until 1918 and was the cornerstone of the Central Powers. Bismarck's motives in negotiating the alliance cannot be defined with precision.

By 1879 Bismarck was satisfied with Germany's boundaries; his policy aimed not at expansion but at consolidation, and he wished to shape a protecting shell for his creation, the German Empire. Historians claim that he was alarmed at the attitude of France or that he wished to snub the Russia of Czar Alexander III. Neither claim is wholly credible. Witness that in 1879 France's military recovery was just begun; note also that two years later Wilhelm I and Francis Joseph joined Alexander III in signing the Alliance of the Three Emperors. "Bismarck always loved balance," his biographer A. J. P. Taylor wrote. "He never committed himself irrevocably to any course. His alliances often led to wars; and his wars were the prelude to alliances."

There are indications that the German Court was troubled about that same cycle. Bismarck had great difficulty winning approval for the alliance with Austria. Wilhelm I didn't like it; several ministers were strongly opposed. For many days the treaty lay on Wilhelm's desk with only the signature of Emperor Francis Joseph affixed. Reflecting on old battles and the benevolent neutrality extended by the Czar during the wars of 1864, 1866, and 1870, Wilhelm I was loath to offend the Russia that had stood by

Prussia. When at last he signed, he said bitterly: "Thinking of what it means I feel like a traitor."

At first the rest of Europe reacted indifferently to the arrangement. Three years later, in 1882, Italy joined the two Central Powers in the Triple Alliance. Austria's object was to avoid a double collision, should there be war with Russia. Italy, a fledgling state, wanted assistance if she were attacked by France. Since these obligations were not only secret but tissue thin in any case, there was still no jar to the other powers.

Another six years passed with no sign that the alliances had put Europe, irrevocably as it proved, on a deadly course. Then, within three years, occurred the events that made the pivotal change. Rapidly thereafter the Continent, blessed with the most mature society, took form as an overarmed camp divided against itself.

As 1888 opened, the aged Wilhelm I, a steady monarch, was ailing, but Prince Bismarck still held power as Chancellor. Frederick, the Crown Prince and heir apparent, was also bedridden and incurably stricken with cancer of the throat. His eldest son, Wilhelm, so plagued the invalid father, bedeviling him to waive his rights to the throne, that even the Crown Princess had to protest the "heartlessness, rudeness, and cruelty" of her eldest.

Modern psychiatry might find some excuse for the second Wilhelm. He was aged two when his grandfather became King of Prussia, aged twelve when Wilhelm I was made German Emperor at Versailles. Born with a withered left arm, he was reared in the shadow of his hero-Emperor grandsire and told by everyone that he must be a warrior to prove worthy of him. It was a terrible burden for a small boy, who also, it has been written, grew up unloved by his mother. His early life is of passing interest only as it bears on his behavior as ruler of Germany. Writers have described him variously as a dangerous paranoiac, an incurable megalomaniac, or an egotistical simpleton. It suffices to say that he was not a good risk.

On March 9, 1888, Wilhelm I died. From Berlin, one diplomat cabled a friend: "Lord abide with us for the evening draws nigh." There followed a brief interlude in which Frederick III had the crown but could not rule; he was in a coma for ninety-nine days. The Empress Victoria, daughter of Queen Victoria of England, escorted visitors to the side of the dying monarch. He made no sign except occasionally to point a finger toward heaven.

Wilhelm II mounted the throne in midyear. Alexander III of Russia soon let it be known that he detested Germany's new ruler because of his "aggressive amiability." But for Europe that was one of the lesser sensations in a rather frenzied summer. France had spun into a nationalistic-monarchistic convulsion, due to the strutting of her new tin-plate hero, General Georges Ernest Jean Marie Boulanger. The fever that hit France also gripped Russian nationalists, who sent Boulanger a sword with the Cossack inscription: "Dare! God helps the bold!"

Berlin became worried. There was renewed talk at court about staging a preventive war against France. It receded as quickly as did the passion of France when her hero, Boulanger, suddenly fled the scene in April, 1889, leaving his followers deflated. Bismarck stood steady, convinced that his earlier handiwork had destined France to remain in a political isolation ward.

But in March, 1980, Wilhelm II dismissed Bismarck. There are many explanations given for his "dropping of the pilot." Under the influence of his own favorite, Count Alfred von Waldersee, Wilhelm, while still a prince, had insulted the Iron Chancellor, accusing him of closing his eyes to the danger threatening Germany from Russia. Prince Bernhard von Bülow, who some years later became Chancellor, wrote: "The authentic reason was that Wilhelm wanted to play Bismarck himself." Be that as it may, few Germans protested or voiced regrets.

Waldersee, a man with a mind of his own, a strong will, and a flashing personality, had already been designated Army Chief of the General Staff. A German contemporary described him as "excessively ambitious, both on the military and political sides, and inclined to intrigues." In line with Bülow's theory of how Wilhelm intended to rule, it does not seem odd that he chose for Chancellor a colorless, better disciplined, less precocious soldier, General Leo von Caprivi. One immediate consequence of the change was the German refusal to renew the Russian Reinsurance Treaty, which had replaced the Alliance of the Three Emperors in 1887. Caprivi explained: "Bismarck was able to juggle with three balls but I can only juggle with two." Alexander III, on hearing the news, said that against his own convictions, he would have to seek an alliance with republican France.

Waldersee's tour at the top was brief and dismal. Late in 1890 army maneuvers were held in Silesia. Wilhelm insisted on commanding one of the field armies. As Chief of Staff, Waldersee presided at the postmaneuver critique. In front of the assembly he said to Wilhelm: "The plan had many traps and Your Majesty fell into every one of them." Shortly after, Wilhelm relieved him, saying: "In war I will be Chief of Staff; in peace the Chief of Staff is but one of my secretaries; you are too old for that."

Waldersee smiled, and then commented: "My successor, Schlieffen, is but one year younger." On that note, the man nicknamed the Fox made his exit. But he left his mark on the German Army while lengthening its shadow across Europe. Prior to Waldersee, compulsory service in Germany had many loopholes and exemptions. Waldersee gave Germany true universal service, every able-bodied young male being required to do military duty for three years. Further, he reorganized the General Staff on modern lines. His tragic failure was that he could not restrain Wilhelm's saber-rattling and martial strutting and that, when he attempted to curb it, he lost out. The Kaiser's image over Europe, at once comic and frightening, did more to spread alarm than the total of German armament programs. Having been warned by Waldersee's fall, Count Alfred Von Schlieffen thereafter merely humored Wilhelm's mailed-fist antics.

In August, 1891, Russia and France agreed to consult if either party were menaced by aggression. Seventeen months later, in January, 1893, the partners also bound themselves to mobilize together should any member of the Triple Alliance (Germany, Austria-Hungary, and Italy) first take that step.

Speaking for France, General Boisdeffre had difficulty in explaining to the Czar: "Mobilization means declaration of war." That the statement was exaggerated made it all the more baneful. It was exactly the spreading of this idea through Europe—that mobilization made war inescapable—that presaged catastrophe. Myth became fact when it generated war planning that allowed no instant of pause. War *had* to come of mobilization.

After the signing of the Franco-Russian agreements, Europe's design against itself simply tightened. Each power's protective armor became its chains. The web of entangling alliances might have been broken. No nation truly tried. Once Russia swung to its side, France bristled with new confidence. Seeing too late that

A spry octogenarian, Emperor Francis Joseph
takes a brisk walk in his royal gardens
in 1914, the sixty-sixth year of his reign.
Although he ruled until his death two years
after the onset of the war, he had long
ago turned away from his empire's problems
and, save for a small band of loyal followers,
died a lonely man.

he had blundered, Wilhelm tried to patch things up with Alexander III. The Russians spurned the German overture.

From 1890 until 1914, various incidents that threatened war arose between the Great Powers, the greater number being connected with strategy in the Mediterranean area. There was never a mobilization. Each crisis was resolved with lip service to conciliation and a further diminution of mutual good will. Throughout Britain's long struggle with the Boers in South Africa, German imperial sympathy was blatantly aligned with Britain's enemy, as for that matter was most public sentiment in Europe.

A still greater strain on Britain's policy of nonalignment was Wilhelm's determination to build the German Navy to a position of challenging strength. The fleet was a wonderful toy. On every ship Wilhelm had his now royal stateroom, the walls adorned with portraits of his kinsmen and court favorites. The formidable shape and threat of that navy began to impress Britain right after the turn of the century. Then, in a flamboyant speech at Reval in 1904, Wilhelm styled himself the Admiral of the Atlantic. Englishmen began to ask what use Germany had for such a navy other than to break England's sea power.

In 1904 the United Kingdom became semiattached to the Franco-Russian combine by an *entente cordiale* with France. Nothing more concrete was affirmed on paper until November 22, 1912, and then the two governments agreed only that if the general peace were threatened, or if either one had reason to fear an unprovoked attack, they would consult and decide what to do. So fragile was this tie that from the beginning it appeared to promise nothing of great consequence.

During the years of which we speak, the armies of the Great Powers knew varying fortunes, only those of France and Germany staying nonengaged. The British, after thoroughly muddling the show in South Africa at the beginning, at long last redeemed themselves with a victory over the Boers. In 1904–5 the Russians fought the Japanese in Manchuria and Korea, only to humiliate themselves by demonstrating that their weapons were inferior, their troops poorly trained, and their leaders unfit. The French Army, which after 1871 attained for a while to that estate, unique in a democracy, where no politician dared attack it, became buffeted by various scandals, such as the prolonged Dreyfus affair. Even so, it suffered very little. A graph of its fortunes covering the years 1871–1914 would show that the trend was upward and onward. By 1905 the French Army was well within control of a relatively young group of reformers espousing a training doctrine called the School of the Attack. They were a little more than half right, which wasn't enough, and their views were to cost France dearly. The Germans continued to train hard. Soldiers of the Dual Monarchy, their ally, tried to do so according to their lights, which burned not too brightly.

The ups and downs of armies, diplomatic crises, the braying of Wilhelm II, the small wars in the Balkans—all are related in some degree to what eventuated for Europe. Each of these subjects has a large place in a history devoted primarily to analyzing the causes of World War I. Here we are concerned mainly with the circumstances that put the Great Power crisis—once it became manifest—beyond solution by reasonable and peace-minded men. Europe was ensnared by the alliances that nations, of their own choice, had entered, each one wishfully believing that it had taken a step to insure its own future well-being.

INQUEST AT SARAJEVO

On the morning after the crime in Sarajevo mobs of Croats and Moslems rioted against the city's Serbs, smashing their homes, business places, clubs, and schoolhouses. One man was killed; fifty other persons were wounded. Within four hours the storm subsided.

Nothing in the immediate aftermath suggested that there was any great violence to come. Governments went through the usual motions. King George V ordered seven days' mourning by the British Court. Czar Nicholas II of Russia outdid him, making it twelve days. President Woodrow Wilson of the United States cabled official sympathy. But few persons, high or low, truly mourned for Francis Ferdinand. Due to his controversial activities, he was considered expendable. In a typical reaction, the British Ambassador to Rome reported to London that "People generally regard the elimination of the late Archduke as almost providential." Right at Sarajevo occurred the first sign that Austria might turn the other cheek. Over the objections of Potiorek, Finance Minister Leon Von Bilinski directed that Government funds be used to compensate Serbs for property damaged during the riots.

Under police questioning, Princip and Čabrinović, both of whom had been instantly seized, at first kept faith with their friends. Then Danilo Ilić, jailed by pure chance in a roundup of suspected subversives, volunteered to tell all about the conspiracy if he were promised that his life would be spared. When this one frightened man broke, so did the prospect that the danger to the world could be contained. Three other conspirators were arrested by July 5. Only Mehmedbašić escaped.

Yet with six conspirators to work over, the authorities bumbled, missing the most sinister portions of the evidence. No affair of such gravity was ever more mismanaged than this investigation. The standard of government within the Dual Monarchy has been described as "absolutism mitigated by sloppiness." It fits the handling of the affair. Taking no part in the inquiry, Vienna left it to a petty police judge in Sarajevo, who knew as little about such work as the average village coroner. Judge Leo Pfeffer proceeded as causally as if he were holding an inquest on a neighborhood dog-poisoning. At the pace of a tortoise, following no system, he interrogated the prisoners individually through that hot July while time ran out. The conspirators continued to shift their stories in a manner best calculated to confuse him and kept in touch with one another by rapping coded messages on the jail walls. Many promising leads appeared in their statements, but Pfeffer did not follow them up.

By the end, Pfeffer still did not know that the conspirators were the instruments of a Greater Serbia terror society called the Black Hand. Originally that secret society had been linked to, and encouraged by, the War Ministry in Belgrade. When friction later developed between the two, the Government still remained well informed on Black Hand operations. Pfeffer did learn that the bombs, pistols, and cyanide were brought into Sarajevo from Serbia; also, he established that the weapons had been supplied to the conspirators by a secondary figure in the Belgrade Black Hand, one Milan Ciganović. But beyond that he did not go. No proof was adduced that showed higher-up complicity in the murders, either by direct instigation by persons acting for government or guilty knowledge. When a Vienna bureaucrat, Friedrich von Wiesner, at last went to Sarajevo to see what had been uncovered, he felt compelled to wire home: "There is nothing to indicate that the Serbian Government knew about the plot."

25

Yet, in arming the conspirators so that they could kill Francis Ferdinand, Ciganović had been acting for Colonel Dragutin Dimitrievič, nicknamed Apis, the Bee. This Chief of Intelligence of the Serbian Army held membership card No. 6 in the Black Hand. Furthermore, at some time around June 1, Serbian Prime Minister Nikola Pašić had gotten wind of the plot, and had sent out secret orders that the conspirators Princip, Grabež, and Čabrinović should be intercepted at the frontier. When that cast failed, and Pašić knew that the plot was on, he still did not come clean with Vienna, or do anything to bring the mob into custody. Instead, he decided to warn Vienna through his own ambassador there, Jovan Jovanović, who being a radical pan-Serb was cold to the mission. All he did was visit Finance Minister Bilinski and suggest that the Archduke would be ill-advised to attend the maneuvers, since "some young Serb might put a live rather than a blank cartridge in his gun, and fire it." Bilinski thought Jovanović was trying to be kind. In any event, it was none of his business. So Bilinski dismissed Jovanović with the words, "Let us hope nothing happens," and forgot about it.

Most of these facts came to light long afterward. Austria-Hungary indeed had a tremendous grievance against Serbia. There was a heavy burden of guilt on some members of the Belgrade Government. But little of this became known during that fateful July. As the crisis intensified, world sympathy swelled for poor little put-upon Serbia. Except for Germany, there was almost none for her antagonist, the giant Dual Monarchy, bullying and belligerent.

Count Berchtold's Folly

In the week after the Sarajevo murders, while most European capitals knew a normal calm, scenting no major crisis out of the Bosnian incident, Belgrade and Vienna tensed. To soothe Austria, and damp the popular emotion, the Serbian Government forbade public assemblies, closing all dance halls and theatres. But it made no move to censor a national press that raged against Austria, praised the deed at Sarajevo, and otherwise incited war fever. Austrian newspapers were no less violent. But in their tone they echoed the Government. On the same day Ilić confessed, the Austrian Chargé d'Affaires in Belgrade, Wilhelm Ritter von

Storck, wired Vienna: "Serbia must learn to fear us again. Otherwise, our old border regions, and not just the annexed provinces, will be in danger." Vienna had no need of this advice.

Count Leopold von Berchtold, the Austrian Foreign Minister, already favored sending a punitive column straight into Belgrade. Such warlike counsel has seldom come from a less becoming source. Regard him well, for Berchtold, not Wilhelm II, is the deep-dyed villain of the 1914 summer's tragedy.

Other principals, by their gross blunders or failure to act, contributed to the ruin. Berchtold is unique. He betrayed the peace deliberately by lying, deceiving, double-dealing, and committing folly unequaled. Berchtold was a dilettante, a snob and society blade, owner of a racing stable, a ladies' man, and a lover of the soft life. Nicknamed Poldi by his intimates, he was outstanding even in their company for his vacuity of mind and shabbiness of character.

Yet his first impulse was good, in a way. By taking a great risk immediately, Austria might have kept the quarrel localized. General Franz Conrad von Hötzendorf, Chief of Staff of the Austro Hungarian Army, and the court's major war hawk, opposed Berchtold's first proposal. But not on principle; his army just wasn't ready for a quick jump. "Order a mobilization against Serbia at once and send her an ultimatum," was his counteradvice. Count István Tisza, the Prime Minister of Hungary, was opposed to both of these ideas: Serbia might beat back a half-armed blow, and a formal mobilization was likely to provoke Russia as Serbia's traditional defender. Tisza also feared that a victory over Serbia and any subsequent annexation of Serbian territory would weaken Hungary's role as an equal partner with Austria in the Dual Monarchy.

So Berchtold hesitated, not from a faint heart, but to plan the next maneuver. Austrian mobilization required about sixteen days. Before he could get it ordered, he would have to consolidate his position, by persuasion if that was possible, or by deception if need be.

In consequence, on July 5, the same day the last conspirators were jailed in Sarajevo, there appeared before Wilhelm II in Potsdam Count Szögyény, the Austrian Ambassador in Berlin. It was a salubriously fair Sunday and they talked over lunch. Szögyény had been prodded into action by the arrival in Berlin of Count

Alexander Hoyos, Berchtold's *chef de cabinet*, who came bearing a letter from Francis Joseph to the Kaiser. Austria needed to know: Could she count on Germany's support if she mobilized against Serbia?

The details of this tête-à-tête were never recorded. None of Wilhelm's ministers was present. We know mainly that Hoyos got what he wanted. Wilhelm assured Szögyény, according to the latter's official dispatch, that "even if matters went to the length of war between Austria-Hungary and Russia . . . Germany, in her customary loyalty as our ally, would stand at our side." Later that same day the Kaiser strolled under the trees with his Chancellor, Theobald von Bethmann-Hollweg, and told him what he had pledged Austria. There were no objections then from the Chancellor, or later from the Foreign Secretary, Gottlieb von Jagow, or the War Minister, General Erich von Falkenhayn, when they were given the news.

Having handed Austria a blank check to deal with Serbia as she pleased, Wilhelm, on the day following his talk with Szögyény, embarked on a North Sea cruise. The outing had been scheduled for months. It was not a ruse intended to deceive Europe into believing that the wind was abating. The Kaiser did not deliberately isolate himself while the crisis mounted. He was guilty only of carelessness amounting to criminal negligence. For with his departure most of his ministers also took off on their holidays, and Germany slept as the time bomb ticked on. Wilhelm was twenty days at sea, an idyllic cruise, better described as one of the great maritime disasters of history.

From the hour of Hoyos's return to Vienna, the die was cast. Count Tisza was won over to the war party on July 14 when Berchtold assured him that no territorial demand would be made on Serbia. This was an outright lie; Berchtold was already planning the partitioning of Serbia. Francis Joseph had blessed the aggression even before Tisza yielded. His decision pivoted on Wilhelm's promise of support. When Berchtold told him that the Kaiser would back Austria all the way, the old man said simply: "Now we can no longer hold back. It will be a terrible war." The Emperor didn't get to see letters from Tisza to the Crown urging leniency with Serbia; Berchtold had pocketed them.

Having gained his way through German support, Berchtold didn't bother to return the courtesy. Along with the blank check,

Wilhelm had given Austria two pieces of sage counsel: Whatever move you make, do it fast! Before going at Serbia, be sure to placate Italy! Berchtold not only chose to ignore this advice, he deliberately kept Berlin in the dark about what he was plotting, disregarded most of its requests for information on developments, and on those rare occasions when he made reply, did so tardily or with evasions and half-truths. Among the mysteries is why Bethmann and Jagow, in the absence of Wilhelm, tolerated Berchtold's contemptuous effrontery.

There is also the question of why Britain did not use her influence more positively on the side of restraint during the days when a firm warning might have deterred Austria or startled Bethmann into pressing the brake. There are several reasons. The London Government didn't know about the blank check and hence did not sense the magnitude of the danger until too late. Foreign Minister Sir Edward Grey's cautious middle course, deriving from this misestimate of the crisis on the Continent, was equally constrained by domestic political considerations. There was little or no sentiment in Parliament for any statement that even by implication might commit England, and, furthermore, the British Cabinet was preoccupied with a threat of civil war in Ireland.

On July 19 the Austrian Ministerial Council met in secret. It was decided that Serbia would be "beaten to earth" and that parts of it "would go to Bulgaria." These were the words used several days later by the Austrian Minister in London when he confided what had happened to Prince Karl Max Lichnowsky, the German Ambassador, who forwarded the information to Bethmann-Hollweg.

In this roundabout fashion, while time ran out, there trickled into Berlin fragments of intelligence indicating that Vienna was risking a double game that fully jeopardized Germany's highest interests. At last Bethmann noted indignantly: "This duplicity of Austria is intolerable." Still, the intolerable was tolerated.

AUSTRIA BAITS SERBIA

At 6:00 P.M. on July 23 Austrian Ambassador Baron Vladimir von Giesl, a fire-breathing nationalist, carried his country's ultimatum to Serbia's Foreign Ministry.

Austria demanded that the Serbian Government formally condemn all anti-Austrian propaganda, expel from office anyone fomenting it, and accept the collaboration of Austrian agents—on Serbian soil—in the suppression of such propaganda. Legal action against the instigators of the Sarajevo murder plot was demanded, with free entry into Serbia for Austrian officials who would steer the investigation. Although these terms totally affronted sovereignty, Belgrade was given only forty-eight hours in which to comply.

In England, Sir Edward Grey read the ultimatum and called it the most formidable demand ever imposed on one state by another. Wilhelm II, loafing aboard the *Hohenzollern* in a Norwegian fjord, also scanned the text and commented to his naval aide: "A spirited note, what?"

Premier Pašić and most of his cabinet were away from Belgrade electioneering in the provinces when the note arrived. In their absence it was read by Ljuba Jovanović, the Minister of Public Information, who commented: "Well, there is nothing to do but die fighting." By the next day, the cabinet had reassembled in Belgrade. In the meanwhile, the Regent, Prince Alexander, had wired an appeal for help to Czar Nicholas II, and Serbia had published to the world the terms of the ultimatum.

In the brief time remaining, the cabinet worked out its reply. Pašić had heard from Russia; he was advised to proceed with "extreme moderation." From the beginning the ministers were unanimous that the Government could not wholly yield to the Austrian demands. They realized that anything less than that would be deemed unsatisfactory, and Austria would probably attack in any event.

These things considered, they strove to compose a document that would win world sympathy, if not Great Power protection, for their country. With minutes to go on the second day, July 25, they were still rewording and amending the note in longhand, the only typewriter having jammed. When the last word was written, Pašić asked: "Who will deliver this?" Their silence, and the pained expressions of his colleagues, left him no choice. Paper in hand, the old man walked in on Giesl five minutes before the 6:00 P.M. deadline. Pašić said to him: "Part of your demands we have accepted. . . . For the rest, we place our hopes on your loyalty and chivalry as an Austrian general."

Giesl had anticipated a qualified reply and had orders to reject

Similar yachting attire emphasizes the
resemblance between first cousins Nicholas
II of Russia (left) and England's George V
(then Duke of York) in this 1904 photograph.
Forced to abdicate in March, 1917, Nicholas
II found a niche in history as Russia's
last Czar, although during his reign he
had incurred a reputation for being an
ineffective ruler. Later he and his entire
family were murdered by the Bolsheviks.

it as unsatisfactory. The legation papers and cipher books had already been burned; the loaded baggage and cars were ready to clear away. The Austrians caught the 6:30 P.M. train out of Belgrade that same day.

Wholly conciliatory in tone, the reply was more yielding in form than in substance. Most of what Serbia could honorably concede, she did. But she could not agree to Austrians officially waging political warfare against her on her own soil. As to all points remaining in contention, Serbia proposed submitting them to the International Tribunal at the Hague.

Just over the border at Semlin, Giesl left his train to notify Vienna via Budapest that he had broken relations with Serbia because the note was unsatisfactory, with the added information that three hours before the rupture, Serbia had declared a general mobilization. Francis Joseph was given the news a few minutes later. He muttered: *"Also doch!"* (It has come after all.) Berchtold was at the Emperor's side in a few minutes, urging that Austria must immediately mount a countermobilization against Serbia, or look weak, thereby tempting Russia to come on. Though the argument was specious, the Emperor yielded. At 9:23 that night Conrad von Hötzendorf had the order for the call-up, with July 27 set as "alarm day" and July 28 as the starting day for troop movements. Everything was going in a rush. Vienna hadn't yet seen the Serbian reply, and Berlin didn't yet know about the reply or the Serbian and Austrian countermobilizations.

As to why Serbia jumped the gun, there is first the fact that the cabinet was certain Austria was determined to have a war. But that's not all. Pašić was confronted with an election. The Serbian officer corps, allied to the Black Hand, was shouting for war and ready to ditch Pašić if he stood in the way. He shied from the political risks of a conciliatory reply unaccompanied by some warlike gesture, and thus played into Berchtold's hands.

The publication of the Austrian ultimatum, followed at once by news of the two mobilizations, sent a shock wave across Europe exactly four weeks after the Sarajevo murders. All governments awakened to the gravity of the crisis. Sir Edward Grey at first proposed that the Ambassadors of Germany, France, and Italy seated in London meet with him to search for a solution. For various reasons that offer fell on stony ground. Grey's next try was an appeal to Berlin to use its influence with Austria to mediate the quarrel. The reply was friendly but equivocal. Grey and Bethmann were thinking of two different things. Grey wanted no war at all. Bethmann was still going along with the theory of a "localized war," as approved by Wilhelm II. This, as Under-Secretary of State for Foreign Affairs Sir Arthur Nicolson noted in England, meant that "all the powers are to hold the ring while Austria quietly strangles Serbia." So while Grey assumed that his proposal was being supported in Vienna by the German Ambassador, Bethmann was sitting on it and letting events take their course. That gave Wilhelm time to see Grey's note, and as was his habit scribble comments on the margins: "This is a tremendous piece of British insolence. I am not called upon to prescribe to H. M. the Emperor [Francis Joseph] how to preserve his honor."

Wilhelm had cut short his cruise and returned hastily to Potsdam on the afternoon of July 27. The Army Chief of Staff, General Helmuth von Moltke (a nephew and namesake of the great Moltke who had won the war of 1870), and Navy Minister Admiral Alfred von Tirpitz also returned prematurely from their summer holidays. Tirpitz was convinced that Bethmann had bungled the situation and was helping provoke a Great Power war. The Kaiser was furious at Bethmann. The Chancellor, kept out of the picture by Berchtold, had forwarded to the *Hohenzollern* too little information, all of it colored with optimism. Together again, and taking fresh measure of the crisis, the returned vacationists had reason for anger and alarm.

That same day, British dailies had published the news that the Grand Fleet, earlier assembled for annual maneuvers, had been directed not to disperse but to proceed to war stations, a precaution initiated by the First Lord of the Admiralty, Winston Churchill. The Italian Foreign Minister, the Marquis di San Giuliano, had notified Berlin that since Austria had not consulted her as an ally before making a move "so portentously aggressive . . . Italy could not consider herself bound in connection with the further consequences." Russia, encouraged by France, was reacting more ominously than had been anticipated. From Ambassador Lichnowsky in London came the message: "Nobody here believes in localizing conflict. . . . Start mediation along lines suggested by Sir Edward Grey." Wilhelm, Bethmann, Jagow, and Moltke conferred about alternatives to "localization." Finding none, they convinced themselves they could have a small war and peace also.

But at last Bethmann felt chastened and worried. That night he wired Berchtold asking him to consider Grey's proposal and suggesting that Austria accept the Serbian reply as a basis for further discussions. Bethmann thought he still had time; due to the sixteen-day requirement for mobilization, Austria was not expected to jump off before August 12. But Berchtold had already decided to plunge immediately "to cut the ground from any attempt at intervention." In Vienna the war declaration was being drafted at the same hour Berlin was making its first move to restrain its ally. At Ischl, Berchtold tricked Francis Joseph into signing the paper by lying; he told him that Serbia was already attacking.

At 11:00 A.M. on July 28, one month almost to the minute after the Sarajevo murders, Austria-Hungary notified Serbia by telegram that she had declared war. This manner of announcing hostilities was so out of keeping with diplomatic tradition that Pašić, on reading the message, at first regarded it as a hoax. The declaration was signed by Berchtold. Germany had not been notified. Wilhelm II that morning had for the first time gone over the Serbian reply, exulting as he read, then sent along his comment to Bethmann and Jagow, saying among other things: "A great moral victory for Vienna, but with it, every reason for war disappears." Still, he had a war, not yet knowing.

Along with his comment, the Kaiser rushed an instruction to Jagow: the Foreign Secretary was to propose to Austria that Wilhelm II mediate the quarrel with Serbia (as Grey had suggested); to assure satisfaction, Germany would advocate a "temporary occupation of a portion of Serbia" by Austrian troops (which Grey opposed). Jagow got busy, and though before the morning was over the news came through that Austria had declared war, he still went ahead. Thanks to fresh information coming in from London and Rome, Bethmann in these same hours was finally becoming aware how shamelessly Berchtold had double-talked and double-dealt him. Angered, he took on the main task of trying to restrain Austria from attacking.

The key message in this attempt was a telegram Bethmann sent to the German Embassy in Vienna on the evening of July 28: "Serbia has in fact met the Austrian demands in so wide-sweeping a manner that if the Austro-Hungarian Government adopted a wholly uncompromising attitude, a gradual revulsion of public opinion against it in all of Europe would have to be reckoned with." Diplomatic language could not put it more plainly that Austria was going to war in a bad cause. But if that is correct, honor could not require Germany to join an ally who had deceived her.

The way out was there, wholly consistent with honor, if Germany cared to take it; and it widened through the next sixty hours. Berchtold ignored Bethmann's telegram, while the men in Berlin waited and sweated. On July 29, Bethmann wired Berchtold: "We must refuse to let ourselves be drawn . . . by Vienna into any general conflagration because she has ignored our advice." That it was said too late to be effective still leaves unanswered the question of why Germany plunged into the conflict.

RUSSIA MOBILIZES

From the time of the murders, the Czar's Court and the Russian press had used the Sarajevo incident mainly to stir public indignation against Austria.

On July 6 Russian Foreign Minister Sergei Sazonov had sent for Count Ottokar von Czernin, the Austrian Chargé d'Affaires, to tell him that an unreasonable attitude by the Vienna Government toward Serbia would not find Russia indifferent. Russian awareness of the probabilities thus coincided with the mounting of the Austrian war party to the driver's seat. But Sazonov was no Berchtold blasting with a trumpet. Having uttered his warning, he retired to his country place till July 8. On returning, he reiterated the warning to Counts Friedrich Szápáry and Friedrich von Pourtalès, the Austrian and German Ambassadors. Szápáry assured him that Austria would do nothing to worsen the situation, and so Sazonov relaxed.

Due to an accident of timing, the good-will mission to Russia of French President Raymond Poincaré and Premier René Viviani coincided with the thickening of the crisis through mid-July. At a reception in the Winter Palace, on July 21, Poincaré discussed the Serbian affair with Szápáry. The Count's truculence, his words, "We cannot tolerate," warned the Frenchman that Austria was plotting some sudden stroke. Poincaré turned to his own Ambassador, Maurice Paléologue, and said: "Sazonov must be firm and we must support him." These words reflect his appreciation of Sazonov's character—ardently Russian, fiercely nationalistic, but at heart a timid soul who wanted peace. Poincaré's presence, and his stiffening influence on Sazonov, strengthened the hand of militarists at court, who were urging that preparatory measures be taken.

Russia's great handicap was the slowness of her mobilization. The country was so vast, the railways so inadequate, the local administration so inefficient, that in times past the Russian war machine had cranked up at about half the speed of the Teutonic forces. To reduce the time lag, a reform had been instituted in 1913, at the urging of France. It listed steps to be taken short of mobilization when danger seemed imminent and the Government opted not to assume a threatening posture. The procedure called for "trial mobilization" of certain reserve units, the preparation of frontier posts to receive troops, the recall of furloughed soldiers, the reshoeing of horses, and the return of naval vessels to harbors. Not even these limited measures had been ordered when Poincaré sailed for home on July 23.

The next morning the news of the Austrian ultimatum to Serbia reached Saint Petersburg. Berchtold had craftily timed his master stroke to coincide with Poincaré's departure from Russia, so that the French and Russian leaders would not be able to confer in person about the consequences of the move. On reading the terms of the ultimatum, Sazonov consulted General Janushkevich, Chief of the General Staff, and suggested that preparations for partial mobilization were in order. With Nicholas II present, the Ministerial Council approved the step on the afternoon of July 25: thirteen army corps to be readied, but only in the districts fronting on Austria-Hungary. The orders were supposed to go out that evening; Russia was about to beat Austria to the draw.

On the next day, a Sunday, Sazonov and Count Pourtalès found themselves on the same train, returning from their summer residences. They talked long and earnestly, each trying to convince the other that his Government had no hostile intent. The German Ambassador went further, persuading Sazonov that he should send a message through channels to Berchtold, requesting direct conversations to stop the drift toward war. It was done, but Berchtold answered that talks had become impossible, since Austria had already declared war on Serbia.

Sazonov and Pourtalès are not exceptional figures in the drama of late July. Sufficient good will was still active in the embassies and chancelleries of Europe at that late hour to avert a Great Power war, had feelings been communicable. Berchtold had only lit a fuse. Wilhelm had been careless. Bethmann had been weak. Poincaré, by stiffening Russia, had helped spread alarm. All along the line things had begun to slip. The hour was at hand when every man's effort to save the peace would prove vain because procedures had taken over.

Laws, regulations, and precedents largely determine what should be done for the security of the state when danger threatens. Its servants, civil and military, are constrained by them. It is the obligation of the statesman to delay the use or the parading of force for as long as possible. The duty of the soldier is to see that his nation is not caught off guard; he must urge that proper protective steps be taken in time. While in an emergency these are divergent approaches to a common problem, they are usually reconcilable at a certain point. Custom, process, and mutual concern so make them.

In 1914 diplomats and strategists shared in the key decisions that made a world catastrophe of the Serbian incident. When in later years historians accented the "champagne mood" and martial ardor that gripped the military when at last the gage was down, it was to imply that in this spirit was the genesis of Europe's ordeal. Things are not that simple. Generals and admirals must play their part. Should they undertake the gravest of all their tasks doubtfully, morbidly, as if driven, they would be unfit to command.

News of the Austrian declaration of war against Serbia reached Saint Petersburg late on the afternoon of July 28. French Ambassador Paléologue, another of the volatile diplomats who must bear a share of the responsibility for the spread of the war, hastened to assure Sazonov of his Government's complete readiness to fulfill its obligations as an ally. Was it an absolute commitment that strengthened Russia in the hour of decision? Afterward Paléologue glossed over the incident in his memoirs. At any rate, soon after the Ambassador departed, Sazonov went to the Czar to report the Austrian action, to acquaint him with the general situation, and, no doubt, to inform him of France's offer of support.

That night Nicholas II telegraphed his cousin, Wilhelm II: "An ignoble war has been declared to a weak country. The indignation of Russia, fully shared by me, is enormous. I foresee that very soon I shall be overwhelmed by the pressure brought upon me, and be forced to take extreme measures that will lead to war." To cousin "Nicky," cousin "Willy" replied in a friendly, sympathetic spirit.

There were more telegrams back and forth, and, at one point, Nicholas became so impressed with Wilhelm's protestations that he temporarily suspended an order for general mobilization, urged upon him by the Chief of Staff. But in his return wire, he included this line: "The military measures that have now come into force were decided five days ago for reasons of defense." Those words ended the dialogue. The Kaiser exploded: "I cannot agree to any more mediation, since the Czar, who requested it, has at the same time secretly mobilized behind my back. . . . My work is at an end!" Wilhelm had reached the end of his emotional reserves, which were never abundant. With his retirement to the sidelines the wheels ground on.

During the Nicky-Willy correspondence, the Russian General Staff had been trying to shift gears. There were second thoughts about partial mobilization. It was breeding confusion that would only be compounded should general mobilization follow swiftly. On the morning of July 29, General Janushkevich went to the Czar with two ukases, one decreeing general mobilization, the other partial mobilization, both of which he would keep in his pocket in case of need. Nicholas II tended to go along with whatever minister had his ear at the moment, and so he signed both papers. However, three other signatures were required to validate them and for the moment General Janushkevich did nothing.

In midafternoon Sazonov again received Szápáry: the Austrian was calling to urge a quick end to Russian preparation. As they talked, the telephone rang. Sazonov answered and heard the latest news flash: Austrian monitors plying the Danube were shelling Belgrade. He turned to Szápáry, shouting: "You only wish to gain time by negotiations. But you go ahead and bombard an unprotected city!" Szápáry rushed from the room.

Like Wilhelm, Sazonov had in one moment exhausted his psychic reserves, and would do nothing further toward preventing the war. He told Janushkevich to go ahead with the ukase for general mobilization, then tried to get to the Czar to expedite action; Nicholas II was too busy to see him. By late afternoon, the Chief of Staff's paper was almost complete. The final cabinet signer, Interior Minister N. A. Maklakov, commented: "With us the war cannot be popular deep down among the masses, to whom revolutionary ideas mean more than a victory over Germany. But one cannot escape one's fate." On that prescient note, he crossed himself and put pen to paper.

Almost ready now, the fateful order stayed suspended overnight. In Berlin, Bethmann and the others were convinced that Russia was already on the move. From the Chancellor to the German Embassy in Saint Petersburg went the message that evening: "Further continuation of Russian mobilization measures must force us to mobilize." Pourtalès got to Sazonov with it somewhere around midnight and tried to convince him that Russia must hold off a little longer. Whether nervously exhausted or finally hardened, Sazonov shook him off. His mind was on the ukase; it required a second signature by Nicholas and the hour of their meeting was already set.

In midafternoon on July 30, Sazonov told Nicholas that there was no longer any choice—Russia must have full mobilization. The Czar blanched and cried out: "Think of what awful responsibility you are advising me to take! Think of the thousands and thousands of men who will be sent to their deaths!" For more than one hour he resisted the Foreign Minister's argument.

One General Tatistchev, who had been attaché at Berlin, had accompanied Sazonov. Nicholas deliberately snubbed him, acting as if he were not present. At last Tatistchev opened his mouth only to say: "Yes, it is hard to decide." A bit of lese majesty, these wrong words to the wrong man in the wrong moment drained Nicholas's last drop of resistance. Blazing with anger, he shouted: "I will decide!" and forthwith signed the order. Sazonov gave the news to Janushkevich by telephone and then added: "Now you can smash your telephone. Give your orders, General! Then disappear for the rest of the day."

This time it was final for everyone. There were no more counterorders. The mobilization office was ready with its sheaves of messages. That evening of July 30 the overloaded wires dot-dashed their summons to soldiers. Though mobilization wasn't scheduled to start until the next day, reservists in Warsaw, Odessa, and other main cities were already moving on their appointed stations to draw arms and form up by 7:00 P.M. of July 30. In a remote Siberian village at 4:00 A.M. on July 31 an English traveler was awakened by a great commotion outside the train window. Said an excited bystander: "Have you heard the news? There is war!" Before dawn broke, the red mobilization posters proclaiming the call-up had been raised in Saint Petersburg (soon to be renamed Petrograd) and throughout Russia. Nicholas II made an entry in his diary: "A gray day, in keeping with my mood."

THE BREAKUP

The news of full mobilization by Russia fixed Europe's fate. Its military leaders had for so long accepted the maxim: "Mobilization means war!" that there could be no other result. They believed it and thereby made it true. After the Russian steamroller went into motion, the diplomats toiled on. Little or no hope remained that peace could be saved. They worked mainly that history might say they were not responsible for what came.

But the relating of cause to effect must not be oversimplified. Austria-Hungary ordered full mobilization at 12:23 P.M. the next day, July 31. General Conrad von Hötzendorf virtually demanded it. But when the order was published, Conrad and Francis Joseph still did not know that Russia had mobilized. It was done because Conrad did not want his front door left open when he went at Serbia through the back door.

Because Pourtalès slept at his post, the grim news from Saint Petersburg was also surprisingly slow in hitting Berlin. The message arrived at 11:40 A.M. on July 31; Wilhelm heard of it during the noon hour. At 10:00 P.M., Bethmann, Moltke, and other principals acting with the Kaiser decided to proclaim *Kriegsgefahr Zustand*, or "Threatening Danger of War," which must lead automatically to mobilization. A wire went off to Pourtalès so advising him; he would deliver an ultimatum to Sazonov, giving Russia twelve hours to call off mobilization. His duty done, Wilhelm was suddenly atremble as he thought of what war would do to his beloved East Prussia. He consoled himself by reading a staff

Soldiers of Czar Nicholas II pass in review during a parade held on July 22, 1914, near Saint Petersburg, in honor of the French President Poincaré and Premier Viviani.

memorandum from Major Bernhard von Eggeling, the attaché in Saint Petersburg, who forecast that the Russians "planned no tenacious offensive but a slow retreat as in 1812."

Berlin, via the Ambassador in Paris, Baron Wilhelm von Schoen, also got off an ultimatum to France. She was given eighteen hours in which to say whether she would stay neutral if Germany fought Russia. If the answer was yes, then Schoen should demand the turning over to Germany of the fortresses of Verdun and Toul as hostages to her pledged word. There was no possibility of France staying neutral at such a price, and Schoen carried out his mission in such a manner that the issue did not arise.

Schoen simply went to the Quai d'Orsay and told Premier Viviani that France had eighteen hours to say whether or not she would stay neutral. Not till later in the war, when the French broke the German secret code, did they learn the most shocking part of Schoen's instructions. He acted as gently as possible, and Viviani responded equivocally, saying: "Let me hope extreme decisions may be avoided, and give me time to reflect." He already knew what France would do in the crisis.

Earlier on that same afternoon of July 31, General Joffre had talked to the French Cabinet and had pounded the table. The army corps covering the frontier with Germany had to be mobilized. Said Joffre: "Every delay of twenty-four hours in calling up reservists means . . . a retardation of the concentration forces, that is, the initial abandonment of ten to twelve miles of territory for every day of delay." Here he was talking only of how fast a mobilized German Army would come on if unopposed. But when generals pontificate about time-and-space problems, of which civilian ministers profess ignorance, they are apt to carry the day. At 5:15 P.M. the cabinet authorized Joffre to start mobilizing. That was some little time before Schoen made his first call on Viviani. When Schoen returned the next day for his answer, Viviani said only: "France will act in accordance with her interests."

How France stood, Russia learned during the minutes when her own ultimatum from Berlin ran out. A late-night wire went from the Russian military attaché in Paris to the War Ministry in Saint Petersburg: "The French Minister of War has declared to me in a tone of hearty enthusiasm the firm decision of the French Government for war and begged me to confirm the hope of the French General Staff that all our efforts will be directed against Germany."

The last vain try for peace was being made in the Russian capital at about the time that the message arrived. On instruction from Bethmann, Pourtalès called on Sazonov early in the evening of August 1 to press the question: Would Russia call off the mobilization? They faced one another. Three times Pourtalès repeated the question. Three times Sazonov replied: "No!" Then the German took a paper from his pocket and handing it to the Russian, said: "In that case, I am instructed to give you this note." It was the declaration of war.

Sobbing like a child, Pourtalès walked to the window, and cried out: "I never, never could have believed that I would quit Saint Petersburg under these conditions." They embraced one another, and Pourtalès asked when his passport would be ready, adding: "I am not capable of thinking and talking of anything else at the moment."

In Paris, General Joffre, surmising that Germany had decreed full mobilization, though he had no such firm information, told the cabinet that unless he was authorized to call all forces, he would quit. There was no debate on this ultimatum. They told him to proceed and the hour was set for 4:00 P.M. that day, August 1. Germany's mobilization order followed France's by less than one-half hour. Two days later Germany declared war against France.

THE OPPOSING FORCES

Everywhere on the Continent mobilization was swift and sure, compared to the difficulties of all previous wars. Even Russia massed its army with greater efficiency than ever before. The acceleration was partly due to the modernizing of military personnel systems. Processing had been speeded up because it was believed that once mobilization began, war became inescapable. Every general staff was bent on winning decisive advantage in the opening round, an extravagant aim in any era. Recent expansion of the European railway systems to keep pace with industrial growth made possible the assembly or reconcentration of millions of men promptly. That was what gave the war unexampled dimension. Out of the growth of civilization came the unprecedented toll in human life. The record shows that in France alone between August 2 and 18, some 3,781,000 persons under military orders were transported in 7,000 trains, which in certain periods succeeded one another at the rate of one train every eight minutes.

Toward France on August 3, Germany was already wheeling 1,500,000 men into line to form seven field armies. Another 500,000 were mobilized to face eastward. Even so Germany took the plunge with no assurance that she would have superior numbers on either flank. Across Europe more than six million men were getting orders and moving either toward the frontiers or to their support stations. Outside of Serbia, however, not one shot had been fired. Although the alignment of belligerents was still far from complete, the event itself was already awesome. Never before had there been such an initial massing for Armageddon. There has been none such since.

Germany's opening advantage was in the fitness of her troops, the greater realism and vigor of her training methods, and a heavier, better balanced armament. Also, the German General Staff had a clearer grasp of the impact of new weapons, especially the machine gun, upon battlefield movement. But it is not true that the German command system was more autocratic, less human, than others. From the time of the first General Moltke, relationships between officers and men had been closer and more comradely than in the democratic armies.

At war's start, Germany fielded eighty-seven divisions, with an average strength of 18,000 men. These formations, and the field echelons above them, were well fixed with medium and heavy artillery, required for long-range bombardment or siege operations. Behind the formidable artillery array was the strongest armament industry in Europe, centered in the Krupp works at Essen, a complex of sixty different factory buildings where 41,000 workers were employed—"a city within a city, with its own streets, police force, fire department, and traffic laws." Germany was assured a steady flow of heavy weapons. In its infantry regiments, the Mauser rifle, which was more rugged than precise, and the Maxim machine gun, invented by an American-born Englishman, were standard equipment. German cavalry regiments, to be used mainly for deep reconnaissance, still carried the somewhat archaic saber and lance, but had been trained to put these weapons aside in favor of the carbine when fighting dismounted.

Austria-Hungary mustered forty-nine divisions in an initial mobilization of just under 500,000 men. When later she went to a full war footing, summoning the reserves, the number rose to 2,700,000. But the cold figures are deceptive; they do not reflect hard strength. Many of the younger serving officers were adequately trained; but the majority of leaders, regular and reserve, were not tempered for fighting operations. The commander, General Conrad von Hötzendorf, was reputed to be "the most brilliant soldier in Central Europe," which description survives despite lack of proof that it was merited; he was chronically a reckless plunger. The Austrian Army's artillery was superb, thanks to the advanced technology of the Skoda works. The "Austrian 88" was one of the phenomenal guns of the century. Few other assets were impressive.

The Austrian Army was far from homogeneous. Three fourths of its officers were of German stock; but only one soldier in four spoke German. The Dual Monarchy was a melting pot on a cold fire, "eight nations, seventeen countries, twenty parliamentary groups, twenty-seven parties," one of its statesmen sighed. When a nation cannot develop organic unity because its people have too few interests in common, the warrior spirit languishes. That was the weakness of the Austrians. Staff work was slipshod; command control, at best, was intermittent. The Austrian official history confesses: "Often a platoon commander could not make himself intelligible to his motley collection of men." Too many of them were like the fictional Good Soldier Schweik, who always preferred rheumatism to duty.

France had only 60 per cent of the potential military power of Germany (5,940,000 to 9,750,000), which deficit compelled her to call all able-bodied men to the colors. She began the war by mustering sixty-two divisions, or a total of 1,650,000 men, and later built up to 3,500,000 men, after heavy losses. The combined figures approximate her aggregate of trained men when war started. But whereas the German High Command placed great trust in the citizen soldier and shaped its war plans on the premise of his immediate full employment, the French General Staff did not. The French counted mainly on the active army of about one million men to strike the blows in the short, victorious campaign they expected.

On the Continent, the French Army was rated in quality and fighting power second only to the German. It had military ardor, great dash, and utmost confidence in its own moral superiority. The belief that French courage was matchless was especially strong among the generals and staff. Like strong wine, their *élan* made them insensible to their own weaknesses.

One of the French Army's shortcomings was the lightness of its artillery establishment. Their 75-mm. gun was the finest quick-firing light field piece on earth. But its shell could do little more than batter and slow infantry moving in the open. Its blast was not sufficient to break down even nonreinforced earthworks. Of medium and heavy cannon, the French Army had only three hundred or so to Germany's 3,500. Each German army corps could back up its divisions with fires from thirty-six 105-mm. howitzers and sixteen 150-mm. howitzers. The French had nothing like this. They regarded artillery as a supplementary force, as did the U.S. Army during the Civil War. That is clearly shown in the composition of the French division, which aggregated 17,000 men of whom 13,300 were foot soldiers. Furthermore, the French General Staff had grievously underestimated the stopping power of the machine gun against deployed infantry. On mobilization day France had only 2,500 automatic arms against Germany's 4,500. It was even outnumbered in light artillery, 3,800 75's, compared to 6,000 77's. This disparity in firepower, unit for unit, was the consequence of the French General Staff's own mistaken doctrine. It was truly believed that, in combat, moral superiority would outweigh advantage in firepower.

Russia started by fielding 114 divisions, or 1,400,000 men, and later built up to a peak strength of about six million. Its great threat lay in numbers, the so-called Russian steamroller, an almost inexhaustible reserve of men, unlettered for the most part, but willing enough, physically stalwart, and phenomenally courageous. Like other European powers, Russia had compulsory military service, drafting men at the age of twenty and releasing them from reserve duty at forty-three. Infantrymen served three years actively, members of other branches four.

Such was Russia's manpower abundance that, though exemptions were granted with a free hand, the peacetime army was twice the size of Germany's, while behind it were more than two million trained reserves. The nation had taken a great defeat in the war with Japan. Radical reforms had been ordered. But how much actual progress had resulted, the rest of Europe did not know. It was suspected that a large part of the new credits had been misapplied, graft and malfeasance being rife within the Czar's Government. The artillery organization of the army was sound; the guns were modern, the fire control was efficient. But it was known that the nation was technologically backward. The likely prospect was therefore that ammunition might prove deficient or inadequate, and there could be no rapid expansion of war industry.

Formed largely of aristocrats and sons of wealth, the officer corps was superbly trained in the niceties of drill, horse handling, the use of sword and saber, and minor tactics. But the supply of professionally trained leaders was far too small for the masses now mobilizing.

Its great size and the physical endurance of the rank and file were the Russian Army's chief assets. Being of the peasantry, the soldiers had more phlegm than flame, and displayed little initiative. When once won to a cause, however, their battle ardor burned fiercely, as Napoleon had discovered. These latent strengths in the soldier also involved a danger for the command. Russian ranks had to be tightly controlled, or else their discipline would erode.

In his ignorance, the average Russian private soldier could not possibly imagine the kind of war toward which he was marching. A beachcomber might more easily foresee what would follow in the wake of an onrushing hurricane. But in his unawareness of his personal fate and the ordeal awaiting his country, this peasant rifleman was no less understanding than the most intelligent of his superiors, and they in turn were no more blind than the wisest of Frenchmen, Austrians, and Germans. Totaling the numbers, all could see that a mighty collision impended. About what would follow it they could only guess, and all their guessing proved wrong.

It is an old story. War cannot be tested ahead of time. That its mystery may be penetrated in advance is merely the persistent illusion. This form of human conflict invariably continues to change just enough to make its developments eternally surprising to planners and participants. But in 1914 there was something else. The scale of operations was incomparably so much greater than anything men had experienced that the generals and general staffs were beyond their depths when they started. Like the schoolboy who merely reads about the massing millions, they were awed by what they saw approaching. But they could not fathom it. France at mobilization had 4,000 artillery pieces. This was thought to be enough for victory. She had to build another 36,000 before the war ended. Her 2,500 automatic weapons were a token of the 315,000 machine guns to come.

It was the same in every camp. The mightiest of mobilizations became dwarfed by the consequences.

BRITAIN'S HESITATION

While these vast pools of armed men responded to orders in the last days of July and took form to become armies on the march in the first days of August, there remained unanswered the question of what England would do.

The doubt was caused by Britain's somewhat ambiguous mutual defense covenant with France, described by Winston Churchill as a "veiled coalition." Their compact dated from the period of Russia's ignominious defeat by Japan in 1904–5, which had surprised the world, proved Russia's military impoverishment, and revealed a precarious power imbalance in Europe. Russia's eclipse clearly left Imperial Germany as the Continent's strongest power, a fact that drove Britain and France toward one another. For these ancient enemies, however, a full-hearted embrace was impossible. While there was time for them to arrive at a common policy deriving from a concrete political aim, they eschewed that, and therefore neglected to tighten their military arrangements before the emergency. There were joint staff rides and increased partying together, but it was all very informal. Britain was not honor bound to support France unless war was fixed on her in a way that also compromised British honor.

Yet from the moment the first spark flew upward from Sarajevo, British statesmen, most notably Sir Edward Grey, the gentle bird watcher who was Foreign Secretary, sensed that this might well happen. So did Churchill at the Admiralty, who penned a note to his staff, "There is real danger; there may be war," then set about checking dispositions of the fleet. Lord Kitchener, the foremost soldier of the empire, was at sea returning from Egypt in that hour. A note awaited him from Prime Minister Herbert Asquith: "I am anxious that you should not get beyond the reach of personal consultation and assistance."

But England had not yet hardened and was only being cautious. French Ambassador Paul Cambon repeatedly tried to find out what course England would take in a war between Germany and France. He got a chilly reception from Grey, who knew that both the people and the Parliament were indifferent to the Austrian-Russian rivalry in the Balkans and were indisposed to support France unless some unavoidable issue arose. German financial interests were influential both with the cabinet and with the City in London. In Paris, Poincaré sent for the British Ambassador and said: "If England will make an immediate declaration of her intention to support France, there will be no war and Germany will at once modify her attitude."

It went unheeded. By July 29 the British Cabinet had become convinced that a European war was inevitable. Asquith, speaking to the Commons, outlined a Continental situation "of utmost gravity." But England still intended to live with it rather than die for it. Beyond the Channel there had been no declaration of war; the British declaration for peace was already articulated as firmly as possible. But one transcendent anxiety threatened

ARMÉE DE TERRE ET ARMÉE DE MER

ORDRE
DE MOBILISATION GÉNÉRALE

Par décret du Président de la République, la mobilisation des armées de terre et de mer est ordonnée, ainsi que la réquisition des animaux, voitures et harnais nécessaires au complément de ces armées.

Le premier jour de la mobilisation est le *Dimanche 2 Août*

Tout Français soumis aux obligations militaires doit, sous peine d'être puni avec toute la rigueur des lois, obéir aux prescriptions du **FASCICULE DE MOBILISATION** (pages coloriées placées dans son livret).

Sont visés par le présent ordre **TOUS LES HOMMES** non présents sous les Drapeaux et appartenant :

1° à l'**ARMÉE DE TERRE** y compris les **TROUPES COLONIALES** et les hommes des **SERVICES AUXILIAIRES**;

2° à l'**ARMÉE DE MER** y compris les **INSCRITS MARITIMES** et les **ARMURIERS** de la **MARINE**.

Les Autorités civiles et militaires sont responsables de l'exécution du présent décret.

Le Ministre de la Guerre,   *Le Ministre de la Marine.*

   IMPRIMERIE NATIONALE — 3-158-1896.

This official order, alerting France's
Army and Navy to prepare for war, was
posted on August 1, 1914. Only a few hours
passed before Germany declared war on
Russia and, two days later, on France.
With tensions boiling and Europe's armies
at the ready, the maxim "Mobilization
means war" had come true.

this resolve—would the Germans violate Belgium?

Britain, like Germany, was a guarantor of the neutrality of Belgium and had been since the foundation of that small kingdom in 1831. But more than national honor was at stake. British strategy could not tolerate the threat of a strident and overarmed Germany solidly positioned on the Channel coast and master of its greatest port, Antwerp, and its largest industrial complex. Belgium, grafted onto Germany, meant menace unlimited.

Germany too late saw that she must go the whole way. Wilhelm had returned to Berlin from his northern cruise on July 27. On the station platform he cried out to Bethmann-Hollweg: "How did it all happen?" Pale of face, utterly cowed, the Chancellor admitted to the Kaiser that all along he had been deceived by Berchtold and forthwith offered his resignation. Wilhelm replied: "You've cooked this broth and now you're going to eat it."

After that word Bethmann not only ate, he gorged. It was the Chancellor who rushed the ultimatums to Russia and France on July 31. To justify the precipitate declaration of war against France three days later, he faked the story that a French airplane had bombed the railway station at Nuremberg.

To Grey in London on August 1 went the German Ambassador, Prince Lichnowsky, a confirmed Anglophile, who had worked long and hard to build friendship with England. Grey told him somewhat obliquely and vaguely, which was his official manner —though by now he felt that words could not reverse the tide —that if Germany would hold off, he would promise to keep France neutral. Lichnowsky wired Berlin that "in case we do not attack France, England will remain neutral and will guarantee French neutrality," which wasn't what Grey had said.

But the Kaiser, getting this straw, clutched hard. He read it as a carte blanche for a one-fronted war against Russia. To the sixty-six-year-old Chief of Staff, General Moltke, he read the message and cried in triumph: "Now we simply march the whole of our army to the East!" "No, Your Majesty," said Moltke, "it cannot be done. The deployment of millions cannot be improvised. The arrangements took a whole year to complete."

History has labeled General Moltke a war-seeker because he did not give in to the Kaiser at that moment. It is an empty accusation. Process was in command; to oppose it was to substitute chaos by unhinging preparations on every front. The momentum of a great army in mobilization is like any machine at its highest velocity; it cannot be stopped on call without incalculable damage.

When finally Wilhelm was convinced of some rather elementary truths known to an average staff major, the group drafted a message to England explaining that the advance on France could not be recalled but promising that the border would not be violated before the evening of August 3—which was exactly according to the German march schedule. Wilhelm then fired off a telegram to King George V: "If France offers me neutrality. . .I shall of course refrain from attacking France and employ my troops elsewhere. I hope France will not become nervous. The troops on my frontier are in the act of being stopped."

With Moltke in despair, the Kaiser next ordered that the troops at Trier, mounted for an invasion of Luxembourg, be halted in place. Once Luxembourg was violated, Germany's intention to invade Belgium would become signaled in the clear. Feeling like Pooh-Bah that to say it was to get it done, Wilhelm returned to the palace. When an aide put the stop message before Moltke, he cried: "Do what you like with this telegram, I won't sign it." The movement into Luxembourg was not halted. A young lieutenant commanding the lead company of the 69th Infantry Regiment crossed the border at 7:00 P.M. on August 1 and captured the railway station at the village of Ulflingen. Luxembourg became fully occupied within twenty-four hours.

In London Grey already knew the worst. On July 31 he had tried to relieve his doubts. Separate notes were sped to Paris and Berlin requesting assurances that Belgium's neutrality would be respected. France said yes unequivocally. Jagow returned the answer that he could not possibly say without consulting Bethmann and the Kaiser, and that he rather doubted that they could answer without disclosing part of the plan of campaign. With that, the cat was out of the bag. Resolving in his own mind that England was now honor bound to take sides, Grey warned Lichnowsky that "if France becomes involved we shall be drawn in." But he still refrained from spurring France and merely gave Cambon the word that the violation of Belgium might alter public opinion in England.

August 2 became the Sunday of resolve for Britain. The cabinet sat through the day. Decision turned on the delivery of a letter at noon from the Unionist Party pledging support if the Government voted for war. Taking one step at a time, the cabinet then sanctioned use of the Royal Navy to keep the German fleet from approaching the French coast; even that was too much for two members, who resigned in protest. At an evening meeting, the cabinet made the more pivotal decision to intervene if Belgian neutrality were violated. Later the orders for mobilization the next morning were signed.

At 7:00 P.M. on August 2 Germany demanded free passage for her troops through Belgium while giving Brussels but twelve hours in which to reply. The pretext given was that Germany had secret information that the French were about to invade. Unless Belgium remained benevolently neutral, "Germany would be obliged, to her regret, to regard the Kindgom as an enemy." Waiting until the last minute, the Belgian Government gave a categorical refusal and warned that any invasion would be resisted. With this act of defiance, the tide of world sympathy began shifting against Imperial Germany, never to turn back.

On Bank Holiday Monday, August 3, Albert, King of the Belgians, appealed to King George for diplomatic support of his country's neutrality. By then not all the monarchs of earth could have saved it. But the hope that springs eternal still pervaded Belgium. Within the palace, as among the street crowd, it was believed that Belgium's stand would compel Germany to reconsider rather than risk condemnation everywhere. By this time German policy had nothing in reserve; the Great War was bound to come.

That afternoon Grey talked to the House of Commons, asking that it approach the crisis in an awareness of "British interests, British honor, and British obligations." At last he got to the vital issue—whether England could hold off and see Belgium struck down. He borrowed a ringing sentence from Gladstone, which in the Franco-Prussian War of 1870 had served to protect Belgium's neutrality: "Could this country stand by and witness the direst crime that ever stained the pages of history and thus become participators in the crime?" There was more than an hour of this. The House listened quietly. At the end it arose cheering. Grey had his answer.

The British ultimatum to Germany followed the next day —either Germany halt its invasion of Belgium or Britain would be at war by midnight. Bethmann-Hollweg called the British Ambassador and cried his astonishment that London would go to war over a "scrap of paper," which unhappy phrase, picked up and amplified by the propagandists, plagued Germany ever after. Grey's saddening words, "The lamps are going out all over Europe; we shall not see them lit again in our lifetime," mordantly prophetic, became a requiem for peace.

But at the marshaling yards or collection points, and apart from the naval stations, it was not a formidable host that responded to Britain's mobilization order. The small professional army was still khaki-clad, as it had been for the South African War. There were 125,000 of them, well-trained, disciplined professionals, adept in musketry and night operations but woefully lacking in commanders knowledgeable of the handling of vast forces. The numbers made possible the dispatch of six slender infantry divisions and five cavalry brigades overseas. Of heavy artillery, the British could take to the field only four 60-pounder (5-inch) guns per division, and but two machine guns per infantry battalion or cavalry regiment, with no spare tubes and no reserve. But sixty-three aircraft were available to serve the expedition. In contrast to this improvident preparation by land, Britain's authority over the seas was unquestioned. In the heavier ships of war, from dreadnoughts down to cruisers, the count of the fleet was 177 to Germany's 87, and the greater part of this strength was already concentrated in home waters.

In England there was no rejoicing or effervescing of war spirit. "Life seemed to stand uneasily still," wrote Churchill, "and in no direction was there any prospect."

II
Appointment at the Marne

A company of French soldiers cross a pontoon
bridge over the Marne on September 10, 1914,
after forcing the Germans to retreat.

When the clock struck midnight on August 4, Britain was at war, though the first armed German had not yet invaded Belgium. Her entry in no way dismayed the German General Staff. They had already allowed for it and discounted it, confident that they could smash through Belgium to a decisive victory in France within four months, before Britain could get major forces to the Continent. Said the Kaiser to his departing troops: "You will be home before the leaves have fallen from the trees."

He was not alone in that gross miscalculation. Sir Edward Grey, the gentle dreamer who knew nothing of armies, guessed that the road would run on interminably, ever darkening. But few literate people in Europe felt that a Great Power conflict would be sustained; its consequences would be too frightful. Moreover, the Germans expected to win conclusively and quickly while holding the fighting and war damage to a relatively limited area.

Of all the legends arising from that gamble, the most persistent and most false is that the Germans struck forth with a perfect plan, created by an all-time genius of war, a wizard in his understanding of the influence of terrain on military operations —and that they fatally blundered by deviating from his infallible formula for success.

A fetish with historians of World War I, this theme is reiterated tiresomely. But it is wrong on all counts. The former Chief of the General Staff, Count Alfred von Schlieffen, was not a mastermind, and his original design for German victory in the West, drafted in 1905, was more elementary than inspired. Moreover, the Germans, going at Belgium, were not even adhering to the Schlieffen Plan. By 1912 that plan had become so far altered by Schlieffen's successor, General Helmuth von Moltke, that it had become another strategic concept altogether. By war's start Schlieffen was dead. But even if he had been present and empowered to execute his own plan, it is idle conjecture to assume that the German Army would have been assured victory. Schlieffen was either blind or indifferent to the political effect of strategic decisions, such as the deliberate violation of a small neutral because it blocked the broad highway. So the main and ruthless idea that became his legacy to Germany brought fatal consequences that were inherent in his planning from the start.

Schlieffen's 1905 memorandum, which is the genesis of the campaign into Belgium, was written while Russia reeled from its defeat by Japan. Reasoning that Russia was finished, if not through the wreck of its military power, then by revolution at home, Schlieffen was not contemplating how Germany should deal with a war on two fronts, but how it should engage Britain and France together. It was an old thesis with him. From 1891 onward, he had argued that the French fortresses, such as Toul and Verdun covering the Eastern frontier, were too formidable and that entry via the Low Countries was the softer alternative. He even sought to justify this morally: the law of "self-defense" was on Germany's side. These are his words: "Belgium is regarded as neutral, but in fact is not so. More than thirty years ago it made Liège and Namur into strong fortresses to prevent Germany from invading its territory, but toward France it left its frontiers open." Schlieffen spoke truly to the point. What he ignored was that Belgium so reacted because she knew no reason to fear France, but a rampant German militarism made her mistrust her other great neighbor. That Schlieffen's casuistry convinced other German soldiers and statesmen shows Belgium had reason. Therein is the root of the matter. The charge that Germany deliberately plotted a European war is unfounded. But it is beyond doubt that Germany had long since endorsed an unconscionable war plan, which by its nature exacerbated the crisis beyond hope of peaceful solution and gave the conflict its terrifying dimension.

But Schlieffen, planning to outflank France through Belgium, and Moltke, ordering that it be done, were bold and original only in their defiance of civilized opinion. There was nothing otherwise novel in their choice of a main route of advance promising the surest return because it was the swiftest. Any foot traveler seeking the easiest road from Germany to Paris must go the same way. That was determined millions of years ago. Nature made it a beaten path, the traditional road of conquest for armies out of Central Europe coveting that part of the mainland that dominated access to the coast and the mysterious seas beyond.

Only via Belgium into northern France is there a level pathway, clear of obstacles, of imposing breadth for most of the distance, and laced with every facility for the rapid deployment and continuing supply of large military forces. Highways, railroads, and canals all stream in the decisive direction. Military plans are influenced by various factors, economic, political, or tactical in character. Even so, the determining considerations have their ultimate basis in the physical features of the areas; troop movements are largely regulated by topography, even as the growth of civilization and the pattern of population distribution conform to the direction in which rivers flow and the way in which goods are transported to markets at least cost. The Schlieffen-Moltke victory design, far from being recondite, was as simple as a geometric axiom, though for armies a straight line is not always the shortest distance between two points. Metz, the German city nearest the French border, is 180 air miles from Paris. Via the Belgian plain, the German armies had to march 250 miles. But the route promised smooth going. Once the Liège gateway was forced, the invaders could spread westward around the northern Ardennes Forest, through Louvain and Brussels, and on an expanding front continue southwest past Mons, Cambrai, Saint-Quentin, and on to Paris. Said Bethmann-Hollweg: "He who is menaced as we are can only consider the one and best way to strike." In the same vein, the Kaiser cabled President Wilson: "Belgian neutrality has to be violated on strategic grounds." He was right according to the saying that there is no morality in strategy. But when military necessity displaces it, one must be sure of winning.

Moltke, who executed the plan, was one of the few who had no illusions about a short war. His General Staff associates had a pet name for him, the German equivalent of "Gloomy Gus." He saw ahead only "the long, wearisome struggle," come a Great Power war, and in that he agreed with his opposite number, General Joffre. That makes it the more inexplicable that, taking up where Schlieffen left off, he grasped for the shadow of the existing plan and rejected its substance. If it was to be a protracted conflict, he was doing the worst possible thing in the beginning by giving the ultimate provocation to the greatest possible number of Germany's enemies. In the light of history, there is no possible explanation of Moltke's vagaries except lazy-mindedness, awe of the establishment that he was supposed to master, timidity about putting himself in opposition to political authority, and the desire for high honor through vainglorious timeserving.

By 1914 Moltke was sixty-six years old, a near invalid, and a captive to the command ideas of his uncle, the great Moltke, whose concepts of staff management and battle direction he slavishly imitated. The younger Moltke did not believe that after armies were deployed it was incumbent on him to control the battle. He thought of his position as being too remote for that; after he had fired the starting gun, decisions as to movement would be regulated by the field commanders forward. Fear of his own capacity no doubt played a part in his abdication. Said a German critic: "He actually drew some comfort from the Emperor's frequent declaration that in the event of war he would himself command in the West."

Moltke did not modify the Schlieffen Plan; he buried it. As drafted in 1905, that plan called for the German left wing to have but 15 per cent of the strength of the right wing, the one to be deployed through Belgium. According to plan, the left wing was later to be cut to 9 per cent by shifting two army corps across the front to the flank irrupting Belgium, after the main weight of the French Army had become committed in Alsace and Lorraine. That would necessitate the left wing retiring to German soil, tantalizing the pursuing French with an illusion of victory, while drawing them ever farther away from the arena of decision.

The weakness of the plan, beyond the political jeopardy that it risked, was its logistical absurdity. Schlieffen took no account of human limitations; superhuman endurance was being asked of the German soldier. Further than that, an excessive load was shifted to the roads and rails of the right wing, which could produce indescribable congestion. Schlieffen had intended to violate the Netherlands also; thus he might have spread his troops and eased the jam. But when Moltke nay-said the invasion of Dutch territory, the plan had to be altered, and once the redrafting began, the new cooks prepared quite a different broth.

By the end, Moltke had brought the strength of the left wing up to 42 per cent of the right wing. Through that distribution, the German plan of campaign was so radically altered that there is no reason, other than humanity's love of legends true or false, for identifying the Schlieffen name with what transpired. Moltke, in fact, had persuaded Germany to try for victory through a double envelopment instead of through a single one.

Still, Moltke took enough from Schlieffen to hang himself. One fatal miscalculation by his predecessor stands out. Schlieffen had reckoned that Russian armies would not menace East Prussia until after the completion of mobilization, which would take thirty days or so; with luck, it would afford a sufficient interval for conclusive victory over France. Moltke banked on that, never dreaming that the despised antagonist to the east was taking the superb gamble at the beginning, and would throw two field armies at him before they were ready and while Russian mobilization was less than half completed. Nor was it only in Russia that audacity and recklessness, which ever open the door to catastrophe, displaced normal military caution. Not even the German Army was prepared in spirit, plan, and material resources for swift recovery after initial defeat—though nothing in war is certain.

Every General Staff in Europe on the eve of collision was self-duped. Each one overestimated the capability of its own forces and held too cheaply the fighting power of its field enemy and the endurance of the nation behind it. From this came the shallowness in the plan and preparation; while there were doubters in all camps, policy was managed by the optimists who believed that the issue would be determined in one great thunderclap of action. The advantages to be gained from greater mobility were disregarded; the question of what effect the proliferating automatic weapons and increased artillery fire would have upon troop employments was not so much ignored as despised. In the British Army the entrenching spade had been abandoned as no longer necessary in war, despite all the digging that had so recently occurred in South Africa and around Port Arthur. The French Army had disdained instruction about the use of the same tool. "To dig one's self in diminishes the intensity of one's fire and depresses the offensive spirit." In this way, as in many others, the armies had failed to train for the unusual war that they were about to fight, despite the important lesson of military history that every war is by comparison with all others largely abnormal. It was not a blindness peculiar to European staffs in those days. An early victim of any prolonged peace is military realism. It happens in every system. The hard truths of the battlefield, indelibly imprinted on the minds of leaders who learn by experience, are too soon diluted by their successors, who know their subject only in theory. As in civilian life, sound planning in the military world is ever bedeviled by new managers espousing change for the sake of change.

The French war plan (called Plan XVII) was the product of such hit-or-miss calculation. "A piece of backstairs jobbery," it is called by J. F. C. Fuller, the genius among strategists in this century. The words fit. General Joffre's General Staff did not even try to read the German mind or anticipate the enemy plan of campaign. It was deemed unnecessary. Once it became an article of faith with G.Q.G. that the French *poilu* ("hairy one") was irresistible in the attack, all balance was lost. Reasonable defensive precaution became taboo. The plan called for the French armies to go headlong at the enemy, deploying between Mézières and Epinal, to advance straight forward against the German center—or rather, where the French guessed the center would be. Having smashed it, they would go on and paralyze German communications in Lorraine.

Britain's one cavalry and four infantry divisions would come in on the left and mop up such German forces as were to be found between that flank and the Channel. This plan for joint action was initiated around 1906, evolved during the next seven years, and was, in 1914, still incomplete.

THE INVASION OF BELGIUM

On the afternoon of August 4, 1914, there appeared in the mouth the the Liège gateway the cavalry advance guard covering six reinforced German infantry brigades out of General Karl von Bülow's Second Army.

The first major mission of the invaders was to smash the defenses of this narrow pass and win admission to the Belgian plain. The gateway is only twelve miles across. Batteries in the forts of Liège dominated the railway lines that funnel through this corridor before spreading out again on the plains beyond. Until Liège was won, the main body of invaders could not pour through the pass and traffic would daily become more congested.

There were 60,000 Germans in the spearhead; 25,000 Belgians manned the works around the city. Behind them, the forced-draft mobilization was still less than half completed, though the sudden call had choked every artery of travel. Beyond Liège, the Belgian Army counted but 117,000 men, formed in seven divisions, with no reserve backup, compulsory military service having been in effect less than one year. Equipment and training were inadequate; ammunition was so short that range practice had been limited to one bullet per man per week; the army was critically short of machine guns, the equalizing weapon that best serves an undermanned defense; the parliament had refused to appropriate money for field guns to cover the open space between the Liège forts. Soldiers and units braced to their tasks unsustained by any tradition of military courage, Belgium never having fought a war.

But Liège was no soft mark. The Meuse bridges above and below the city had already been wrecked by Belgian demolition crews. The heights above them on both shores glared at the German infantry. A dozen modern forts, thick-walled and fitted with four hundred guns, breathed menace from the high ground. Energizing the garrisons was a snowy-haired diehard, General Gérard Mathieu Leman, who had received a "hold to the end" order from King Albert, and was determined to die trying.

The Germans cracked Belgian soil that evening. The next morning Leman spurned a surrender demand. By nightfall the invaders had crossed the river at Visé, far north of Liège and next to the Dutch border, spurred on by a relatively unknown colonel of fusiliers, Erich Ludendorff, who had become separated from his own unit in the confusion of battle. He was already complaining about armed resistance by Belgian civilians. German soldiers were to execute these so-called *francs tireurs* (civilian snipers) by the hundreds without trial; their wanton slaughter was the basis of the "Belgian atrocity" stories, which in later years were discounted as propaganda. On the first day, before anything was clear, the Germans instituted the organized butchery not only of innocent civilians but of Belgian priests, whom, with no shred of proof, they accused of instigating resistance. These Germans were first-time fighters. Their nerves were jumpy. They imagined that anything that moved was an armed enemy. This was nothing new with green troops. Little more can be said in mitigation, and it leaves not half explained the fact that the German campaign through Belgium was sullied by orgiastic frightfulness, a pagan saturnalia of burning and killing. No wonder Moltke wrote on August 5: "Our advance in Belgium is certainly brutal."

Liège died hard. The Germans tried to cross the river on pontoons. To the astonishment of survivors, the effort collapsed bloodily in Meuse water. The brigades hitting in the center were checked and beaten back by the guns in the four forts farthest forward. The Germans, who knew no better at this stage, tried to charge the slopes in a run straight at nested machine guns. The resulting carnage was grim and great, before General Otto von Emmich, who directed the siege, pulled back his troops.

Alexander von Kluck (left) and Karl von
Bülow were both sixty-eight years old
when they led the German First and Second
armies in the Battle of Mons at the Belgian
frontier in August, 1914. If left to his
own devices, Kluck, described as arrogant
and unapproachable, might have bypassed the
British defenses and—due to his superior
numbers—left the B.E.F. utterly ruined.
Unfortunately for him and for the larger
German campaign, he was temporarily under
the command of Bülow, a white-haired,
nervous fellow who seemed to need to pull
everything in around him to feel secure.
Ordering Kluck to stay close, forbidding him
to swing wide, Bülow made it impossible
for Kluck to attempt anything but a head-on
attack. Although the Germans inflicted
heavy losses, they sounded the cease-fire,
allowing the British to claim this battle as
their first small success.

Still, luck was with him. Put on the right road by Ludendorff, the German cavalry out of Visé struck south and got on the rear of the Liège defenses, where the Belgian plain opened. This threat, more hollow than real, shook Leman immoderately. He forthwith ordered the mobile division and brigade, which had come to him as reinforcements, to quit Liège and rejoin the main body of the Belgian Army behind the Gete River. That denuded his front in the areas between the garrisons tied down in the right forts.

Again Ludendorff became destiny's darling. At precisely the right moment for Ludendorff, General Wussow, commanding the 14th Brigade, was killed by a shell. The sightseer took over and, after almost coming to grief by losing his direction, got on the right road again and led the brigade under cover of darkness to the inner citadel of Liège. For this limited success, he spared himself no credit, saying of it: "I gathered that the faith of troops in this undertaking was slight." The heart of the city was no longer close-guarded, owing to Leman's order, but on this stroke Ludendorff rocketed to fame. Before Ludendorff was through with the business, Emmich had passed two additional brigades into the city.

But the figure of Ludendorff, "first seen through the fumes of Liège by the German people," was better understood than the deed. He had not broken Liège, for the forts still held out. Even so, Berlin hailed the new hero with delight, and Moltke ceased quaking for the first time.

Cut off from the main body of the army, the three brigades at last won freedom of maneuver by capturing Fort Barchon from the rear on August 10. That partially cleared the way for the advance of Germany's first surprise weapon—the 420-mm. siege guns that wrecked the remaining forts one by one. On August 15 General Leman was felled and carried unconscious from the ruins of Fort Loncin. The next day the defense ended.

What the ten-day stand at Liège did for the Allied cause remains a question. Sentimentally, it gained much. The example of "brave little Belgium" steeled green troops of other nations, and the image won hearts around the world. The legend lasts that it also gained extra time, stopping the German field armies long enough to allow France to deploy and permit the landing of the British Expeditionary Force on the Continent. Thereby heroism at Liège is made to underwrite victory at the Marne.

The Germans deny it absolutely. Ludendorff is one witness: "We got possession of all the works just in time to permit the march of the army over the Meuse without hindrance." General Alexander von Kluck, commander of the First German Army, is less assertive in his memoir. He did not get orders until August 10; he marked time at most for forty-eight hours after his army was formed and he felt it ready to march. He says of the later fight for Brussels: "Had the German Army been *mobilized* and deployed three days earlier, a more decisive result might have been obtained." But there is no hint that Liège wrecked the schedule, and basic logistics makes it seem implausible. The great concentration did not start until August 6. Thereafter each day until August 12, 550 troop trains crossed the Rhine, putting more than one million soldiers in the forward zone.

On August 5, the same day that Emmich first bruised his knuckles on Liège, General Joffre joined his fifty-officer G.Q.G. staff at Vitry-le François, a village on the Marne. Twice a day this entourage pondered a general situation report, discussed what it meant, and prepared orders, in undeviating routine. Joffre's right bower was a fiddlestring-taut soldier, General Belin, but he inclined more toward 250-pound General Henri Mathias Berthelot, who like himself "couldn't understand difficulties." The French were not yet in contact with the enemy, and G.Q.G. for the moment was even more remote from the war's realities.

On August 7, for instance, Joffre sped the Belgian liaison officer Major Collon homeward to present his views. The Belgian Army was advised to form on the Meuse, attempt delaying any German effort to cross, and then either attack the enemy columns in flank or fall back on Namur to help the French. Joffre was just 180 degrees out of phase with the possibilities. Hardly had Collon departed with this *aide mémoire* when a wire from Brussels carrying an appeal for help from the Belgian Army hit Joffre's desk. Joffre had only one cavalry corps in the north and he ordered it posthaste to Beligum to see what it could do. Then he settled back, "there being nothing more that I could do." That evening he heard from his own War Minister, Adolphe Messimy, that the Belgian Government was seeking an armistice—the war's first dangerously tall story. Last, he published the attack order to the French Army. Next day he calculated that the German main body was concentrating behind the Moselle river; Liège he regarded as a feint or a sideshow. Because the commander of his own VII Army Corps was advancing cautiously in Alsace instead of rushing upon the enemy, he suggested his removal—this before one blow had been struck. It was all rather dreamlike.

In England, Lord Kitchener, though just back from Egypt, saw things more clearly. On August 5, in front of the War Cabinet, he argued with ten other generals about the placement of the Expeditionary Force. His military colleagues pressed for a concentration around Maubeuge, which was far forward. Kitchener wanted it at Amiens, seventy miles closer to Paris. He said it was wrong to expose the B.E.F. to an initial retreat; to his mind, he added, the violation of Belgium signified that the Germans were launching their knockout blow east and west of the Meuse. Thoroughly right as to his premise, he was nonetheless mistaken in his tactical conclusion, and in any case was voted down because the French military advisers in London sided against him. Kitchener mistrusted their plan wholly and expected the Germans to scatter the French "like partridges." Here he was guided on intuition, for he was as strange to European armies as to his home establishment. A son of Mars, he extended his contempt to the British Army, "the preserve of gentlemen who dislike having to take their own profession seriously." Yet so great was his prestige that when he was named War Minister on August 6 (the first serving soldier to sit in any cabinet since the Duke of Albemarle in 1660), the British public for the first time reacted ecstatically to the war news. Already he was telling his cabinet colleagues that the war would be won only with the aid of "the last million men," and they listened less in shocked dismay than in indulgent disbelief.

Another popular choice, lionized by the press, Sir John French, the former Chief of the Imperial General Staff, got away to France on August 14. This first commander of the B.E.F. is described with reasonable accuracy as "a weak-willed man of medium height, amiable enough, though petulant when thwarted." Expedited smoothly by the Royal Navy, his small 100,000-man army got to the appointed ground in good time and just across the border in southern Belgium formed a front hinged on the coal mining center of Mons. Its east-west line extended for approximately twenty-seven miles. There, nonengaged, the army (Corps I and II) for almost one week marched and fired its weapons to harden the lately received reservists. Sir John made great plans for smiting the weaker side of the oncoming Germans. One brief visit to G.Q.G. had sold him on Joffre's optimism. The various parts of his own army were not linked by telephone; it was a lazy signals job; G.H.Q. did not even have a line to the corps commanders. Already, Sir John had met General Charles Lanrezac, who commanded the French Fifth Army on his right, and had rated him "a pedant whose 'superior education' gives him no idea how to conduct war." Lanrezac loved French no better. Inspired snap judgments, they boded ill for the two Allied armies.

Waiting time for the B.E.F. ended on August 22. A British air pilot reported seeing field-gray columns swinging out to the west of the twenty-seven-mile front, beyond which there was only French cavalry. Sir John recorded his "disappointment and disillusionment" at hearing the Germans were coming on in large numbers. The French Fifth Army was being pounded all along its front. Its bridgehead force guarding Namur, the fortress city at the strategic triangle where the Sambre joins the Meuse, was broken and driven off. Both rivers were falling rapidly and could be forded in many places. Lanrezac, already spinning toward emotional collapse, appealed to Sir John to attack in flank the enemy columns coming at his army. Bearing in mind the air report that the Germans were swinging wide enough to bag the B.E.F., Sir John prudently refused. If he turned to aid Lanrezac, the movement would put the enemy on his rear. Though that threat was more fancied than real, the danger for other reasons was greater than Sir John knew. Lanrezac's army had already been driven back an average of ten miles from the Sambre, which put the B.E.F. alone and unsupported the same distance forward; that displacement Lanrezac concealed from French. Yet on the same day that he appealed to Sir John to attack across the front that he had vacated, Lanrezac in a signal to Joffre reported on "the British Army which is still in echelon to the rear of the Fifth Army." It was a ludicrously clumsy attempt to alibi defeat by shifting the blame elsewhere. Sir John, with his G.H.Q. at Le Cateau, twenty-six miles from his rifle line, was too remote from the war to plumb the depth of Lanrezac's duplicity. He agreed to hold at Mons for an additional twenty-four hours. But that night he decided on retreat although he had not even been hurt.

After cracking Liège, the German First and Second armies (Kluck and Bülow) had rolled on through southern Belgium. Brussels, perfunctorily defended, became the stage for a German victory parade. King Albert drew off his shattered army into fortified Antwerp, where it regrouped and licked its wounds for a time.

Kluck's mass to the west of the Meuse river, Bülow's to the east of it, the German right wing then attacked straight south-westward, following the valleys of the Meuse and the Sambre, its tributary. This valley line, when extended, points straight to Paris. As the two invading armies were heading, their combined strength converged more directly on Mons than on the British right flank, left dangling in air by Lanrezac's withdrawal. For the defenders, it was not an ideal situation. Superior ability to concentrate is the almost invariable advantage of the army in movement; the Germans were abreast of their march tables and keyed high by the successes that followed Liège; their supply problems were half solved by the bounty of the countryside; their horses foraged on the uncollected harvest. The surprise of overwhelming numbers, with its devastating shock, had been withheld till the last moment, due to the nigh total breakdown of the information flow between the Allied fighting line and higher headquarters. The British line's first warning came from a phenomenon that continued to plague the beaten armies during their most desperate hours—the terror of an uprooted people in mad flight. "A grey mob, grey because the black clothes most of them wore were covered with dust, was filing endlessly by; they occupied the whole width of the road . . . [going] in absolute silence, the only sound being that of very tired feet dragging. . . . Each individual in that slowly-moving mass looked the embodiment of a personal tragedy; men and women with set staring faces, carrying heavy bundles, moving on they knew not where, formed a background of grim despair." So wrote an eyewitness, Lieutenant Edward L. Spears, in *Liaison, 1914.*

Still, with all this fortune, the German giant nodded. Kluck, an irascible old man, was the relentless driver and gambler of the pair; Bülow was the nervous type, the tidy tactician, prey to his fears. Kluck's army had more than enough power to sweep around the British; out of it would have come the B.E.F.'s ruin. But Bülow, for purposes of coordination, was temporarily commanding the group, and Kluck was ordered to stay close. So instead of attempting a decisive maneuver, he came like a bull with head down, straight at the British front.

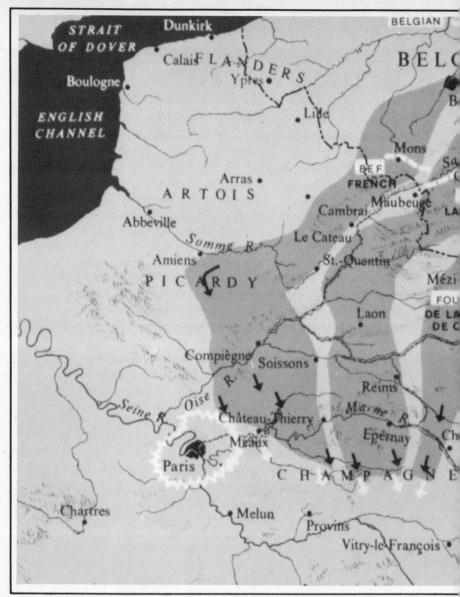

The five armies of the German right wing and
center cut a wide swath through Belgium and
France in August, 1914. The great Belgian
fortresses of Liège and Namur, reputed to be
impregnable, fell within days. This map
depicts the futile efforts of the B.E.F. and
French Fifth Army to check the invasion

at Mons and at the Sambre River (broken
white lines), as well as the abortive French
offensives in the Ardennes Forest and Lorraine
(broken white arrows), and shows the Germans
(black arrows) pursuing the French and
British south of the Marne about September 4.

Sir John had not backed out of Mons in time, though being far to the rear at Le Cateau, he did not know it till later. That Sunday opened pastorally, church bells ringing, townsfolk going to early Mass. The rest of the day was battle. The blow fell directly on the British II Corps under General Sir Horace Smith-Dorrien. The Germans tried what had worked against the Belgians, their standard practice, the buildup of a fire line, followed by an infantry charge. Nothing worked. They were cut down in windrows by British rifle fire. The onslaught withered amid slate dumps, slag piles, and oat fields. But it was not all one way. Around Mons the unremitting cannonade took hard toll and by midafternoon, to escape it, the British pulled back to a line of villages south of the town. Sir John arrived in early evening to confer with his corps commanders, in time to hear enemy buglers sound the "Cease fire!" as if on maneuvers. He found II Corps hurting badly. The British paid with 4,244 casualties for this first small success. Still, Mons became a famous victory. B.E.F. veterans were called Mons Men, and Britain's battle medal for the early days is known as the Mons Star.

Just before midnight Sir John ordered his army to hit the road. The "Retreat from Mons" is better known than the battle. It began unpromisingly. Lanrezac had already ordered another fallback by his army, again without advising the British. The French Fifth, counting one-quarter million men, had been battered throughout the day by Bülow's Second Army, though its losses south of the Sambre and in the climactic fight for Charleroi were but a flesh wound compared to the carnage of later battlefields. Even so, the Fifth was not without honor, being the last French army to go into recoil following defeat on the forward ground. Retreat was the word everywhere. But Joffre was still blind to the number of Germans in his theatre and refused to believe in the collapse of his illusionary plan.

In the west, British and French retired as they had fought, almost without reference to one another. The initial estrangement between Lanrezac and Sir John soured into outright hostility, for the Frenchman was behaving abominably, and the Englishman, knowing he was being crossed, withdrew unto himself. For that part of it, Lanrezac is without excuse. His personal failings were ignoble. Not so the retirement of his army. It drooped between two fires—the French Fourth Army under General Fernand de

70

Langle de Cary, fronting on the Ardennes, having already been crushed by General Max Klemens von Hausen's Third Army.

Smith-Dorrien's battered corps closed on Le Cateau after midnight August 25–26, with the enemy not far behind. The men were dead beat, their condition made worse by a violent thunderstorm. Their General ordered a bivouac in the town, an ineluctable decision when troops are exhausted. Sir John had bucketed on to Saint-Quentin, twenty-six miles closer to Paris. By 2:00 A.M. Smith-Dorrien knew that the enemy was on him, and he must either resume march with a sleepwalking corps or accept battle soon after dawn. He said to his people: "Very well, gentlemen, we will fight." Two factors mainly influenced his judgment. The corps was spread out among the town houses and outlying farms; to get an order to units would take hours, there being no telephones between them. And refugees clogged the roads. The fact was that Sir Horace had no choice. The battle of Le Cateau was unavoidable.

The Germans hit soon after first light. The British had no time to prepare defenses. But there were stone walls at hand and they picked the ones that commanded the best fields of fire, as American militiamen did between Concord and Lexington. Fighting began in the streets of Le Cateau, the enemy having crept in under cover of fog. These skirmishers were hunted down and destroyed. But again the enemy superiority in artillery told heavily. The British were still holding most of their line when dusk set in. Midway, they had received gallant support from the French cavalry corps under General J. F. A. Sordet. The day is best summed up in the words of the British official history: "In fact, the whole of Smith-Dorrien's troops had done what was thought to be impossible. With both flanks more or less in the air, they had turned upon an enemy of at least twice their strength; had struck him hard, and had withdrawn . . . practically without interference. . . . The men looked upon themselves as victors, some indeed doubted whether they had been in a serious action."

If a victory for Britain, Le Cateau was like that of King Pyrrhus. Smith-Dorrien's defense cost 8,077 men and thirty-six cannon. By these losses the fighting parts of the B.E.F. were cut by half and Sir John's soul became gutted of hope. The British II Corps limped away, still less crippled in body than was Marshal French in spirit.

Turning now to the denouement of Joffre's wishful planning

for his own army, we must backtrack two weeks. The records of France's ordeal—the repulse to her thrusting armies, the trembling of her Government, the misery of a people invaded, and the collapse of the dream that the readiness of soldiers to die in futile attack is sufficient insurance for victory—leave much to be desired. There were no press correspondents; no one who understood, fully observed, and was free to report what he knew. No official process insured that this be done. The main sources are memoirs written by principals who had axes to grind, or letters by inconsequential participants who saw but one acre of a vast landscape. They are equally undependable. History therefore resorts to that logic by which mistaken intentions become reconciled, perhaps too easily, with nigh catastrophic developments.

Joffre was certain that the Germans were advancing with a relatively small army. His intelligence bureau had told him that no enemy reservists would be fed into the battle formations, and this he believed. So by adding two columns of figures, he concluded that the French would be in superior force all along their frontier. That basic reasoning guided his every battle order up till August 23.

What came of Plan XVII's mistaken intentions is called the Battle of the Frontiers, a name as vague as is human knowledge of the slaughter in which France lost about 300,000 soldiers from the initial collision. Joffre proposed to get his five field armies approximately in line from the Swiss border to Abbeville on the Somme by August 25. Three armies would seal off the rest of the country while the two armies of the right wing dealt the hammer blow. By August 11 the French First Army (General Auguste Dubail) struck with six divisions in Upper Alsace, captured Mulhouse, and was then beaten back from it with heavy loss. On August 14 the French First and Second (General Noël de Castelnau) armies attacked northeastward past Metz. Without giving battle, the German Sixth Army retired to draw them on. By August 20 the French were winding through difficult country where narrow roads wind crazily and small hills, lakes, and forest partition an advancing front. There the German Sixth and Seventh armies fell upon the Second Army and one flank of the First. In the battles of Morhange and Sarrebourg, the Second Army was thoroughly defeated, and by evening both French armies of the right flank were in full retreat. Despite this setback east of Metz, the French Third and Fourth armies attacked west of Metz on the following day, and, crossing the frontier, deployed into the formidable Ardennes plateau, a region of sharp hills and dense forest. The German Fifth and Fourth armies (under the German Crown Prince and Albrecht, Duke of Württemberg) were already situated in the Ardennes and were informed of the French advance; their nested machine guns covered the sensitive points and defiles. (The French counted twenty divisions, the Germans twenty-one.) But the invaders had stopped and taken up defensive positions because the uplands were wrapped in fog. The French blundered into this defensive front and, true to their doctrine, tried to crush it at bayonet point. They were mowed down by machine guns. In these grotesque encounters, the French were everywhere beaten. The two armies retreated.

The French showed ardor and nothing else. They did not try to advance in short rushes or to wiggle forward or to make a stealthy use of ground in their approaches. Their battle kits contained no grenades. They charged straight in, expecting by audacity to stampede the enemy. By today's view, that is madness. But these soldiers tried to do what they had been taught. History tries to explain why they were so stupid. It blames as their evil genius Lieutenant Colonel Louzeau de Grandmaison, a firebrand and chief of training on the General Staff, later killed in battle as a brigadier. Grandmaison was the main voice of the oversimplified preachment that wars are won by the unconquerable spirit. Though he has been damned for half a century, he was more than half right. In prolonged periods of peace there is no other way to keep high the power of an army than to kindle an aggressive spirit in combat troops, while judiciously instructing them about the techniques of defensive action. Yet, when one colonel is blamed for the near ruin of five field armies, it proves only that scores of generals have abdicated their main responsibilities.

One of them was Ferdinand Foch, who in the wrong hour amplified Grandmaison's voice insensibly, and then late in the war arrived at the supreme position at the right time, when the same voice rang clear as a bell over every battlefield. Foch in 1914 was but the commander of the French XX Corps in the Second Army, which failed east of Metz. The greater offender was Joffre, who commanded all armies. He could have cut Grandmaison down, had he known enough, and been confident of it, to disagree.

Joffre not only swallowed what Grandmaison offered but based his battle plan upon it. In this individual, whom capricious fortune had elevated to the throne of responsibility, there were combined intellectual dullness and emotional phlegm in heroic or disastrous proportion. His failure to see and understand almost doomed France and her cause from the beginning. His personal obliviousness to the cost of his own blunders in the end became France's salvation. It is not always thus that world-shaking reputations are made. But the controversy over Joffre goes on.

Langle de Cary, the commander of the French Fourth Army, used the word "disorderly" in reporting to G.Q.G that he was retreating. Joffre merely concluded that troops only misbehaved when they were badly led, and urged him to relieve some of the officers. When the flow of bad news continued into the night of August 23, Joffre at last sat down to reestimate his situation. He arose quite satisfied that there was nothing wrong with his plan. According to the numbers, his armies were in superior strength all along the front. The repulse was due to "lack of energy on the part of local commanders."

Moltke, now headquartered in Luxembourg, read the progress reports from his field generals and felt little relief. Wracked by illness, in his own words "knowing pain indescribable," he viewed all things darkly. Yet at this stage some instinct properly warned him. Great German victories were being reported by his converging armies. But where was the large take of prisoners and where the toll of captured guns? These are the tokens, the forfeits, of a beaten, broken foe. If the French Army was not demoralized from battle losses and early defeat, the farther it fell back on its own main bases, the stronger would become its unity, the firmer its control, the better its supply, and the easier its replacement problem. The German Army, by contrast, was paying the normal penalty of too rapid extension. Battle forces were having to be pared off to guard every main city, river crossing, and highway juncture in the wake of the march. Such detachments had already cost the Germans more mobile force than the French had lost in the frontier fighting. One other equalizing factor not entering into German calculations was at work. It is a biological, a glandular thing. Troops backpedaling from a fight retain and regain more energy than troops prodded to attack, meaning that pursuit is always more wearing than retreat, though the latter sounds more grim.

By the next day, August 24, Joffre knew! G.Q.G. had gone over all the messages of the prior night from the field armies. There was not one shred of comfort. From flank to flank it was the same story—defeat and retreat. The offensive was dead; Plan XVII was a chimera. For more than an hour, the bulky old man paced up and down in the garden at Vitry, hands clasped behind his back, his pink, bewhiskered face immobile, the person seemingly lost in thought. His awakening had come on reading a gloomy report from Langle de Cary, whose integrity and nerve he deemed unshakable, though he so credited few others. He sensed at last that his main peril lay on the left. That galled him more because only the British were in position to offset the menace, and this was the one army to which he had no right to give orders. So he set in motion a scheme to form a new French army based at Amiens.

In Paris, War Minister Messimy, a soldier and graduate of the Staff College, was playing nobly the role of the steadying civilian superior. Amid the gloom, he spoke no reproof, sending Joffre only words of encouragement. But he went beyond that. Read one wire of the day: "Send back officers relieved of command by motorcar and have them court-martialed. There are only two punishments, dismissal and death. You want to win; to do so, use the most rapid, brutal, energetic, and decisive methods." Joffre shuddered at that and decided that the normal processes for eliminating combat weaklings would be sufficient. More constructive, more decisive, though it encroached on strategy which generals regard as their domain, was Messimy's next communication: "If our armies are forced to retreat, an army composed of at least three active corps must be directed upon the entrenched camp of Paris." That was an order, not a suggestion. The contingent situation had already arisen. But the concept was too broad for Joffre; he hadn't three corps to spare and he was still thinking fuzzily about a new army at Amiens.

Paris was blessed in having the one right man as military governor, General Joseph Simon Gallieni, a veteran colonial, pulled from retirement to command the capital's defenses. There were none; he started the barricading and entrenchment on the day of his appointment, August 25. But it was on his own terms. "They don't want to defend Paris," he said to Messimy. "In the eyes of our strategists Paris is a geographical expression—a town like any other. What do we have in troops to defend this heart and brain of France? A drop in the bucket. Give me an army of three active corps and I will agree to become Governor of Paris. On this condition, formal and explicit, you can count on me." That was what swayed Messimy. Thereafter the two men worked together to raise the vital garrison, ordering new reserve formations to the spot, pressuring Joffre to release active divisions as his front narrowed. In this way the French Sixth Army came alive as a last-minute improvisation. It was not Joffre's creation; he suffered it.

Not unbroken, the retreat continued. On August 29 Lanrezac's Fifth Army turned and hit back hard in the battle at Guise, then broke off and got away little hurt. Stunned, Bülow's Second Army stayed rooted to its tracks for two days, while its chief cried to Kluck for help.

The same day better news came from the right wing. Among the French Army reforms that had followed the 1870 defeat was the construction of a fortified line that ran in an arc around the east-facing scarps inside the frontier. This barrier of sunken forts, anchored on Belfort next to Switzerland, continued to Epinal, past Toul, and on to Verdun, by nature the stoutest bastion in the system. Between the Epinal and Toul nodals, the engineer general in charge, Seré de Rivières, had left a forty-mile gap called the *Trouée de Charmes*, which device was intended to attract, canalize, and trap any German invasion. A tactical absurdity since forty miles affords too wide a deployment, surprisingly, it worked. Crown Prince Rupprecht's Sixth and Seventh armies, flushed with victory, struck south to Epinal, then turned west into the *Trouée de Charmes*, where the attack broke down completely, although Castelnau's Second Army was in the process of detaching divisions for the Paris garrison when called to battle. With that, the eastern door slammed shut against the Germans, never to open again. Concurrently, out of Verdun, the French Third Army, now under General Maurice Sarrail, smote in flank the Crown Prince's army when it tried to pass the fortress. Bleeding hard, it recoiled.

These counterblows, warning that the French were not done, came too late to save Moltke from a catastrophic blunder. Wilhelm had been at him again. This time he had better reason. The Russians were about to overrun Prussia. At Gumbinnen on August

The massive Joffre seems to be lecturing the mercurial Sir John French (center) while Sir Douglas Haig, apparently amused, looks on from the right. Despite his many errors in judgment, French Commander-in-Chief Joffre generated great respect from his countrymen.

20, three German army corps had been whipped, two divisions quitting the field in such panic that 7,000 prisoners passed into Russian hands. Five days of straight German success in the West had bespoken to Wilhelm that the game there was already won; it remained but to reap the harvest. Moltke, still doubting, fearing more the displeasure of the All-Highest than the consequences to his soliders, took the weak way out. On August 25 he decided to withdraw two corps from his armies in France and speed them to Prussia. The irony was that the Russians, after Gumbinnen, entered a prolonged tactical pause.

This while Joffre still groped. He had no scheme yet for recovery, and while his left wing fell back, he simply calculated where it might make a stand. By August 25 he defined the line as Verdun-Laon-Amiens-Abbeville. But between the B.E.F. and the Channel was only vacant country. It was this gap, not Paris, that prompted the idea for a new army at Amiens. One division, pulled back from Alsace, and five reserve divisions, newly raised, actually got there. They made it just in time to join the retreat. They fell back on Paris, squeezed toward it by the general retirement, and there joined an Algerian division and a Moroccan brigade to form the Sixth Army under General Michel Joseph Maunoury.

Something else that happened to benefit the left wing was not so inadvertent. After Le Cateau, Sir John French played the booby, wholly fed up by his experience with Lanrezac. On August 31, the B.E.F. being no longer in contact with the enemy, its commander wired Kitchener: "I have decided to begin my retirement to-morrow in the morning, behind the Seine, in a southwesterly direction west of Paris. This means marching for some eight days. . . . " What it actually meant was that Sir John was quitting the war and pointing his soldiers toward the port of Saint-Nazaire, where he proposed to reembark them for England. When Kitchener hurried to Paris, ordering Sir John to meet him there for a conference, the commander bridled at the War Minister for interfering with his strategy. There was a painful, private scene between them, after which friendly relations died. What mattered was that Kitchener ordered Sir John back into battle and he complied.

On that same day, September 1, Kluck was writing to his army: "The forces in front of us are now known to be the British;

there's still a chance of reaching this enemy." He couldn't have been more wrong. Earlier, he had let the British slip away from his front when he might have reached out his hand and gathered them in. Now he sent his troops on a wild-goose chase, though, feeling they were exhausted, he had previously scheduled a day of rest.

But that was a sideslip, not a deviation from the grand design to which Moltke still held with nervous fingers. His directive of August 27 outlined the army missions: First Army to advance on the lower Seine, keeping west of the Oise; Second Army to march on Paris; Third Army to march on Château-Thierry, Fourth Army on Epernay; the Fifth Army was to invest Verdun; and the Sixth and Seventh armies would stand on the defensive in Lorraine and Alsace. That still left it to the overmarched right wing to harvest quick victory. Moltke's order ended on the equivocal note: "If the enemy puts up strong resistance on the Aisne and later on the Marne, it may be necessary to abandon the southwestern direction of the advance and wheel south." That was asking for trouble, since Kluck and Bülow were already at loggerheads over the direction to be taken. Bülow thought it best to stop extending the line because the right wing, weakened by the withdrawal of the two corps sent to fight the Russians, had already lost cohesion. Kluck was so certain of victory that he did not even report the fresh forces (French Sixth Army) gathering off his right flank and was prepared to press on by whatever road promised the swiftest reward. When in the evening of August 31 Bülow besought the First Army's cooperation by wheeling inward "to gain the full advantage of the victory," Kluck was happy to comply because it fitted his own headlong mood. When Kluck wirelessed Moltke about the change, he got the High Command's blessing. There is no accounting for Moltke's mental processes in this, the critical hour of his professional life. The rational explanation is that he saw no option but to eliminate the French Army, calculating that the right wing was too weak either for a drive west of Paris or to invest Paris.

With Moltke's concurrence, the whole concept was changed, and the plan that the Germans had followed since Liège fell by the wayside. With the Third Army converging toward the Aisne, the two armies of the extreme right wing were to form a common front and drive the French forces of the left flank southeastward away from Paris. Herewith was abandoned the main idea of crossing the Seine west of Paris and taking that city, the hub of all communications arteries, the citadel of French resistance. Instead, the now partly fortified capital, and its garrison, would be left to threaten the flank of Bülow's armies. Kluck, power-intoxicated, didn't get it at first. Three days later, the light dawned and he lamented: "To drive the enemy away from Paris southeasterly is difficult and risky. But the Supreme Command seems firmly convinced that the garrison of Paris need not be taken into account."

The German change of direction started at once. That evening, Kluck's wheeling movement was detected by a British pilot. The shift was also confirmed by a captured order. Still unseeing, Joffre was given the momentous news late on August 31. On the following day, September 1, occurred the key moves and decisions that culminated in the series of widely separated but hard-fought actions called the Battle of the Marne. No great event was ever more ingeniously shaped out of human fumbling and error. It could not have been fought but for the presence of the French Sixth Army on the right ground, more through accident than design. Had Kluck not wheeled eastward, his weight might have been enough to smash Maunoury's four divisions. But that is mere conjecture. When the Germans changed their plan and lost, it magnified the significance of every blunder on the road to failure. Yet it is beyond proof that had Kluck stayed west of the Oise, he would have known fortune. The German right wing was already dangerously overextended; its troops were played out. Every mile they marched produced greater compaction in the Anglo-French forces, simplifying Allied communications, easing their supply problems, and bringing their commanders into closer hour-by-hour contact with each other, this being of utmost importance. Physically, the Allies were at last becoming a collected camp at the same rate that greater diffusion beset the Germans. That Kluck failed wholly to understand that the balance was shifting is the real measure of his obtuseness as a tactician. His orders to his army, his entries in his diary, during this period, are worthy of a train dispatcher.

In Paris, there was a cabinet crisis. That colorful figure, Messimy, who deserves so much more credit from his countrymen than has been given, was replaced by Etienne Alexandre Millerand; then Messimy changed uniform and became a soldier in the line. Joffre asked Millerand to put Paris directly under his own command, which was done. Then he directed Maunoury to concentrate his troops within the capital. Through Millerand, he advised the Government to quit the city. His Instruction Général No. 4, published that day, September 1, to the field armies, is a catchall reflecting only vagueness as to future plans. The armies of the left would return to the offensive "once Lanrezac's Fifth Army escapes the menace of envelopment." The First and Second armies might be summoned in due course to resume the offensive, should the opportunity arise. The concluding words, "Finally, mobile troops of the fortified camp of Paris may also take part in the general action," are the basis for the claim that Joffre foresaw the Marne and already envisaged Maunoury's scratch army as the counterattack force. It is not credible.

The next day, September 2, Kluck got an order from Moltke: "The First Army will follow in echelon behind the Second Army, and will be responsible for the flank protection of the armies." It was normal precaution; to ignore it meant risking that the rear of both armies would become exposed during the wheel from southwest to east. But Kluck was already one day's march in front of Bülow, who prudently had rested his troops while imprudently failing to command Kluck to do the same. With the bit in his teeth, Kluck rejected his appointed role as flank guard, preferring the post of honor, and pushed hard for Château-Thierry, still farther away from Paris. That this town was to have been the Third Army's target under the original order defines the breadth of the German displacement.

Joffre still groped and bumbled. His secret instruction to his commanders on September 2 contains a striking aberration. Preparatory to the decisive battle, the generals were told to establish their forces on the line Pont-sur-Yonne–Méry-sur-Seine–Arcis-sur-Aube–Brienne-le-Château–Joinville. The key word in this order is Joinville. It implied that for line-shortening purposes, the French Third Army was to abandon Verdun, the anchor upon which the whole French left flank pivoted. Had it been done, Joffre's front would probably have been split asunder, despite Kluck's blunders; and no sortie out of Paris could have saved it. That dour character, General Maurice Sarrail, put Joffre's order aside, held to Verdun, then halfway complied by swinging his left flank rearward fifteen miles, so that it faced due west. The movement left a wide gap between the Third and Fourth armies.

The French Government was more than ready to oblige Joffre and get out. But the signs of its impending departure stirred panic in Paris, where previously there had been mild alarm. Censorship was in full sway. G.Q.G. communiqués never admitted defeat or retreat. Getting its first small air raids (fewer than a dozen persons were killed), the city by night was wrapped in impenetrable gloom. Not knowing anything about the Sixth Army, the populace became suddenly and acutely aware that the forts of Paris dated from 1876, as did most of the guns. Crowds formed and clamored for the Government to declare Paris an open city. There was no reply. On September 2 the rumor raced through the streets that the Germans were encircling Paris from the southwest, though they were already past it driving eastward. Masses of fugitives crushed one another in railway stations as if in a theatre ablaze. At sunset a German airplane dropped propaganda leaflets with the message: "There is nothing you can do but surrender."

In the ministries, just before the getaway, the gloom was hardly less than in the streets. Joffre put to his superiors the blackest possible interpretation of the situation. The German wheel eastward meant only a "brief respite." Millerand passed along to Poincaré his commander's appreciation of the situation. "All our hopes are defeated. We are in full retreat all along the line. Maunoury's army is falling back on Paris." Thus by forcing the Government to take flight, Joffre acknowledged that he expected to lose Paris and that on September 2 he had no plan for a counterbattle that might save it. Nor did Gallieni at the moment. But after saying his adieus to the weeping ministers, Gallieni let it be known to the Parisians who still remained that he intended to die hard. His first order, plastered on walls all over the city, read: "The members of the Government of the Republic have left Paris to give a new impulse to the national defense. I have received a mandate to defend Paris against the invader. This mandate I shall carry out to the end."

THE CLASH OF GIANTS

As for Gallieni, the confusion existed only because until early afternoon of September 3, Joffre had failed to take him into his confidence, both with respect to the German wheel eastward and the secret order published the previous day. When Gallieni at

82

last grasped the situation, he also saw the possibilities that Joffre but vaguely glimpsed. The two minds were better than one; Gallieni's conception changed like a flash when he got full information; he then became the catalyst urging Joffre to use Maunoury's army as a maneuver force. This was happening elsewhere in the Allied camp: in extremity, unity of will was developing out of closer physical contact between the commanders, all thinking on one problem. In battle crisis, the hardening of decision is rarely a one-man thing, though history commonly so treats it. It matures out of suggestion, acceptance, discussion of means and approval. Joffre's attention had drifted to his left wing because there only was the German grip loosened. Gallieni's intentness kept his gaze riveted there. That night the French Foreign Office passed Joffre the information that two days earlier (it was in fact five days earlier) the Russians had taken a major defeat in East Prussia (Battle of Tannenberg). But why had the Imperial Headquarters suppressed news of a great German victory?

It was another straw in the wind, helping to confirm conclusions that Joffre had reached tentatively through that busy day. "Chaotically out of a confusion of conferences," as J. F. C. Fuller puts it, there had proceeded the Allied realignment that was the essential prelude to the counterblow, though Joffre was still thinking defensively. A new army, the Ninth under General Foch, would go into line between the Fourth and Fifth, as soon as it could form. Sir John French, whose B.E.F. had pulled away from the Germans and held an east-facing line not far from Paris, was sent an exploratory message asking if he would be ready to deliver battle the next day. A like question went to the new commander of the French Fifth Army. Joffre that day had replaced Lanrezac with General Louis Franchet d'Esperey, his ablest corps commander. But was Joffre finally and fully resolved to strike back immediately? In these same hours, he wrote to Millerand: "Our duty is to hold out, gain time, and contain the strongest possible German forces."

But Sir John had also conferred with Franchet d'Esperey that day and they had talked with Sir Henry Wilson, French's subchief on the General Staff. At Joffre's request, Gallieni and Maunoury had also called on Sir John. Out of all this stir and bustle came a warrior's consensus that reacted on Joffre like a goad. The time was now, not later. Kluck's army was "in the air," its communications exposed. The gap between it and Bülow's army yawned

On September 5, Kluck's IV Reserve Corps clashed with
France's Sixth Army (1). The next day Kluck's II
and IV corps (2, broken black lines) joined the
fighting on the Ourcq (solid black line). The German
III and IX corps withdrew on the seventh, and the
B.E.F. and French Fifth (3) moved in (broken white

84

FIRST MARNE
September 5 – 9, 1914

Rethel

Reims

Marne R.

Châlons-sur-Marne

SECOND
BÜLOW
Epernay

THIRD
HAUSEN

Montmirail

MARSHES OF
ST. GOND

④ Sept. 8–9

III

IX

⑥ Sept. 5–8

Main

NINTH
FOCH

FIFTH
FRANCHET
D'ESPEREY

Sept. 8

Provins

PARIS TO REIMS, 77 MILES

lines). On the eighth, d'Esperey's attack at Montmirail
(4) forced Bülow back, the B.E.F. hit the German
cavalry (5, dots), and Foch's Ninth Army was pushed
back (6). On the Ourcq (7), the French Sixth and German
First fought to a standstill by the ninth, and the
Germans began retreating to the Aisne (8).

wide; it would not stay open long. Generals become emboldened when they rub elbows. The upsurge of ardor in the army chieftains infected Joffre, who in turn carried along his staff. Several offensive plans were drafted and scrapped. Shortly before midnight Joffre published his Instruction Général No. 6, calling for an attack against the exposed wing of Kluck's army on September 6.

The general plan did little more than rough out boundary lines. It was phrased with the object of enveloping Kluck's First Army. But all depended on the readiness of the Sixth Army. If the trap was to be sprung, the decisive maneuver would have to be made by the force having the least battle experience, the fewest Frenchmen, and the smallest count of regular units.

When the order got to Gallieni later that night, he called Maunoury and told him to move only when he knew that Sir John was marching the B.E.F. also. That made sense; still more to the point, G.Q.G. was at last listening to Gallieni. Because he stayed convinced that Kluck continued to advance southeastward past Paris, he argued that now was the time to strike out of Paris.

But counsel stayed split. The last hours had found Joffre at loggerheads with Berthelot, normally his mainstay, who wished to delay longer and lure the Germans "deeper into the net." In a camp about to be netted, this was sheer bravado. Sir John maintained a discreet silence, confused by the confusion in the French tent. When Joffre swung over to Gallieni's view, so great grew his anxiety about Sir John's attitude that the next day he visited him at Melun. His impassioned talk ended: *"Monsieur le Maréchal, c'est la France qui vous supplie."* Sir John tried to answer in French, then sputtered: "Damn it, I can't explain. Tell him that all that men can do our fellows will do."

While the Allies thus contrived a brief, blessed harmony, the seams parted wider in the enemy camp. Through September 4, Moltke in Luxembourg grew more agitated as he read reports of French troop trains arriving in Paris. Responding to his anxiety the staff got out a new order, the sense of which was that Moltke, while winking at Kluck's disobedience, sought to redress it by pulling the First Army back into contact with the Second Army on stronger ground. To reinforce the order, Moltke then dispatched by motorcar Lieutenant Colonel Richard Hentsch, his intelligence officer. It was an odd choice. Moltke inclined to

Hentsch because he, too, was ridden by doubts and fears, which is not unusual in this branch of the staff. But it was more properly a mission for an operations man. In his conversation with Hentsch, Moltke used the words "possible retirement" and "retreat," whereas he had but ordered a realignment. From what followed, Moltke became the goat of the Marne defeat and Hentsch is blamed for his undoing.

Moltke's order reached Kluck soon after dawn. Earlier Kluck had disregarded the same authority. Now he worried. By wireless, he badgered Moltke to let him know what the other field armies were doing; this is the act of a general trying to square his own record.

Moltke's order was sped to General von Gronau, commanding the corps of reservists that, thinly spread, covered Kluck's dangling flank northeast of Paris. Gronau's troops took off at once to see if any new danger threatened. This was not compliance with the order; it was a search for proof that Kluck was right. Attacking some heights near Monthyon, this screen drove off French pickets masking the front of the upcoming Sixth Army. Then Gronau was himself surprised when Maunoury's army arrived in superior numbers along his front in early afternoon. Feeling the heat, Gronau fell back six miles. His call for help alarmed Kluck, who turned his II Corps around and marched it northwest to get IV Reserve Corps out of trouble.

In this way, accidentally, was begun the Battle of the Marne, twenty-four hours before Joffre intended that any of his troops should attack. More than the order itself, the opening of the fight steeled decision.

From Monthyon, the small fire mounted skyward until it raged for seven days all along the Western Front. Following a great curve, it spread from directly north of Paris, along the Marne and its feeder streams, eastward to the heights of Verdun. Beyond that fortress, and on eastward almost to the Swiss border, there was fought at the same time another great battle, equally demanding and costly.

Within this flank-to-flank collision were scores, yes, hundreds, of separate engagements, many without clear tactical purpose, most of them only indirectly bearing on actions occurring elsewhere. Men battled over worthless ground, ignoring great prizes close at hand. Artillery was fired, often wastefully, because shells were available though reliable target information was not. Generals advanced their troops who might better have spared them, fearing to miss their moment of glory. That's how war is made. But the cockpit of all this fury was the Marne, where the fate of France was staked on the attempt to turn the German right wing. Here we are concerned only with the decisive engagements fought on that flank, where one relatively small river gave its name to the unfolding event.

The Marne joins the Seine hard by Paris, draining the countryside northeast of it. Its deep trench is the strongest topographical barrier within the Île de France, and its main tributaries, the Ourcq, Petit Morin, and Grand Morin, are also deeply moated. Describing the shape of a fan, the tributaries pour into the Marne not far above Paris. Farthest north, the Ourcq flows south into the Marne, extending the main trench. The other streams flow westward, the Grand Morin being farthest south, so that its valley points directly at Paris. The town of Meaux, prominent in the orders to the Sixth Army, nestles in a sharp bend of the Marne between the two Morins, but on the west bank. It is like an interchange, so placed that a force out of Paris pivoting on Meaux may move laterally along the course of any of the four rivers. There is one other main feature. The Petit Morin originates in the waters of the extensive Marshes of Saint-Gond, an east-west-running belt all but impassable for troops.

When the battle opened, Kluck's main body was already established along the heights south of the Grand Morin, fronted south, with Paris directly to the west, and the Marne River system at its back. From the plateau south of the Grand Morin, Kluck's light screening forces curved in a northwest-running arc through Meaux and well beyond the confluence of the Ourcq and Marne. In driving for Meaux, the Sixth Army was therefore taking the shortest line to turn Kluck's right flank and get on his rear. For his part, Kluck had moved beyond the Grand Morin to sever the French left wing from the center.

Colonel Hentsch got to Kluck shortly after the fight began at Monthyon. They discussed the situation and Moltke's order. Kluck agreed to pull in his horns some—but later, since there was a fight on. Hentsch told him that the other German armies weren't all advancing victoriously; they were held or hard pounded. Kluck expressed amazement. That made possible a shift of troops from the French right to his own front. But he still chose not to pull back.

So the French Sixth drove for Meaux, and the German First spread wider to stop them. Gronau's IV Reserve Corps pulled back from Monthyon to northwest of Meaux on the first day; General von Linsingen's II Corps, after a six-hour march, entered the battle at dawn of September 6, near Trilport and Meaux, on the opposite bank of the Marne. There Linsingen's troops became so heavily engaged by Maunoury's rapidly gathering forces that he called for help. Half of Kluck's army by now was standing in suspense south of the Grand Morin; the other half was being fought to a standstill east and west of the Marne. But he fed another corps, the IV under General Sixt von Arnim, into the fire on his left; it arrived next to Linsingen on September 7. By now Kluck's whole army was dangerously off balance, with its weak wing too far forward, the other four embattled corps deployed at right angles to it, with no strength at the hinge, and the rear lines of both flanks thoroughly entangled. Kluck had to order his two remaining corps—III and IX—out of their defensive ground and into the battle, to save himself. But in realigning his divisions so that they faced westward, an average of thirty-five miles from where they had fronted southward, he sold out the German order of battle. Corps III and IV were just coming under fire from the French Fifth Army when Kluck withdrew them to join the fight around the Marne. Their northwestward march left a hole where Kluck's left flank had been and doubled the already yawning gap between his nearest tactical forces and Bülow's Second Army. The vanishing of III and IV corps at the French Fifth Army's first lunge roused its tired fighters as nothing else might have done. Kluck made this final move, which both cast his own army adrift and put the Second Army in full jeopardy, without either consulting Bülow or advising Moltke. By ignoring Hentsch, he had made his own problems; by scorning his superiors, he had robbed his soldiers and theirs, Bülow's and Moltke's. There is no question who lost the Battle of the Marne.

Kluck's army now held the high ground running north from the angle where the Ourcq joins the Marne. Maunoury's divisions fronting east were strung out from Trilport to Crépy. For two days Germans and French locked in a death struggle. Giving and taking great blows, the Sixth Army's line began to bend. On September 8 Maunoury tried to get around Kluck's right, reckoning to rush forces up the Marne-Ourcq valley behind him and close the bag. It was too late. Arriving at the right moment behind this flank, the German III and IX corps blocked the road. Maunoury called for help. Gallieni collected some 1,200 taxicabs in Paris and rushed reinforcements to him. There is no more cherished episode than this in French military history; little else is remembered by average citizens about Gallieni's generalship or what made victory. "The Miracle of the Marne" is the familiar label for the mysterious moves of armies out of which Paris was saved. But when people ponder the miracle, they have their minds on taxis rather than on soldiers.

With the First Army going it alone but not enveloped, the German Second Army got no breathing space in which to stretch toward it. The French Fifth Army, back in the fray again, became fired up by its seeming success in the one-day fight against the German III and IX corps. The German withdrawal and the French rush forward uncovered Bülow's right flank. Bülow pulled back behind the moat of the Petit Morin and entrenched his army as the French Fifth Army kept driving for Montmirail. On the night of September 8–9, the French XVIII Corps under General Louis Ernest de Maud'huy got a bridgehead at Marchais-en-Brie. When that impingement made Montmirail untenable, Bülow was far enough out on the limb to hear the wood cracking. He retired eight miles eastward and formed a north-south-running front, like Kluck's way to the westward. With that, all possibility ended of closing the gap between the German First and Second armies anywhere in the vicinity of Paris.

The issue was decided. Paris was already saved. Kluck had lost. It is of no more importance that he kept battering away at Maunoury's army, telling himself that opportunity still glittered and one more charge might prove it, than that scholars and strategists, impressed with his attitude, date the crisis later. While his army wasn't broken, it had been maneuvered to the brink of obliteration, and if it was to be saved, there was no way to go but out.

Foch's new Ninth Army, deployed to the right of Franchet d'Esperey but given no time to shake down, had moved up at the same time as the Fifth. So placed, their flanks joined around Villeneuve. Fortunately for this hastily improvised newcomer, a great part of the army front was covered by the Marshes of Saint-Gond; this twelve-mile center of the twenty-mile defensive zone was a maze of hummocks, clearwater pools, and reed patches, traversed only by a few dirt roads bedded on narrow causeways. But on the Ninth's right the Gap of Mailly afforded the enemy a wholly favorable route of advance and Foch had only a cavalry division to screen it.

On September 6 General Hausen had launched his Third Army at the sensitive corner where the Fifth and Ninth joined flanks, aiming to roll up Franchet d'Esperey's army. The loosely tied-in units bent under the blow, fell back a few miles, but did not break. Hausen had too few troops in that sector to renew the attack. On September 8 Hausen tried again, with an attack in main aimed over the clear ground on Foch's right. This assault, which was joined by Bülow's corps nearest Hausen, progressed steadily through the day, the French repeatedly counterattacking without seeming to stem it. When it stopped from exhaustion of German energy, Foch turned to the offensive. Legend has him wiring Joffre: "My right gives. My center yields. Situation excellent. I shall attack"; but that is apocryphal. What happened is more exciting. Foch made the inspired guess that to mount his attacks on the ends, Hausen had stripped his center of men. Intensive cannonading from across the marsh through the day strengthened that suspicion. So he withdrew an army corps from behind the Petit Morin gorge and launched it across the east end of the marsh, off the flank of Bülow's corps. The result was a bull's-eye. The attack smashed through Hausen's center and his army had to recoil.

Throughout this time the twenty-mile free passage between the German First and Second armies, created by Kluck's maneuver westward while Bülow was being forced to the east, was beckoning to the B.E.F., the only force near Paris not fully committed to battle.

But though the gap yawned, so did Sir John. With him by now were three solid army corps. British losses had been replaced. The Tommies were longer rested than the *poilus* already engaged. All Sir John had to do was ride hard to transform a tactical advantage into an overwhelming victory. Yet this cavalryman did nothing to urge his formations forward. They marched slow-step to golden opportunity, doing twenty-five miles in three days, by which time this solid army at last came even with the entrance to the gap. Its river crossings were lightly opposed; little time needed to be wasted on reconnaissance of infantry in that era. It was not for Sir John.

Joffre sensed Sir John's timidity and the costs thereof. The bulky Frenchman shone like a star throughout the crisis of his one supremely great operation. Of a sudden, all the fog was gone. Seeing that Sir John was dawdling, Joffre, on the evening of September 8, ordered the Sixth Army to try to keep Kluck pinned along the Ourcq while the Fifth Army was ordered to close flanks with the B.E.F. and then set the pace. It was already too late.

At Luxembourg Moltke, by now in collapse, had sent Hentsch forth on another mission. This time he was authorized to visit all army headquarters, and, in the name of Moltke, issue such orders as were necessary to give the embattled Germans a future. Never before or since was more power confided to a staffer of such low rank. But Hentsch was ready to swing his weight. Moltke put nothing in writing. Hentsch said later: "The Chief of the General Staff empowered me, should it be necessary, to order the five armies to fall back behind the Vesle River along the heights north of the Argonne." He did not go that far, nor did they.

Midday of September 9 he reached First Army headquarters at Chézy. Kluck was away somewhere visiting his troops. Hentsch talked to General von Kuhl, Kluck's Chief of Staff. Speaking in the name of Moltke, he told Kuhl that the First Army had to retire; it was a direct order; the reason given was that the gap between Kluck and Bülow had widened to thirty miles. Kuhl did not argue. Nor did Kluck when he returned and Kuhl gave him the news, though earlier Kluck had egregiously spurned operational orders directly from Moltke. His submission is eloquent of this general's predicament; Kluck at last knew he was beaten and was but looking for a chance to shift the blame elsewhere. Hentsch had gone on his way, continuing his rounds of the other army commands to bring off a coordinated retirement. In this way began the German retreat to behind the Aisne River.

It was a badly battered army that fell back. Its generals had been outmaneuvered in this most terrible of all chess games. But something far worse had happened. The people lower down had made the same mistakes that the French had made weeks earlier in the Battle of the Frontiers. Recklessly, they had scorned normal protection against massed fire, failing to entrench and advancing upright, fully visible. On the immense battlefield of the Marne, they repeatedly attacked without prior reconnaissance, with no artillery preparation and no artillery support. So doing, they were cut down in waves.

Now came time for the English and French infantrymen to surge forward, heads high, fresh hope in their eyes. They knew at last that they could beat the Germans; shortly they began to understand that they had stumbled to a great victory, and it was only one step from that to believing that the worst was over. Moving north, the Germans, who had thought themselves invincible, began slowly to comprehend that they had suffered a great defeat by enemies whose fighting abilities they despised.

Edward Spears ends his *Liaison, 1914* a week after the victory of the First Marne with the words: "I am deeply thankful that none of those who gazed across the Aisne on September 14th had the faintest glimmer of what was awaiting them. . . . There was nothing to show them that the most dramatic period of the war was over. . . ."

III

Guns East

It seemed as if the lines of tramping
soldiers, like these Russians, would never
end. The most important ammunition in the
war was not artillery, but massed humanity.

Germany had no plan for the Eastern Front except to stand where possible and play for time. Yet there, also, the storm struck with full fury right from the beginning. And that was how things went all around the horizon—the unique condition distinguishing World War I from every other conflict. All four of the Continental powers suffered delusions; all tried at the same time to swing for a knockout blow; all four failed. "The most terrible August in the history of the world," the novelist Sir Arthur Conan Doyle called it. "One thought that God's curse hung heavy over a degenerate world."

As the month of August opened, the German front covering East Prussia was lightly held by the one cavalry and eleven infantry divisions forming the 135,000-man Eighth Army. In command, General Max von Prittwitz und Gaffron had as his Chief of Staff, General Count von Waldersee, the nephew of Schlieffen's predecessor. The army was critically deficient in heavy artillery, medical service, and field telephones. Prittwitz, nicknamed the Fat Soldier, venerable in years and testy in temper, was a clever enough general, but, like his army, not soundly wired together. In crisis, he had to lean on someone, and Waldersee, a sick man, had knees like jelly. Still, Prittwitz had the one great talent that many an otherwise dull commander has parlayed to fame: he knew a good man and would follow his advice. On the first day of mobilization one such officer came to him by sudden transfer from an infantry battalion in Alsace. Lieutenant Colonel Max von Hoffmann, a roly-poly staff officer, long in wisdom, canny about Russians, destined to command this army, joined it in the nick of time.

Already forming to come against Prittwitz faster than Russians had ever moved before was an army group of 650,000 men under General Jilinsky. Its two armies, commanded by Generals Pavel Rennenkampf and Alexander Samsonov, counted thirty infantry and eight cavalry divisions, which gave the invaders a numerical superiority of more than four to one.

In all else, the advantage lay with the Germans. Samsonov and Rennenkampf had feuded since the day during the Russo-Japanese War when they had come to blows on a station platform at Mukden. Hoffmann had intimate knowledge of their vendetta and saw its significance. They carried their grudge into the march, which was difficult enough without that. Between their armies and the German front lay a moraine-strewn countryside, broken by forests, lakes, marshes, and rolling hills, traversed only occasionally by dirt service roads. These natural obstacles canalized the Russian advance right up to where the Germans waited behind the north-south line of the Masurian Lakes. Restricting the columns, compelling the Russians to deploy over relatively narrow fronts, the terrain both slowed their pace and diffused their mass. Behind the water barrier, the German Eighth Army, making use of a highly efficient network of railways, could shift weight and concentrate against whichever invading army struck first. In these circumstances, Samsonov and Rennenkampf owed it to their armies to synchronize their movements, arriving abreast, hitting together. But their bitterness precluded cooperation and on this the Germans reckoned.

Prittwitz and Hoffmann talked it over. They calculated that the Eighth Army would become embattled some time between August 15 and 20. But that was just an educated guess. The German espionage apparatus in Poland had evaporated. Further, this strange enemy was marching by night and sleeping by day. Just why it did so is a mystery Air bombardment was in its infancy, and since surprise was out of the question, observation was not to be feared. So the eccentric invader lost time fighting the countryside when haste was essential. On entering East Prussia one army would have to march north of the Masurian chain while the other advanced south of it. Hoffmann and his associates estimated that Rennenkampf's northern army from Vilna would appear sooner than Samsonov's army from Warsaw because its path was more favorable; and they were not disappointed.

But something slipped in the German camp that had vast consequence. On August 14, the army headquarters prepared to move out of Marienburg to a field location more central to the planned battle. The same day the first Russians appeared opposite the northern flank. The order went out for the army to reform behind the Angerapp River to complete the defensive alignment. That meant baring the extreme eastern corner of East Prussia. In command of I Corps there was a Prussian, General Hermann von François. To give up any of the sacred soil was to him intolerable. So instead of dropping behind the Angerapp he marched the corps east to attack the Russians. Thunderstruck, army headquarters heard about it three days later. Meanwhile,

François had joined battle with a larger Russian force at Stallupönen and beaten it, taking many prisoners. But while stalling the enemy advance in the very hour when the headquarters wished it to roll forward, he had also suffered severe losses. François was hastily pulled back. But now Prittwitz worried that his whole plan was falling apart.

Still, he stayed with his first purpose, to defeat Rennenkampf in the north before turning on Samsonov in the south. That brought on the battle of Gumbinnen on August 20. The three German army corps under Generals François, August von Mackensen, and Otto von Below did not wait for the Russians to close; they attacked. It was a mistake. The two outside corps were everywhere successful, but the center under Mackensen became impaled on solid Russian earthworks east of the Rominten River. By midafternoon Mackensen advised that his corps was defeated and its position gravely compromised.

Steeled by the success on both flanks, Prittwitz would have resumed battle on the same line the next day, but for a "rude interruption." It made Gumbinnen go down in the books as a defeat for the German Army, and the news sped around the world. The statistics warrant it. Enough German fighters had been bagged to flesh out a division, and out of Mackensen's corps the word "panic" appeared for the first time in German dispatches. But Rennenkampf also was licking his wounds, reluctant to lay on again, least of all to help Samsonov. The "rude interruption" to Prittwitz was that Samsonov's Second Army from Poland was now knocking at his other door.

TANNENBERG

Hoffman got the message while standing in front of the Nordenberg Command Post early that evening: "The Warsaw Army with five corps is crossing the frontier now." He remarked to his companion, General Grunert: "I am afraid the nerves of the commander and the other chiefs are not strong enough to hear this. If we could suppress it, tomorrow we would end the battle here and then turn on our Warsaw opponent."

This was Hoffmann having his little joke. A minute later Prittwitz and Waldersee emerged from the building. Hoffmann could tell from their faces that they already knew the worst. Moreover, Prittwitz had learned it too soon for his own good.

He said: "The Warsaw Army will advance on our rear if we continue the battle and cut us off from the Vistula. This army shall therefore break off the fight and retire behind the Vistula."

Both Hoffmann and Grunert argued that the field at Gumbinnen remained favorable and that Rennenkampf could be finished within two or three days. That would leave just enough time to move the main body around the lakes to the southern flank if General Friddrich von Scholtz sparred vigorously with his corps, not yet committed. Prittwitz cut them short; he would have none of it.

The two soldiers then got out their compasses and showed their chief that a simple retreat to the Vistula couldn't work because Samsonov's army was already closer to the barrier, which meant that the Eighth Army would either be intercepted or embattled most of the distance. It was elementary. They proposed the alternative: stop Samsonov's Warsaw Army by an attack in main against its left flank. This did not involve a long and complex displacement, but a sideslip rightward. Even so, Hoffmann and Grunert were double-talking their chief. Their case, though they did not state it outright, was that the Gumbinnen fight could be resumed and won, and that the army could still redress to beat back Samsonov.

In his one shining moment in history, Prittwitz saw more clearly than his aggressive lieutenants. He gave up the idea of retiring behind the Vistula. He agreed to the attack in main against Samsonov's flank. But he ruled that the battle at Gumbinnen had to be broken off instanter, so that troops could refresh and re-form. Out of his decision came German victory at Tannenberg, though all of the credit was passed to other hands.

For that, Prittwitz could blame himself. Men around him, chiefly Waldersee, had erred by yessing him in weak moments. Before Hoffmann ever talked to him about Gumbinnen and the new threat to the old plan, Prittwitz had been on the telephone to Moltke in Koblenz. After hearing from Mackensen in mid-afternoon, his heart went down. It sank more on learning of Samsonov's approach. So he got on the telephone and told Moltke, before ever discussing the situation with Hoffmann, that the Eighth Army must retire to the Vistula. Compounding the error, Prittwitz failed to tell Hoffmann about the talk he had had with Moltke at G.H.Q.

Worse followed bad. After the conference, neither Prittwitz

nor his assistants thought to call Moltke to tell him that the general retirement was canceled, and a new, firm counteroffensive plan was afoot. The main actors were too busy writing and scanning the orders that went from army to troops that same night.

Moltke, who was already falling apart himself, decided that Prittwitz had disintegrated. This is the average reaction of weak men trying to play strong parts. Moltke's eye was on the German advance through Belgium and the French lost provinces. So far so good. But it wasn't good enough if, in consequence, Russian armies were to overrun East Prussia because of a spineless commander. Within the military, it is unfortunately true that the frail reed seeks to shift blame more quickly than the resolute and knowing commander. On the basis of one phone conversation, Moltke decided that there had to be an immediate and dramatic change in the command on the Eastern frontier. For this paper soldier who knew nothing of battle, it was one of the few inspired guesses of a lifetime.

To Ludendorff, the hero of Liège, now approaching Namur with Bülow's army, went a message from Moltke: "You may yet be able to save the situation in the East. I know of no one in whom I have such absolute trust. The Kaiser, too, has absolute confidence in you. Of course you will not be made responsible for what has already happened." The date when Ludendorff fed his ego on this encomium was August 22. It was forty-eight hours after the Council of War had steadied Prittwitz at Gumbinnen and nothing even verging on disaster had happened to the Eighth Army. The call for help was but a measure of the vacuum in German communications. Higher commanders were not saying enough to one another to be understood.

By motorcar he sped to Koblenz, well knowing that he would have the power but not Prittwitz's title of commander, because his social position, like his military rank, was too lowly. En route he wrote these notes: "I passed through Wavre. The day before it had been a peaceful town. Now it was in flames. The populace had fired on our troops." None but a genius may authenticate such hearsay on the fly.

In Koblenz, Ludendorff bent Moltke's ear and had his own bent. The Eastern Front, he heard, was a shambles, the Eighth Army having been ordered to fall back behind the Vistula. "It would spell ruin," said Ludendorff. Therefore he proposed that in the southeast of Prussia a strong group should be formed to take the offensive immediately against Samsonov. The Russians should not be let off without another battle. The orders went out; they changed nothing, Prittwitz having disposed his army that way two days earlier. But from there on Ludendorff spoke of the arrangements as "my plan." That night he hobnobbed with the Kaiser, who decorated him with the order Pour le Mérite. Later he caught a special train bound for the Eastern Front. On the station platform he heard that General Paul von Hindenburg, called from retirement, had been given nominal command of the Eighth Army and would board the train at Hanover.

Hindenburg boarded. Ludendorff reported, saluted. They talked over the situation and Ludendorff's conclusions. Then to bed. That was about the way it happened. As Ludendorff wrote: "All other versions belong to the realm of fiction." Yet the story of the meeting collects more embroidery with the years.

Even so, their meeting was a grand event in that it made both men tall, compounding the worth of each as an individual. So history was changed. Soon it came to pass that the figure of Hindenburg incarnated all that was best in the German people, in their nature and in the resolute character of their fighting forces, so that he towered as the great national hero above the land. For that, he could thank Ludendorff, the prideful man of lowly origin, stiff-necked in his determination to reach for the stars. At first meeting each gave ground a little bit. One was a thruster, the other a has-been. Their mutual respect man-for-man surmounted their instinctive reservations deriving from status, which was their great triumph. Ludendorff was the hero of the moment, the warrior with battle prestige. H-L became the symbol of team play because the two men pulled equally together.

But Ludendorff had shaken Moltke, where he might have steadied him. In the clutch, he was not the strategist weighing the forfeits all around the circle, but the tactician ready to risk all else to further his personal interest, now tied to the Eastern Front. If his plan was good, then the forces already at hand would so prove it. Reinforcements could not arrive in time to do more than stem further invasion after a lost battle. He would have put this to Moltke had he been a selfless saint rather than a general. It was expecting too much. Yet in not doing so Ludendorff became a chief contributor to Moltke's worst blunders. To assure success for H-L in the days that immediately followed, he stripped manpower from the marching armies in France and shipped them to Prussia.

By the afternoon of August 22, the Eighth Army Staff knew of the change in the command. The news came first to the transportation office: prepare for a special train bearing the new Commander in Chief. From there it spread through the army. No one told Prittwitz. Later came the formal order from His Majesty relegating him and Waldersee to the unattached list. On its heels arrived a wire from Ludendorff directing all commanders to meet him in Marienburg next day. To have complied, they would have had to trek far west, leaving their troops; Ludendorff still believed that this army had retired behind the Vistula. Twenty-four hours later, with their arrival at the field headquarters, he and Hindenburg at last realized that the situation was far more favorable than they had supposed, with the army holding hard to the decisive forward ground, and aggressively disposed. Still, they did not notify Moltke, although Ludendorff well understood how false was the impression of the Eastern battle in Moltke's mind, and how vital was the character of the new information.

Hoffman knew Ludendorff personally. They had served together on the staff at Posen and dwelt at the same quarters in Berlin for four years. Here was a break; among soldiers acting under pressure, prior service together outweighs all other credentials. Hoffmann made the report, outlining the situation and the plan already in motion. Ludendorff forthwith approved.

By this time, the main body of the Eighth Army had pulled back from Rennenkampf's front an average distance of thirty miles, in order to regroup against Samsonov. German cavalry maintained a stakeout of Rennenkampf's troops, with infantry in blocking position farther back. But the Russians did not stir.

Far more incredible fortune attended the change in command. One of Jilinsky's staff officers had been found dead on the battlefield; in his pockets were papers outlining the march table and proposed movements of both Russian armies. Yet more fabulously, the field wireless sets connecting the three higher Russian headquarters kept clacking out operation orders in the clear, with the German camp getting every word. Such stupidity even on the part of the two battlers of Mukden may strain belief.

What doubts Ludendorff had, centered in one great question. Dared the Eighth Army wholly withdraw the two army corps from their blocking position in front of Rennenkampf? They were needed if Samsonov was to be crushed rather than merely stopped. But if they were sent south, the Russian right wing could roll into the void and compel a German retreat midway in the maneuver to envelop the Warsaw Army. It was a dilemma.

From one small incident came sudden light. On August 24, General Scholtz, commanding the German XX Corps centered around Tannenberg, asked permission to move his 37th Division rearward with Samsonov's forces. It was granted. The Russians saw the 37th pull out and mistook it for a general retreat by the Eighth Army. By wireless, Samsonov ordered his army to pursue and German field headquarters intercepted the message.

So the great chance was taken. The XVII Army Corps and I Reserve Corps were shipped south and when they cleared away, only one cavalry division remained in front of Rennenkampf, facing twenty-four infantry divisions. Russian cavalry continued to thrust forward from Rennenkampf's front, but if it learned about the German departure, its commander paid no heed.

By August 25, H-L could contemplate their first battle array together. The German left wing had railed southwestward about one hundred miles during the two days. Now reconcentrated, the army stood nine divisions spread roughly in a great crescent extending upwards of sixty miles and facing southeast. Toward the center of this arc Samsonov's columns were advancing, still under the impression that the Germans were pulling away westward. There was nothing elaborate about the German plan, though all depended on whether Samsonov's intentions were correctly divined. Both wings had been strengthened tremendously at the expense of a thinned center. That lightly manned middle ground was the lure; the heavy flanks were expected to close around the enemy with crushing weight. With the parlor all set, the next question was whether the fly would walk right in. He seemed headed in the right direction, marching north rather than west.

Now on the last leg of the approach, Samsonov had premonitions. Cavalry screening his front returned with the word that enemy infantry columns indicated a sudden buildup against the Russian left flank. Reacting to this menace, Samsonov sped a staff officer to Jilinsky to ask whether he should not veer, and advance westward, feeling his way. From the top brass came the brazen reply: "I will not allow General Samsonov to play the coward. I insist that he continue the offensive." One hundred and sixty miles to the rear of his fighting troops, Jilinsky couldn't be intimidated. For the unpardonable insult, Samsonov should have pistoled him, but the distance was too great. So he followed orders and kept marching, thereby missing the chance to save his army and a great deal more. There is unending dispute over who deserves credit for victory at Tannenberg; there should be none as to the placement of the blame for the defeat. Jilinsky is the villain in the piece. Being in command, he made no effort to control. Rennenkampf was allowed to dawdle at the wrong time; Samsonov was driven pell-mell when he should have been pulled up. How can one account for this man's folly? Two years earlier Jilinsky had been Chief of Staff over the Russian armies. Visiting in France, he had promised to reform mobilization procedure so that his armies would give battle fifteen days after the starting gun. His vanity had to be fed, though his troops stumbled forward half-rationed, half-armed, many of them unbooted, their feet bound in rags. The harvest was not yet ripe and the artillery horses starved. Such unpleasant detail in no way eased the itch of his ambition.

The drama began to unfold at sunrise on August 26. But it was a play of many parts, with diverse scenes that were little connected. On the German side, there was no continuous front, the lakes blocking one corps from another. The Russian advance was split by the far separation of the approach roads so that there were wide gaps between the center and the wings. Like the Marne, Tannenberg was not one great shock collision between armies meeting front against front (modern battles never are), but a succession of independent actions, extending for sixty miles and lasting for four days.

Samsonov drove straight for the trap, aiming his opening assault at the weak German center. There the German XX Reserve Corps was formed of men fighting on their own heath; their homes were around Allenstein. Their line reeled under the onslaught, gave ground, and fell back westward but did not break.

Fearing the consequence, Ludendorff ordered General François to counterattack immediately with I Corps, aiming at the Russian left wing near Usdau. But again there was trouble with François. He protested that his heavy artillery, most of the light guns, the munitions trains, and some of the troops had not yet arrived on the battlefield. Ludendorff summarily ordered him to

TANNENBERG

August 20 – 31, 1914

GULF OF DANZIG

Danzig

Vistula R.

Marienburg

Elbing

EAST PRUSSIA

Passarge R.

EIGHTH

**PRITTWITZ/
HINDENBURG**

3R

Allenstein

Osterode

XIII

Löbau

XX

Tannenberg

XV

Frankenau

6 Aug. 29

Seeben

Neidenburg

Lahna

XXIII

Willenberg

Soldau

Usdau

Aug. 26

3 Aug. 24

Chorzele

SEC

SAMS

5

Greenspan

Mlawa

TANNENBERG TO KÖNIGSBERG 83 MILES

After the defeat at Gumbinnen (1), Hindenburg took command of
the German Eighth Army. Leaving only a cavalry screen (black
dots) to block the Russian First, he moved his I, XVII, and
I Reserve corps (2) to meet Samsonov's Second (center bottom:
Russian movements in white, German in black). Samsonov's XV
Corps moved (3) to attack the German XX at Frankenau, while the

SEA

Königsberg

I

XVII

② Allenburg

I R Aug. 23

Bischofstein

XVII

Bischofsburg

VI

Aug. 26

④

Sensburg

Pregel R. Insterburg

Nordenberg

Angerberg *Angerapp R.*

Lötzen

FT. BOYEN

Masurian Lakes

Johannisberg

Kolno

POLAND

Niemen R. Tilsit

Gumbinnen

① Aug. 20

FIRST

RENNENKAMPF

Russian VI Corps advanced (4) to Bischofsburg, where it was routed by the Germans. Samsonov's I Corps (5) was defeated at Usdau, and his XV forced to withdraw (6). Only remnants of Samsonov's Second Army escaped to Poland through François's picket lines between Neidenberg and Willenberg.

go anyway. But the hardhead was biding his time. His compliance on this day was the capture of one outlying ridge.

Amid the clamor, there came to Ludendorff a telephone call from G.H.Q., Colonel Tappen, Moltke's Chief of Operations, speaking. Hoffman got on the extension. To their astonishment, they heard Tappen say: "We are sending you three corps and a cavalry division as reinforcement." Both men knew that these troops must be transfused from the German body in France. Moltke was doing it, still believing that Gumbinnen was a disaster and that hordes of Cossacks were about to ravage Germany. For three days Ludendorff had let him sweat and brood, instead of picking up the phone to lay the specter. Now he merely protested feebly that the peeled-off army (such was its aggregate strength) wasn't "positively" needed in the East and would arrive too late for the decisive battle. That did not change Tappen's mind. In war, it is much easier to initiate troop movements than to recall them. But these forces were still tramping toward the railway stations when Ludendorff might have barked: "No, don't do it!"

On Samsonov's right flank, which was two days' march from the rest of his army, the advance on August 26 collided with the arrival on the battlefield of the two German corps under Generals Below and Mackensen, which had slogged overland from Gumbinnen. Both sides were near exhaustion from their travels, but the Germans at least had been fed. There followed a trancelike struggle, decided by the superior weight of the German artillery. The Russian infantry fell back in confusion, without having closed to small-arms range. Too worn down to pursue, the Germans watched them depart. But the elements of one Russian division had attacked with their backs to Lake Bössau. In the panicky getaway a few soldiers dashed into the lake and drowned. From this one isolated incident rose the legend that Hindenburg drove the Russian Army into the lakes and marshes, where it perished in the water.

That evening occurred a crisis of nerves in the German camp, precipitated by two phantasmagoric intelligence reports: a great body of enemy cavalry was in movement to the south and coming around François's flank; and, out of Rennenkampf's army, one corps was advancing on Mackensen's rear. Ludendorf's resolution was suddenly like water. Now he wanted to recall François, which meant abandoning the entire battle plan. Hindenburg and

Hoffmann discouraged him from doing so.

By sundown, Samsonov realized that his cast had missed and his own army was in peril of becoming enveloped. But he determined to continue the struggle through the next day, renewing his attack against the German center. To his corps on the left flank, opposite François, he signaled: "Hold at all costs." But his real hope was that Rennenkampf would be ordered up. Dim as that chance was, he dug himself in deeper. German wireless operators heard message after message from Samsonov pleading, praying that the other army be loosed westward. But there was no answer from Jilinsky or Rennenkampf. Churchill describes Samsonov's situation on that night in terms of utmost melancholy: "On both flanks rout, and in the center, far advanced in danger's jaws, a doubtful battle. . . ."

It became that bad only after François and his corps went after Samsonov's left wing hard the next morning; dawn cracked to the full thunder of the German artillery. François's infantry drove toward Neidenburg, which target was on the rear of the Russian center. But a counterattack against the German outer flank forced it to wheel toward Soldau, which was on the escape route of Samsonov's left wing. That day, the attempt at a shallow envelopment failed. François was held as the Russian I Corps fought desperately to cover the army's line of retreat. Artillery took frightful toll of Samsonov's left wing. Still, when night came, the battle remained in equipoise. The Germans got little cheer out of their few local successes; there had been no grand decision. Again Ludendorff's nerve faltered, and when he spoke shrilly about holding back François, bolder men once more dissuaded him.

Now look at Samsonov. Through the day the pressure against his left had all but cracked it; there was still time and room to start extricating the center. But he reacted to the threat of doom as if mesmerized, ordering the center in this last moment of reprieve to resume the attack.

When dawn came, the Russian left had vanished from in front of François. The greater part of one corps had fled toward the frontier. So where the German I Corps had been denied Soldau the day before, it could now go the whole distance to Neidenburg against relatively light opposition. Neidenburg was the vital rail and road center; beyond it stretched the lakes. Once the Germans had Neidenburg, the sack would be closed on the Russians hammering at Scholtz's XX Corps, and the battle would be done except for the mop-up.

So François drove on. It was the key move. That night he had Neidenburg. Next day he gained Willenberg, well to the east of it. For these successes, he is overpraised as the real victor of Tannenberg. He literally fell into them, for as Hindenburg said: "The enemy was no longer seeking victory but [his own] destruction." Ludendorff, still cautious, tried to bring François in on a shorter bite, pointing him toward Lahna; not yet sensing he had the battle won, Ludendorff worried more about overextending his own forces than about widening the sweep of the fleeing enemy. François shrugged off that order, either because of a contrary spirit or a sharper tactical instinct. Along the road that he had won, his twenty-five battalions were strung out as a line of entrenched pickets stretching for thirty-five miles. Into these armed posts during the final three days staggered thousands of unarmed, emaciated, bone-weary scarecrows who shortly before had been enemy soldiers. It was an impressive, if unheroic, catch, in the backwash of the Russian debacle. Of 92,000 prisoners taken at Tannenberg, 60,000 were hauled in by François's roving patrols and line of pickets.

One main prize they missed. Samsonov was seen not far from Neidenburg by the British liaison officer Major General Sir Alfred Knox, in midmorning of August 28. He knew now that his army was shattered. With his staff, he mounted to get away, telling Knox not to follow. Through the afternoon he rode the riptide of his own refugees, pondering the wretched fragments of the quarter-million-man army he had led west. With those hours fled the last wisp of glory and of wanting. At the end, he said good-by to his retinue and walked into a stretch of woods. They heard a pistol shot but did not bother to search for the body. It couldn't have ended otherwise for the soldier "never regarded as brilliant, whose main assets were his simple kindliness of character and the devotion of his men."

Northward, there was no such ingathering. Most of the Russians of the right wing got away to the forests east of the frontier. Below's and Mackensen's corps moved too slowly in their attack east of the lakes to join hands with François while the enemy still held the field. For that failure to close quickly, Ludendorff's nerves were blamed. True, he kept Below and Mackensen check-reined.

The wire sent Moltke on the night of August 28 reflects his mood: "Battle won. Pursuit continuing. Surrender of the two Russian corps may well not be achieved." That message refers to the still footloose Russian right wing. But greater caution had to be exercised on that flank, for Below and Mackensen had advanced with a solid Russian army (Rennenkampf's) at their back. The more recklessly they had lunged, the greater had become the jeopardy.

For security reasons, Moltke bottled up news of the famous victory. It was released as a timely antidote to German disappointment over the Marne. When the fog lifted around the Masurian Lakes, Germany beheld towering sky-high a new national hero, Hindenburg. Tannenberg was cheered as the greatest German victory of all time. The victory was first called Ostroda. Then at Ludendorff's suggestion, it was rechristened Tannenberg, a propaganda move to remind Germans that the 1410 action fought there, in which the Poles broke the power of the Teutonic Order, was now gloriously avenged. Men are superstitious. Therefore governments ever strain at war's beginning to raise new heroes and drain fresh magic from old symbols.

Yet Tannenberg changed nothing. For a few days the victors rested forces, tidied their field, then resumed the pursuit. After Samsonov's fall, Rennenkampf abandoned the scheme to attack Königsberg, quit his elaborately entrenched base of operations, and retreated eastward. The Niemen River was to be his line of defense. The Germans got close enough to engage his rear guard once or twice before he was back on friendly soil. Overrating the importance of the victory and holding too cheaply Russian power within Poland, Hindenburg, counseled by Ludendorff, determined to press on. It was their first major blunder. The same abnormal difficulties of the countryside that had oppressed Jilinsky were now turned against the Germans. Their columns became far separated by the rocky hills, forests, and lakes. The Niemen, a broad river, ran south to north directly athwart the line of advance. On its banks, at either end of the Eighth Army's path, stood the fortresses of Grodno and Kovno. In the German camp these obstacles were scorned. Tannenberg had been as heady as strong wine. Now that Paris was beyond reach, Berlin was clamoring for a quick march to Warsaw by Hindenburg and his victorious forces. To the German public he was the invincible commander.

Moltke had been eased out, protesting bitterly that the fault for the defeat in the West was not his. There was some truth in this. The Kaiser, Tappen, Kluck, Bülow, and Ludendorff had all contributed to his failures. In his place now sat General Erich von Falkenhayn, an enigmatic soldier, Moltke's own protégé. Out of the Pomeranian nobility, he was eye-filling, seemingly cut for the part of the peerless military leader, fairly exuding dash, energy, and steadfastness. Much of it was false front. Falkenhayn was as ridden by anxiety and hesitation as Moltke, the difference being that in him his weakness was not apparent.

AUSTRIAN OFFENSIVES

By no means dismayed that his chronic longing for "a bright, brisk little war" had helped fire a colossal conflict, the Austrian gamecock, General Franz Conrad von Hötzendorf, tried to do all things at one time.

One of history's small jests is that it mentions him favorably while sighing that he deserved a better army than the Austrian. This is like saying that he could adjust to everything except what counted most. To demand of mediocrity more than it can give is itself mediocre. Conrad so acted from the beginning. Even before mobilization, he had decided that he would open the war by striking down Serbia while at the same time concentrating the main weight of his army in Galicia to take the offensive against Russia. In aiming for this double knockout, he threw to the winds the value of the natural defenses of the country, exceeding also his proper role as the junior partner in the Central Alliance. It was far more rash than Joffre's launching of the French Army headlong into Lorraine.

More from hatred than from considered policy, Austria attacked Serbia at war's opening with two reserve corps, less than half of the expedition previously earmarked to attack across the Danube. The commander of this small army was Major General Potiorek, who as governor of Bosnia had by his carelessness helped make the Sarajevo tragedy. His credit at court had survived that business, but not his nerve fiber. Where Conrad overreached from bravado, Potiorek but dissipated his forces out of timidity. There had been given him two armies; he wasted one on police duty in Bosnia and excursions against Montenegro, as if his main object were pacification. That left him with six divisions of relatively soft troops to go against ten divisions of Serbs, or about 70,000 men, hardened by their mountains and the recent rigors of the

Balkan Wars. Another Austrian army (the Second) was kept demonstrating near the Serbian frontier but was ticketed for shipment to Galicia on August 18. Conrad and Potiorek imagined that this bustle and dispersion would dupe the Serbs into equal foolishness. Pure wishful folly! The Serbs had an obstinate general, Radomir Putnik, who worked by rules and ruled by work. Less is known of this shadowy figure than of any military leader in World War I; but he was a positive genius at compelling the enemy to fight on a field of his own choosing. Putnik kept his three armies concentrated under his hand and, maneuvering just enough to draw Potiorek's Fifth Army away from ready support, waited at the central position.

His defensive campaign is a classic of operational adroitness. By August 16 Putnik was set and ready within the Drina-Sava River bend southwest of Belgrade. He there engaged full-length in what is called the Battle of the Jadar, fought over a thirty-mile front along the river of that name. By nightfall, the Austrian center was shattered and driven back upon the Drina, and the left had retired after heavy losses consequent to the smashing of the center. That same night Conrad had departed Vienna for Przemyśl, which fortress in Galicia was to be his headquarters in the campaign against Russia; he got the bad news by wire next day. His dauntlessness for the first time wavered; instead of cutting losses, Conrad hedged his bets. The question was how to employ the Second Army, seated next to the Danube but already mounting for the ride to the northern frontier. He ordered Potiorek to use one corps from the Second Army to redress the situation. Now Potiorek demanded permission to use all of the Second Army but Conrad refused it. So but half of the force needed was sent to the going battle and the other half entrained for Galicia. Fighting resumed the next day and continued one week in excruciating heat. The extra corps got to the field two days too late to save Potiorek's Fifth Army and became so entangled in fighting around Šabac that it couldn't be extricated until August 30. The Fifth Army meanwhile had been fought to an exhausted standstill, winning nowhere, though avoiding annihilation. By month's end, the Austrians were back on their own soil. The campaign had cost them 40,000 casualties and the respect of the neighborhood; relatively little hurt had been done to the Serbs.

The first repulse in Serbia is the more dramatic, if less thunderous, half of Conrad's attempt to serve his Emperor by charging in two directions at one time. We look now at the other venture. Galicia was an appendage of Austria-Hungary in empire days, lying next to the Russian frontier. That put it beyond the protecting barrier of the Carpathian Mountains, which curved like body armor around the northern side of the Dual Monarchy. That well-forested range, which strongly resembles the Appalachians, is about sixty miles wide in its central part. No river valleys cut through it, but there are six or so serviceable passes that cut the crest line, the most prominent being the Dukla, Lupków, and Uzhok. North of the Carpathians, the fortress cities of Jaroslaw, Przemyśl, and Kraków cover the approaches to these passes and afforded the Austrians strong anchorage on the lower ground.

Altogether, the defender's advantages in Galicia were impressive. The Carpathians frowned on any movement southward of bulky supplies and heavy artillery. The few militarily useful roads could be blocked and the rails cut. Heavy snows would soon close the passes. Beyond the fortress cities, the plateau was fronted by a broad trench where the Vistula and San rivers flowed from opposite directions to meet in the center. The obvious strategy was for the Austrian armies, pivoting on the cities, to entrench behind the river line and let the Russian waves break against the barrier.

It was too sensible for Conrad. The Russian armies were bound to be concentrating somewhere east of Warsaw beyond the Vistula. So an Austrian thrust out of northeast Galicia pointed between Lublin and Kholm ought to cut the railways between those two fortified bases and the cities of Warsaw and Brest Litovsk. Then if the line of advance was maintained and the German Eighth Army rolled east and over the Niemen River, Russian forces in Poland would be trapped. These were the mighty prizes Conrad glimpsed and their dazzle blinded his eyes to the probable drawbacks. They were substantial. Should the Austrian Army be mauled and routed in its attempt to slash through Russian Poland, the prospect faded that it would be able to re-form and hold behind the San. Once the Russians were over the San they would be within reach of Kraków, the gateway city near the western end of the Carpathians, whence broad highways opened north and south into the heart of Bohemia.

On August 9 Moltke advised "Dear Friend" Conrad that there couldn't be a German offensive mounted from East Prussia. It deterred Conrad not at all. By August 18 he knew that his own Second Army was mired in Serbia. It didn't faze him. On August 22 he loosed his three field armies, each ten divisions strong, and they marched north toward Lublin as if bound for a fire. Austrian cavalrymen forming the screen were soon leading their galled horses. But they encountered no Cossacks. General Ivanov was using his horse regiments as decoys in the gaps between his four advancing field armies, trying thereby to suck the Austrians deeper into Poland. This was a better-than-average use of cavalry: at least it was good for the horses. When collision began between these vast forces, it was more by accident than design. Each side had totally misunderstood what the other was trying to do. The Austrians were pushing north out of Galicia; the four Russian armies were coming from the east and west against Galicia's flank frontiers. But the Russian commanders, in particular Generals Russki, Dmitriev, and Brusilov, were bold, competent leaders, unlike the pair to the north under Jilinsky. Though greatly outnumbered, Brusilov's army drove the Austrian right wing back through eastern Galicia and by September 1 had enveloped Lemberg (Lvov), the fourth city of the empire, capital of the province, and the hub of Galician travel routes. The city fell September 3.

There was no halt after Lemberg. Brusilov split his army and sent his left wing straight for the Carpathian passes, while his center and right drove west for Przemyśl. Part of Russki's army, on Brusilov's right, slid in between the Austrian Third Army (which had defended Lemberg) and its home bases, so that it couldn't retreat; the other half marched northwest in a defensive maneuver. Bulgarian-born Dmitriev drove toward Rava Russkaya, the main railway juncture west of Lemberg. Raveling the Austrian right flank, these marches out of eastern Galicia threatened to cut away the whole army. But the Austrian center, under General Baron Moritz von Auffenberg-Komarów, who was insensible to the warning, drove deeper into enemy country. The attack by the Austrian First Army under General Baron Viktor von Dankl (their ablest commander) on the left wing was better restrained. All that saved these two armies from ruin was that unwittingly they were charading too far west of the Russian mass to be pinched off. When on September 10, coincident with the German retreat to the Aisne, Dmitriev took Rava Russkaya, they hastily went into reverse, thus at last abandoning an offensive more pantomime than real. The retreat ended when the San was crossed. Jaroslaw fell, and the other fortress city, Przemyśl, was invested; so began a siege that lasted, on and off, six months, visiting on the penned-in garrison of 150,000 Austrians deprivation and misery indescribable. Just off the shoulder of Rumania, Brusilov slashed deeper into the Dual Monarchy and grabbed the eastern passes into Hungary. His van overran Bucovina Province and his soldiers bivouacked in Czernowitz, its capital, a pawn that ran the cycle of capture and liberation fifteen times during the war.

There are no authentic figures on manpower costs in this campaign. But at least 120,000 Austrian soldiers were marched off captive, and in the wasting battles Conrad had lost the cream of his relatively few competent junior leaders. While he had gained nothing, and nearly lost all, the Russians stopped far short of decision. Their armies had bounded too far too fast and were suddenly drained of energy and supply. They turned to broadening the gauge of Galician railways to fit their own rolling stock.

Conrad's attempts to invade without first looking, although ghastly failures, neither humbled him nor caused Austria to relieve him. Within two months, he tried once more against Serbia with no better result. But the two opening defeats for Austria, and the two-hundred-mile-long retreats by her armies, were not mere temporary setbacks. The Dual Monarchy remained militarily a chronic invalid, without vitality or inspiration, though its ability to resist final dissolution passed understanding. Too soon Germany realized that the choice was one of carrying Austria or watching it go down. Austria was supported patronizingly but not too kindly, an attitude best expressed in a grim phrase soon to be common among German officers: "We are fettered to a corpse."

TURKEY AND THE CRUISERS

Turkey did not go reluctantly to war on the side of the Central Powers, wooed by Germany, offended and finally alienated by Allied blunders. Like the story of the maiden wronged, that apology, while lending spiceful suspense, obscures the long-standing nature of the seduction.

Turkey got in through a secret treaty signed with the German Government on August 2, the day when all of Europe beçame convulsed by the general mobilization. That the Turks, for rea-

After Tannenberg, Russia retreated beyond the
Masurian Lakes (top). The broken black lines
trace Conrad's movements in Galicia; meanwhile
Austria formed a bridgehead in Serbia (bottom).

sons of self-advantage, saw fit to conceal the design until October 29 is as incidental as are the dramatic episodes that created the historical illusion that they chose sides reluctantly after painful slight to their national honor.

For several years Wilhelm had sedulously courted Turkey. German generals were in command of the Turkish Army; Turkish ranks, wearing field gray and *pickelhaube* helmets, had learned to goose-step smartly on parade; six months earlier the army had been an undisciplined rabble. Wilhelm had to have Turkey. It was the only way to cut the threat of the Franco-Russian alliance. With Turkey committed, the Central Powers could close the Dardanelles, the only practical line of supply between the Western democracies and their equipment-hungry imperial ally. If compelling to Wilhelm, the arguments for the contract were no less persuasive to the Turks, although for traditional reasons. Russia was the natural enemy, then as later under Stalin and Khrushchev. Ever since Peter the Great, the Czars had coveted the Turkish Straits and lunged toward them whenever the hour seemed opportune. As Turkish power and territory diminished, these fears became exacerbated.

But there was more to it than that. Turkey was in the grip of a totally debauched government. The forty men who had title to power in Constantinople were a cast suited to *Ali Baba*. They were the last and hardiest of the Young Turks, a band of revolutionaries who in 1908 had come out of the mountains of Macedonia, stormed into Constantinople, and deposed the bloody butcher, Sultan Abdul Hamid. It was supposed to have been a cleansing, democratic reform. The ideal has seldom anywhere been more hideously mocked and degraded. In office, these men behaved like the worst of the Chicago mobs in Prohibition days, using murder, torture, and terror to consolidate their gains. Massacres of minority groups and wholesale deportations were common. Opponents, that is, all who dared protest, were garroted or hanged. It was a government with character—all bad.

Leader of the band was Talaat Pasha, an ex-mailman and telgrapher who wielded power from the Ministry of the Interior. Nothing was certain about his pedigree; rumor identified him as a Bulgarian gypsy. He had the physical endowments of a heavyweight wrestler and knew how and when to throw them about.

His second was a dandified thirty-two-year-old, Enver Pasha, who in 1914 became Minister of War. He glorified in the popular title, "Hero of the Revolution," although his intimates called him Napoleonlik, or Little Napoleon. The pretensions are a sufficient portrait. Enver's record as a conqueror had one entry; in the Balkan Wars, he had recaptured Adrianople after the Bulgarians had completely abandoned the city. But there is no doubt about the sincerity of his belief that he was born to rival the Great Captains of History. Sent on a mission to Berlin, he hobnobbed with the Kaiser and returned to Constantinople with new facial herbage, a spiked, upturned mustache. Soon afterward, he was named chief of the armed forces. It was regarded as a German triumph.

The more fastidious ambassadors to the Sublime Porte felt a certain distaste for these *opéra bouffe* types, an attitude that furthered the game of the German Ambassador, Baron von Wangenheim, who knew what the Kaiser wanted, and stopped at nothing to gain it.

By late spring of 1914 Talaat and Enver were well along in the rascally business of exiling the Greeks from the port of Smyrna and the islands nearby because they were rated security risks. Although people of Greek origin predominated in the coastal area, most of them were Turkish citizens. The impetus to their deportation to Greece came directly from Berlin. The Athens Government bridled, but felt powerless to intervene. Then in June, out of the blue sky, Greece negotiated the purchase of two well-used American battleships, the *Idaho* and the *Mississippi*, old but still more powerful than anything in the Turkish fleet. Wangenheim did his best to block the deal, warning U.S. Ambassador Henry Morgenthau: "The sale of these ships may bring on a European war." But through a broker, the sale was consummated for $12,535,276.98, and the dreadnoughts took their place in the Greek line.

That made Talaat and Enver strain all the harder for the delivery of two dreadnoughts, built for Turkey in England, which were completing their tests and just about to be delivered. The *Reshadieh* was to be handed over in August; the *Sultan Osman* would come a few weeks later. Money for the vessels had been raised by popular subscription several years earlier, and Turkey made the last payment at the time of Sarajevo.

Whether the ships would be released as promised was the great question in Turkey in the hour that Vienna fired the ultimatum at Belgrade. It dangled unanswered through the hours when every minute weighed decision and made of record who kept faith and who did not.

On July 27 Turkey voluntarily and secretly proposed to Germany a mutual defense pact against Russia. Knowing nothing of it, Winston Churchill on July 28 requisitioned the two Turkish warships for the Royal Navy, because he believed war with Germany had become unavoidable and he saw no present and pressing threat to Turkey. The Turks mobilized July 31. Germany returned the signed treaty to Constantinople on August 2. In that same hour, Britain, still believing that Turkey was undecided, offered, on behalf of all members of the Alliance, including Russia, a solemn guarantee of the integrity of all Turkish territory in return for a pledge of neutrality. It was a waste of breath.

Wangenheim, who knew all about the Turkish-German treaty, went to Talaat and Enver, raging about British perfidy; they knew all about it, also. But it was a good act, done straight-faced and carrying conviction until the full story came out years later. The Turkish press fulminated and stirred the public to war-fever pitch, which was the main object. There were still cards to play, and while luck held, Wangenheim knew how to deal them. The chance was at hand to make Germany appear as Turkey's best friend and protector, in contrast to England, the betrayer. The German cruisers *Goeben* and *Breslau* were then steaming around in mid-Mediterranean, possibly in anticipation of this very contingency, and certainly too far from home base to risk returning. Wangenheim suggested to Talaat and Enver that Turkey should go through the form of purchasing the two ships from Germany.

The prospect gleamed on August 3, the day of the British ultimatum to Germany. From Admiral Alfred von Tirpitz in the German Admiralty went a signal to Admiral Wilhelm Souchon, commanding in the Mediterranean: "Alliance with Turkey concluded. Proceed at once to Constantinople." That was all to the good with Souchon; he scorned the alternative of making for the Adriatic port of Pola to spend the war playing second fiddle to Austrians. But agreeing was easier than complying.

Signals had also gone out to the British Mediterranean fleet and to the French fleet steaming from Toulon to North Africa to intercept the *Goeben* and the *Breslau*. But the unique conditions of a war not yet exploded stultified the admirals. Still short of a full war footing as to munitions supply and still uncertain whether by formal declaration it was not open season on German vessels, the two fleets proceeded hesitantly, without coordination, on what should have been an easy sweep. The *Goeben* was having boiler trouble and both vessels were low of fuel. The still greater affliction to Souchon was a confusion of signals from Tirpitz. In Constantinople, divided counsel developed right on the verge. Enver stood for bringing the German ships on, through hell or high water. Talaat wished to maintain the show of a feigned neutrality for as long as it took to square Turkey around for the most favorable possible start. The Grand Vizier, Saïd Halim, an Egyptian-born puppet, was not a party to the grand design; so he wanted no German ships at all lest England be offended. In Berlin Tirpitz breathed alternately hot and cold to Admiral Souchon, while Wangenheim in Constantinople urged on Enver an immediate declaration of war.

While Allied warships searched the western sea and covered the middle passages, Souchon nonchalantly coaled at Messina. He made forays against the French seaports in Africa. For one week, there was a chase round about the eastern sea, more galling than great. The *Goeben* sighted. The *Goeben* pursued. The *Goeben* slipping away. Much is made of the episode in naval histories, because it was the first suspense-filled incident of the Great War.

All that matters is that the *Goeben* and the *Breslau* arrived at the entrance to the Turkish Straits still fight-worthy, still pursued, and were admitted. This time Enver didn't bother to consult the Grand Vizier.

Then the German attaché, Colonel von Kress, pressed him for one more decision, asking: "If the English ships follow, shall the forts fire on them?"

Enver at last replied: "Yes."

A Turkish destroyer led the way, after the mine fields were lifted. This happened on August 10. Upon getting the news, Britain and France still believed that Turkey might be persuaded to keep to the middle of the road. The Grand Vizier continued to cable friendly messages to the cabinet in London. But the Allied Ambassadors protested in vain to Talaat and Enver that the *Goeben* and the *Breslau* should be interned and disarmed. The *Breslau* was a token nuisance, but the 24,000-ton *Goeben* could outgun and outrun anything in the Russian Black Sea fleet.

Turkey went through the act of completing purchase of the

ships. They were rechristened with Turkish names. A few of the sailors aboard donned red fezzes, just for fun. When photographs were taken, some Turkish naval officers were piped aboard to pose alongside the turrets. But it was all part of a deadly, though somewhat silly, game of make-believe. The vessels were never fitted into the Turkish Navy. Rather, the Turkish Navy subordinated itself to Souchon's command. While the pretense lasted, the *Goeben* steamed one day up the Bosporus to drop anchor in front of the Russian Embassy. The sailors doffed their fezzes and donned their own flattops to sing *Deutschland über Alles* and other German airs while the ship's band blared. The act completed, the *Goeben* sailed away.

Not all of the Turks cheered. On the day King Albert of Belgium had to withdraw his army to Antwerp, a Belgian visiting the Sublime Porte was stopped on the street by Djavid Bey, the Finance Minister. "I have terrible news for you," said the Turk. "The Germans have captured Brussels."

"I have more terrible news for you," replied the Belgian. "The Germans have captured Turkey."

It all came clear enough soon enough. Souchon repeatedly sent his ships on prowls into the Black Sea, trying to provoke an attack. They got nowhere. The Russians played dumb. October 29 was a Turkish religious holiday, the festival of Bairam. German sailors relieved some of the crews. Three Turkish torpedo boats in their custody made for Odessa, entered the harbor, sank the Russian gunboat *Donetz*, shelled the French freighter *Portugal*, and then bombarded a sugar factory, wrecking it and killing or injuring a large number of Russian workers.

In the Sublime Porte there were perfunctory gestures toward prolonging the sham. The Grand Vizier, genuinely wanting peace, sent a question to Russian Ambassador Giers: "What guarantees are needed?" Giers replied: "Russia will guarantee you don't again enter the Black Sea." Talaat came to Morgenthau, in the name of the Vizier, to see what he could do.

Said Morgenthau: "Why don't you drop the mask as messenger and talk to me as Talaat?"

Replied Talaat: "All right. Wangenheim, Enver, and I all prefer that war should come now." So at last came forth candor equaled in measure only by stupidity. The members of the racket mob that managed Turkey were amateur gamblers in the largest game of all. They could not understand the odds against them. By now the Marne had been fought and lost. From Tannenberg had come no thoroughfare for Germans through Poland. Austria had been humiliated all around its border. Even so, at this stage, Enver and friends plunged, not because any principle was at stake, but because they calculated that Germany was bound to win. The decision was as cold, crude, and careless as that. But this triumvirate of political brigands was denied its one moment of cockcrowing; suddenly, on November 2, Russia declared war on Turkey.

Thereupon, again, the war changed its dimension dramatically. No other event contributed so directly to its agonizing duration. None more heavily influenced the postwar transfiguration of Europe, or induced such vast changes in its political, social, and economic structure. When the Dardanelles were closed to Imperial Russia (the German commander, General Otto Liman von Sanders, had forced Enver to take that step tentatively on September 27), she became doomed as an economic and military power. Russia could no longer dispose of surplus grain; imports slowed to a trickle; there were lacking both the finance to pay for war and the goods to energize it. Within one year thereafter, Russian soldiers were going into battle without cartridges, and the Romanov dynasty was tottering.

The war ultimately cost Turkey one fourth of her population. Of 4,000,000 adult males, about 1,600,000 were called to service. More than 1,000,000 families were left without breadwinners. A multitude of women, children, and old folk died of starvation and lack of medical care. But it didn't bother Enver Pasha. Wrote Ambassador Morgenthau: "He was more impressed by his success in raising a large army with no money, which no nation had ever done before."

None of these trials was plain at the beginning. Once the Turks were in, their war started in slow motion. Their leaders had no initial plan and the strategic possibilities were frustrating. Mainly, Talaat and Enver were thinking about banqueting on war spoils after playing supernumerary in a clash that would be quickly won by Germany. So they would have preferred to fight in Europe and go after the lost province of Thrace. But Greece and Bulgaria stayed neutral, which deprived Turkey of a good target up close. That left two possibilities, equally unpleasant. An attack toward the Suez Canal might force Britain to rush support

Turkey's Minister of War Enver Pasha,
shown here sporting the upturned
mustache he had acquired in
Berlin, was largely responsible for
leading his country into war. Often called
"Little Napoleon," Enver thought of himself
as a great conqueror and hoped to resurrect
Turkey's days as a glorious empire.

to the Indian and Australian brigades in training there; or an attack could be staged into the Russian Caucasus, which might divert Russian troops more direly needed for the great battles shaping in Poland. This is what Liman von Sanders and the other Germans wanted.

Neither prospect was attractive. In both directions nature was hostile. The arid Sinai peninsula, which was the only approach to the Suez, is a waterless, dune-heaped belt 150 miles across, so harsh that only a few Bedouins, ravens, and jackals suffer it through the seasons. There is no more repellent fighting country anywhere on earth. Within the great range of the Caucasus, running from the Black Sea to the Caspian, are the tallest, driest, hardest mountains in Europe. Logistically, the Turkish Army was as poorly tied to these remote areas of its own frontier as to the supply depots of Austria and Germany, on which it was so greatly dependent. War stocks from the Central Powers could be fed to it only via the rail line running through Rumania, and the Rumanians either cooperated or blocked passage according to their whim and the shifting fortunes of the war. No rail line out of Constantinople traversed Palestine; away from the coast, a narrow-gauge served this territory only as far as Nablus, north of Jerusalem. The Russian border in the Caucasus was five hundred miles beyond Konya, the closest Turkish railhead.

But the Young Turks, twice vanquished in the Balkan Wars, operated more by sight than by information. With their planlessness, they combined a ruthlessness that they expected would carry the day. Otherwise, they would have shirked the venture against Transcaucasia, based on their own province of Armenia, whose Christian inhabitants had been tormented, massacred, and humiliated for centuries by the Moslem oppressor. Enver knew a way to handle that and avoid harassment to the army's rear; it is more correct to say that this was his excuse for mass murder. In 1915 the Turkish Army tried to exterminate the Armenians. More than one million were slaughtered. By the thousands, Armenian women were violated. Children were sold into prostitution. Old folk were driven into the desert. Except for Germany, the civilized nations voiced their outraged protests.

About two thirds of Russia's Caucasian border fronted on Persia, the other third on Turkey. Along their common frontier, Russians and Turks were fortified against each other. To avoid these battlements, the field forces on both sides swung eastward, violating and overrunning the Persian province of Azerbaijan, as Russians had oft done before, and were to try again in 1945. Kurdish troops advanced through Suj Balak, took Tabriz, and meeting no resistance, struck northward toward the Russian frontier. This was in December, 1914. The Russians had left no garrisons east of Mount Ararat. But they quickly remedied that blunder. Their forces came down like the wolf on the fold, broke the first Turkish invasion among the snow-clad peaks at Sufian, and by late January had a solid hold on Tabriz. Enver Pasha had already taken the field elsewhere as generalissimo, rallying four Turkish corps around the Lake Van area for the grand offensive that was to consolidate his military reputation. From it came debacle and frozen death for the great part of one Turkish army. Yet that folly was to have less influence on the course of the war than an earlier, intrinsically trivial incident. In a moment of weakness, after the Kurdish troops took Tabriz, the Czar's Government messaged London requesting a diversion against Turkey to ease the threat in the Caucasus. By the time the British cabinet came to consider its response to the message, the diversion was no longer needed. But the ministers continued to gaze anxiously eastward as if following immemorial law. So a great oak popped out of an acorn, planted by Winston Churchill. Let us not oversimplify how things developed. From the moment the war against Turkey started the English trustees of empire were rightly concerned about protection for the "jugular vein" at Suez and for their other strategic holdings in the Middle East. Within five days after the break, one British brigade out of India arrived in the Persian Gulf to extend its protecting arms around Kuwait and Bahrein, place names whose significance in that time meant little to the outside world. No less promptly, a British battleship moved to engage one of the outer forts protecting the Dardanelles and in a half-hour bombardment wrecked it, silencing all guns. This exchange at Sedd el Bahr, like the Russian cry for help, distracted the official gaze to the Eastern threat and prospect, but no more than that.

For better or worse, every early development inclined the British toward the Middle East. The Turkish commander in Syria, Djemal Pasha, got away to a slow start, but by the end of February, 1915, had put about two divisions across the Sinai desert and was threatening the Suez Canal. A few of his soldiers actually crossed into Egypt before the threat recoiled, defeated more by overextension and lack of food and ammunition than by fire from the defenders.

In the Caucasus, winter and 100,000 Russians ruined Enver's dream of sharing a niche with Alexander the Great. He started with a bold plan and 150,000 troops, at the wrong time in the wrong countryside against the wrong enemy. The passes and valleys around Sarikamis were deep in snow. General Woronzov's army was dressed for it, not so Enver's. In great battles around Kars, Karai Urgan, and Khurasan inside Russia, Turkey's Third Army was crushed. One army corps was annihilated and more than 50,000 Turks froze to death. Unhelped and nigh helpless, still they tried. The campaign was fought in terrain not unlike the California Sierra around Donner Pass. After three ghastly weeks, it ended in a Turkish retreat. With the frozen bodies of their comrades, the wretched survivors left behind in the ice Enver's dream of rolling back the Czar's armies.

Thereupon, the pendulum of British strategy-making swung from apprehension to anticipation. Attracted at first to the threat of Turkish strength, the gaze was now fascinated by battlefield proof of Turkish weakness. About this, there was a certain inevitability. Papers were circulating in the War Council calling attention to the "remarkable deadlock" on the Western Front. Europe had seen nothing of its kind before. The reality was fearsome. It kindled visions of a more hopeful alternative. Already, David Lloyd George was badgering his colleagues and contending that the only sensible course was to withdraw the entire British Army from France and ship it to the eastern Mediterranean.

Change was in the air. There was no one clearly to foresee that the gleam of opportunity could be no less deceptive than the glare of menace.

IV

Seeds of Stalemate

Touring the Western Front in 1916, George V of England (left) chats with Albert, the tall, youthful soldier-king of Belgium.

By the end of September, 1914, the battle between German and Allied armies along the line of the Aisne had trenched itself into immobility. Armies drained of energy and supply incline to dig in for a respite. In this case, neither side realized that in one autumnal fortnight there was being scratched in earth the first faint tracing of a pattern that would curse millions of soldiers throughout four years.

Frantic optimism remained abundant. In late September Sir John French cheerfully predicted that his soliders would be in Berlin within six weeks. Wholly convinced, his G.H.Q. Staff railed at Kitchener for not sending every available soldier to France instead of preserving a nucleus at home for the vast forces that he believed would be needed. Joffre was less sanguine than Sir John, if only because his artillery was starved for 75-mm. rounds and the war plants were producing only about 10,000 shells per day. In fact, the shell shortage forced him to mark time on the Aisne while the Germans fortified. The French followed suit so that they might live longer, and the novelty, while offensive to their doctrine, swiftly became a habit.

After the Marne, the spirit of the French people was marked by a "grave enthusiasm, a disciplined exaltation," in the words of novelist Maurice Barrès. But the people were unaware that already 90 per cent of their iron mines, 83 per cent of their heavy industry, and 40 per cent of their sugar refineries now lay in enemy country. In Germany there was no sudden public awakening to the turn of fortune. How could there be? Never having heard of the magic plan for quick victory, the people could not understand that it had gone awry from Kluck's careening. To the average German a strategic reverse was incomprehensible, when headlines spoke only of battles won. But Falkenhayn grasped, perhaps too well, that the outlook had blackened, obscuring the goal. At the start his mind was more on security than on reinvigorating the offensive. Measures that would avert defeat outweighed what might be done to restore opportunity. Immediately on taking over active command from Moltke on September 14, he moved his headquarters from Luxembourg far forward to Charleville on the Meuse. There, reviewing his situation, he realized that the German right flank was in great danger of being enveloped unless it promptly extended westward to the sea. That meant loosing Kluck once again to turn the tables on Maunoury, if possible. But at the same time, he directed that the German First Army should fortify its front.

This conflict in Falkenhayn's thought became the seed of the Western Front's enduring dilemma. For fortifications are death to mobility; an army cannot apply its force downward and forward effectively at one time. German pioneers are perfectionists; their protective measures are always far more elaborate than those of other armies. So the scarp of the great plateau north of the Aisne, where Kluck's Germans first dug, became honeycombed with deep works. The trenches were man-height deep and broad enough for two to pass. There were underground dugouts for men and horses; galleries were run into the reverse slopes of the hills to accommodate stores and minor headquarters. Concrete strongpoints, or pillboxes, began to rise. With the first appearance of this system, the Germans started that rotation of rifle companies in and out of the first line position, for brief spells of support duty, that shortly would be in fashion all along the Western Front. With these changes, as munitions dumps were replenished, the night and day bombardment was heightened. It was a tactical pause, just an interlude. But the Aisne, not the Marne, was the premonitor of all the shock, horror, and monotony to come. Few guessed it. The young American poet Alan Seeger, nearing the great adventure as a volunteer in the Foreign Legion, wrote his mother: "Imagine how thrilling it will be tomorrow marching toward the front with the noise of battle growing continually louder. I go into action with the lightest of light hearts."

But it wasn't all long-range hammering. In late September the Crown Prince attacked Sarrail's Third Army, captured Saint-Mihiel (liberated exactly four years later by the Americans), and cut two main railway lines. In consequence, the great fortress of Verdun was left dangling and dependent on one narrow-gauge railway running from Bar-le-Duc. The jeopardy to Verdun did not become apparent to Joffre until February, 1916.

What started Joffre thinking of his left flank while diverting his gaze from Verdun comes clear in his memoirs. German wireless kept leaking information to his intelligence desk. From it, he got the tip that a new Seventh Army was forming under General Josias von Heeringen to come in on Kluck's right. Having more confidence in Castelnau than in his other generals, he mounted the Second Army in little boxcars and shipped it north to hook the German right wing. The order called for "a direction of march that will be outflanking in relation to any new forces that the enemy may add to his front," which is like saying, "lead boldly but don't get caught off base."

THE RACE TO THE SEA

In this way, more or less haphazardly, began the stretching-out operations by which the battlefront was extended to the North Sea coast. This series of attempted outflanking maneuvers to the north is given the graphic name "The Race to the Sea." Strangely, the Germans had not thought initially to plunge for the Channel ports, and stranger still, the British had not troubled to outguard them. In the movement, which was not a race but a succession of lurches, neither side gained main advantage, although the Germans swung outward with the heavier concentrations. As the line stretched more and more toward the breaking point, it was spliced with fresh formations or units pulled from the line where trench warfare had already set in. Consequently, even with the resumption of maneuver, the generals leaned on their earthworks. There was hard fighting around the chalky slopes of Bapaume, where Castelnau thought he had at last rounded the German right. Louis Ernest de Maud'huy's Tenth Army got hit heavily a few days later around Arras and remained embattled there for some time. The greater menace was still farther north. Masses of German cavalry, under General Georg von der Marwitz, were heading toward the lower River Somme between Amiens and Abbeville.

The B.E.F., now six divisions, had stayed awkwardly wedged between two French armies on the Aisne. Pressed by Sir John, who was still dreaming of a fast "ride into the blue," Joffre agreed that the British should be shifted as rapidly as possible to the extreme north end of the line. By that stroke, made without consulting his London superiors, Marshal French served the cause brilliantly, moving rapidly to Flanders, where his strength was most needed. By October 9, one British corps had detrained at Abbeville and moved posthaste to Béthune. Another corps, which had been rushed to France to relieve Antwerp but had arrived too late, also deployed to help guard Flanders. But by midmonth the left of the line was still a scattering of fragments holding grimly to a wide-open and tactically difficult countryside. As the

German Army made its first power drive toward the Channel ports, the B.E.F. bore the brunt of the fighting, with none of its parts performing more gallantly than that anachronism the British cavalry. In South Africa the cavalry had learned to fight afoot with rifles. When all was in flux in Picardy and Flanders, it was this extra talent of the British horse soldiers that saved the Channel ports.

Now about Antwerp. Until early October that great port had been not only the one stronghold of the Belgian Army but the potential anchor of the Allied front next to blue water. But on September 9, the same day Kluck and Bülow fell back beaten from the Marne, the German Emperor ordered that Antwerp be taken. Missing the preparation wholly, Allied intelligence first knew of the oblique move when on September 28 Antwerp was brought under seige. One-ton projectiles from 17-inch howitzers rained on the city; though they were as buckshot compared to the V-2's that blasted Antwerp thirty years later, they terrorized the population. By October 1 the German fire had wrecked two of the Antwerp forts, with German infantry taking over the trenches between them. Justifiably alarmed, King Albert called on London for help; his 150,000 soliders were too few to man the perimeter.

Winston Churchill rushed to Antwerp to see what was needed. From there, on October 4, he wired the cabinet, urging that the Government speed reinforcements, volunteering to take command of them himself, and suggesting that Walter Runciman, Chairman of the Board of Trade, replace him at the Admiralty. It is reported that all members laughed uproariously except Kitchener, who proposed that Churchill be made a lieutenant general, provided that Asquith would release him from the Government. When the suggestion was overruled, it was agreed that a British corps under General Sir Henry Rawlinson would be sped to the relief.

But Churchill was a little late. The outer forts were falling one by one. Belgium's army was demoralized, having fought too long in isolation. Ever sort of matériel required for defense was either lacking or running short. To King Albert and his ministers, weighing the odds, it seemed a questionable gamble to stake the future of the nation on the army's prospect of holding the city. There was one line of retreat still open, running parallel to the Dutch frontier and then down the seacoast. Three Belgian divi-

**Wounded British marines leave Antwerp in
October, 1914. Most of Britain's professional
soldiers—members of what the Germans called
the "comtemptible little army"—were killed
in these early battles, but survivors proudly
called themselves the "Old Contemptibles."**

sions held back the German threat in that quarter. But their time was running out and a decision had to be made.

Some British marines arrived and took their place in line. British naval guns and bluejackets joined the action. But, with the collapse of the forts, these driblets didn't help much and Churchill knew that Rawlinson's corps wouldn't be debarking around Ostend and Zeebrugge until October 7 at the earliest. The first question was whether the Belgian Army would be able to hold that long. Above and beyond the question was the greater gamble: unless with the aid of Rawlinson's corps Antwerp could be secured until the Allied flank extending westward from the Aisne closed on it, an army would be wasted. These were issues to make the bravest heart tremble. But Churchill pondered them in solid company, as is witnessed in this evocation: ". . . the King and Queen through these tense and tragic days [were] magnificent. The impression of the grave, calm soldier King presiding at Council, sustaining his troops and commanders, preserving an unconquerable majesty amid the ruins of his kingdom, will never pass from my mind."

Two British naval brigades came up and joined the defense. Rawlinson got there ahead of his troops on October 6, and was all for staying till hell froze over. But that night the Belgian Council of War decided a final stand on Antwerp could not be justified, and it was best for the army to move, while it still had an escape route, and join hands farther down the coast with the relieving forces. Churchill felt no inclination to dispute that view and left the city the same night. The Belgian Army began its retirement, with one division and the British naval brigades staying behind to cover the retreat. They got away on October 8 and the Germans swarmed into the city.

Albert and his battered forces pulled up behind the Yser River still holding to a fragment of their own soil. There they dug in, fortifying the embankments as if they were guarding earth's greatest treasure. Four years later they were still holding to the same ground when U.S. divisions joined them to finish the Big Push.

But the Antwerp victory was a windfall for Falkenhayn. The end of the siege released the greater part of a German army (four reserve corps) for employment against the undermanned and loosely strung Allied left flank between Ypres and the sea. All of the heavy guns that had battered Antwerp (seventy-five miles from Ypres) were also free to pour their metal into the offensive.

Falkenhayn proposed to win the war in Flanders before the westward shift of Allied forces could equalize defensive strength along the Western Front. That is why Marshal French's decision to displace his army westward was of such vast consequence. He rode for the gate that had to be closed, although Joffre, Kitchener, and Churchill did not mark the imminent danger. A breakthrough to Calais, mounted between Menin and the sea, was in Falkenhayn's mind, with the troops out of Antwerp doing the hammering. It was a sound calculation that if Germany could possess Dunkirk, Calais, and Boulogne, that would be more damaging to the Allies than any blow manageable before winter closed, even if it did not trap the B.E.F. or force it to embark for England.

By about October 18 the German assault forces were reassembled and ready. Their opening shock was directed against the Belgians along the Yser, which is hardly more than a drainage ditch curving through flat country so waterlogged that the roads and rail lines traverse it on causeways ten to twelve feet high. German infantry wallowed through this muck, while from off the flanks old British battleships and monitors enfiladed them with heavy shell. The marshes turned red, but the German reservists persisted. Wholly outranging the defense, the German artillery took terrible toll. Belgian units had become scrambled during the retreat from Antwerp and the army was scarcely more than a mob when the attack hit; even so, it lost 35 per cent of its strength to enemy fire in the fight along the Yser and did not break. In late October the sluices of the sea dikes were opened at the suggestion of General Foch and the sea gradually flooded the field of fire between the river and the railway embankment running from Dixmude to Nieuport. Thereby a belt of water two miles wide and shoulder high intervened between the Belgian defense line and the besieging Germans. That shallow flood alone preserved the Belgian Army.

FIRST BATTLE OF YPRES

Sir John was still feeding on raw meat and seeing offensive opportunity where it did not exist. Even as the lightning hit the Belgians, he loosed Rawlinson's III Corps in an attack toward Menin, aiming for a breakthrough by which he might reach Ghent. In so doing, he thrust at dead center of the German massing. While that bad guess wasted soldiers' lives, it also misled Falkenhayn as to the strength of the Allied left wing on the eve of his first effort. The curtain was rising this October 20 on the First Battle of Ypres, the name given to the other half of the two-shafted German attempt to crash through to the Channel.

"Wipers" it was called by the Tommies. To the Yanks much later it was "Yeeps." But however pronounced, there is no other ground on earth more sanctified by the blood of soldiers. It was, in 1914, a quiet Belgian town of 22,000, little visited by strangers, a religious center where life revolved largely around Saint Martin's Cathedral and the Cloth Hall, two gems of Gothic architecture. The making of Valenciennes lace was Ypres's principal business, which is about as remote from the stuff of war as any occupation can be. Ypres was already laden with war wounded, collected from the Belgian retreat and from British cavalry actions around nearby Armentières.

The Germans wanted Ypres because it was a communications hub. Their roads funneled into it and the roads to westward went to the Channel ports. If Ypres could be broken, there was no linchpin beyond it that could give the Allies the advantage of radial lines.

Belgium's army was tied to the Yser and could not advance. Ypres itself could not be defended from trenches at the town's edge. So the higher ground directly east of it became the battlement, making a bulge in the Allied line called the Ypres Salient. Around its rim were little villages like Hollebeke, Hooge, Langemarck, Passchendaele, Poelcapelle, Wytschaete, and Zonnebeke. The syllables in these names, even today, ring like a dirge.

The salient was shaped like a human skull; German cartoonists pictured the jaws crunching on Ypres. A man could walk that cranial outline in the sunlight of one day. Yet within this narrow compass, more than one million human beings were to suffer death and wounds. Most were British, but there were Frenchmen, Belgians, Algerians, Senegalese, Canadians, and, finally, Yanks. The blood and bone of the races enriches the earth of the pastures beyond Ypres la Morte, the City of the Dead. In that salient through four years soldiers were expended at triple the rate of any other sector.

The British I Corps settled in on Ypres on October 20—just in time. Its commander, Sir Douglas Haig, would soon be challenging Sir John French for leadership of the B.E.F. The British Cavalry Corps under General Edmund Allenby—another Great

Captain on the rise—found it and IV corps "like a frigate between ships of the line." Opposite it, similarly wedged, was the German Cavalry Corps. Animals were left behind, Germans and Englishmen both moving to collision as foot soldiers. Still the terms are deceptive. Allenby's two divisions counted but 9,000 men. The German corps mustered 24,000. Elsewhere, the odds were more even, though not by much. The German artillery, which included the Antwerp siege train, far outranged the British 13-pounders. The French Army had come to the battle also; the French divisions joined flanks with the British at both ends of the salient, and French *poilus* held the rampart of its northern face.

There were two stages to the battle. The first German drive for Ypres opened October 20, raged ten days, and spent its fury on October 31, just as the British line neared the breaking point. Then, after a brief lull for regrouping and replenishment, the gray tide rolled forward again, the violence at last dying amid the blizzards of the third week in November. After October, the Germans never got so close again. The first onslaught built up gradually, starting with small attacks against the north face of the salient, then extending toward Zonnebeke and sweeping southward. Their forces converged more and more toward the Menin Road, and the battle climax was a full-scale bid for a breakthrough along that avenue, repeatedly hurled back only to be renewed.

After the early warning fire, Sir John stayed ecstatically optimistic. Instead of pulling in his horns, on October 21 he loosed Haig's I Corps in an attack north of Ypres, pointed toward Poelcapelle but intended to break the German back by knifing through to the coast. Two French divisions struck along with the Tommies. On the second day the movement was stopped dead by a German counterattack. Sir John had already launched Rawlinson's III Corps on another equally ill-timed strike toward Menin, where the enemy was massing.

Kaiser Wilhelm had moved up front to Courtrai to inspirit his troops for their touchdown try. What they needed more was common-sense tactical guidance. They continued to attack in mass, charging straight in against bunched machine guns and volleying rifles. At Ypres, generals belatedly began to understand what soldiers already knew—that the bullet was sovereign

By December, 1914, the Western Front had become
consolidated along a 400-mile trench line
from the North Sea to Switzerland, with seven
German armies (black) facing eight French
armies (white), the B.E.F., and the Belgian Army,
which had retreated (white arrows) from Antwerp.
The inset shows the First Battle of Ypres, October 20
–November 22, in which the B.E.F. and Belgian
Army stopped the German thrust toward the
ports of Dunkirk and Calais.

along the Western Front. The German folly of putting men forward in droves was somewhat offset by British carelessness. There was no systematic entrenching within the salient, although soldiers in that unwholesome position are vulnerable to artillery fire from four directions. To be held without inordinate sacrifice, every narrow salient requires deep works. The Tommies, in shallow ditches or behind ditch banks, were protected only against small-arms fire.

Largely due to these conditions, First Ypres fragmented the original B.E.F., stripping it of its best and bravest junior leaders. At the inquest, the generals delivered only the sterile verdict: "We must dig deeper!" Ypres thereby confirmed the inkling from the Aisne. All that saved the British hold on Ypres, beyond mortal valor, was the extraordinary defensive strength of the salient, a maze of small wood plots, dikes, ditches, and canals. But the excessive attrition was not really the fault of those much-maligned individuals, the British brass hats, tabbed "The Donkeys" by a latter-day critic. The battle had arisen too soon. Its dimensions were far beyond anything for which their life training had prepared them. Troops in a death grapple can be helped or hurt by the behavior of subalterns and sergeants. But generals can do little more than regulate the support and advance the reserves, which at Ypres were preciously few.

So we weep for Sir John, alternately glowing and forlorn. Once the futility of his offensive was demonstrated beyond doubt, he must have felt as frustrated as the women of Ypres, who tearfully prayed and sought sanctuary in the cathedral. Soon enough, it was made a target of the enemy howitzers. The aid staiton set up for wounded civilians was blasted apart. So were little children at play in a schoolyard. The poorer sections of town were fired by the shelling. The Gothic towers took their first hits. The exodus of townsfolk from Ypres was slow in starting; before long, the town was only a warren of rubble where tired fighters huddled. Every day of the attack heightened the crisis of nerves. At G.H.Q. in Saint-Omer, Sir John drew comfort from his new and steadfast friend, General Foch, sent west by Joffre to coordinate the Allied effort. They were together at the climax of the first German assault. Of their communion has been handed down a fragment too melodramatic for belief. Said French: "All that remains for me to do is get killed." Replied Foch: "You must not talk of dying but of winning." It would have had greater dignity coming from a foxhole.

In their shock effort as October waned, the Germans put five new divisions opposite the southeast angle of the salient, giving them numerical advantage of three to one in the chosen sector. The commander of this new group, General Max von Fabeck, proclaimed to his troops: "The breakthrough will be decisive. We must and will conquer, ending the war against our detested enemy." But the words couldn't do it. Allenby's soldiers were driven back more than a mile around the Messines Ridge. French troops under General Victor Louis d'Urbal were rushed to the impact area and stiffened the British line. This was the first heavy repulse to the Prussian Guard, the elite of the army.

There were other hard trials through early November. The British were beaten back from Messines, the blow falling on the London Scottish, the first territorial force to engage. Then Wytschaete was lost and with it went all the high ground on the southeast shoulder of the salient. On November 11, thirteen German divisions attacked on a nine-mile front running from Messines to the Menin Road. They made a thousand yards, then came to grief amid the brambles of Nun's Wood. Cooks, clerks, engineers, and oddments of every kind were thrown into the British counterattack.

When finally the battle died like a tempest spending itself, the Germans doubled their artillery pounding of the heart of Ypres. Systematically, the guns worked over the sluices and lock gates of the Ypres Canal until the flood broke loose, inundating the low ground and compounding the misery of forces committed to the salient.

First Ypres cost Germany at least 130,000 soldiers; British casualties were 2,368 officers and 55,787 other ranks. French losses made the blood toll nearly one quarter million. Kitchener, appalled, cried: "This isn't war!" But by whatever name, the unexampled carnage collaborated with the coming of winter to drive the contending forces to ground. Soon the opposing trench systems, fitted with deep artillery-proof chambers (dugouts) where soldiers existed like rodents, extended from the Alps to the North Sea. Every supreme effort that aimed to break the deadlock produced the opposite effect, intensifying the paralysis. Soldiers no more understood the war than did the politicians.

Take one factor. Neither the artillery array nor the shell output of any nation was yet extravagant. England, for example, had only one ordnance factory turning out 30,000 rounds per month, at Woolwich. Factories had to be built and technicians trained to accelerate production in proportion to the indicated need. So within less than one year England was turning out 1,200,000 shells per month. For France, Millerand, at Joffre's urging, expanded production to 30,000 rounds daily for the 75-mm. gun. Germany went through a like buildup.

As the munitions multiplied, so did the manufacture of field pieces. Artillery structure in support of infantry broadened and deepened because the tubes were available. In all armies a brigade of artillery or more became an organic part of the division, this for the first time. Behind the division was more artillery serving with the corps, and still larger guns with the field army. The guns were worked from deep earth pits to foil counterbattery fire. The stronger the artillery establishment became, the less was the chance of infantry closing against infantry. The guns kept the rifle companies confined to deep earthworks during tactical pauses and cratered the middle ground so that it became tediously difficult for infantry to advance at all. Then when troops were launched on an offensive, the enemy artillery pounded them at the start, and if by rare luck they closed to within accurate small-arms range, they were caught between automatic fire and barbed wire. Here was the vicious circle. Barrage fire by artillery did most of the killing; machine gun fire, delivered line-of-sight, made the sacrifice unavailing. As for indirect machine gun fire, for which so much was claimed in World War I, it was mainly a waste of ammunition.

The young American historian Richard M. Watt writes: "The generals are to be blamed not so much because they failed to open up the trench war as because they went on trying to do it, wasting thousands of lives with each attempt, long after it should have been apparent that they could not succeed with the old methods." This is fair criticism and puts in a proper light the High Command failure. But the other half of it is that politicians have no patience with generals who only mark time or hesitate.

Only colonels and under (excepting a few brigadiers) took the extreme punishment of the Western Front. Generals were usually comfortably billeted in châteaux or manor houses safely back from the fortified zone, though within sound of the guns. They saw little of the butchery. The immobile front actually simplified command and staff duties. Reliefs and changes of position were almost automatically administered. Old hands stayed on to familiarize new hands with all operating procedures. It was a kind of nursemaid arrangement. When a green, untried unit moved forward, its place in line and hour of arrival were designated well beforehand. Guides and staff officers who knew the area waited to help the newcomers settle in, and acquaint them with their own and enemy gun locations, alarm systems, and housekeeping routines. Work parties were led by the hand to pick up their first rations, locate water points, and check munitions and signal stores. Just behind the fighting front, narrow-gauge trains brought forward shells, wire, food, and revetment timbers from the nearest railhead. Coal for cooking and warming, and candles for lighting the shelters, were also at the forward dumps. Ambulances could usually run as far forward as the light railways. The routines were as habitual and closely regulated as the morning stir in a college dormitory. While men lived, higher commands had chiefly the job of seeing that their animal wants were satisfied. When they died, burial parties would be provided.

As the First Ypres Battle died, all of this development was in embryo. Except for a few sectors like the Aisne, the opposing trench systems had hardly scratched the earth's surface. But as soon as the respite occurred, the military engineers took over and began to elaborate them. European armies had long neglected the science, and the general design came about empirically. The traversed trench line with its alternate fire bays and earth bulkheads was soon in vogue, its design purposing to prevent enfilade and confine the damage of any one shellburst to a small area. Communications trenches by which troops and supply moved up to the front line were cut zigzag for the same reason. Support trenches, one hundred or more yards back of the front line (and sometimes used for messing), were less pretentious. Every conveniently sited knob along the front line was made a strong point—usually a slotted, thick-walled bunker or a concrete turret, housing crew-served weapons. Machine guns were placed to fire diagonally across the front so that one bullet swarm interlocked with another, splintering an attack with cross fire. Where high ground was convenient, battalion command billets were usually aboveground in defilade on a lower reverse slope. So-called listening posts were pushed forward into no-man's-land to warn of night attack or to ambush small enemy patrols. The enemy normally had all of these features spotted. They were pet targets.

As any voluntary yielding of ground was anathema to the higher commands, the meandering of the front line did not always conform to the best protective use of natural features. Too often, the front line rested on a marshy flat, with strong slopes and fair fields of fire at its immediate rear. But wherever placed, the trench was shielded forward by a thicket of barbed wire strung in broad aprons or collapsible concertinas. These barbed belts were frequently 150 feet or more in depth. Pioneers strung the barricades by night; enemy artillery tried to blast them apart by day. Distances between the opposing front lines varied from sector to sector. In some places Germans and Frenchmen fought at talking distance from one another. Elsewhere the lines were more than a kilometer apart. The pattern followed no sensible criterion. Where the lines were farthest separated, both sides pounded hardest with artillery. Great gun duels would arise and go on for hours, often starting from nothing more significant than a nose-thumbing from a soldier on outpost observed by a lynx-eyed marksman in enemy country. First the small weapons would get into play; shortly would follow the complete orchestration. Where the opposing trenches were close-joined, they were mutually immune to the big guns, but they suffered all the more from grenades, mortars, automatic fire, and trench raids.

Still one other effect of the tactical deadlock more immediately multiplied the frictions of the war, causing division within the military command and fomenting bitterness among the political chiefs. The terrible cost of the first months, with no turning point in sight, made the probable bill for victory on the Western Front too grim to contemplate. Somewhat chastened, the military leaders no longer came forward with sure-fire plans for a quick ending. Not through default by the military, but from anxiety over their own faith and credit, the political leaders felt tempted to dabble in strategy. So the Allied camp split between "Easterners" and "Westerners." The first group looked for a field of decision somewhere other than in France; the second opposed any diversion, seeing no path to success but the defeat of Germany in France.

Because of a like conflict in interest, the German camp was somewhat similarly divided. The Easterners were Hindenburg and Ludendorff. They wished the army to go on the defensive in the West and ship all reserves to Prussia for a knockout blow against Russia. Falkenhayn had to be a Westerner; his fear of the rising influence of the two heroes of Tannenberg was enough to keep him one. Kaiser Wilhelm swung first one way, then the other. He had to back Falkenhayn but he couldn't afford to let down H-L.

THE EASTERN FRONT

After Tannenberg, Germany knew indifferent fortune in its attempt to exploit the victory. Following the battle around the Masurian Lakes (September 5–13), in which it was driven out of Prussia, Rennenkampf's army quickly recovered its muscle behind the Niemen River. Hindenburg's bridges were blasted apart by artillery when he tried to cross the river. The Germans retreated uncertainly, clumsily. Rennenkampf moved faster and almost rapped them wholly, forty miles west in the forest of Augustów. Most of the Germans got away to their entrenched line along the Masurian Lakes—where they had started.

Great events elsewhere wrought wholesale change in this seesaw contest. For one thing, Conrad had suffered his crippling reverses in Galicia, and with the Grand Duke Nicholas massing his armies toward Kraków, the gateway to mineral-rich German Silesia, it became clear enough that the H-L forces had to go to the rescue of the faltering Austrian ally. The means were at hand. With the arrival of the corps pared from the Western Front at the wrong moment and other troops from Posen and Königsberg, there were bodies enough to field an additional army out of Prussia. The Eighth was given to General von Schubert and left to cover East Prussia. The Ninth formed under Hindenburg and Ludendorff. Then, when the Kaiser named Hindenburg "Commander in Chief, East" with Ludendorff as Chief of the General Staff, Mackensen took command of the Ninth as H-L moved up one rung. H-L weren't happy about their two armies. Right from the start Falkenhayn was pressured to send east more forces. He said no. The Ninth was transferred to Austria by rail and fitted onto the left flank of Conrad's forces, north of Kraków. What H-L had in mind was to get hold of every bridge and crossing on the Vistula from the juncture with the San to Warsaw and then go after Warsaw; supported by General Viktor von Dankl's Austrian First Army on his right, Mackensen started his advance as September closed. The Grand Duke also had a vast offensive underway; his plan was to hold the whole line of the Vistula, and out of Warsaw throw the greater part of four field armies at Prussia and Silesia.

Head-on collision should have resulted—bulldozer against steamroller on the same main line. But the plot unfolded as Hollywood might have written it. In the wallet of a dead German officer the Russians found papers that revealed to the Grand Duke all he needed to know. A few days later, on October 9, before the feeling-out process was well begun, a German scouting party discovered a Russian corpse and found on it a copy of the Grand Duke's operational order. It almost shocked Hindenburg into tightening his habitual glower. The Grand Duke had sixty divisions, Hindenburg eighteen. Ludendorff summed it up: "Mackensen was to be opposed by fourteen divisions; the Grand Duke projected his strong encircling movement from the north against the Ninth Army. There would be simultaneous frontal attacks against it and the Austrian armies. If this plan succeeded, the victory of Russia was assured."

As forbidding as was this prospect, Hindenburg had little choice but to dare it, if the Grand Duke's armies were to be diverted from smothering Austria. Had the German Ninth Army tried the weaker course, going on the defensive alongside its ally, it might have saved Kraków and blocked the passage to Silesia. But it would have opened wide the gate to East Prussia.

Audacity and cunning, speed of movement combined with care in technical preparation, marked the approach. These were the features of H-L generalship. As the Ninth Army struck forward, every bridge crossed was prepared for demolition; stores and control points were preset to accommodate a probably rapid retreat. That was as it had to be. For more than 250 miles an almost unbroken line of Russians, extending from Warsaw to Przemyśl and covered by the Vistula-San trench, awaited. The rivers were unfordable; there were only two bridges, at Warsaw and Ivangorod. Extensive marshes edged both streams. From the embankments the Russian guns could sight on the German columns as they came up. But that was not the worst part of it. Most of Warsaw is on the Vistula's west bank. So was the Grand

Duke's maneuver mass and it rested on the fortresses ringing the city. Against this formidable target almost two million soldiers vainly strained. By October 6 the Germans had closed on the Vistula below Warsaw and the Austrians had breasted the San. But that was as far as they got. The German right wing was held, fiercely embattled by the Caucasian Corps, which worked its guns from the shoreline amid the infantry, in Napoleonic style. Against lesser resistance, the tired Austrians still could not get one bridgehead across the San.

The German bid was centered in the effort to force the Vistula crossing near Józefów while also striking for Warsaw. By midmonth Mackensen, with the main weight of the Ninth Army, got within twelve miles of the city and seized a main rail junction on the perimeter. That was when the Grand Duke launched his counteroffensive and the German left wing gradually bent back away from Warsaw until it faced north along the Pilica River. The great battle raged five days as the Hindenburg headquarters at Radom prayed for the Austrians to get over the San and ease the pressure. For four days there was rain unceasing. Entrenchment became impossible. The bogged guns couldn't be displaced. But the foul weather also clutched at the Grand Duke, disarranging march tables and upsetting coordination. Otherwise Warsaw might have been a German catastrophe. By October 17 Mackensen knew that he was done, and the only choice that he had was to get out or be destroyed.

The Ninth Army retreated sixty miles in six days, and by October 23 was back at the starting point, 40,000 men fewer. This was Hindenburg's first great defeat and he couldn't understand it. Wrote Hoffmann: "Our retreat from Warsaw was naturally treated by the Russians as a victory." Well, it was. Flushed with success, the Russian armies rolled on toward Posen, Silesia, and Moravia. Conrad blamed the Germans for having broken off the Warsaw battle: German headquarters laid it on the Austrians for not having crossed the San. That neither slur was better than a half-truth didn't ease the sting; the Austro-German combine was simply up against too many Russians and too vast a countryside.

But the campaign did ease the pressure on Austria by creating the illusion of larger opportunity to the westward. Ludendorff had figured on that. By General Staff calculations, the Russian field armies would become beached if drawn approximately eighty

The dapper Winston Churchill (right) and
David Lloyd George walk to the House of
Commons in 1910, when they served together
on the Board of Trade. Both men became
known for their persuasively eloquent styles
and their bold, aggressive war policies.

miles beyond their closest railheads. So, as the Germans pulled away, all bridges were blown and all rail lines razed by pioneers moving with the rear guard. Ludendorff had the satisfaction of seeing the Grand Duke's offensive trail out at the distance calculated. Though the Russians again broke into East Prussia and fought the Germans around Mlawa, shortly there was a logistically enforced pause in campaigning. In the interval, Ludendorff visited Falkenhayn and tried to persuade him to send several extra army corps to the Eastern Front and engage the Grand Duke in an all-out trial. It was the first showdown between them, and Falkenhayn had to say no because the Kaiser's heart was set on capturing Ypres.

While the point-blank refusal exacerbated a rivalry that ultimately changed the course of the war, it did not stop H-L. Plans for resuming the offensive were already well advanced before the visit. Secretly, the Ninth Army was shifted north by rail to join hands with the Eighth Army and the group re-formed along a seventy-mile front before the Russians learned of the movement. There began in November the second German drive for Warsaw. This time the Germans were in superior numbers in the zone of action, Russian massing being limited by the terrain and ravaged communications. The Russians withdrew south so that their defensive front would be covered by the marshes of the Bzura River, whence they hoped to protect both Warsaw and the fortress of Lodz. It didn't work; the Germans forced a causeway crossing at Piatek. The battle for Lodz lasted until December 6, when the fortress surrendered and the Russians fell back.

More dramatic than the victory was the mushrooming of the Hindenburg legend from it. He was made a field marshal. Grand Admiral von Tirpitz would soon write in his diary: "Oh, Blessed Hindenburg, help us soon, we are in sore need of it." The ugly fact remained that though H-L had won Lodz, the Russian right flank still rested inside the East Prussian border. As trivial as was the impingement compared to the German grip on northern France, H-L would exploit it to play on German heartstrings in continuing their power struggle with Falkenhayn. But that smoldering affair, like the Eastern Front, would be relatively quiet for the next several months.

Frustrated in his campaign against Russia, Conrad could not forgo another attempt against Serbia. As November came, the bungling Potiorek took off again. The campaign opened promisingly, and on December 2 the Austrians captured and occupied Belgrade, the Serb defenders having pulled out when ammunition ran low. The next day, General Putnik regrouped his forces and struck back. Buffeted by blizzard and blistered by bullets, the Austrians were totally routed. By campaign's end, another 100,000 Austrians were dead, and as many Serbians. But for the wastage of bodies and bombs, nothing was changed. It was the end of Austrian attempts to whip the little kingdom singlehandedly and the end of Potiorek as a soldier.

THE DARDANELLES

Toward year's end, the stalemate all around and winter's grip upon the armies in the more northern theatres superinduced a main change in the drama.

Come cold weather and the mind of the strategist turns to the possibilities of action where the sun bears down. Environment does condition decision in matters great and small. It is easiest for soldiers and sailors to stay hopeful about prospects when and where weather is brightest.

Much more than that entered into the calculations by which the spotlight turned to focus upon the eastern Mediterranean, the British Royal Navy, and two of the Great War's most forceful personalities: Admiral Lord Fisher, the First Sea Lord; and his minister, Winston Churchill, who had returned Fisher to the Admiralty from retirement at age seventy-four.

Until December, 1914, the Royal Navy had little reason for satisfaction with its role and record, its majesty over the high seas considered. Of that, the Allies could claim so far only the supreme advantage that the oceanic lanes remained open for their commerce, a material triumph but with too little glory.

The *Goeben* and *Breslau* had evaded larger forces that easily should have snared them. Then in late August the score was more than evened when Vice-Admiral Sir David Beatty pressed his flotilla of battle cruisers into the Heligoland Bight "right up to the enemy's gate," and sank the light cruisers *Köln*, *Mainz*, and *Ariadne*, and one destroyer, without losing a ship.

But after that brilliant raid, things continued to go badly. In September the British cruiser *Aboukir* was torpedoed off the Dutch coast and the same U-boat later sank the *Hogue* and *Cressy*, with most of their crews drowned. In October the battleship *Audacious* hit a mine off the Ulster coast and went to the bottom.

Worse followed. The German Far East Squadron under Admiral Count Maximilian von Spee crossed the Pacific and refueled from colliers at the island of Más Afuera, four hundred miles west of Valparaiso, Chile. Vice-Admiral Sir Christopher Cradock, with the cruisers *Good Hope* and *Monmouth*, and the light cruiser *Glasgow*, was in these same waters. He got orders from the Admiralty to "search for" and "be prepared to have to meet" Spee's raiders. To Cradock, these words meant engage at all costs, and no mind the sacrifice. It was his death notice. Spee's *Scharnhorst* and *Gneisenau* had Cradock's ships far outgunned, outranged, and outarmored. They met by night off Coronel near the Chilean coast on November 1. The *Good Hope* and *Monmouth* were gunned to the bottom, leaving not a single survivor.

The battle cruisers *Invincible* and *Inflexible* under Vice-Admiral Sir F. Doveton Sturdee were detached from the home fleet and sped to the South Atlantic to hunt down Spee. The German Admiral rounded Cape Horn on December 1 and, instead of plowing homeward, detoured via the Falkland Islands, intending to bombard the British base at Port Stanley. So doing, he overreached; Sturdee's ships were coaling inside the port as Spee came up. Too late, he tried to flee. Speedier, heavier armed and plated, the British battle cruisers pursued, firing leisurely at long range. The *Scharnhorst* and *Gneisenau* were sunk. Later Sturdee's ships got the German light cruisers *Nürnberg* and *Leipzig*, though the faster *Dresden* escaped. This last German cruiser at sea was finally cornered and sunk the following March off the islands of Juan Fernández, where Robinson Crusoe is supposed to have met Friday, and near the spot where Cradock undoubtedly met death.

Most daring, and most effective, of all the German commerce raiders was the German light cruiser *Emden*, commanded by Captain Karl von Müller, who for three months played the game as if knighthood were still in flower. From August 22 till November 9, this 3,500-ton craft ravaged Allied shipping in the Indian Ocean and almost paralyzed commerce with India. In the first fortnight, Müller captured thirteen ships. Wherever the ship made port, it spread propaganda against the Allied cause among the native peoples. But Müller and his men scrupulously observed international law, treated all prisoners with utmost courtesy, and opened fire only against legitimate targets. In the end the *Emden* was overtaken near the Cocos Islands by the Australian cruiser

148

Sydney, three knots faster, 2,000 tons heavier, and with bigger guns. After a fair fight, the *Emden*, fully ablaze, was driven onto a reef. Müller and his officers were allowed to carry their swords into captivity because of their extreme gallantry.

There were other naval excursions and explosions in 1914. The German cruiser *Magdeburg* became grounded in the Baltic and so fell prey to the incompetent Czarist fleet. In December German battle cruisers raided into British waters and shot up Scarborough and Hartlepool. The French battleship *Jean Bart* was sunk in the Strait of Otranto by an Austrian submarine on Christmas Day.

It was all fairly small change, give-and-take, blow-for-blow, when compared with the land battle, though thousands of seamen died. Adding the score, the youthfully ebullient First Lord of the Admiralty and his no less pugnacious teammate, the veteran First Sea Lord, had no reason for prideful reflection.

There is something almost dangerously kinetic about this fascinating combination—the abundantly energetic and ambitious, militarily gifted young politician, and the hard-driving Father of the Fleet, sure of himself, proud of his ships, yet grateful to his young chief and more than eager to yield him head space. Both were given to the penning of eloquent buckslips. Both loved to have their voices ring in council. They were bound to pull hard together so long as they rowed in the same direction and as a pair they irresistibly outglowed their company.

It was Fisher, not Churchill, who first suggested in a memo to the latter on January 3, 1915, that the navy should try to force the Dardanelles using "Admiral Sturdee . . . with ships of the *Majestic* and *Canopus* class." Churchill had previously felt that taking the Turkish Straits was an affair for soldiers. But here was his professional adviser arguing the decisive advantage of possessing Constantinople employing the navy as the main instrument. Later the same day, with Fisher's approval, he cabled Admiral Sir Sackville Carden, commanding in the Mediterranean, asking for his estimate of the possibilities. In this way began the weaving of the fateful web. Carden returned the answer that he felt the project was feasible with navy force alone, but that it could not be rushed and had to be envisaged in four stages. They were: (1) destruction of the forts guarding the entrance, (2) silencing of the forts inside the Straits, (3) clearing of the mine fields, and (4) neutralizing of the defenses of the Narrows and the smaller works beyond. For his task Carden wanted twelve battleships, three battle cruisers, sixteen destroyers, and a vast armada of auxiliary craft. The demand seemed not excessive to the cabinet.

Nothing was said, either by Carden or the men in London, about what would follow after the navy broke into the Sea of Marmara. They assumed that the Turks, confronted by the fleet, would quit. The ministers warmed to Carden's optimism and ignored his omissions. By mid-January the operation was "in the works" and awaited only final approval. France agreed to cooperate and to provide a naval squadron.

Kitchener simply went along with the scheme, voicing no enthusiasm, saying that he had no troops to support it. To his mind, it was an admirals' affair. Time came when the venture perforce pivoted on Churchill's personal force and influence, his authority over the admirals, and his persuasiveness with other ministers. For suddenly Fisher went cold, opposing his chief, renouncing his own memo. He proposed an opposite adventure for the fleet: put it into the Baltic to land a Russian army on Germany's north coast. With the German fleet intact, such a stroke was too foolhardy to take seriously. There was a painful scene between Churchill and Fisher, with Kitchener playing conciliator. Fisher returned to the War Council grumbling, a sound that steadily amplified to a stentorian rumble.

Hallowed by history, the scene of the play about to unfold is also glamorized by myth and romance. Once Leander swam across the strait for love of a woman, and, centuries after, Byron did it for love of love. The Hellespont, renamed the Dardanelles in modern times, after fortifications near the entrance, is the most important narrow passage in the world. The channel is two miles wide at the entrance, broadens rapidly to more than twice that, then closes to an average width of two and one-half miles, short of the Sea of Marmara. These are deep waters, twenty-five to fifty fathoms throughout. All the flood of the Danube, Don, Dniester, and Dnieper forms its mighty current, which surges at three to four knots.

The Gallipoli Peninsula, which guards the European side of the Straits, is cliff-sided and steep-to around most of its rim, and almost everywhere fixed with an imposing scarp overlooking sea and channel. The high ground forms a spine running down the center, its higher ridges rising to 1,200 feet and more. The twisting shoreline is scalloped at only four points by sharply ramped and heavily shingled beaches. Inland the ridges are fairly covered with dense scrub standing up to six feet, with stunted pine forest in the hollows. Little of the ground can be cultivated and the few villages are deprived and primitive.

In 1915 only one dirt road ran the fifty-four-mile length of the peninsula. Being on the inner side next to the Straits, it roughly linked the forts. These were permanent works of an ancient vintage, partly modernized in the nineteenth century, and last fitted with heavy artillery of German make during the Turkish-Italian war four years earlier. The Germans had been improving the defenses for six months and steadily thickening the mine fields. There were two groups of forts, the first pair covering the entrance, the second pair fourteen miles higher up at the Narrows. But there were also other guns, emplaced artillery along the heights adjacent to each fort.

British warships had been demonstrating outside the Dardanelles for weeks. The Turks lived in anticipation of the strike up the Straits. They feared it would succeed and the threat hung heavy. Even General Baron Kolmar von der Goltz, the German who knew more about the defenses than anyone else, made of record his view that the British could force a passage if they were willing to lose ten ships. Concerning this operation, however, it is singularly the case that there was equal reason for pessimism on both sides, and that all prophecy proved to be gratuitous folly. In 1906 Britain's Committee of Imperial Defence studied the problem of forcing the Dardanelles and concluded it would be impossible to land an army on its hostile shores. Yet no one referred to the old paper at the time, for this was to be a naval show.

On January 28 the fateful decision was taken and thereafter the undertaking against Turkey proceeded on a crash basis. There wasn't time to think things through, to plan methodically, to arm and load systematically, and to balance forces judiciously. Seldom, if ever, has such a vast enterprise been launched as haphazardly, with eyes so riveted on the glittering object that means were only superficially attended. Something akin to euphoria enveloped the deliberations, and it is conceivable that the Turkish Army's dismal showing in Sinai and the Caucasus but intensified it. When Churchill said of it later, "Not to persevere, that was the crime," it was invidious criticism. No civilian minis-

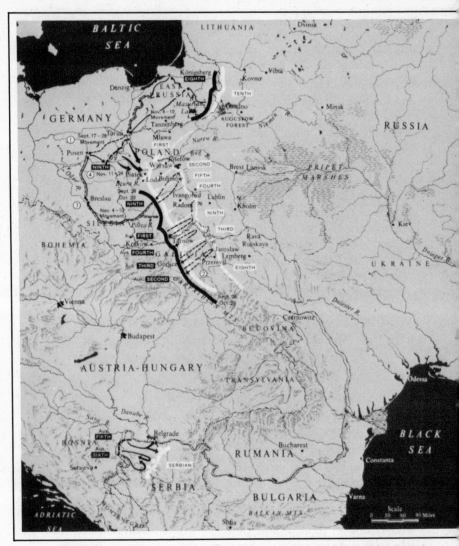

The Germans moved south (1) to join the September, 1914, assault (2, broken black arrows) on the Russian-held Vistula-San position (broken white line). By late October, the Austrians and Germans were back at their starting point (solid black line). Going north (3), the Germans attacked Poland (4, black arrows), and at Lodz halted the Russian drive (broken white arrows) on Silesia. Serbia repulsed an Austrian attack (black arrows at bottom) in December.

ter can carry along an entire government in that spirit when there is lacking an awareness of almost insuperable obstacles to be overcome. The beginning should have warned him: undeviating resolution never hardens out of cloud-walking. Thus the operation got away to a piecemeal start. It wasn't that sufficient forces couldn't be scrounged; the fault was that no one advanced a realistic appreciation of what would be needed.

Admiral Carden, who had agreed to try with naval forces alone, started his attack on February 19 and continued, with interruptions by foul weather, until March 16. Despite the frequent blocks, halts, and fresh starts, it was an auspicious start. At long range the battleships pounded the outer forts and their auxiliary batteries into a submissiveness that allowed shore parties of marines and sailors to land, blow the remaining guns, and roam the nearby heights. There was one hitch apart from the recurrent lash of bad weather. Mine sweeper crews had been formed of civilian fishermen from the North Sea fleets. When they shirked the danger, refusing top sweep near the shore, they had to be replaced by unskilled naval volunteers. So additional time was wasted. By the Ides of March, however, all was ready for the decisive thrust against the Narrows. At that point Carden fell apart, physically whipped, nervously exhausted by the strain of the undertaking.

But already it was apparent that London was wavering on the initial intent—to blast through with ships. On March 12 Kitchener had called in an old friend, his Chief of Staff from South Africa days, General Sir Ian Hamilton, and said to him: "We are sending a military force to support the Fleet now at the Dardanelles, and you are to have command." With little more instruction than that, no plan in his pocket, and no balanced staff to draw on, Sir Ian went bucketing off to the eastern Mediterranean to witness the navy battle. It was an odd choice. Sir Ian was sixty-two, a valiant spirit, greatly traveled, a keen observer of armies over the world, and, beyond that, the army's great man of letters. He was more interested in analyzing and recording his own reactions than in writing thorough orders based upon fullest possible knowledge of the developing situation. There is never time for both; no proper commander has that much genius, that much energy. Sir Ian's planning at Gallipoli reveals throughout an amazing ignorance of, or indifference to, major factors that should regulate operations.

Vice-Admiral Sir John Michael de Robeck took over from Carden. A still more remarkable man was his young Chief of Staff, Commodore Sir Roger Keyes, one of the great fighting characters of the century. Together, they swung into action on March 18, a clear day of light wind and calm sea. Save for the weather, there was nothing good about it. Near noon the first four battleships began the offshore bombardment of Fort Chanak at the Narrows. It lasted two and one-half hours. Behind them came the French Squadron, the *Bouvet, Charlemagne, Gaulois,* and *Suffren.* Under the combined fire, the forts were silent. Then the French ships were ordered to retire to make room for the British battleships *Albion, Irresistible, Majestic, Ocean, Swiftsure,* and *Vengeance.* That movement exposed a vast target area in the narrow channel, and the Turkish forts with the auxiliary batteries suddenly resumed full fire again. Only one gun ashore had been dismantled by the shelling. It is not surprising. Sailors are ever inclined to overestimate the effectiveness of their artillery against landward targets.

One Turkish salvo struck the *Bouvet;* she heeled over and quickly sank with most of her crew. Next, the *Irresistible* turned out of line with a heavy list, the victim of a mine; she lasted more than an hour and a destroyer rescued most of the ship's company. One-quarter hour later the *Ocean* bumped another mine, and went to the bottom in a few minutes. Both the *Gaulois* and *Inflexible* were badly mauled, with hard damage to structure and some loss of crews. Still, the remaining ships continued the bombardment until the light faded. When at last the sun dropped behind Gallipoli, and targets were no longer distinguishable, the Allied fleet slipped away, with the fire from the forts following after. It was a greater defeat than any man aboard yet realized.

De Robeck was not whipped; as he pulled off, he had every intention of resuming engagement at the earliest practicable hour. He worried some that he would be relieved for the loss of his ships. But Keyes, who was all afire, said to him: "There can be no question of that; the First Lord will rely on us to see this matter through." Then he went forth to shave and to read Kipling's "If," pasted by his mirror, as was his habit when plying a razor.

But on the next morning, General Hamilton, who had observed part of the fight, wired Kitchener that he felt compelled, reluctantly, to conclude that the Straits could not be forced by battleships alone. A more striking irregularity is hardly to be found in English history. No general is a qualified judge of such business; decision was for de Robeck and the Admiralty. Sir Ian was in the position of a special pleader; having gained command, he was overeager to employ the army. To put his point across, he not only ignored de Robeck but he disregarded channels.

Yet the campaign turned on this mischievous intervention. After getting Hamilton's message, London queried the Admiral. De Robeck had now either to take the weak way out and go along with Hamilton or stake his career on an opposite estimate. So far he had merely carried out Carden's design. It was asking too much of the man on the spot. On March 22, de Robeck messaged that he agreed with Hamilton. That fixed Lord Fisher's opinion and left Churchill with no choice but to bow to professional judgment or alienate all support around him through bullheaded assertion, which couldn't carry the day.

Ever since, controversy has raged over whether the British Navy stopped short of triumph. Those who so insist muster the evidence from the other side of the hill—Turkey's acute shortage of heavy shell, the demoralization of the Constantinople populace, the avowal of the defending chieftains that they were at rope's end, and so on. It is all meaningless and unavailing. It is enough to know that the navy drew off and waited for the army to assemble and attempt what its General Staff had called impossible. Hamilton had charge of the whole show now, though his forces for storming the peninsula were not even at hand. There had to be a wait. Like Churchill, he had worked himself into the dangerous position of the man who has promised victory if things are done his way.

NEUVE-CHAPELLE

Sir John French and all other high commanders on the Western Front were from the outset opposed to the Gallipoli gamble. Their strategic argument was elementary. France was the main theatre; Germany could be beaten decisively only where her main armies fought, irrespective of the fate of Turkey. Every man, every gun, shipped east perforce squandered resources best conserved for the main battle and thereby prolonged the war.

Among military men this argument is older than the most

ancient shard buried in the sands around Jericho. In strategy, there is no one approved solution, either justifying or condemning the indirect approach. All depends on circumstances. Sir John's case against Gallipoli would have been sounder if British sea power were strained to breaking point supporting the war in France, or if the tactical deadlock in France could fairly be blamed on a shortage of Allied manpower. But these conditions did not exist. The B.E.F. commander had no formula for ending the war in the West; the sea lanes to France were comfortably short. Gallipoli was indeed a rare opportunity which, fully exploited and enthusiastically supported at all levels, might have won limitless fortune. So the foot-dragging in France, by Sir John, Joffre, and the camp-in-whole, must be otherwise explained. It comes back to prideful human nature. How generals view strategy is more often determined by self-interest than by impersonal evaluation of time-space factors. By disposition and professional training, Sir John wished to be the center of the show, ever extending his authority over greater numbers of men. An egregious fault? Yes, he should have been a saint.

Joffre, who was a peasant's son, was not more modest. Taking advantage of his glory, he had in effect compelled the French Government to abdicate its authority for six months, during which he would make all main decisions on the higher conduct of the war. Between Napoleon and de Gaulle no Frenchman ever wielded greater power. Though a French minister commented cynically, "Modern war is too serious a business to be entrusted to soldiers," France did exactly that.

When despite their best effort to block it the trend to the eastern Mediterranean became an overpowering urge in England, Sir John and his generals saw it both as a challenge and a reproof to their own inaction. The B.E.F. front had remained quiet after a brief, bloody fracas around Messines in early December. Winter was conducive to this hibernation. Trenches were waterlogged, no-man's-land was a morass, and soldiers were overburdened with the creature task of staying alive. But for some time General Sir Douglas Haig had been toying with the idea of staging a limited objective offensive on his army front. It was to be one of those "narrow, knife-edge" affairs, with infantry cutting the fortified line on a limited sector, then rolling back the enemy flanks so that cavalry might charge forth "into the blue." What was to come later was never precisely defined, although there was a vague idea. The British hoped finally to reach the Aubers Ridge and threaten Lille as half of a team operation in which French troops under General Foch captured the Vimy heights and overran the plain of Douai. That done, they would so compromise German operations that the enemy would have to retire from Noyon. But the French command had to cancel because of heavy commitments in Champagne. Thereupon, Sir John decided to go it alone.

By thinning their front to extremes near Neuve-Chapelle, the Germans invited attack. There were only six companies, or about 1,500 men, and about twelve to fifteen machine guns covering the chosen sector. Haig had forty-eight battalions stacked up for the assault. They were to be supported by sixty batteries of light guns, forty medium howitzers, and eighty-two pieces of heavy artillery. This was the beginning of that vast elaboration of artillery support that gave the later main battles of World War I in France their unique thunder, as of a world riven.

Haig's first fourteen battalions were launched on the desperate gamble on March 10 and the fight ended three days later. Neuve-Chapelle was for many reasons a remarkable small battle. The frontage of the attack was only 3,500 yards. But due to the overpowering preliminary bombardment, which lasted but thirty-five minutes, a clean penetration was achieved, one of the three times it was done during the war in the West. The attack was mounted with a proper understanding of what penetration required— complete surprise. It failed because the plan was too cautious; the frontage attacked was so narrow that exploitation of the breakthrough was foredoomed. The few troops who got on the enemy's rear couldn't get the word back that the opening was there. In any case, the avenue of penetration was so small that substantial support could not be rushed forward through the German shell and automatic fire that closed in from the flanks, and the attack simply withered on the flanks under the storm of German artillery.

At the end, the British had captured 1,600 Germans, and remained in possession of Neuve-Chapelle village, a bit of shattered real estate. For these prizes they paid with 13,000 casualties. Also, they had expended 100,000 artillery shells. Haig's attack had wasted one fifth of the B.E.F.'s total supply of ammunition. Neither a defeat nor a victory, but a two-sided blood sacrifice, Neuve-Chapelle happened just in time to encourage and popularize the swing toward Gallipoli. Sir John's strategy was thus impaled on its own pike.

But it cannot be said of Neuve-Chapelle that the negative result came from cumulative small slippages here and there by leaders great and small. The soldier did more than his part. But he had no chance from the beginning because the generals had misread their problem. The war was taking a form for which human experience provided no guidelines, and confronted by the reality the staffs remained blind.

HINDENBERG VERSUS FALKENHAYN

In the German camp, as with the Allies, the rift between the opposing schools of strategy (it would be more accurate to say the conflict between rival groups of ambitious men) steadily widened.

Admiral von Tirpitz, the truly brilliant chief of the German Navy though he became a favored target of Allied ridicule, pushed controversy to the limit of absurdity. Working secretly, but with the support of the Kaiserin and the Crown Prince, he conspired to have Bethmann-Hollweg and Falkenhayn dismissed. The Emperor would vacate his powers temporarily and Hindenburg would step in as dictator, supreme over all German affairs, military and political. Naturally, nothing came of the plot.

But it steamed for a while, following by some weeks differences between Falkenhayn and the Eastern Giants that brought their feud into the open. The boil started in January and once again Conrad's seething ambition for his Austrian Army was at the center of the brew. He proposed to stage a winter offensive in Galicia and he wanted German divisions along to put muscle in the push. Two fears motivated him—that the Russians were preparing an attack and that Italy was about to enter the war on the Allied side. Falkenhayn flatly refused to help. Thereupon H-L just as flatly defied him for the first time. They notified the Chief of Staff that, with or without his consent, they were sending the German divisions to Galicia.

This was naked insubordination. When both sides appealed to the Kaiser, the All-Highest was put in the middle. He did not dare dismiss the Eastern heroes; but he could not override his chief commander. Then Falkenhayn made what seemed a concession but was really a dagger thrust at H-L. He proposed that the

In this Ludwig Dettmann sketch, a heavily
burdened German drags a comrade to safety.
Casualties ran higher than in any previous
war and, after only five months of fighting,
there were more than one and a half million
dead, wounded, or captured on both sides.

divisions should be sent to Galicia, provided Ludendorff commanded them: that would break up the H-L combination. Clutching at straws, the Emperor approved. Desolated, Hindenburg got on his knees to frustrate the design, writing to Wilhelm: "I venture most respectfully to beg that my war comrade may graciously be restored to me as soon as the operations in the south are under way." The Kaiser gave in and Falkenhayn's prestige never recovered from the blow. Completely affronted, he went to Breslau to confront H-L and try to impose his will. They merely scorned him. Their plan for offensive operations was approved by Wilhelm over Falkenhayn's head. Ludendorff stayed wedded to Hindenburg, his posting to independent command being canceled. Thereafter they openly joined their voices with the claque at court urging Falkenhayn's dismissal. The wonder is that he lasted as Chief of the General Staff another eighteen months.

One reason for the delay was that having promised decisive victory, H-L couldn't bring it off. There were too many Russians. Conrad's plan for a little show rapidly evolved as a theatre-wide spectacular—a double-pronged offensive out of Prussia and Galicia against both wings of the Grand Duke's array of armies. H-L dreamed of another Cannae, something far more devastating than Tannenberg. "Our trusting wings were to surround the enemy," wrote Ludendorff, "and the sooner the better." But alas, between the blocks imposed by the Russian shots and the fury of the February blizzard, the pincers couldn't close. The Austrian push was stopped at the departure line on colliding with a Russian offensive already rolling. In Prussia the second battle of the Masurian Lakes blazed through February into early March. At its height the Tenth Russian Army was destroyed in the forest of Augustów, 110,000 prisoners and hundreds of guns passing to the German side with its surrender. With that, the battle ended. Hindenburg's armies had fought to exhaustion and there was no energy left to exploit the opening. "A great tactical success," wrote the Field Marshal, "but we failed strategically." As a result both Czarist Russia and Falkenhayn were assured a longer life. Hindenburg was more revered than ever by the German people when the news of the Augustów Forest spoils blazoned. But Falkenhayn, too, was scoring battle points: not only had the British been knocked back on their heels at Neuve-Chapelle but the concurrent French offensive in Champagne had been repulsed with heavy loss. So for the time being the inner power struggle between the Chief of Staff and his Eastern Front rivals remained a standoff.

One footnote to the Masurian winter battle, little marked by history, was heavier with portent than its grim statistics. Walter Nernst, Professor Chemistry at the University of Berlin, had been working with German Army ordnance. Though there are no monuments to his glory, he was an original thinker. In pursuit of his ideas, 18,000 very special artillery shells were put at the disposal of the Ninth Army. They were used to barrage the Russians at a place called Bolimów on January 31, 1915. Hoffmann watched the attack from a church window and was chagrined not to see thousands of the enemy laid low. This first gas attack in history was a failure. Being ignorant of the new weapon, Hindenburg's people didn't know that gas is innocuous in subzero weather. So the new era of frightfulness dawned wanly. But if the Russians saw or smelled anything when the low-charge shells burst around them, and if they guessed that a new agent of death had enlisted for Germany, they failed to communicate their suspicions to their allies; troops were left unprepared. How it could happen is one of the enigmas of the war.

V

Spreading Conflict

Australian troops in pith helmets line the
decks of a British ship carrying them toward
the landing on the Gallipoli shore.

By the spring of 1915 the contagion out of Europe had spread fear around the globe. The peoples still at peace far outnumbered those belligerent. But they could not escape the war. Its unparalleled dimensions awed them, and its far-reaching effects changed everywhere the patterns of casual conversation, altered living costs, stimulated interest in military training, exacerbated mistrust of strangers, whetted partisan frictions, and reconditioned the outlook of great men in finance, industrial magnates, and average householders concerned with the future well-being of the family group.

Beyond doubt, there were farmers in Sinkiang and tribes in Central Africa who heard nothing of the conflict. But in the civilized world, among literate people, the war overshadowed all daily life. That was only in part due to the magnitude and fury of the collision. A world for the first time electronically connected with the battleground could hardly follow the distant struggle in emotional detachment. Unhidden persuaders such as Richard Harding Davis, Wythe Williams, and Granville Fortescue sweated overlong at copy to make sure that Americans would feel deeply about the war. But there was something else. Though the world was not afire, and only Europe was being put to the torch, there existed a universal presentiment that the horror must spread.

The war's anodic sputtering across the Eurasian land mass had little to do with this. Japan had joined the war on August 23, 1914, on the side of the Allies. It was a variety of scavenger hunt. Japan wanted Kiaochow, the German-held mortgage on Shantung province. To get it, the Japanese Army and Navy had to attack the token-garrisoned port of Tsingtao. They did it with trumpets on October 31, and, after some days of ostentatious bombardment, the German governor ran up the surrender flag. The Japanese went on to grab the Mariana, Caroline, and Marshall islands of the Central Pacific, but the Australians beat them to German-owned Neu-Pommern, later known as New Britain. These actions ended the story of German authority in Asia and throughout the Pacific.

What happened in Oceania premonitored the shape of things to come. On land the European war had gradually settled into a joint siege operation. The armies could not unclinch to swing for the knockout. So statesmen and warriors had to think about other means, as all voices predicting early victory became muted. Both camps hoped that sea power might change the balance. In the beginning, there had been no broad thinking on this subject, owing to excessive expectations of a land battle moving swiftly to a thunderclap of decision. When the armies became deadlocked, it was inevitable that the navies would step forward to promise more than could be done. Their line-tightening might not bring victory, but a crueler war had to result. Also, the horizons would be pushed back.

By the end of 1914 German shipping and its protection were all but gone from the seas. The widely separated actions by which it was routed, while dramatic, did not immediately compound international tensions. Instead, difficulties accumulated over Allied command of the seas. Economically, America was beginning to prosper from the war. Its markets and munitions plants were open to all belligerents. But except for a very few militarily useful commodities, such as cotton, which could be transhipped to Germany through Holland, only the Allied nations could take delivery. Vainly Wilhelm's Government protested that this single-track supplying of the Allied camp violated neutrality. That the charge was false and the American course wholly legal were from the German view irrelevant. In retaliation, the German diplomatic and undercover apparatus in the United States undertook to hamper Allied purchasing by fomenting trouble in the war plants. Although in the early months German submarine warfare and the mining of international waters were not intense or systematically directed toward the wrecking of international commerce, this threat steadily mounted. As the squeeze on the German economy tightened, more U-boats came from the shipyards and the two factors combined to produce a greater violence.

On January 24, 1915, occurred the naval battle of the Dogger Bank, sixty miles off the English coast. The British battle cruiser fleet under Vice-Admiral Sir David Beatty engaged a greatly outgunned German squadron under Rear Admiral Franz von Hipper in a five-hour running fight. Germany lost one capital ship, the *Blücher*, and 951 of her seamen met death. British losses were phenomenally light, fourteen men killed, six wounded.

In proclaiming the victory to the House of Commons, Churchill forecast heavier naval pressures against Britain from an enemy "who places herself outside all international obligation." His remark was ingeniously timed. On the day after, Germany announced that henceforth all grain and flour would be contraband of war, subject to seizure. Until then neutral vessels carrying foodstuffs had been allowed to proceed to Germany. Now, the British Government promptly seized the American freighter *Wilhelmina*, docked at Falmouth, with a food cargo bound for Germany. From this small action began the decline of the German masses to a near-starvation diet, one of the more hideous aspects of the war. Enraged by the miscarriage of her own undertaking, Germany declared war against all goods moving into Britain. The warning was given that, after February 18, the seas around the British Isles would be dealt with as a combat zone. Enemy merchant vessels found therein "would be destroyed without it always being possible to warn the crews and passengers." Ten days later, Prime Minister Asquith declared a counter-blockade by Britain against Germany. After March 1 no neutral vessel would be allowed free way to enter a German port or even to return from it. In this manner, rather suddenly, after seven months of relatively desultory fighting, the war at sea approached its climacteric.

American public sentiment followed these mutually strangulating maneuvers with interest rather than anger. From the beginning, the majority of Americans favored the Allies, though the Teutonic cause had its supporters. Yet the outnumbered pro-Germans were highly vocal. Toward them, for the most part, there was a slightly annoyed tolerance. After the violation of Belgium, the tide of sympathy swung heavily to the Entente, and following the Marne there was a satisfied feeling that the Allied combination must win. But there was no national disposition to rush to the fire. The Washington Government believed that vigilant neutrality was the path of national interest, honor, and virtue. The public, despite its emotional inclination, heartily agreed. A strong cheer-leading part for the nation seemed good enough to most Americans. There were exceptions, notable among them former President Theodore Roosevelt, the staunchest advocate of direct intervention. Toward all such oblique pressures, President Woodrow Wilson stayed coldly aloof, convinced of the rightness of the middle course, persuaded he could maintain it. When the double blockade was begun, Mr. Wilson called a plague against both houses, warning both Britain and Germany that American opinion was boiling against them. It was a vast overstatement, but with regard to Germany it was only a trifle premature.

In late April the popular Cunard liner *Lusitania* prepared to sail from New York. The German Government published a warning that such British ships might be sunk en route. But she cast off with a full company, only one passenger, a clergyman, having canceled his passage. At noontime on May 7, the great vessel was off the Old Head of Kinsale on a straight run toward Liverpool; why the master did not follow the precaution of zigzagging was never explained. The German submarine *U-20*, at the order of Commander Walter Schwieger, let go two torpedoes. Just eighteen minutes after the first one hit, the *Lusitania* went to the bottom. Of the 1,198 persons who died with her, 128 were American citizens, most of them women and children.

America shook with rage. From that day, hatred toward Germany mounted and public sentiment for an interminable neutrality, or peace at any price, visibly declined. Nothing that Germany could do, by way of official apology, moderation of policy, or offers of compensation—as she made when the White Star liner *Arabic* was later sunk—could stem the tide of bitter resentment.

It was different with Mr. Wilson. His personal emissary, Colonel Edward M. House, was visiting in London when the *Lusitania* went down. He wired the President: "America has come to the parting of the ways." To U.S. Ambassador Walter Hines Page he said: "We shall be at war within a month."

But he was wrong on both counts. In calm detachment, Mr. Wilson rode high above the tumult. Then, when in trying to explain his attitude, he used the unhappy phrase, "There is such a thing as a man being too proud to fight," it rebounded. Americans couldn't quite swallow that. "It had an ugly air of cant," wrote John Buchan. Worse, it sounded outright craven.

Winston Churchill in his book *The World Crisis* attributes German defeat directly to the ravaging of Belgium and the sinking of the *Lusitania*. "Only to these two grand crimes and blunders of history, were her undoing and our salvation due." It is an immutable judgment.

Germany tried to turn back, but it was too late. Appalled by the surge of anger in America, Chancellor Bethmann wanted to abandon U-boat warfare. Admiral Tirpitz stoutly opposed him. For months, while the exchange of notes across the Atlantic went on, the Kaiser veered like a weathercock between these views.

Then on September 1 Germany announced that the sink-on-sight campaign was off. But it could only be a brief respite. Essentially, Tirpitz was right. For Germany, there was no other chance.

THE GREAT GAS ATTACK

It was a lovely day at Ypres, with golden sunshine, and a balmy breeze blowing lightly off the German trenches. The morning had been marred by a more than routine shelling of the town and the Allied salient. But little attention was paid to that. During the preceding two days, after weeks of quiet, the heart of Ypres, around the cathedral and the Grand Place, had been the target of a terrible cannonade. The Germans had brought up the monstrous 42-cm. mortars—the guns used to crush Namur and Liège. Every twenty minutes a salvo fell. All the road crossings were blasted into interlocking craters.

After forty-eight hours of this horror, the morning of April 22, 1915, when only the little guns spoke, seemed like a respite. Through the afternoon the salient was somnolent and men in the trench line heard larks and thrushes singing. Then at five o'clock sharp, the big mortars once more zeroed in on Ypres. The bombardment went twenty minutes. But the men in the trenches, four miles east of the city, heard it as a distant rumble, which did not obliterate a hissing sound arising from the enemy line. Opposite the village of Langemarck, which was held by French Turcos and Zouaves, appeared two greenish yellow clouds, which gradually merged. Then almost as a fog rolls forward, over five miles of the front, the cloud leveled out and came on, stretching from Steenstraat to Poelcapelle. At first it was scarcely higher than the head of a man and it moved as gently as "mists seen over water meadows on a frosty night." Some who witnessed were transfixed by its beauty. Then gradually it swept over them, visiting slow death, excruciating invalidism, and shock panic on more than 15,000 men.

The emission of the chlorine gas lasted only fifteen minutes. But the heavier-than-air poison cloud dropped into the trenches and lingered, some parts of it sweeping on as far back as Ypres. The surprise, while complete, need not have happened. Some days earlier a German deserter had revealed to the French that the enemy line was fixed with tubes of asphyxiating gas placed in batteries of twenty for every forty meters of the front held down by the French Colonial Corps. The command had simply refused to believe him. So the poor Africans got all the worst of it, and the few who escaped the cloud bolted in mad terror, fleeing a manifestation of the supernatural. One flank of the Canadian Division was in the main path of the gas, but a freak twist of the current threw the cloud across the division's rear area as the Canadians moved back with the wind. Where the chlorine was thickest, some men died where they stood, retching into unconsciousness. A few saved themselves by urinating on handkerchiefs or shirts and using them for masks. By dark the remnants of the French were wandering along the west bank of the Yser Canal. Their stampede left a four and one-half mile gap in the Allied front, east of the Canadian Division. In Ypres, civilians panicked. Still, no one really understood what had happened. Several Canadian reserve battalions in the town were rushed forward to do what they could.

Allied disaster was averted by their gallant try and the failure of the Germans to steel themselves for a main effort. Their commanders had too little confidence in the new weapon; the troops feared asphyxiation if they drove too fast and too deep. Only German local reserves were thrown into the attack that came after the gas cloud. No strength had been stacked up rearward in anticipation of a breakthrough. The oversight typified the German way in war. All was perfectly laid on only to miss at the decisive point. Throughout the night the massive bombardment of Ypres and the salient persisted. On Canada's sector, attack and counterattack continued. The exodus of the innocents from Ypres mounted. Wrote an eyewitness: "Children wailed, and men's voices cursed and growled in uncouth *Flamand* accents. The sky seemed a vault of flame, and the tall budding poplar trees that made an avenue of the causeways rustled and whistled eerily in the wind."

The German attack waves got to within 2,500 yards of the town and there they stopped, though there was no one to oppose them. While they hesitated, the Canadians and reserve battalions from two British divisions pressed forward toward the crackle of their fire. Thin as these units were, their spreading manned the sector and revalidated the defensive line. In this way the gap at Ypres was closed, never again to be opened. There were no trenches to protect the few soldiers who closed it; the line was preserved by their deathless courage.

That was only the beginning. The cloud of Ypres rose as if loosed from the genie's bottle. Until the end of the conflict, gas warfare continued and grew more complex. Soon all troops were wearing protective masks, and antigas discipline became a main technique in all combat forces on the Western Front. The first attack out of cylinders gave way to gas barrages fired by artillery. There was also a weapon called a projector, which lobbed a great gas-loaded receptacle into an enemy trench line, where it exploded. It looked like a drop-kicked football during flight. The gases were given odd names like yellow cross and white cross, according to their shell marking. Country-boy sergeants who knew nothing of chemistry had to memorize tongue-twisting words like dichloroethylsulphide. It was all part of getting along with a strange new war. The Allies decided that they would have to embark on gas warfare, just to stay even. In early September, 1915, the British released their first chlorine cloud at Loos. It was no sensation, for already they were running a little behind. Easily obtained, chlorine is also easily foiled. The Germans that summer had decided to use phosgene. It is supposed to be deadly when present with 9,999 parts of normal air. Chlorine is rated a killing dose if mingled with 4,999 parts of atmosphere at very best. That made phosgene twice as effective and hence doubly desirable.

ENTER ITALY

In the two World Wars, Italy's story is much the same. Neither ideals nor irresistible outside pressures compelled Italy to abandon neutrality and become a belligerent. In both cases, the Government in Rome dallied, waiting to see how the fight would go, then carried the people into war for the spoils. But the jackal-like nature of the entry was recognized as such only when Mussolini ordered it.

When the other powers mobilized, Germany demanded to know how Italy would stand. The Foreign Minister, the Marquis di San Giuliano, replied that since Austria was waging an aggressive war against Serbia, his country was not morally committed to join, its ties to the Triple Alliance being purely defensive in scope. That sounded righteous enough, but was sheer flummery. Under the secret treaty arrangement, if Italy made war on France, due to colonial rivalry or any other issue, Germany was bound to

169

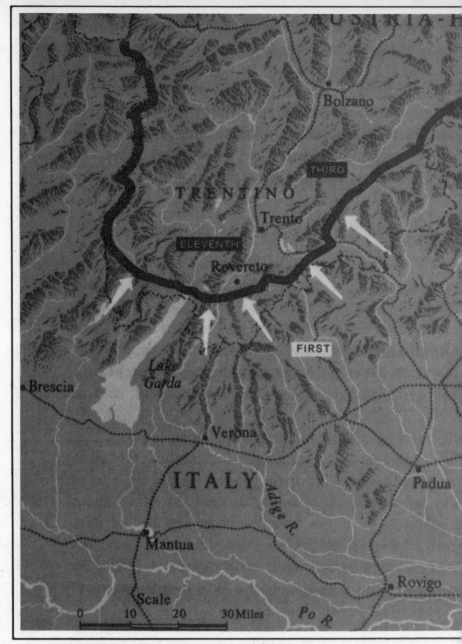

Italy's 1915 war effort was limited to futile thrusts (white
arrows) at Austria's Trentino region (left) and Gorizia (right).
Italy captured the rim of the Trentino salient, but to the

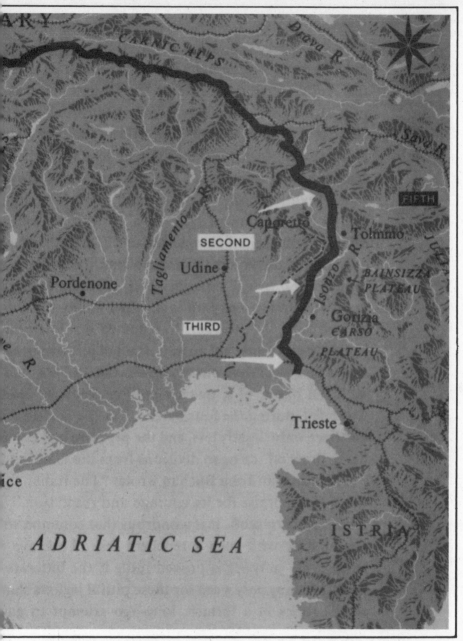

east its advance was halted at the Isonzo River. Elsewhere, the combat line (solid black) followed the peacetime borders.

fight by her side. Italy's abstention was made certain when the Austrian Foreign Minister, Count Berchtold, declared brusquely that he would rather have it that way than compensate her with any of the bones of Serbia for joining. San Giuliano was dead in less than sixty days. The wooing of his successors began at his funeral. But Prince von Bülow, the broker extraordinary sent to Rome by Wilhelm to keep Italy appeased, had literally nothing to offer. Although to some extent they were working in the dark, not knowing Italy's exact relation to the Central Powers, the British, French, and Russian Ambassadors had no competition as they collaborated in trying to buy Italy out of her old treaty obligation.

That statement of it is no cruder than the deal itself. The sordid bargain was not revealed until after the war. The contract, called the Treaty of London, was signed by British Foreign Minister Sir Edward Grey, and the Ambassadors of Italy, Russia, and France, on April 26, 1915. It was a real estate mortgage. Italy was pledged the Trentino, Istria with Trieste, Dalmatia, Cisalpine Tyrol, a base in Albania at Valona, and permanent title to the Dodecanese Islands, which she had recently wrested from Turkey. Of German colonies, and whatever would be taken from Turkey in the Middle East, she was also promised her fair share. In payment for the plunder, Italy promised to fight alongside her new allies against all enemies. Surfeited with riches still to be earned, Italy declared war against Austria on May 23, 1915, but didn't pronounce against Germany until August 27, 1916. Bülow, quitting Rome unchastened by the defeat that he regarded as inevitable, returned to Berlin and synopsized the wartime situation of his own country in few words: "Morale and attitude of the German people—A-1. Political leadership—Z-minus." Gabriele D'Annunzio, the poet and latent swashbuckler, was making a more melodious assessment of Italy: "No, we are not, and we will not be, a museum, an inn, a village summer resort, a sky painted with Prussian-blue for honeymoon couples, a delightful market for buying and selling, fraud and barter." But words rose up and thoughts remained below.

Italy was ill-prepared for the decision, short of war matériel and capital, with a run-down and outdated munitions industry. Under King Victor Emmanuel II, the chief of the army was General Luigi Cadorna, a venerable artilleryman. In his establishment when war came were 875,000 soldiers, enabling Italy to field thirty-six infantry divisions. Gripped by the Russian vise in Galicia, Austria could not send more than 100,000 troops to outguard the limited portion of the common frontier that was susceptible to the maneuver of tactical forces. That was the real problem. The fierce mountain barrier so constricted operations that Italy's greater numbers were no real advantage. Could the Italian Army have laid on immediately, that would have made a difference. But the machine was too run down to afford quick massing and surprise while the frontier was lightly covered. With only a few troops, Austria could hold the crags as a bulwark against Italian aggression. Once her concentrations became superior in any sector, she could pour men down across the Italian northern plain with little difficulty. The problem of this mountain menace defied solution. For the Italian Army, every campaign would be a backbreaking struggle upgrade.

A main effort against the central rampart of the Dolomite and Carnic ranges clearly would yield nothing. Yet some of Italy's best mountain troops had to be doled out to a containing effort there. For reasons that combined sentimentality and grim geographic necessity, Cadorna had to look at the operating possibilities of the two flanks. In the northwest, the "lost province" of Trentino, inhabited mainly by Italians, was an enemy salient biting deep into Italy. In general an imposing mountain barrier, the Trentino is bisected by the broad and flat-floored Adige Valley, a glacial trough affording the easiest and most natural passage north and south through the Alps. Deceptive in its promise, the sector that first gained attention lay on the extreme east, where the sluggish Isonzo River meanders through mud flats and marshes to the Adriatic. There the Italians could come to grips with the enemy initially on flat ground. But there was a forfeit in this. Any attack toward the Isonzo had its flank already exposed by the curvature of the frontier. So if main operations were to be staged there, the frontier had to be kept strongly garrisoned all the way from the Trentino to the Julian Alps.

Just beyond where the Isonzo washes the plain there rises the steep Alpine wall. The fortress city of Gorizia (the Austrians called it Gorz) guards the angle where the river pours from its deep gorge to form the flood plain. Elimination of the wide enemy bridgehead covering Gorizia became inevitably the first grand object of the campaign. It was easy enough to point that way.

But south of the city the Carso plateau rises like a protecting battlement, "a howling wilderness of stones sharp as knives." Directly north of Gorizia is the Bainsizza plateau. Nature couldn't have done a better job for the defenders. Gorizia was a deadfall. To win it was a superhuman task, and, once won, it became a portal to nowhere, though like a mirage, Trieste beckoned temptingly from the distance. Getting only to Gorizia was far beyond Italy's capacity.

There were four Italian offensives in 1915, all staged in the same area, all monotonously ineffective, all mournfully wasteful of blood and bravery. They are called the First, Second, Third, and Fourth Battles of the Isonzo, titles aptly measuring the stall in the death march. The Archduke Eugen was nominally in command of this theatre for the Austrians; but defense of the Isonzo line was committed to a competent Slav, General Borojevic von Bojna. Austria sent its southern Slav, Hungarian, and Tyrolese troops to this front, and they had no love for Italians. The battles varied in intensity but the result was always the same. Fighting began June 23, and, with brief interruptions for replenishment, clearing of forward hospitals, and minor alterations of plan, lasted until December 2.

In their attacks on the Isonzo line the Italians maintained a numerical superiority of approximately two to one. There was no payoff in it; when finally the front became frozen, the attackers had dented the Austrian position here and there, but no important object had been won. For a few worthless pieces of soil, the Italians had paid with the blood of a quarter-million soldiers, dead and wounded, during the four battles. Yet the cost to Austria had been only slightly less, and the pressure had compelled her to draw off ten or so divisions from the Galician fronts.

The historian John Buchan wrote: "The Italian fighting was beyond praise for its courage and resolution." There is no reason to scoff. It is wondrous that common soldiers would stick with such a repellent task. To brave death when every purpose is proved futile is the bitterest of all trials. We may only weep for these pitiful legions shattered on the rocks in a forlorn, long-ago attempt to gain the Ljubljana Pass. Allied strategists were lured by the same glittering goal in World War II but never tried to attain it.

Why was it done in 1915? What made Cadorna continue to throw his army away? Prior to the war, the Italian General Staff had considered the insuperable difficulties of the ground and concluded that a defensive strategy toward Austria was clearly indicated. Italian troops could have been usefully employed elsewhere by the Alliance; for example, against Turkey. Italy had a grievance there. The Young Turks had violated all rights of Italian nationals, herding and hounding them more relentlessly than the French, British, and Russian subjects stranded by the war. No conclusion about the change to an offensive strategy is possible except that military prudence was sacrificed to political cupidity. Having contracted for Trieste, the Trentino, and the other tantalizing prizes, the Rome Government felt obligated to win them by armed conquest, whatever the cost. Cadorna had no choice but to throw his armies into the meat grinder. Two of them were deployed against the fifty-five-mile-long Isonzo front. The other two, spread out over 130 miles, struggled vainly to eliminate the Trentino salient.

Years went by, but that was the war for Italy. Its armies, trying to do the impossible, wasted away. The bleeding and brooding by millions of men swelled the resentment that brought postwar fascism to flower. Victory didn't turn sour; it hadn't been won. There were eleven battles of the Isonzo before the end. Gorizia, the first objective, remained distant. No Italian rifleman, dodging hot steel amid the crags, could understand an ordeal that even in the light of history remains incomprehensible.

GALLIPOLI

Having discouraged the Royal Navy from trying again against the Dardanelles after March 18, General Sir Ian Hamilton then was compelled to stall more than a month before striking at the Gallipoli shore with his army.

It was an unavoidable lag, due no less to Kitchener's refusal earlier to dispatch dependable field forces, such as the 29th Division, to the scene than to the logistically faulty loading of those formations that were sent.

When the fleet disengaged, amid the unmistakable signs of an Allied troop buildup on Mudros and in Egypt, the Turks knew their shore would be invaded either along the peninsula or on the Asiatic side around Besika Bay. Shortly, the larger British warships would sail away; admirals are loath to keep their main chariots standing by amid a preparatory hustle and bustle in hostile waters. It is too apt to attract submarines.

"If the English will only leave us alone eight days!" General Liman von Sanders exclaimed when the fleet quit the Narrows. The grace allowed him was eight days, plus one month. That gave Enver Pasha more than enough time to form a separate army for the land defense of the Dardanelles, with Liman in charge. It counted six divisions, or 84,000 men—six times the strength deployed along the shores when the fleet had bombarded the forts. Two divisions were put at Besika Bay, and two near Bulair in the waist of the peninsula; the others covered Gallipoli's lower end. One of these, kept on a string as the general reserve, was commanded by a little-known lieutenant colonel, Mustafa Kemal. The genesis of his greater fame as the father of a reformed Turkish Republic after the war was his inspired leading and bold fighting in this campaign. So his efforts were not without dividends.

The home governments and military councils of the Allies were still divided over making a main effort at Gallipoli. Sir John French stayed flatly opposed and Joffre was no less obdurate. But having sent Hamilton east as a token of fresh resolve, Lord Kitchener had to give way, if slowly, to his demands for more troops. That carried the ministers along. The stalwart 29th Division was loaded and shipped to Sir Ian. Thereupon the French Government, despite Joffre's objections, sent forward a division in the interest of comity, and possible future claims in the Middle East. Joffre wrote: "Confronted by my refusal, the War Minister directed the General Staff to form the division from details found in the depots." Then another French division was formed out of such oddments and sent along, making a corps under General d'Amade, who soon gave way to General Gouraud. By dint of all this dredging, Hamilton at last had 70,000 men. Their job was to open a path for the fleet through the Narrows, and not to conquer Turkey. Hamilton moved to Cairo to see how it should be done, while the quartermasters got the misloaded forces squared away.

All of it came hard. Gallipoli positively glared. Nowhere along its lower shoreline was there room for a supply buildup with a protecting perimeter to keep it beyond enemy gun range. But the insuperable task that awaited them in no way damped the spirit of the men collecting for the great adventure. Never was there higher zest to dash forward into shot and shell. We are told by Alan Moorehead that: "Rupert Brooke, with his romanticism, his eagerness and his extreme physical beauty, is the symbolic figure in the Gallipoli campaign . . . among all these tens of thousands of young men, this was the one who was perfectly fitted to express their exuberance, their secret devotion, their 'half joy of life and half readiness to die.' " We may well believe it. They had gathered zealously against the Turk as if bent on a modern crusade, though not all of them had traveled east. The two divisions of the Australia–New Zealand Army Corps, under General Sir William Birdwood, were at hand, having wintered in Egypt. The Anzacs are a breed apart. Lusty, irrepressible, they go at fighting as if it were a soccer match, to be won for the sheer hell of it. Their drive is only exceeded by their contempt for the forms of discipline. Also straining at the leash was the Royal Naval Division, which had gotten only enough of the smell of battle at Antwerp to feel thwarted. Brooke was one of its junior officers. On April 23 he died of blood poisoning brought on by sunstroke, just before the fight, and was buried in an olive grove on the island of Skyros by a party of intimate friends. They were an extraordinary lot, these his pallbearers—Arthur Asquith, the Prime Minister's son; Aubrey Herbert, the orientalist; Bernard Freyberg, taking his first stride to the military pantheon; Charles Lister and Denis Browne, more genius that died too soon.

At the hour of the burial, the warships and the troop-loaded transports were already steaming to their rendezvous off Gallipoli. Hamilton wept when at midnight he got a signal reporting the event. The weather had been stormy throughout the shakedown period, then it eased off just as readiness was reported. The staging was so scheduled that thirty-six hours after the eleven transports started moving, the attack on the Gallipoli shore would begin.

Hamilton fired with a scatter-gun, aiming at every nook along the lower peninsula that promised a toehold. The Royal Naval Division was to make a pass toward Bulair, impossibly rough and heavily manned ground. The French, held in reserve, were to land one regiment at Kum Kale, on the Asiatic shore. But these were feints only, intended to mislead the Turks, which they did not. The inexorable tasks were committed to the Anzac Corps and the newly arrived 29th. Four small and unconnected beaches around the toe of the peninsula (Cape Helles) were the designated touchdown spots for the 29th, and provided the division could seize them, its people were then to march on the hill mass of Achi Baba. The Anzacs were to go in north of the promontory Gaba Tepe, drive the Turks from it, and, swinging inland, take Hill 971. These were thought of as immediate objectives, something to be carried by the momentum of an unchecked attack. They eluded the Allies until the end of the war.

In this strangely managed operation, Hamilton permitted lower commanders to decide, within limits, when to hit the shore. The plan was adjusted to suit their views of what was tactically expedient. Birdwood believed that it would be better to risk the confusions of a night landing against fire than to offer the Turks clear targets in a daylight shoot. Major General Sir Aylmer G. Hunter-Weston, who led the 29th, preferred a daylight landing, so that he could be helped by offshore bombardment. In the event, neither was proved wrong, and although the vital statistics of the landing somewhat favored Birdwood's judgment, the meager achievement of his troops during their nocturnal floundering hardly proved that he was infallibly right. Wanting to stage the whole show by night, Hamilton still humored Hunter-Weston. All of the British generals were groping, since there existed no informed doctrine on amphibious operations. One was mothered by necessity in World War II and it still has many grave gaps.

There were no LST's in those days. For lack of anything similar, Navy Commander Edward Unwin hatched a scheme to beach a troop-loaded collier, the *River Clyde*, at the sand strip called V-Beach. It was imagined that a mass outpouring from this awkward device would stun the Turks; instead, it bunched helpless victims for Turkish fire and there ensued a slaughter grim and great. Hamilton added his personal bit to the improvisations —the landing of two battalions at a supposedly inaccessible cove called Y-Beach, whence this force, in the manner of 1944 Rangers, was to get on the rear of the Turks defending the southern beaches. The detachment gained Y-Beach all right—and thereafter did nothing. Up in the Gulf of Saros, where the Royal Naval Division staged its charade, the ruse was made good by one man. Commander Freyberg swam ashore from a small boat three miles out and lit a line of flares along the beach, this to alert the Turk defenders inland that invasion was coming—which it wasn't.

For the Gaba Tepe landing, the Anzac troops were loaded on battleships. Five miles out the first wave of 1,500 men got into the small boats just after midnight, with April 25 coming up. They were then towed by the battleships halfway to the shore. There the tows were cast off and a steam picket boat took over the leading of the cutters, or lifeboats, each holding about 125 men. But a strong current both slowed the approach and spoiled the aim. First light was just beginning to show when the forty-eight boats grounded on the strand, and the Australians scrambled ashore more than a mile north of the intended spot, in a shockingly churned-up country, gully-riven, scrub-covered, and boxed by cliffs. Very little fire came against them. The second wave, which came off seven destroyers, was landed even farther from the target, and, hitting at dawn, suffered heavier losses in crossing the water line. But some of its men persevered, and one party penetrated far enough inland to see the Straits glistening in the early sun. It was a vision too soon blanked out. Birdwood's night landing had scrambled his troops, dropped them in an area for which they were not briefed, and isolated them from their main object. During the crisis hours, this vital force simply milled around along the slopes next to the sea, trying to get organized. The time thus lost could never be regained, and with it went the prizes.

Only two Turkish rifle battalions were on guard over the country south of Achi Baba. They were too few to smother Hunter-Weston's four-pronged landing; they were enough to deny it all but a desperate clutch along the shore. The main stroke by the 29th was aimed at beaches V and W. Two companies of Turks beat it back. The disaster at V-Beach came from the ill-conceived grounding of the *River Clyde*, though the author of the plan, Commander Unwin, who won his Victoria Cross that day, proved a lion under fire. Only a handful of men managed to wiggle ashore and crawl for protection to the shingle; they had to be taken off that night. Hundreds died trying to follow them. At W-Beach the Turks withheld fire until the small boats arrived. Then the bullet blast became withering. The brigade commander made shore with a few men and they started to move toward the scarp. For only a little while they held. Then the commander was wounded and the whole brigade recoiled.

According to plan, seven and one-half battalions were in the initial assault, followed by five in the second wave, with one French division in the floating reserve. Only one battalion was sent against S-Beach, the landing on the extreme right, at the eastern face of the peninsula's tip. It was such an unlikely spot that the Turks had posted less than one platoon to cover it. They fled. The battalion made shore without too much difficulty and by 8:00 A.M. was simply squatting on its claim. It might have marched around the bend and from the rear skewered the few Turks at the other end of Morto Bay who were dealing death to the *River Clyde*. But nobody thought of that, and Hunter-Weston had such an exaggerated impression of the Turkish strength along the tip that he wouldn't order the advance.

A more savage irony than the situation of that day cannot be imagined. In the center at V and W, the futile death of hundreds of men threatened collapse of the whole operation. Off the ends of this holocaust, the three battalions at Y and the one at S were doing parade rest, though they could hear the battle crescendo and could have marched to the sound. No natural obstacle obstructed them. There were only 2,000 Turks at this end of the peninsula; their whole force was outnumbered by the British already safely ashore, and only a minor contingent was standing off the two critical landings. But nothing was done. Hunter-Weston, offshore, couldn't grasp his situation, and Hamilton was too gentlemanly to impose his own will.

By midmorning two more battalions were safely ashore on X-Beach, another unguarded spot. But they immediately dug in because Hunter-Weston had earmarked them as the division reserve. After another thrown-back attempt to land at V-Beach, the two and one-half battalions of the support force tried W-Beach and at last beat the Turks back. Cruising by on the *Queen Elizabeth*, Hamilton observed the comfortable bivouac of the three battalions ashore at Y-Beach. So he signaled Hunter-Weston: "Would you like to get more men ashore at Y-Beach? Trawlers are available." Some hours later the division commander replied that any such deviation from plan would interfere with existing arrangements. But not even Sir Ian dared suggest that his extra-insurance force had been staged into Y-Beach to be used. The rest of Y-Beach is a sad story. The Turks stormed against it a few hours later. There was hot action and several bayonet charges back and forth, with fairly heavy loss on both sides. Then the Turks withdrew, feeling they were beaten. Not sensing the withdrawal, the British counted their dead, and also decided that they were whipped. So they called for shipping to take them off and were shortly at sea again.

The one sadder entry in the tangled tale is that during their twenty-nine hours ashore, the battalions at Y-Beach heard not one word from their own general, Hunter-Weston. He was too busy knocking down Hamilton's schemes to reinforce the men ashore. Just before evacuating Y-Beach, Sir Ian suggested there could be no better place for the French brigade (six battalions) then loading to join the attack. Hunter-Weston ignored him and sent the French into the cauldron at W-Beach. The failure of the overall commander to insist on compliance in a vital matter is as glaringly obvious as is Hunter-Weston's resentment of his superior and of the Y-Beach enterprise which was Hamilton's idea. Y-Beach was the magic key to victory, and it was tossed away.

At Anzac Cove, as the northern beachhead came to be known, the corps had 8,000 men ashore by 9:00 A.M., and there were only two Turkish rifle companies to resist them. Inland four miles was the immediate reserve of two battalions and one light gun battery. Several miles beyond it was the general reserve, eight battalions and three batteries under Mustafa Kemal. Several anonymous Turkish heroes who had watched the landing did the sensible thing, throwing down their rifles to run and carry the word.

One hour later, they got to Kemal, who was exercising a regiment. When they gasped out the news, he turned to his soldiers and said: "Have we got ball cartridges? All right, follow me." They took off for Chunuk Bair, some five hundred of them, Kemal leading, and they got to the crest of this commanding height just in time to beat back the first Australians who were straggling up the western slope. It was the determining move of the day's action, the struggle for the northern beachhead, and the campaign. The fight wore on through the day, fire, charge, and counterattack, both sides repeatedly lunging, both sides steadily building up, with more riflemen and guns manhandled upslope. By nightfall, the loss in both forces exceeded 2,000 men. The Turks still held Chunuk Bair. There were at least 16,000 Australians ashore but they remained compressed in a tight crescent on the lower ridges. The sense of defeat thickened in the invading camp. Troop commanders reported to Birdwood that their men were wholly demoralized by the rain of Turkish shrapnel from the heights. He sent a signal to Hamilton: "There is likely to be a fiasco. If we are to re-embark, it must be at once."

Hamilton returned the reply: "You have got through the difficult business. Now you have only to dig, dig, dig until you are safe." Read in any light, it is an odd admonition. The difficult business was only beginning, to dig meant mere resignation to it, and there could be no safety so long as the beachhead was but a strip suitable for burrowing.

For the next forty-eight hours Liman von Sanders, who had

British soldiers—the blind leading the blind—shuffle toward an advanced dressing station. Photographed near Béthune in April, 1918, they were the victims of a German gas attack during the Lys offensive. The brutal new weapon, gas, caused over 79,000 deaths.

rushed to Bulair when the British battleships opened their preliminary bombardment of the beaches, withheld his main forces from the battle, waiting to see what else might develop. But the invaders could take no advantage of this interlude of relatively low pressure. After the exertions of the first day, Hunter-Weston reckoned that his troops were so exhausted that it would be useless to press them. Further, he was expecting momentarily a full-scale Turkish counteroffensive. His first supposition was probably right and cancels the significance of his second assumption, which was unmistakably wrong.

The Turks simply were not yet deployed for the riposte. On April 28 the Franco-British force on the southern beachhead mounted an all-out attack. By then the enemy reserves had filled out the frontal positions and the attack was beaten back with heavy loss. Then for two days as May opened, Liman von Sanders launched his forces in main assault with the bayonet, the order reading that they were to "drive the invaders into the sea." In the end they recoiled, leaving their dead piled high in front of the Allied trenches. Two new brigades of Anzacs arrived at the Cove. The southern beachhead was augmented by a brigade of territorials out of Egypt. The stiffening encouraged Hamilton to try for a breakout once more on May 6. For the first two days he let Hunter-Weston manage the battle, giving him control over all reserves. This *ad hoc* elevation to commander in chief did not increase Hunter-Weston's combat luster. The net result was great slaughter on both sides. The enemy outguard line remained undented. Too late, when all energy was depleted, Hamilton took over again and ordered his troops to "fix bayonets, slope arms, and move on Krithia precisely at 5:30 P.M." When the attack collapsed, the forward bayonets were no closer to Krithia than before, though in three days one third of the Allied assault force had fallen.

The digging continued. So did the wasting attacks by both sides, though they tapered gradually to probing operations. The Anzacs stayed straitjacketed in their cove by the sea. At Cape Helles, a force equal in size to a modest city remained bound to a strip of earth too mean for a village. The Allies couldn't break out of their two prisons at Helles and Anzac Cove; the Turks couldn't break in.

Hamilton realized at last that he was trapped; hope lay only in a fresh start by greater forces. He cabled this view to the home Government, which was quite startled to learn that the Gallipoli venture was on the rocks. Up till then the messages had breathed optimism. Agonized by the army's frustrations, the Allied admirals announced themselves ready to put their fleets against the forts of the Narrows again. It wasn't to be. While decision held suspended on May 13, a Turk destroyer slipped down the Straits by night and put a torpedo into the battleship *Goliath*, which lay in Morto Bay giving gunfire support to the French brigade on the Allied flank. *Goliath* sank immediately and 570 of her people died. Twelve days later the battleship *Triumph*, anchored off Anzac Cove, was killed in the same way by the German submarine *U-51*. Two days after, the *U-51* destroyed the battleship *Majestic* while she supported the forces at Cape Helles.

The explosions at Gallipoli were muffled by the heavier detonations in London. Lord Fisher erupted to Kitchener in a note fused with an ultimatum: either the *Queen Elizabeth* would be withdrawn from the east Mediterranean or he would resign. Trying to placate Fisher, Churchill had already sent the signal ordering the ship's return. Wholly disturbed, Kitchener wrote in a note to Asquith that if the navy was giving up on the Dardanelles, maybe all of the troops should be shifted to Egypt. The Prime Minister felt that he had to support Fisher. The *Queen Elizabeth* would be pulled out. But Fisher resigned anyway, and in a huff packed his bags for Scotland. Thereupon Bonar Law informed Lloyd George that the Conservative Party could no longer suppress its mistrust of Churchill.

Asquith agreed to remove Churchill from the Admiralty and form a new coalition cabinet. His Liberal colleagues all tendered their formal resignations. The British press then redoubled its attack on Kitchener, who told Asquith that he was ready to leave the War Office. Although his hold on the country remained too great for that, control over munitions was taken from him and vested in a new ministry under Lloyd George. Churchill's place at the Admiralty was taken by Arthur J. Balfour. To the reconstituted Dardanelles Committee, the inner cabinet directing war policy, Kitchener circulated a memorandum warning that withdrawal from Gallipoli would shake British prestige throughout the world. So the campaign had to continue though its mainspring was out.

At the scene the navy acquired a new look. The battleships cleared away. Replacing them were awkward, shallow-draft craft called monitors, little more than floating platforms for heavy guns, but with bulging, torpedo-resistant sides. There was also the "beetle," a new type of landing boat, with a droppable ramp for quick getaway, the far forebear of the ducks, rhinos, and alligators that carried men onto hostile shores in World War II.

When the fleet displaced, Hamilton lost his headquarters afloat. There was no room for his establishment ashore on Gallipoli. So he set up shop on the island of Imbros, one hour's run by torpedo boat from the beachheads.

More troops were promised from England. France forwarded fresh forces. There were more battles through June, mainly at Cape Helles, chiefly with the object of breaking out if possible, but in the end they accomplished only a shortening and straightening of the Allied line by finally tying together the several small beachheads. Like the earlier engagements, all were prodigally wasteful of human life and distinguished equally by command lapses and phenomenal heroism. By June 9, one regiment (Royal Fusiliers) had lost every officer and NCO except one sergeant major, and only 140 men remained of those who had stormed the beaches. In all commands, brigadiers and colonels were being expended at a faster rate than other ranks. The new territorial battalions arrived to flesh out the line; immediately committed, they did bravely. Indian brigades settled in, to fight loyally, ignoring the propaganda line of the Moslem enemy: "You are at liberty either to desert to us and save your lives or get your heads cut off to no purpose." Gouraud's French troops, at grim cost, won a few of the acres that made possible a rounding out of the Helles position, and Gouraud was himself horribly mangled by an artillery round. There were no longer any truces for burying the dead; the corpses bloated and shriveled in no-man's-land and their stench fouled the air. By July's close battle casualties had passed the 50,000 mark, not counting French losses, or the several brigades of men evacuated to hospital with fever or dysentery.

There was barely enough water for drinking and cooking, and never enough for hygiene and sanitation. The fighters stayed dirt-encrusted, save when they could clear away for a dip in the sea within reach of the Turk artillery. Kitchens and latrines went half-cleaned and ill screened; bloated flies (troops thought that they fed on the dead) swarmed everywhere. There just wasn't enough water on Gallipoli; most of it had to be brought in lighters from the Nile. A canteen per day per man was about the ration; in such heat it wasn't one fourth enough to quench thirst.

We come now to Suvla Bay and to the situation on the Gallipoli

Peninsula at the beginning of August, 1915, the first anniversary of the war. By then Sir Ian had, either on base or arriving, thirteen divisions, or approximately 125,000 combat men, from an overall force of one-quarter million, with which to expand his holding ashore. Although the expedition stayed chins up, the army had now to break out or eventually perish.

The Anglo-French forces hardly more than finger-held the harsh margins of the shore. At Anzac Cove the beachhead was a shallow crescent 2,000 yards long, its entrenched perimeter enclosing less than 400 acres. Yet within these shallow diggings, 17,000 Anzac soldiers survived by struggle or died in fighting back the enemy, three times as numerous in this sector. At Cape Helles there were six divisions, or 35,000 soldiers. The beachhead at the snout-shaped end of the peninsula had more than three times the area of Anzac Cove but was no less desperately placed. Both positions were intrinsically hopeless.

Opposite these forces garrisoning the peninsula were thirteen Turkish divisions, 63,000 men, about half of them Nazim, or first-line Regulars. But in the vicinity of Suvla Bay was only a minor troop body called the Anafarta Detachment, embodying three rifle battalions, a squadron of cavalry, a labor battalion, and nineteen artillery pieces. This is more than enough weapon power to instill the shock fear that paralyzes green soldiers. There were better reasons than the light manning that made Suvla Bay the chosen spot for landing. Besides affording secure anchorage for the invasion fleet, it was to the eye the one fair target on the peninsula; at Suvla, no rugged scarp directly commanded the shore. A salt lake more than one mile wide lay directly inland from the Suvla beaches. But it was known to be dry in summer, though the wide fissures in the cracked surface barred walking. Sir Ian planned that the troops would skirt the edges; he didn't know that they were dune-stacked.

Long before July ended, the plan was "on ice." It was too ingenious, having as its fatal flaw Hamilton's aim to do all things with all forces at one time. His own habit of limited control would thereby be further diluted. On the appointed night, a task force from the six divisions at Helles was to make a limited attack against the nearby village of Krithia. The Anzac Corps, augmented by one and one-half divisions fresh from Britain, was to feint toward the knob called Lone Pine, then, under cover of dark, drive for the commanding ridge of Chunuk Bair. The landing at Suvla was scheduled for one hour later, or 2230, just in time to beat the rise of a waning moon, just in time to make the expedition land blind. By midnight the Allied front would be in eruption all around.

Wonders were accomplished in the safeguarding of the multiple-chambered surprise at Anzac Cove, though the Turks guessed that a big blow was coming somewhere. The reinforcement of Birdwood's beachhead—men, animals, and vehicles—had to be smuggled ashore at night by the navy in stealth and silence, then kept hidden by day during the preceding days, so that the Turks would not sense the buildup and interdict the shoreline with night fires. Somehow it was done, though the navy's beautifully contrived deception deserved a better return by the army. With hardly more trouble, the sea service, given Sir Ian's blessing, might have shifted places between the Anzac Force and the 25,000 untried soldiers shipped from Britain for the try at Suvla. That would have delivered dependable strength against the decisive target.

To command IX Corps going in at Suvla Bay, there was sent from England Lieutenant General Sir Frederick Stopford, old for his sixty-one years, kindly complacent, remote from troops. He had never commanded in combat in his life. Kitchener had picked him because he was senior on the list; there couldn't have been a sorrier choice. By comparison with him, the ranks had at least youth in their favor. Yet they had never felt fire. Their junior leaders were equally ignorant of the very special tactical problems of the venture—shore organization, preservation of identity, and collection by night.

Where lies their unique complexity? Simply in this, that command power derives only from recognition of authority, which in daylight is conveyed by the face, manner, gesture, and spoken word. Men see and know their leaders and in turn are known by them. Any good junior leader can memorize the names and faces of two hundred men within thirty days. But in that same period he will not be able to identify more than ten or twelve of them by voice. Yet in the dark all is dependent on voice recognition. Let troops become scrambled and authority evaporates. Men will not obey, not knowing who speaks. Leaders hesitate to give orders, not knowing whom they address.

No more wretched scene can be imagined than such a breakdown by night on a strange beach under fire. Each man feels lost in the crowd, and his personal panic is exacerbated by the bedlam confusion of the milling mass. There is no brake against mounting terror and the physical depletion it induces. These men had been subjected to excessive pressures earlier in the ordeal —the enervating heat during the mount-up, the churning approach by the small boats, the vomiting from seasickness and fright, the awful sweat of anticipating the unknown.

This was the situation into which Hamilton and Stopford delivered 25,000 soldiers at Suvla Bay just before midnight on August 6. Armies have learned much since then about these motor forces that was not known at the time of Gallipoli. So in justice to the two generals, it must be said that they probably did not know what they were attempting (the impossible), or one commanding voice would have cried: "Stop it!" In default of knowing what to do, they did only what they knew, and from their ignorance came the nightmare.

There was relatively little Turkish fire against the landing melee, but it was enough, though by dawn the Turks had withdrawn inland toward the high ground. Such was the inertia that settled on the troops from their night of shock that when morning came, a score of Freybergs and Unwins was needed to get groups on their feet and boot them along to the ridge crests on the horizon. But at the working level there were too few of these stalwarts, whose drive is as insatiable as their instinct for doing the right thing. A few brave parties struck out eastward; the mass stayed put not far from blue water. They were still inert, still scrambled and worrying about getting sorted out. Some were a little euphoric, what with the coming of day and the pullback by the Anafarta Detachment. But there was now a worse drag. They had made shore with only a canteen of water apiece, long since drained dry. Parched men can't swallow salt; saltless, dehydrated, they reel on the edge of sunstroke and cannot march.

The tactical details of how the operation fell short need not be repeated here. Sufficient is the appalling fact that given two days as a gift, the Turks closed first in strength on the nearby ridges above Anafarta Sagar, which all along had beckoned to the stranded invaders. Incredible? Not at all, when we get the picture of Stopford, dawdling on his command ship, distant from the wrought confusion, messaging Major General Frederick Hammersley congratulations for getting his division ashore, not caring what he does with it afterward. Here is a general definitely not commanding. (His leg was bothering him.) But when Hamilton belatedly gets up to Hammersley, he neither takes over his sector of the battle nor relieves the man who is toying with it. He is too gentlemanly even to voice a mild protest, much less breach chain of command.

From Cape Helles the corps commander did not carry out the limited holding attack toward Krithia as ordered. Overreaching, he tried to capture both the village and Achi Baba. So doing, he paid for his failure by losing half his task force of 4,000 men. There are no braver tales in war than that of the gallant try for breakout by the forces of Anzac Cove. Wrote the war correspondent Ellis Ashmead-Bartlett: "It was launched against positions the like of which had never been attacked before under modern conditions of warfare." So it was. Masefield, Moorehead, and others have paid eloquent tribute to the superhuman valor attending this intricate, overdemanding operation. Deathless courage was abundant. But more so was death. And glorious failure is failure still.

The strike for the commanding ridges missed, partly because men lost their way, baffled by the twisted ridge folds in the dark. That so much gallantry became mischanneled into dead ends was the heartbreaker. Of the new troops, the Warwicks, Gloucesters, and Worcesters lost every last officer. General Baldwin and every member of his staff were killed. Four brigadiers were wounded. One New Army Division, the 13th, lost 10 commanding officers out of 13, and 6,000 men of 10,500. The total casualties in Birdwood's corps were around 18,000, or approximately half its strength. It was no comfort to the survivors that the Turkish slain also littered the crags and gullies.

There and at Suvla the fighting continued for about one week. When the fire sputtered and died, Anzac Cove was just a little roomier, the sector extending eastward to enclose Lone Pine and northward to tie in, near Azmak Dere, with the Suvla beachhead, which now ringed the salt lake and anchored in Kiretch Tepe. Walking from one to the other was possible, though enemy snipers skulked in the brush. On the Suvla perimeter, the British clung to Chocolate Hill. The Turks had Scimitar. That meant they were right off the edge of the ground the British tramped the first morning. More than 40,000 Allied soldiers fell during the August battles. It was the price paid, one of the generals said, "for five hundred acres of bad grazing ground."

Stopford was sent home. Hamilton remained, not to muddle

GALLIPOLI CAMPAIGN

March 1915 – January 1916

SAROS GULF

GALLIPO

Aug. 7-8

LIMAN
VON SANDERS

Anafarta
Sagir

CHUNUK BAIR

SIMIT
HILL

Fire Line

Aug. 9

LONE PINE

Salt Lake

CHOCOLATE
HILL

AZMAK DERE

ARI BURNU

Anzac
Cove

SUVLA
BAY

IX 8

ANZAC 5

GA

STOPFORD

BIRDWOOD

AEGEAN SEA

KRITHIA TO BULAIR - 50 MILES

HAMILTON

David Greenspan

In March, 1915, the Allied fleets failed
to force the Dardanelles (1). On April 25,
feints at the Gulf of Saros (2) and Kum
Kale (3) screened troop landings at Cape
Helles (4) and Ari Burnu (5). At Helles,
Y-Beach was quickly abandoned, but X-, W-,
V-, and S-beaches were enlarged from first-day
holdings (white dots) to a unified beachhead
(white line) by early May. On August 6, the

Turks withstood an Allied attack at Helles
(6) and rushed troops (broken black arrows)
to repel an Anzac lunge (7, white arrows)
at Chunuk Bair. Other Turks from Bulair met
the August 7 British landing at Suvla Bay
(8). The Allies were never able to break the
Turkish lines (solid black). The arrow on
the inset shows the perspective of the map.

through, but to muck it up at least one more time. What followed for the Gallipoli expeditions were months of misery and tedium, hard duty, and the grinding gamble to stay alive against odds, all of it anticlimactic.

Failure at Suvla made inevitable the ultimate evacuation. Pride postponed it for a little time. All confidence had been lost. The army sagged, not because it was ready to give up ground, but because its light had died. The courage of troops must be reborn every day; but enthusiasm, as Goethe said, can't be kept bottled like pickled herring. In the latter-day phrase of England, the expedition had had it. The shocked ministers in London were loath to believe this. Kitchener sent out Lieutenant General Sir Charles Monro to see what might be salvaged from Hamilton's debacle. The new broom went for a clean sweep, recommending nothing less than total evacuation.

At home there was sharp debate, violent argument pro and con. Among the military bitter-enders such as Commodore Keyes, various counterschemes were hatched to keep the theatre alive and resume the drive on Constantinople. But nowhere was there enough heart to hold the line so readily taken in January. Kitchener went out to Gallipoli to look for himself. He found Birdwood still ready to fight. But he couldn't swing Monro around. Then, when he returned to London, he found that his own sanguinity no longer carried weight with the ministers. They grew ever more agitated. The winter's first blizzard had just swept Gallipoli, drowning 280 men in trenches at Suvla and freezing others to death where they stood.

Evacuation was decided on in late November. Birdwood and Keyes, who alone had played their parts well in the campaign, were put in charge of the arrangements for evacuation. Fate, good staff work, and winter's rigor dropping on the huddling Turks helped them to an astounding success. They had expected heavy loss, if not disaster, during the reembarkation. But the last of the troops were taken off in early January, 1916, from Cape Helles. It was a getaway under the nose of the enemy.

Half a million Allied soldiers were sent to Gallipoli and more than half of them became battle casualties. Turkish Army losses on the peninsula were officially reckoned at only one thousand fewer. So blood for blood, it was practically a drawn campaign. By every other measure, it was a great Allied defeat.

Monro was decorated for recommending evacuation. The soldiers who stuck it to the end got no badge or special recognition.

General Sir William Robertson wrote the appropriate summation: "A wonderful example of gallantry and endurance by men and a calamitous display of mismanagement by authority."

SALONIKA

From the beginning of the war the Balkan states had restively marked time, less concerned with the bleeding from their own pre-1914 struggles than anxious to know where their interests lay. In short, they hesitated because of uncertainty about which side would win.

Turkey's entry, combined with the steadily intensifying German involvement in Turkey's affairs, which led to Allied intervention at Gallipoli, ringed the Balkans with conflict and accelerated the drift toward war.

Appearances, as the ancient Greeks well understood, do govern the world, deciding things more often than reality. The other Balkan states felt little sympathy for Serbia; public sentiment did not incline in that direction and ruling circles were still more aloof. But when Great Power operations began pressing at the Balkan threshold, continued neutrality began to seem like slow death to the minor states of the neighborhood. If they did not join, sooner or later they would be submerged anyway.

Greece, being next door to Turkey and a traditional enemy, was ready to grapple at the start. But when in mid-August, 1914, the Athens Government put all forces at the disposal of the Entente, Britain declined the offer, still hoping to keep Turkey neutral. Later that month, Russia asked Greece to send an expedition to help force the Dardanelles. King Constantine agreed, if Russia guaranteed Bulgaria's neutrality. No answer came from Russia, and, shortly after, Turkey became a belligerent.

Whether these overtures, which historians treat seriously, were sincere or merely exploratory remains a good question. One of the strangest was Enver Pasha's offer to join cause with Russia —this after Turkey had signed its war pact with Germany. There was much of this double-talk. After the Allies took aim at the Dardanelles, Greece again offered troops to help. By then Russia would have none of it. Her strategists had already grown cold on the expedition, which they had nudged into being: it fell athwart their design to be in possession of Constantinople and the Turkish Straits when the war ended.

However, what the armies did spoke more persuasively than

all of the seductive phrases on paper. As early as January, 1915, when the Dardanelles campaign was still in the discussion stage, both Britain and France were considering the alternative of a direct intervention in the Balkans, hoping thereby to get additional backing from Greece as a prop to Serbia. Nothing was done for the time being because the Allies opted to attack Turkey. But the possibilities that might arise from a large-scale venture at Salonika continued to enchant the war councils. It was an amazing illusion, really. Salonika was an inadequate Greek port with only a single-track rail line running north into Bulgaria. To the logisticians it was perfectly clear that the locality could not support an advancing field army. Although the Vardar River valley, which cuts through the Rhodope Mountains to enter the Aegean Sea at Salonika, has been a beaten path for armies throughout history, it is most of the way a palisaded defile. A few troops on the heights can hold back legions. Withal, the Salonika countryside is terribly unhealthy, malaria ridden, subject to heavy flooding in winter and intense heat in summer. Why the Allies imagined it a pearly gate to opportunity is one of the war's enduring mysteries.

Personal politics played a part. In June, Joffre relieved General Maurice Sarrail of the French Third Army; he had commanded Verdun at the time of the Marne. Although they were antipathetical, Joffre said he did it because Sarrail wanted troops. But Sarrail had such strong backing in anticlerical circles that he couldn't be left unemployed. Thereafter, Joffre sought a major command for him somewhere safely away from France. It wasn't mere coincidence that the French Government thus began seriously planning another strike in the Near East in exactly the hour when the Gallipoli Expedition under Hamilton was building up to the Suvla Bay calamity. But France intended to play the lead in this new venture.

One other development combined with these influences to weight the balance of decision. Chiefly out of Rumania, word continued to sift through the Allied intelligence during the late summer that the Germans were massing large forces directly north of the Danube, in Austria. There were other straws in the wind. All commerce with Rumania had been cut off by Austria. German units operating under H-L continued to vanish from the Russian front. So the suspicion grew that the Germans were forming an army to march into the Balkans, and the rumor spread that Mackensen, their most successful general in the violent summer campaigns, would command it.

There wasn't much question what Bulgaria would do if such a thrust materialized. King Ferdinand, a vain and silly monarch, was related to the Kaiser. It was believed that the kinsmen had already made their bargain. Under Ferdinand, who hadn't a trace of soldierly quality, was a field army of about 300,000 rifles, with another 60,000 in reserve. The Bulgars are warrior stock, adapted to fighting in rough country. One thing the army lacked —adequate artillery. By this time the decimated Serbian Army counted no more than 200,000 men. Greece had 18 divisions— 240,000 men under arms—and a stronger artillery. But Greece and Serbia had mulcted Bulgaria as cruelly after the Second Balkan War as had Turkey and Rumania. Still smarting, Bulgaria could not be expected to act nobly toward plundering neighbors. This is not to say that she had acted with greater benevolence in the First Balkan War. What made the Balkans a powder keg was the fact that each of its small states wanted more than a just allocation of territory. Through the summer of 1915, both the Allies and the Germans fanned these mean ambitions.

An army was made ready for Salonika before there was clear definition of its target. It wasn't until September 6 that a Bulgarian delegation visited German Headquarters and at Pless signed a contract to enter the war if Serbian Macedonia and Serbia east of the Morava were given Bulgaria as prizes. Thereafter the wheels spun rapidly. On September 21 Premier Eleutherios Venizelos of Greece asked the Allies for 150,000 troops so that his country could be helped in keeping its pledge to aid Serbia; two days later the Allies agreed to forward the expedition. Bulgaria had already mobilized, calling it a precautionary move to protect its independence. Prophetically, the Agrarian Party leader, Alexander Stamboliski, told King Ferdinand: "This policy will not only ruin our country, but your dynasty, and may cost you your head." The Allied advance parties had already landed at Salonika. On October 2 Venizelos protested what they were doing, a *pro forma* gesture, since Greece was not yet in the war. The landings continued, and on October 3 more than two divisions came ashore at Salonika, the nucleus of what became the Army of the Orient under Sarrail. Next day Venizelos made a speech to the Greek Parliament, its tenor being that Greece no longer had any honorable choice but to league with the Allies. He was wrong. King Constantine forthwith summoned him, renounced the war policy, and forced his resignation. At almost the same hour that the

King was reaffirming Greek neutrality, Bulgaria was breaking relations and taking the plunge to war, blaming the threat from the south. Meanwhile the too-thin Allied columns were extending their trespass northward across the soil of a nonbelligerent toward the outposts of a new enemy they had no chance of reaching. The contorted diplomatic history of the war has no stranger twists and turns than these. Premier Alexandros Zaimis, who followed Venizelos, proclaimed a neutrality that toward the Allies at least would be "characterized by the most complete and sincere benevolence." These were lofty phrases, meaning that Sarrail could exercise squatter's rights at Salonika.

It was too late to help Serbia. Two Bulgarian armies were already at her border, and when on October 12 Sofia declared war on her, they were already invading. Under Mackensen, an Austro-German Army 250,000 strong was simultaneously advancing across the Sava River. Rather than be crushed between these two millstones, General Putnik fell back from the Teutonic armies, burning stores and blowing bridges as he retreated. On October 23 the Bulgarian First Army smashed at Putnik from the east. The Serbs rocked with the blow and continued the march south. Fighting one desperate rear-guard action after another, the Serbian remnants by mid-November had reached that mournful place, Kosovo Polje, the Field of the Blackbirds, where another Slav army had met doom five hundred years earlier. They were not yet wholly enveloped. But the advance of the Second Bulgarian Army across Macedonia and over the Vardar had killed the last chance of a linkup with Sarrail's forces at Salonika. The survivors, with thousands of women and children trailing along, fell back through the icy gorges of eastern Albania in the dead of winter. When at last they collected along the shores of the Adriatic, there were left approximately 135,000 men. This was the last of the war for Serbia; but it was a finish not without glory.

There was little enough of that for Sarrail's Army of the Orient. While the Serbs were being downed, its spearheads got only as far as Krivolak, seventy miles north of Salonika. Then the Bulgar pressure became too great, and with the Greek attitude remaining uncertain, the forward forces were withdrawn to the entrenched camp next to the coast. Then came the question whether the expedition should be scrubbed. Due to national pride and court politics, war's commonest paradox is that it is much easier to start such ventures than it is to stop them. So it proved this time. The Germans wryly called Salonika the Allies' "largest concentration camp," and they were not far wrong. The Army of the Orient stayed there, fighting nothing but disease, and despite its bodily ailments, growing steadily larger. By 1917 it was a force of 600,000 men, mainly French and British, but with Greek, Albanian, Serbian, Italian, and Montenegrin contingents. Its only accomplishment was to keep the small Bulgar Army from breaking out somewhere, though it really had no place to go. How unheroic were its achievements is indicated by hospital statistics. British strength at peak in the Army of the Orient was just over 200,000. But during the three years, 481,262 Britons reported sick at Salonika infirmaries, while only 18,187 Britons were treated for wounds.

At last, in September, 1918, when the defeat of the German armies on the Western Front clearly impended, and the Turks in Mesopotamia were preparing to negotiate the first major surrender of World War I, the Army of the Orient broke through and crushed the Bulgarians. By then the hour was so late that its soldiers might better have been spared the pain. Not why it took so long, but why it lasted, is the question. Not one Allied statesman who contributed to the shaping of the policy ever composed a sensible explanation. The military leaders, in their memoirs, shrugged it off; it was not their idea.

Salonika was without doubt the most ponderous and illogical undertaking of World War I. But even its massive irrelevance could not command public attention. The expedition went almost forgotten except when some other superlative incidental to its wallowing made spot news. There was one such; it gave rise to the greatest maritime disaster in history. Out of Marseille, the 19,000-ton French transport *Provence* (formerly the Hamburg-America's *Deutschland*) was carrying 3,500 troops to Salonika. On February 26, 1916, she was torpedoed by the submarine *U-35* and 3,300 men perished.

The tragedy is not made less by the reflection that General Sarrail would have wasted them at Salonika anyway.

THE WAR IN AFRICA

The war spread to Africa because the colonial outposts of the contending empires wanted their share of the glory and the booty. In all of the resulting operations the salient characteristic was of meager forces on both sides almost overwhelmed by the vastness and formidable nature of the countryside. But it was not all war-

197

fare in slow motion. Out of the Gold Coast, a small Butisi column under one Captain Barker struck into German-held Togoland right after war started. Marching rapidly and outmaneuvering the enemy garrison, Barker got a surrender at Kamina on August 26, 1914, which ended German dominion in west Africa. It was the lightning performance of World War I.

The Germans were the late colonizers in Africa. They got their main holdings from the European Anti-Slavery Conference at Brussels in 1890, wherein the powers, after declaring their "emphatic desire to protect the native races from slavery and oppression," reapportioned the melon as the first step. By arrangement with Britain, contrived without protest or opposition, Germany annexed the large territories that became known as German Southwest Africa and German East Africa.

These were the areas against which British Empire forces turned the sword. Germany had not expected it to work out that way; her colonial experts anticipated that the Union of South Africa, due to its predominantly Boer population, would react passively to the struggle in Europe. It was a naïve assumption. The great Boer leaders, Generals Louis Botha and Jan C. Smuts, were not only soldiers of distinguished military attainments but statesmen with a broad world vision. Also, their loyalty as subjects of the British King was absolute.

Immediately, London decided to recall all imperial troops from South Africa, when Botha, then Premier of the Union, offered to replace them with Home Guardsmen. But in the beginning Botha missed becoming a German war prisoner by a hair. Just before the ultimatums flashed over Europe, he was at Delagoa Bay and about to step aboard a German ship for passage to Cape Town. At that moment he got a message relayed from his great friend Winston Churchill, saying that war was coming. Their careers had crossed at many points and Botha, feeling that Churchill's touch gave him luck, canceled the voyage and returned by train. By that margin, he missed being carried to Germany as a prize captive, and was left free to continue his great exertions.

Botha's campaign against German Southwest Africa got off to a slow start because he had to train forces. But the foundation was thorough. The colony, which extended some eight hundred miles between the Orange River and Angola, was garrisoned by 2,000 German Regulars. It is in large part desert; water for the invading columns had to be tanked over the railway. More than 50,000 South African militiamen and native bearers were used in

In October, 1915, Austria, Germany, and Bulgaria
(black arrows) invaded Serbia and forced its armies
(white arrows) to retreat to the Adriatic. A French
rescue column, sent to aid Serbia, advanced from
and retreated to Salonika (broken white arrow).

the conquest before the end. The army was strong in cavalry—a Boer specialty—and its sweep closed across the enemy line of retreat toward Angola. On July 9, 1915, the Germans surrendered; it was quite a haul—5,000 military prisoners, enough arms to supply a division, and a mountain of stores. The Germans were returned their arms and released on parole. Botha simply destroyed their system and imposed his own.

Out of German East Africa the Germans struck first, due to the organizing genius of a first-rate soldier, Colonel Paul von Lettow-Vorbeck. One column led by the unlikely named Major Kraut went after British East Africa, striking for Nairobi and the port of Mombasa and aiming to cut the Mombasa-Kisumu railroad. A second column, under Colonel von Wehle, had the more exotic task of attacking north against the shores of Lake Victoria Nyanza, and, afterward, occupying Uganda. The third column, led by Count von Falkenstein, was to go south against Nyasaland and Northern Rhodesia and sever all lines between South Africa and the Lakes region.

These ventures met varying fortune. Kraut almost had Mombasa in his hand when he was turned back by British command of the sea, which made possible reinforcement at the eleventh hour. But that did not end his gadfly performance. By September, 1914, Wehle had seized Karungu, a small British port on Victoria Nyanza. Then two squadrons of the South African Mounted Rifles reached the lake and beat him back. The Germans were based in Bukoba. From South Africa, a brigade under Brigadier General J. M. Stewart, and, from Uganda, a battalion of Lancashires concentered against that target. With the capture of Bukoba, the German munitions and stores in that region passed into British hands and the threat to the British Empire in Uganda ended.

But that was just one small facet in the struggle in Central Africa, which went on and on. Across the great lakes of that region there ensued small naval engagements between minor vessels on which the control of the whole region pivoted, with fortune swinging pendularly between the two sides. There is a peculiarly fascinating quality to these operations, a storybook appeal, reflected in later years in romance literature, for example, C. S. Forester's *The African Queen*. Truth remains stranger than fiction. An Englishman, Commander G. Spicer Simson, R.N., smashed German amphibious power on Lake Tanganyika, 6,000 feet above sea level, by portaging two armed launches 2,300 miles from Cape Town, via the rivers, swamps, and jungles of the Congo Free State. Experts thought him mad for trying, but he did it. Another British column of 2,000 men under Colonel P. V. Kelly of the Third Hussars took on the forces of the pro-German Sultan Ali Dinar at El Fashar in Darfur and, in a battle styled like Omdurman, killed him and scattered his army. One German stronghold energizing the fight for Central Africa was anchored on that fabulous peak, Mount Kilimanjaro.

Begun immediately after the declaration of war, the contest for the German-held Cameroons endured eighteen months. This was a territory larger than European Germany, in part mountainous, largely covered by forest, dense grass, or bush, plagued by the tsetse fly, and everywhere fever-ridden. British columns out of Nigeria, French forces out of French Equatorial Africa, and Belgian-led troops from the Congo all struck at the Cameroons. Mainly native troops with white leaders, these motley armies, counting weapons men and porters, must have aggregated 50,000 or so. There was much skirmishing and a few sharp fights at border crossing points. Then one after another the columns slowed and halted, wasted from dysentery, malaria, and other fevers. Motion was restored after the medical services won the battle for health. The end approached at Youandé on January 1, 1916, when the German commander, Colonel Zimmermann, fled south with the main body of defenders, to be interned in the Spanish enclave at Rio Muni. At Mora, a native garrison under Captain von Raben resisted until February 18. For so doing, he and his officers were allowed to keep their swords on going as prisoners to England, a quaint touch of chivalry that distinguished the African campaigns.

But the detailed story of the struggle for the roof of the Dark Continent must be read elsewhere. In the end, Britain and the Allies prevailed, thanks to indigenous help. In this way, the German Empire died in Africa while in Europe millions fought on in the name of the German Emperor.

VI
Deadlock

The real hero of Verdun was the *poilu*,
a front-line soldier in the French Army, as
typified in this photographic portrait of
a self-reliant French veteran.

From the trenches near Ypres in the late winter of 1915 the young American poet Alan Seeger, in a letter to his mother, foretold the future. His words are no less remarkable for their courage than for their wisdom:

"You are quite wrong about my not realizing what I was going into when I enlisted. I knew that it would be a fight to a finish, just as our Civil War was. The conflagration, far from diminishing, seems to be spreading. The lull during the winter has allowed each side on this front to fortify itself so strongly that, in my opinion, the deadlock here is permanent."

Although Seeger's horizon hardly extended beyond the enemy wire, he grasped the essential that famed commanders missed. Around Ypres the German onslaught had continued forty days beyond the first appearance of the chlorine cloud on April 22. For both sides, this Second Battle of Ypres proved a meaningless slaughter. It cost the B.E.F. 2,150 officers and 56,125 other ranks. At the end, the defenders clung to a harshly truncated salient, waterlogged and bestenched with rotting flesh and the sour smell of gas. Their lines north and east of the town were now so far retracted as to put all of Ypres within range of the smallest mortars. By holding the heights outside this semicircle, the Germans made it a shooting gallery to sharpen their artillery. For the British, holding on was immoderately costly and breaking out was impossible. Wrote one soldier: "It is all like some strange city in a dead world, some horror from the Apocalypse."

Even so, British G.H.Q. could scent opportunity not far beyond the graveyard. General Smith-Dorrien, who had acquitted himself admirably from Mons onward, was relieved of command of the Second Army, simply because he doubted that offensive operations were justified and wanted to yield some ground at Ypres so that his troops would be less exposed. He was succeeded by General Sir Herbert Plumer, who was more deferential to his superiors and equally thoughtful of his soldiers, a combination that is universally admired.

Joffre and Sir John French, who together called the tune for the Western Front, rebounded from their hard winter unchanged. Both still believed that the one great battle that would collapse Germany was just around the corner. What they said to each other in correspondence outweighed everything they should have read from their operations. On the morrow of Neuve-Chapelle, Joffre was already writing to his British collaborator that as promptly as warm weather afforded favorable footing, he would stage his decisive attack with the French armies. The storming of Vimy Ridge would open the Douai plain beyond, whence crashing through to Namur would "finish the war in three months." But to clinch things, he would require a push from the British on the left. Sir John was quite willing. And so was General Haig, whose First Army was to mount the offensive. Both looked to May Day as the time in which to make up for past blunders; the chosen ground for the hitting by the British was on both sides of the old Neuve-Chapelle battlefield—a pincers movement by three British army corps. Of that earlier regrettable affair, the G.H.Q. memorandum said: "We have learnt the lessons and shall know how to avoid mistakes." Ringing words these, they underscore only what G.H.Q. thought it had learned —that artillery could blast a hole through the opposing wall for infantry and thereby assure success. After Neuve-Chapelle this idea became an obsession with the Allied command, not only dominating all planning for 1915 operations but exercising a sinister influence on tactics till the end. Generals could not perceive that the concept was wrong; failure was attributed instead to imperfection in the method of execution. So heavier artillery preparation, greater infantry masses, and attacks on wider fronts became the formula. Today it is called escalation. What it means is that the sacrifice of men steadily ascends.

At the same time, in the other camp, General Falkenhayn had reached a wholly opposite appreciation of the possibilities. He wrote: "The English troops, in spite of undeniable bravery and endurance, have proved so clumsy in action that they will accomplish nothing decisive against the German Army *in the immediate future*." The last four words are more significant than the whole. Falkenhayn saw clearly what Joffre and French missed—that the tactical deadlock was unbreakable for the time being, made so by the echeloned depth of machine guns and artillery. He could risk thinning his front in the face of Allied massing; his enemies could afford to take that same risk. From the long view, Germany's one chance lay in the Allies' continued squandering of troops in futile offensives; attrition might alter the balance. Otherwise, as he already saw it, Germany could not emerge victorious. Although it was a realistic appreciation, he did not dare convey it to his war lord or Government. As Chief of the General Staff, he was already under direct challenge from H-L, at odds with the Kaiserin, undercut by Tirpitz, and only tepidly supported by Bethmann. Even had his enigmatic nature permitted frankness, anything coming from him that seemed tainted with defeatism would have insured his removal. Joffre and Sir John French both lacked Falkenhayn's military insight and at this stage were less worried than he about job security. As a result of this difference, the war's tragedy on the Western Front deepened. The Germans simply organized themselves better to beat off the Allied attacks. These sharply contrasting attitudes enabled Joffre to boast of "maintaining the initiative" while deprecating Falkenhayn as a "general unwilling to take a resolute decision." The words make for more impressive reading when they are separated from the comparative casualty figures.

IN ARTOIS

Aubers Ridge was a hill mass lying about one and one-half miles behind the German front line where it faced Neuve-Chapelle. From there the ridges run southeast toward Lille, Roubaix, and the cities of the Scheldt plain. This otherwise unimpressive feature gave its name to the British half of the Maytime battle in Artois because Haig's two assault bodies were supposed to converge there after breaking the enemy front. If the German second line could be carried, the ridges afforded a high road to a linkup with the French who were attacking toward Lens. British I Corps and the Indian Corps would assault on the 2,400-yard-wide front south of Neuve-Chappelle; British IV Corps, jumping off on a 1,500-yard front, would strike to the north of it. These separately plotted penetrations, however, were launched so close to one another in distance that, even if both were successful, they afforded too little latitude for exploitation.

May 9 opened as a day of golden sunshine, and contemporary records say that troops heard larks singing before the guns spoke. If that be true, they did not sing long, and around Lens it is doubtful if they sang at all. For six days, 350 heavy guns and 969 pieces of light field artillery had been bombarding the ground over which General d'Urbal's French Tenth Army expected to advance, along a front 16,000 yards wide. At first it had been planned that Haig's army would assault one day later than d'Urbal's. Then it was realized that the prolonged softening-up fires from the French guns would kill any chance for surprise. So the two assaults were synchronized, though Haig's front was given only forty minutes of preparatory bombardment, his army being short of ammunition and having only half as many guns as the French. This was incredible hardihood. The German works in front of Haig's three corps had not been battered in any of the earlier fighting, and their protection was far too massive to be more than scratched by perfunctory fire. Heavy artillery will not even crash timbers when they are revetted by four or five layers of sandbags, as at Aubers Ridge. Light guns will do no more than spill sand from a few bags. As it transpired, the British shellfire was too lightly laid on to cut lanes through the enemy entanglements. Ninety-two per cent of the British fire was shrapnel, which had no effect upon the works.

Western Front battles in 1915 never ended in a grand climax but drizzled off into unconnected and miserable local actions. It was so with the French in front of Lens. But the artillery opening was the heaviest overture ever played in war until that hour. Through the morning of the assault more than 300,000 shells were loosed against the German positions. Packed like sardines in the frontal trenches, the reserves having been brought forward, French infantry boiled out of the trenches in the wake of this steel tempest and walked forward. By noon they were past the Arras-Béthune road, having penetrated enemy country almost three miles, the deepest advance in France since the beginning of position warfare. It is reported that they stuck sprigs of lilac and hawthorn in their kepis during this surge, so great was their exultation. Had things gone equally well with the flanks as with the center, Lens might have been won in a day. But on the left, resistance was firmer and the countryside more broken. Still, for the next three days, the attack made headway, and then the weather changed, with the onset of torrential rains.

The French Battle of Artois, a struggle in which General Mud intervened on the side of the Germans, went on sporadically through the month of May. Considerable real estate, wherein all shelters were laid flat, changed hands. On a front more than 6,000 yards wide, the French Army had penetrated three enemy defense lines to an average depth of 3,000 yards. But German counterfires had blocked French reserves in emerging from the frontal trenches in time, thereby enabling the defending infantry to close the gap. Enemy guns were still anchored on the ridges that commanded Lens. The French attack played itself out in going against the fortified machine gun nests between the trench system and the artillery. So while trenches had been carried, the line, in effect, was not broken. But even such an able soldier as General Foch drew from the Artois battle only the sterile conclusion that the method was essentially correct and required only a few tactical refinements. This furthered that underestimation of German defenses that hampered Allied generalship for the greater part of three years.

The collateral attempt by Haig's troops to carry Aubers Ridge came to grief and dead stop more quickly and dramatically. Only two German regiments, the 55th and 57th, manned the front against which the British launched three corps. They were enough. The Germans had so engineered their front with switch lines, angular communications trenches, deep protective works to cover troops, and strong points in the rear fixed to fire parallel to the front, that they were perfectly disposed to wither the flanks of the two-pronged converging attack. British I Corps and the Indian Corps were heavily beset from the beginning. British IV Corps, which attacked later from the left, fared a little better, though the difference would more aptly be measured by burial parties than by tacticians. One day's loss in what was called the Battle of Aubers Ridge, or Festubert, was 458 officers and 11,161 men. Wrote the British historian Alan Clark: "It had been a disastrous fifteen hours of squandered heroism, unredeemed by the faintest glimmer of success." But no Londoner would have guessed the truth from Sir John French's official communiqué: "First Army has pierced the enemy's line on a total front of four miles. The entire first line system of trenches has been captured on a front of 3,200 yards." Every word of it was positively true—and absolutely deceptive.

In the Artois battle, the French center that had attacked so brilliantly was formed by XXXIII Corps, under General Henri Philippe Pétain, who had started the war as an obscure colonel. He emerged with all stars shining. But the fight that furthered his fame also cost France 400,000 soldiers. France seethed over the toll. On a visit to the front President Poincaré heard this pleading from the commander of IX Corps: "Pray do what you can to stop these local offensives. The instrument of victory is being broken in our hands." George Clemenceau predicted: "If things keep going this way, there will be a revolt of the Generals against the High Command." Seemingly unperturbed, Joffre circulated the story that enemy losses were higher still, whereas they were only half as great.

In Britain the political repercussions coincided with the detonation over Hamilton's mournful experience in the Gallipoli landing. But Sir John French escaped with head unbloodied, having artfully planted the cover story that the munitions shortage was responsible for the defeat. Kitchener was directly assailed as the man responsible for the shell shortage, and the charge undermined his prestige in the very hour when his protest against the large-scale Allied attacks on the Western Front cried for amplification. So there was less restraint upon a high command bent mainly at staging bigger and more ghastly shows. In June the French and British staffs met at Chantilly to review strategy and decide that, in view of the problems of the Alliance as a whole, "passive defense" in the West was "entirely out of the question." To the generals, that meant that the monstrously wasting offensives must continue.

The B.E.F. by this time had risen to twenty-one divisions (greater numbers than Britain poured into France in World War II) and the Third Army formed under General Monro took over a fifteen-mile sector between Arras and the Somme. The reinforcement provided more splendid material for the meat grinder, and the more that arrived, the more certain it became that the High Commands would not moderate their course.

To describe his strategy, Joffre coined the unhappy phrase *"Je les grignote"* (I am nibbling them), which tacitly acknowledged that he saw no chance to bite through. How the nibbling too often worked out is best revealed by what this grandfatherly figure could write casually about one of his own blunders; "A feeling of uneasiness spread to staff and troops. It would have been advisable to postpone the attack. But men cannot be kept long in flooded trenches. Delay would have lost the valuable element of surprise. Therefore the order was given. The results were negligible. The attacks were continued three days and were everywhere unsuccessful." So in this case thousands were slain simply to prove to their general that the "valuable element of surprise" was wholly an illusion. This was the real horror of World War I as laid bare by the 1915 battles. The unusual length of the war, its

The stalemate on the Western Front remained
unbroken throughout 1915 despite the German
attack on Ypres in April (black arrow); the
French strike at St.-Mihiel, also in April;
and repeated Allied assaults in Artois
and Champagne (white arrows). In both
spring and fall, the opposing armies fought
savagely, and suffered tremendous casualties,
for possession of the villages between
Ypres and Arras (inset).

barbarisms and atrocities, the flood of maimed and mutilated individuals turned back to society, the submarine sinkings, the starving civilians—all of these things are less shocking than that vast armies were raised, maneuvered into annihilation, and achieved nothing through their death.

By the spring of 1915, however, the front line ordeal of the Tommy and the *poilu* was not wholly unremitting. Coupled with the enemy's purely defensive posture, the arrival of the new divisions made possible rotation in and out of line. Within the committed regiments that was done routinely. Battalions in reserve, though only a mile or so to the rear, could live it up during the respite. It was one of the paradoxes of the war that beauty and high excitement were found so very close to squalor and abject misery. The forward battalions, living in dugouts, sloshed through trenches knee-deep in mire. Red slugs crawled the walls of these ditches; frogs splashed in the muck of the floor; rats and roaches plagued the sleeping quarters. At intervals the front-line companies would be run through delousing stations on the regimental rear. Men bathed while their clothing was put through a steam chamber. Then back to the dugouts, and within twenty-four hours they were again lice-infested. Reading one's shirt for seam squirrels was a daily occupation. The battalions out of line got back to leafy villages, trained in fields bright with poppies and buttercups, and slept in splinter-proof huts or haylofts.

Whole divisions would be withdrawn and moved for a fortnight of rest to some countryside out of sound of the guns; fresh cheeses, tasty sausages, white bread, and low-priced wines were available there, which made it seem like paradise. There were portions of the front, for example north of Toul and in Alsace, that by mutual consent became "quiet sectors" where battered divisions, French and German, could be rested and rehabilitated, with hardly more risk than men know at home. In the army rear areas, all kinds of schools came into being, in which NCO's and junior officers were made expert in gas defense, use of the bayonet, trench raiding, handling of grenades (they were called bombs), or some other military specialty. This chance for change made life bearable while it lasted, as did the prospect of drawing a "blightly" wound, just crippling enough to return a man home. Troops were not morose, driven by desperation, or suffused with self-pity. The war kept going because to the uncomplicated mind of its average soldier its dangers remained tolerable. Young Seeger's diary is wholly consistent with troop nature. One day he writes: "Every minute here is worth weeks of ordinary experience. This will spoil one for any other kind of life." Then a few days later he notes in despair: "We are not leading the life of men at all, but that of animals, living in holes in the ground, and only showing outside to fight and to feed." All Western Front soldiers felt that way. The feeling of being debased by the rodentlike environment was the common affliction. In an odd way, this oppression excused them from worrying excessively about the more absolute values.

ON THE HOME FRONT

By early summer Britain's New Army—Kitchener's Mob replacing the Old Contemptibles—was crowding the front in Flanders. This phalanx of volunteers was to become the last stand of the illusion that free societies can hold their own in a disordered world without resorting to compulsory service. Its recruitment was accomplished by a modern advertising campaign that pulled out every stop in working on the emotions of the young British male. Walls in England were plastered with signs reading, "What did you do in the Great War, Daddy?" and "What will your best girl say if you're not in khaki?" These new formations proved hardly less willing and able than the professional army, which, except for higher commanders, was now largely in Valhalla or hospitalized. But, despite all the pressure, the New Army had not grown apace with the requirement imposed by the military command's stubborn insistence on a continuing offensive strategy. A few more actions like Aubers Ridge and Neuve-Chapelle must wipe it out. A few leaders like Churchill and Lloyd George faced the grim reality, but the public and the press simply could not grasp that no terminal point to the slaughter was in sight. Like the generals, they lived in daily expectation of a breakthrough. Soon the joy bells of peace would sound again, and the lads would come marching back to England, home, and beauty, just as they had done in earlier wars. Due to this optimism, the issue of national service, though hotly debated for a time, stayed unresolved. Ministers were loath to stake their political fortunes on it; they sat waiting for a popular demand or a crisis of such magnitude that the need for change would become incontestably clear. But such ground swells, if they are to command events, require impulse from the top, and democracies are rarely fortunate in having leaders who will challenge public opinion on unpopular issues.

Britain took the first step toward conscription through the back door when on June 23, 1915, the Munitions Act was introduced. The law put the nation's whole industrial structure on a war footing. Arbitration was made compulsory in all labor disputes. Strikes and lockouts were forbidden unless thirty days had passed without intervention by the Board of Trade. Employers' profits were limited. The Minister of Munitions was authorized to declare any plant "a controlled operation." Trade union rules were declared suspended where they restricted production or employment. Wage changes could be made only with the approval of the Minister. Employers were forbidden to hire individuals out of munitions plants, which effectively froze war industry workers on their jobs.

In this way, the question of totally organizing management and labor for the war was faced before there was any realistic decision to insure the raising of adequate military manpower. But from the trend must come the sequel. In large numbers, the women of Britain were already displacing men in the war industries, on public carriers, and in communications work. Their adaptability, plus their patriotism, eased the pinch on the labor market and put greater human resources at the disposal of government. France and Germany, having systematized national service, had experienced this shift from the beginning.

Still, it would be false to think of the British in 1915 as a people with backs bowed and nerves steeled, wholly at grips with their problem. It was not yet looked upon as a war of total obligation; sweets and other luxuries had not disappeared from the market. Prices for necessities had not boomed and rigid controls had not appeared. Though nearly one-quarter million British fighting men had died, and the count of grief-stricken homes was mounting daily, the spirit of "carry on," "do your bit," "see it through," and "pack up your troubles" was not elsewhere pervasive. To the masses of London, the bloody sacrifices at Neuve-Chapelle and Aubers Ridge were less poignant than the deaths of two hundred or so noncombatants that had thus far resulted from Zeppelin raids over the city. Frequently in France and Gallipoli that many young Englishmen were meeting death in two minutes. But though the war was costing the nation about twenty-five million dollars per day, it was being financed through floating capital and the people were rallying to the War Loans magnificently, happy that the income tax rose no higher than the standard rate of 10 per cent. No real economies had been fastened on the citizen. Rationing was for the future.

There was considerable disarray in the mind of Kitchener, however. He is the Hamlet of the play, except that Hamlet reveals his confusions of mind while Kitchener's majestic front conceals them. Kitchener believed that Sir John French and Sir Ian Hamilton were bleeding their armies in battles that could not be won; but he never said so unequivocally to his fellow ministers and he continued to scrounge troops here and there to send forward for the feeding of heavier fires. At Calais on July 6 and 7, he, Asquith, and Balfour met with Viviani, Millerand, and Joffre to discuss Allied strategy. Sir John French was also present. The French delegation argued for unity of command on the Western Front; hadn't they generously accepted the principle at Gallipoli? Kitchener persuaded Joffre to table this knotty question at least until the adventure in the east Mediterranean had worked itself out. Then, contending that Hamilton's operation must be given priority for as long as it trembled in balance, he asked the council to agree that there would be no more main offensives on the Western Front during 1915. The Frenchmen were taken aback; that would reverse what their own council had decided at Chantilly; France had to keep hitting until all Germans were thrown from the sacred soil; the soul of France permitted no other course. Then Kitchener and Joffre took a stroll together. What they discussed remained thereafter known only to themselves. But Joffre returned to the council in high humor, announcing that he was won over to the idea of standing on the defensive in the West. He didn't mean one word of it; already he was planning secretly for a mönstrous offensive in the Champagne in early autumn. Kitchener's biographer says: "It is certain that Kitchener knew what Joffre was planning." After all, if Hamilton won through, the other question would become academic. But if this was how he was thinking, he did not reveal it to his British colleagues. They returned to London happily convinced that the orgy of slaughter in the West was effectively damped. When at last they knew that they had been hoodwinked at Calais, their affections toward Kitchener withered further, but the Government didn't dare turn him out. Until death decreed otherwise, he remained the Great Indispensable.

Unlike Britain, Germany did not yield gradually to the grip of the war. At first, wage levels were frozen while prices continued to rise. That couldn't outlast the blockade, which effectively isolated Germany and cut off imports, save from Scandinavia. Controls and rigid economies had to be forced on the citizenry. The poor got poorer and the wealthy landlords funded the Government loans. Sniffing at how Britain did it, the Minister of Finance, Dr. Karl Helfferich, told the Reichstag: "It is not in accordance with the German taste to apply the style of a circus advertisement to the serious matter of war." But for all this appeal to ideals, working-class Germans were hurting too grievously to feel moved. Moltke, having taken to his bed, entertained visitors by damning the Kaiser for not having properly provisioned the nation, as he had urged him to do before the blockade was clamped on. The submarine campaign had done absolutely nothing to ease this strangulating hold on the national throat. Ersatz materials were already flooding the market. All food stocks were rationed and doled out under government supervision. To the possible limit, the industrial plant had been swung over to the making of munitions and other war goods. But as to finance, the majority of Germans still believed that the overstretching of the internal credit would at last be righted through the winning of the war. It was the filial reaction of a regimented people, conditioned by Prussian disciplines to accept on faith the words of their leaders.

Interior Germany was not yet at nadir. American neutrality remained its partial, self-righteous benefactor. The best the British could do was blacklist any bottoms that carried goods to the enemy via neutral ports, deny them coal in British ports, and officially boycott the owners. Washington policy sought to uphold those suppliers and shippers who defied the blockade. Mr. Wilson was equally scornful of the British attempt to collapse Germany by economic pressure and of German encroachment on freedom of the seas. Even so, his admonishments from atop the fence had less bearing on events than the shipyard contest between the great belligerents. The British were better prepared to enforce their policy at sea, but they could not seal off Germany. By mid-1915, the British navy had almost 3,000 armed surface craft of various types available for guarding the sea lanes. The German fleet remained bottled in harbor.

At war's beginning, Germany had had only twenty-four U-boats ready for duty. By the end of 1915, nineteen U-boats had been sunk while fifty-four new ones had taken to the oceans. Having started late, Germany was only now girding for the showdown at sea. On the home front, her critical deficiency was not so much foodstuffs as chemicals. Prior to the war, the Germans had produced more than 80 per cent of their dietary needs. But the great part of their chemical fertilizers had come from abroad. The neutrals to which Germany had access could not take care of this deficiency. German plant capacity couldn't do it because the nitrates were also needed by the munitions plants. So the soil deteriorated, crops fell off, and what was grown became less nourishing. That was the rub. Belt-tightening began in 1915. By 1917 extreme malnutrition had phased into starvation, the chief victims being the poorer classes, the sickly, the aged, and the children. German writers claimed in later years that three quarters of a million of their countrymen were killed by the blockade. No such figure is subject to proof. What is known is that it was America's entry that made the squeeze deadly. As a belligerent, the United States applied with a vengeance the very methods that it had denounced as a neutral. After 1917, there was no further quibbling about the moral issue.

THE FALL OF WARSAW

In the Eastern theatre, the cast of main actors—warriors and policymakers—remained the same except that Count Berchtold, the supreme mischief-maker, had departed the Foreign Office in Vienna.

It happened very simply. Count Tisza went to the Emperor one day and urged Berchtold's dismissal because he lacked decisiveness. Francis Joseph said: "I have long thought so myself." So the man who had worked Europe into a war spent the rest of it strolling in his flower gardens. To friends he said: "Speak to me of peace; I'm sick of the war." In that he was not alone.

General Conrad was as ebullient as ever and continued to press upon Hindenburg and Ludendorff great designs that would require the transfer of preponderant German strength to their front—suggestions that did not lessen their admiration for him.

Falkenhayn's resistance to their pressures grew weaker, despite

"YOUR COUNTRY NEEDS YOU"

Lord Kitchener reminds Britons of a sacred
duty in a prototype of America's famous
"Uncle Sam" recruiting poster. To avoid
legislating compulsory military service,
the British used posters like this one to
encourage volunteers. When the young men
enlisted, women moved into their positions
in the war industries, on public carriers,
and in communications work.

his conviction that Germany would prevail in France or not at all. Looking back now, it seems strange that he could not buck the tide, for the German Crown Prince was solidly in agreement with him. Here is one of the most traduced and least understood figures in the Great War. The butt of Allied ridicule, the Crown Prince was lampooned as little better than an imbecile and nothing of a soldier. The image was grotesquely false. The Kaiser's eldest was a decent man, of good instincts and reasonably sound political insight, possibly not a great commander, but still worthy of his uniform. His qualities, not his lack thereof, denied him credit with his father. But as the duel between H–L and the Chief of Staff intensified, even the Crown Prince had to trim sail. Possibly it would be better, he argued to Falkenhayn in April, to shift major forces to the Eastern Front, aim for a knockout blow there, and then reconcentrate all strength in the West, where finally the war must be won. Once persuaded by this deft piece of soft-selling, Falkenhayn went full length. Conrad had asked for four German divisions. As Falkenhayn reckoned strategy, half enough was not enough by half. He decided that four corps should be shipped east, and that they should be formed as the Eleventh German Army for the unfolding operation between Gorlice and Tarnów. But his about-face did not end the acrimony. Falkenhayn and H–L continued to insult one another at every turn. What went on in the name of devotion to the Fatherland was in fact a venting of private spite. The two headquarters were more intent on outmaneuvering one another than on joining cause to defeat the common enemy.

Mackensen took over the Eleventh Army and the Ninth Army was given to the aging Field Marshal, Prince Leopold of Bavaria. To mask the preparations for the attack that Mackensen was mounting around Gorlice, Leopold's army staged a gas attack at Skierniewice on May 2. His troops knew nothing about the new weapon; they were not supplied with masks; they were told only that the chlorine would wipe out the Russians confronting them. A special gas battalion was brought into the area to handle the gas cylinders. The German infantry advanced directly behind the light-green cloud. Hardly had they trod no-man's-land when a few men were felled by a scattering rifle fire. Thereupon the whole force decided that the chlorine had failed and recoiled to its own trenches. The gas had in fact almost stripped the Russian front of defenders. So the Ninth Army mounted another gas attack. This time the wind turned just as the cloud started rolling. Many Germans were killed, but no Russians.

Mackensen's army and the Fourth Austrian Army struck also on May 2 and that day captured Tarnów, the hub of Russian defense short of Gorlice. In the days that immediately followed, Mackensen broke through the third and fourth Russian lines, thereby compelling a general enemy retirement from the Carpathians. These were tremendous battles, 170,000 men on the Austro-German side, in full collision with the Third, Eighth, and Eleventh Russian armies under the Grand Duke Nicholas, along a 250-mile front. More than 700 light field guns and about 250 heavies supported the attack, so that in the breakthrough zone there was a gun for every thirty yards. No earlier battle in France had massed so much artillery.

But in this smashing success in their neighborhood, there was no cheer for H-L. They had been shoved down the totem pole. Falkenhayn and his headquarters had moved east to direct the battle. It was done in a very roundabout way. Mackensen and his Eleventh Army, which had the gifted Hans von Seeckt as Chief of Staff, were formally placed under command of Conrad. But he had first to agree that he would issue no orders unless they were first approved by Falkenhayn. Should too much time then be lost by this circuitousness for the sake of Austrian dignity, the pitch would be made Falkenhayn-to-Mackensen directly. So H-L looked on sourly from the sidelines. They had been invaded.

From the first blast-off, the Russian front caved in. Dmitriev's Third Army, in the eye of the storm as the Germans struck northeast, was virtually wiped out. When at last the attackers slowed from lack of energy, 150,000 prisoners, 125 cannon, and 300 machine guns had been taken. By mid-month Mackensen's army reached the San, and as June opened Przemyśl fell to it like a rotten plum, the Grand Duke having decided not to defend the fortress, which his siege forces had taken in March.

But on June 3 when Przemyśl changed hands, the event was overshadowed by a glittering conference on strategy held at Pless. The Kaiser, Conrad, Falkenhayn, Ludendorff, Hindenburg, Hoffmann, and Mackensen were all present to review the bidding. There was plenty to talk about. Italy had entered the war. The Allies were ashore on Gallipoli. Conrad wanted to shake divisions out of Galicia and ship them to the Isonzo to teach the Italians a lesson. All the Germans hardened that view. What they had started in Galicia, they intended to finish, though Falken-hayn was looking anxiously toward the Dardanelles and asking what could be done as a counter. Pointing one way and walking in the other, he urged that four of the German divisions be returned to France; at the witching hour of success, he was revers-ing his own strategy. H-L aggressively opposed the transfer; they had the bird in hand and it was certain Falkenhayn couldn't stay around to claim all the eggs. In a sense, they outwaited him. What worked out was that the Kaiser ordered the Mackensen offensive to continue, after it was beefed up with four and one-half additional German divisions. That called for a regrouping with all the attacking armies coming under Mackensen's control. By mid-June the Austrians and Germans were on the move again and on June 22 they took over Lemberg without a struggle. Rava Russkaya shortly was taken by storm and the Russians retreated to the Bug River. At each stage of the advance Falkenhayn re-newed his argument for breaking it off but the weight of council was set solidly against him. However, the offensive was creaking. No headquarters had anticipated that the rupture would be so complete and consequently the supply backup was inadequate. This administrative bind in the German camp enabled the Grand Duke to back away without suffering a total debacle.

Again there was a grand war council, this time at Posen on July 1, and again the Kaiser decided that the offensive should be continued. The Twelfth German Army would attack and head for the Narew River. The Ninth Army would advance on the Vistula. The axis of Mackensen's army was changed ninety degrees, so that it would sweep the broad corridor between the Vistula and the Bug, where the main Russian forces were concen-trated. Ludendorff disdained the plan, objecting that it was aimed too shallowly; it would compress the Russians but it would not bag them. He wrote of it: "I had to keep my views to myself and hope that later the movement I wanted might be carried out." Hoffmann was also growling in frustration, convinced that an opportunity to envelop the Grand Duke's armies was being thrown away. Falkenhayn, reflecting on what had happened to Napoleon, feared to become too deeply enmeshed. An enveloping maneu-ver through Kovno aimed at Vilna and Minsk, which Ludendorff wanted, looked decisive on paper, but it also risked overexten-sion and the prolonged retention of overstrength German armies

Two Austro-German offensives (black arrows) from May to September, 1915, forced the Russians (broken white line) back to the line (solid white) running from Riga south to Rumania.

in the East past the time when another great fire might break out on the Western Front.

So the Kaiser decided, backing Falkenhayn. What came of it made a case for neither party. The Grand Duke did manage to back most of his forces out of the Polish salient before the Germans converged on his main bases there. But he lost one-half million prisoners to the Germans in doing so. On August 5 Warsaw was evacuated by the Russians, in a general retreat from the line of the Vistula. By mid-month the Germans had overrun most of Poland. Much of the civilian mass had fled east toward Brest Litovsk and the Pripet Marshes, stampeded by fear of German brutality, before the Russian armies gave way. The military columns overhauled them and rammed through, shunting the refugees into the ditches.

Amid the din and dirge of battle, however, there was still to be heard the fugue of insatiable German military ambition and camp rivalry. Hindenburg wrote a self-pitying letter to the chief of the Kaiser's military cabinet complaining that his title of Commander in Chief, Eastern Front, had become a "cutting irony." Falkenhayn, hearing about it, made the cut deeper by ordering a regroupment that removed still another field army from H-L's command. Bulgaria was teetering on the brink and about to declare war. The plan to shift Mackensen south and smash Serbia was already in the works. German intelligence had smelled out the forthcoming Allied offensives on the Western Front. These were major considerations with Falkenhayn; he was determined to play for security all around. His great rivals in the East could neither become reconciled to his perspective nor dissuaded from sulking in a corner because of it.

After Poland was overrun, Ludendorff got his Vilna plan back on the rails and put the German cavalry in motion. The new offensive started on September 9. Two German field armies, one under Below, the other under Hermann von Eichorn, attacking on different axes, one northeast, the other slightly southeast, sought to close around the bulk of the Grand Duke's forces. Their mass was in that salient formed by the fifty-mile-wide loop in the Niemen River that has Grodno as its apex. It was to be envelopment on the largest scale.

Grodno quickly fell. The German cavalry had already charged on to Vilna, which put them on the enemy rear. But the German foot strength was too thin and the pincers couldn't close in time to cut the railways running east from the salient. Most of the Grand Duke's soldiers backed away. There followed another such attempt to bag the Russians in the Vilna salient, formed by the line of the Viliya and Shemanya rivers. This time the German infantry made the passage of the fords in time and captured Vilna with the Russians still in the salient, while the cavalry moved on the key railway junctures, seemingly locking the exits. News of the trap closing caused great rejoicing in Berlin. It was premature. The bear shook loose because the jaws were too weak. The German cavalry was driven back from Molodechno, the rail escape route was recaptured, and the Grand Duke's forces successfully retired to a new front farther east. These things happened in September, 1915. Ludendorff perforce suspended operations. His campaign had won much ground, while failing of its main object, and his advanced forces by this time had far outrun their supply. During the progress of these maneuvers to the northward, Mackensen's army had driven through to Brest Litovsk and Prince Leopold's troops had traversed the Bialiowieza Forest. Ludendorff commented: "We had taken a great step toward Russia's overthrow. The Grand Duke, with his strong personality, resigned and the Czar placed himself at the head of the armies." That by-product of the campaign, for Germans, was its most gratifying reward.

Conrad and his Austrians had tried to do their part. On the extreme right of the Teuton alignment, hitting from ironically named Luck, they were to strike east and trap all Russians south of the Pripet Marshes. Begun in late September, their offensive swiftly withered. Conrad tried to renew it in October. The result was further slaughter, the campaign costing Austria another 250,000 soldiers.

When the front at last subsided with the coming of winter, the Teuton armies were dug in on a line running from Riga on the Baltic to Czernowitz on the Rumanian border. There remained for their Slav foeman two years of spasmodic and wasting resistance. But not until 1944 would Russian armies again menace Germany.

It was on September 5 that Czar Nicholas signed the army order reading: "Today I have taken supreme command of all forces of the sea and land armies operating in the theatre of war. We shall fulfill our sacred duty to defend our country to the last. We shall not dishonor the Russian land." Peter the Great, much earlier, and dictator Joseph Stalin, twenty-six years later, took the same action in an hour of national crisis; the proclamation written by Stalin as Hitler's armies reached for Moscow had much the same ring. But the circumstances were quite different. While the armies under the Grand Duke had suffered hard reverses, they had escaped disaster, and their operations in the defense of the Grodno and Vilna salients had been ably conducted. In the three weeks' campaign that had advanced the German Army more than one hundred miles inside Russia's border, the Russian soldier, as in later wars fought by Communist armies, had performed with dogged bravery. The Russian saying, "We have one good weapon—the living breast of the soldier," was sadly true. The Germans prevailed because of vastly superior firepower. For every Russian machine gun, the Germans had four. The Russian field artillery, good enough in design, was also far outnumbered; undersupply limited every shoot by the defenders and a high percentage of the shells were duds. Toward the end, the rifle supply became exhausted, and where there were rifles enough, there were too few cartridges. Unarmed men waited in the fire line for comrades to be shot so that they might arm themselves. One division in the retreat was wholly without small arms and its guns were rationed to three shells per day. Yet there had been no panic, no rout, no sign of mutiny. The armies had retired in good order. No soldiery has looked more solid in such extreme adversity.

Yet the Czar assumed command believing that the danger to the empire was measureless. It was more than a sign to the Germans that there would be no suit for a separate peace while he lived. He meant it as a tocsin to the nation. General Mikhail Alekseev, one of the ablest group commanders facing the Germans, was put in command of the forces manning the winter line. It was his hand, more than the Grand Duke's, that had saved the Russian armies during the retreat.

But if "saved" is the right word for the armies at this stage, the nation itself was in terrible turbulence. Some part of it was due to the tide of refugees flooding back from the stricken border through towns and villages, fearful that it would be their turn next. While there was as yet no outcry against the regime, confusion and dismay were mounting, creating the climate that nourishes suspicion and multiplies ugly rumor.

The Duma, that tribune of the masses, had met on August 1

to voice its defiance of Germany, but it stayed on to debate issues and make speeches that rocked Russia. Charges were heard that German capital controlled Russian banks, which in turn were responsible for the lag in munitions and the manipulation of the commodity market. It was said that Krupp was a heavy shareholder in the main munitions works and it was his hidden influence that kept labor on a five-hour day in some of the plants. Via the Duma these sinister reports were spread to the nation as if authenticated. The net effect was that public anxiety mounted and the Duma did nothing decisive to restore national confidence. Its progressive bloc, in this session headed by Pavel Milyukov, split into left and right wings. The right devoted its energies to crying for the ouster of all pro-Germans from the bureaucracy; the left demanded that the cabinet be made responsible to the Duma. The debate becoming steadily more nasty, the Premier, Ivan Goremykin, went to Nicholas and convinced him that the Duma must be prorogued. When the order was published, there was mass rioting in the cities for the first time, and the munitions plants were struck. The disorders continued for one week. Then the Czar got the Duma leaders together. It was agreed that the Duma would resume sitting. One of its own leaders, Deputy Khvostov, was chosen as Minister of the Interior.

In this way passed the first political crisis in Russia. But it had played its role of a pebble cast into a pond.

CHAMPAGNE AND LOOS

To mount the operations that shook Russia so gravely, Germany had accepted extraordinary risks on the Western Front. Throughout the summer of 1915, Allied combat manpower along the line in France and Belgium outnumbered the enemy by at least three to one.

But it was a calculated risk, based upon hard tactical analysis of the main fighting problem. One year of fighting on the flankless front had convinced the German High Command that decisive penetration was mathematically all but impossible. The Allied generals were slower to learn the secrets of the trade. General Pétain was one of the exceptions. His conclusion, put in somewhat more stilted language, was that the Allies couldn't blast a big enough hole in the enemy wall to pour an army through until many more Germans had been killed.

"The breach," he said, "must be twenty kilometers." That was the distance needed to leave the breakthrough force unaffected by hostile fire from the flanks. But since troops advancing under fire always converge toward the center, reacting to the instinctive craving for company in time of peril, the frontage for the opening offensive would have to be twice that, approximately twenty-five miles, with upwards of fifty divisions in the assault.

The lost battles in Artois during the spring of 1915 had fallen far short of these figures. They failed because, as the attacking infantry toiled laboriously over the shell-torn middle ground (three miles of such going per day is a strong man's limit), enemy reserves were already in motion to the threatened area. By the time trenches were overcome, new trenches were under construction behind them. The whole front, except for the fire zone, could supply reserves to bulwark the new line. The active trench system could be taken because massed artillery could fragment its resistance. But once that stage was passed, the attack again deteriorated into a siege operation.

From all that had happened, Joffre reasoned that his theory on how to win the war quickly was correct, and that failure had come because of faulty application by his subordinates. "Artois had taught me," he wrote, "that simultaneous operations by several armies would prevent the enemy from making full use of his reserves and force him to accept battle with limited means." That was how he was enthusing about the idea in early August, 1915, one month before the Czar replaced the Grand Duke. So the autumnal carnage on the Western Front can hardly be justified as a necessity forced on the Allies by the mounting distress in Russia. Joffre hit because he dreamed that he could win. When he sought Sir John's cooperation, the Field Marshal replied noncommittally, as if at last assailed by doubts. Joffre named Pétain his favored instrument to handle the main battle in the Champagne, and Pétain was laden with tactical misgivings. Sir John called on Douglas Haig, who also looked askance at the assignment, protesting that the slag-heaped, pitted, and heavily fortified area around Loos was no place for an attack. Kitchener, who had damned the blood baths in the spring, was all for another such trial in the autumn. It was a camp strangely divided.

Pétain took over a fifteen-mile front in the Champagne, and was given thirty-five divisions, or about one-half million men for his handling—large figures, but still not enough. This region

Against the backdrop of a burning Polish
village, Austrian soldiers, burdened
with arms, field packs, and bulging sacks
(perhaps filled with the loot all armies
deny taking), continue their devastating
advance through Galicia, May–September,
1915. Some four million Poles were killed
or made homeless by this brutal campaign.

of chalk flats and shallow, treeless meadows was the ideal stage for an infantry massing and the concentrating of a vast artillery. There are no natural defenses in the countryside; to get protection, troops had to dig in as far back as where the reserves assembled. So a great reticulation of ditches had to be spaded, with communications trenches running three to five miles long, and all this work went on in sight of the Germans, who held slightly higher ground. There could be no surprise about what was coming, but only the question of when. Apart from tactics, there was a strategic reason for the choice of scene. The Western Front was not a straight line but a salient, with Champagne forming a reentrant bulge on its southern face not far from the apex. A breakthrough there might cut the enemy's rail communications running across northern France from Menin to Verdun. That done, the Germans would have to retire to Belgium.

The greatest of Joffre's attempts to break the German Army with one blow got under way on September 22 with a full-throated roar from 900 heavy and 1,600 light guns. The bombardment continued three days. Verdun, even, had been stripped of its fortress batteries to compound the fury. Boasting about it, Joffre got off a proclamation to his troops: *"Votre élan sera irrésistible!"* It found an echo in at least one heart. Alan Seeger was in the line. He mused: "A terrific cannonade has been going on all night. I expect to march right up the Aisne borne on in an irresistible *élan*. It will be the greatest moment of my life. I shall take good care to live up to it." Alas, a few days later, he was writing: "Our regiment has been decimated though many of us have not fired a shot."

It had happened to many other regiments. The infantry attacked on the morning of September 25 in a blinding rain. Nonetheless, the bands played the *Marseillaise* at the jump-off and fifers trilled amid the troops as they sloshed and skidded forward. There were great expectations. Arms were carried sloped, so confident were the generals that the enemy defenses had been pulverized. Little hurt, the French swept right on over the German outpost line, made the first line, and insectors cut through as far as the second and third trenches. Then the attack began to bog down as death, wounds, and sheer physical exhaustion neutralized all that marvelous *élan*. The Germans had well husbanded most of their men and firepower farther to the rear and their might came to bear only after the ripe, eager target's expanse lay fully revealed in the open. "Our role," wrote Seeger, "was to lie passive in an open field under a shell fire that every hour grew more terrible, while airplanes and captive balloons, to which we were entirely exposed, regulated the fire." And Seeger's regiment was still back in the reserve, not yet committed.

It went on for ten days, although the show was really over with the first act. Toward the end, a French consolidation over an eight-mile front was effected to strike the German second position. There was another preparatory bombardment. It blew off in air. The Germans were safely bunkered in on the reverse slopes of hills immune to any but high-angle fire. Troops had gone stale, sensing after the first eight hours that nothing of heroic consequence worth the sacrifice remained to be won. So when the second organized assault died, the enemy's improvised bastion stood intact, and it remained only to measure the trophies and the cost. What France heard was that a great victory had been won, and a bag of 25,000 prisoners and 150 field guns certified it. What was carefully kept hidden from the country was that 145,000 Frenchmen had been cut down in the Champagne offensive, which had yielded no strategic advantage whatever.

By the time Joffre cried: "Hold! Enough!" he had no choice. His artillery had leveled its own dumps, having fired, 4,967,000 rounds in one battle, which is enough to feed a war the size of Korea. His only significant comment on the denouement was: "These figures show what progress had been made in the supply of munitions." He could afford to play it cool, for his soldiers remained a loyal lot, more generous with their blood than with their sous. Père Joffre still ran his empire with an iron hand. The Government was allowed to know nothing of his plans. Deputies were shouldered off when they tried to visit the front or were shown only what he wished them to see. Generals who conversed with politicians were sharply disciplined. Even War Minister Millerand feebly lamented: "The Zone of the Armies is not my province. General Joffre does not want it invaded by civilians."

Falkenhayn had rushed back from the Eastern Front to direct the German defense. He need not have bothered. There was no major emergency. In Artois, the Franco-British offensive, which got off on the same day as the Champagne attack, fared little better. General d'Urbal's Tenth French Army and Haig's First

British Army were the flag carriers. So in the combined attack there were eighteen French divisions and thirteen British. Ferdinand Foch was the overall coordinator. The grand objective was little different from the aspirations in the campaign of the spring. The French were to conquer Vimy Ridge, a rather flat-topped feature rising only four hundred feet above sea level, but important because it was high enough to command the railway running from Lens to Arras. The British were to attack convergently toward the mining village of Loos. Provided both strokes cut clean, the combined weight could then break through to Lens, beat the Germans back from the lateral railroad, dominate the Douai plain, and possibly capture Lille. Had everything the planner extrapolated come to pass, the push still would not have won the war. Artois was a sideshow, which in the castle-building by Joffre's staff would prevent the Germans from shifting forces from their right flank to stiffen the Champagne defense in the decisive hour. It now seems weird that planners could thus faultily calculate cause and effect. German forces on the Artois front were already thin and far-stretched. Besides that, Artois was a grotesquely cut-up country, repulsive to the infantryman's eye and morale, unlike the terrain of the Champagne region, which leveled off invitingly.

Confronting part of the French sector was an area called the Labyrinth, best described by a soldier who knew it: "Behind its slight sky line was dead ground where soldiers could mass without being seen. From the ferroconcrete blockhouses of the Labyrinth, which lay no higher than many of the chalk parapets of the maze, the ground held by the French was overlooked for a long way. With its machine-gun cupolas, its deep dugouts and belts of wire, its trench system, like the web of a garden spider, the Labyrinth was one of the many tragedies of the French people." Henri Barbusse was one of the *poilus* sent against the Labryinth. He survived it to write his shocking book, *Le Feu*, which, published a few months later, epitomized the infantryman's agony on the Western Front, his feeling of being trapped beyond chance of escape. From his throne nearer heaven, General Haig had no such view, but he looked at the ground that his men had to take short of Loos and gave Sir John French the word that "a rapid advance would be impossible." When that was reported to

Joffre, he replied that Haig would "find particularly favorable ground between Loos and La Bassée." Be geography what it may, there was no stopping Joffre.

So came the battle. Just before it tipped off, Kitchener visited Saint-Omer to give Sir John and Sir Douglas his deep-freeze version of a pep talk. The terrain remained obdurate. The attack was preceded by the usual "crushing bombardment." The French almost won the crown of Vimy Ridge during the first three days, only to recoil after the weather turned sour. When they broke off, they were 18,000 prisoners ahead, and 190,000 additional Frenchmen were in the hands either of the burial squads or of the nurses. For the British, it was what their average trooper might have called a bloody go. They liberated Loos, which was no great trophy, and in getting it they spent 60,000 soldiers. Strategically, the Allies were no better off than before. Officially, the German losses in Artois were counted at 178,000.

The battle, in the end, put the skids under Sir John French; or rather, Sir John, by playing a silly game, gratuitously rid the B.E.F. of his presence. It was bound to happen anyway because Sir John was too full of contempt, watered by fear for his own position. His downfall came from what should have been a small thing in the management of a battle doomed to be lost anyway— the handling of reserves. There were three divisions of them, two from Kitchener's New Army, and that superb body from the top drawer, the Guards. Having passed to Sir Douglas Haig the buck for the battle, to win or lose it all, Sir John kept the reserves in his own palm, then stationed them so far back that they must perforce dissipate their power on the road in getting forward to the battle line. It was an asinine disposition; after all, what are reserves for? Sir Douglas handled his hitting forces deftly enough and achieved certain local successes that might have been compounded into great gains, had more troops been present to throw in. But Sir John held on to his reserves too long. Then when he released them, they were too far back to exploit the fleeting moment; and when they got forward (except for the Guards), they were too worn down. Sir Douglas quite rightly was provoked.

Sir John posted off to London to mend his fences. Obviously inspired by the presence, an article appeared in the *Times* signed by French's confidant, Colonel Charles A'Court Repington, expressing regret that Sir John had not personally commanded

In September, 1916, David Lloyd George
(right), who had recently become Secretary
of State for War, visited Joffre and Sir
Douglas Haig on the Western Front to assess
the situation firsthand. Looking on at
left is the robust Albert Thomas, French
Minister of Armaments.

at Loos; then things would have been so much better. That was too much for Haig. He wrote his commander a letter demanding that the facts concerning the reserves be made of record. Sir John took to his bed for several days and then sent Haig a letter saying, "This correspondence shall forthwith cease." But it was too late to hush the affair. The quarrel between the champion and the contender was now in the open. The ministers, including Kitchener, and the King moved over to Haig's side. By the end of the year Sir John was out and Sir Douglas was installed in his place.

Sir Douglas was of the whisky-making Haigs. What is to be marked of his earlier career is that the rate of rise was in disproportion to the brilliance. He failed his tests for Camberley Staff College. Because the Duke of Cambridge was a good friend of Haig's sister Henrietta, he got the appointment anyway. Later he married Dorothy Vivian, maid of honor to Queen Alexandra. None of this proved a handicap, especially when he looked the part of a dashing soldier. As a subordinate staff officer, he had helped finance Sir John French out of difficulty. Sir John's gratitude lasted quite a while. Haig was cold as ice. Between him and the troops there was no bond of sympathetic understanding. But it would be unfair to say that anyone excelled him in the art of getting ahead.

There was a last painful scene between French and Haig. Sir John had only one thing to say, one request to make: "Will you give Winston Churchill a battalion?" Asquith had recently dumped him from the cabinet; true to his nature, Churchill had asked for a command in the battle line. Weighing his talents and experience, Sir John thought that Churchill was at least entitled to the command of a brigade. Incredible as it now seems, the Prime Minister gagged on that, Lloyd George whispering in his ear that if Churchill were so honored, there might be a public outcry. So the issue was held in suspension until Haig pondered it. The future Prime Minister and Honorary Citizen of the United States was at last given his battalion and took his place in the rifle line. Rifle bullets were never afforded a better opportunity to thwart history.

Sir William Robertson, a gifted military administrator who had risen from the ranks, had been Sir John's Chief of Staff during the closing months. He was now summoned to London to take over as Chief of the Imperial General Staff. Reporting, he put it straight to Kitchener: he would not move in as CIGS unless the full duties of that office, which Kitchener had in large part usurped, were restored. Kitchener at first agreed, then bridled, threatening resignation, alarmed that his own authority was being scuttled. Robertson kept pressing and at last got it in writing; "All orders for military operations should be signed and issued by the CIGS under the authority of the War Council and not under that of the Army Council."

By December 23 Sir William was settling in his new chair and Kitchener was passing into eclipse. Wrote Robertson gratefully: "He showed a genuine desire that everything should go as smoothly as possible." London's impression in that hour was that the Allies could count on another six months of respite to prepare for one more Herculean effort. The guess was 180 degrees off reality. What made it so was that Falkenhayn was reacting to the war strain like a man haunted by a death wish.

VII
Ordeal of Nations

In this ink drawing, *The Harvest Is Ripe*,
the Dutch artist Raemaekers shows the Grim
Reaper at work in Flanders, August, 1914.

234

General Falkenhayn spent his 1915 Christmas holidays brooding as he penned for the Kaiser an estimate of the problems confronting Germany.

His paper ranged over the war's entire panorama, and whereas in most communications he spoke of himself in the third person or by title, this time it was "I say" or "I believe." Yet there are few stranger documents than this one in the war's archives. It is the reasoning of a soldier at cross-purposes with his own inner convictions.

Germany, he pointed out, could not win a long-drawn-out war because its manpower reserves were too thin. England was the Great Adversary. But there was no way to get at England. So, what was to be done? While there were still troops to afford a concentration, Germany must launch a battle that would bleed France white, compel her capitulation, and thereby collapse the Alliance.

To meet these conditions, the target would have to be either vital to the integrity of the Allied front or sacred emotionally to the French. Two such targets were Belfort and Verdun. Falkenhayn favored Verdun because it was within twenty kilometers of the main railway supporting the German front and if captured would ease that worry.

This was Falkenhayn's brief for staging the greatest battle in world history and doing it in the dead of winter. It ignored every lesson that the same man had drawn from his own failures in the two great battles at Ypres. Believing in those lessons, he had risked thinning his own armies of the Western Front in the ratio of one to three throughout the summer of 1915, and the Allied offensive failures had proved his judgment sound.

Falkenhayn was convinced that the fortified front could not be decisively penetrated. He reasoned that when such an attempt was made the attacker must always bleed more than the defender. In accord with these propositions, Germany's main chance could only be to conserve forces and let the Allies continue their suicidal attacks. Yet his paper argued that France's will could be broken in one great battle of attrition, though protection must favor the French. In his paper, Falkenhayn was not honest about that. He said to Wilhelm that he would attack and still lose only one third as many soldiers as the enemy.

The motives of this tormented mind, while complex, are not inscrutable. Falkenhayn saw no chance to win. He was surrounded by a court bent on nothing less. He had not, like Hindenburg, the gift of forgetting everything except the immediate operations problem; he was more aware than Ludendorff of the dangerous inner workings of world politics. To his gaze, the Western Front deadlock was a monstrous absurdity. Yet confronted with it, the antagonists continued to harden. Very well, then, he would stage one battle, so terrible in its dimensions, so shattering in its impact on both camps, that governments and peoples would be shocked into making peace on terms short of ruin for Germany. If in the light of what followed that was proved a vain hope, it was not the most tragic or inhuman miscalculation made by a World War I high commander.

On Christmas Eve, wrote Falkenhayn, "it was decided to give effect to the views that had crystallized out of this process of reasoning." The operation was given the code name *Gericht*, meaning place of execution. In Berlin, carolers were abroad singing of peace on earth.

Gericht was scheduled to start on February 12, 1916. The German Crown Prince's Fifth Army, which had been confronting Verdun since the Battle of the Marne, would deal the blow. Neither the Crown Prince nor his Chief of Staff, General Schmidt von Knobelsdorf, got to see Falkenhayn's memorandum prepared for the Kaiser. To them he addressed only a directive calling somewhat vaguely for "an offensive in the Meuse area in the direction of Verdun." They took this to mean that he wanted the fortress captured, and the Army Staff set about preparing plans based on that assumption. Falkenhayn had no such idea, for if the city fell quickly the battle would die down, and the "rivers of blood" would cease to flow.

Nothing about Verdun is as astonishing as the speed with which the German Army rearrayed its power, once the decision was taken. That the tremendous shift was brought about without detection is hardly less remarkable. Never before nor since was there such massing of artillery within one limited sector. For Falkenhayn had decided against an attack across the whole front of Verdun. The attack would be directed only against French positions on the east bank of the Meuse, which on its northern course cuts the city in twain. Falkenhayn stated his arguments in defense of this strategy. The frozen and swamplike Woëvre Plain delimited the hitting sector on the east bank; the Argonne wilderness bound it on the other side. That still left a relatively clear thirty-mile sector for the assault on both sides of the river. But this he did not want because he intended to manage the battle. He would keep the area of eruption limited by holding onto the general reserves and keeping them at a distance elsewhere on the Western Front. That would force the Crown Prince to continue the attack on a narrow front of about five to seven miles, which eliminated any possibility of breakthrough. As the forces in the attack became expended, Falkenhayn would release their divisions to the Fifth Army, just enough to keep the battle going but never enough to end it. In this way, the Crown Prince would be compelled to fight with one hand tied. A more diabolical plan is beyond imagining. Falkenhayn's object was to get as many people killed as possible.

During January, 1916, 542 heavy guns, 306 light field pieces, and 152 giant mine throwers were concentrated on the narrow Verdun sector. But these were not the usual corps support heavies. There were brought in thirteen 420-mm. mortars, the Big Berthas throwing the one-ton projectiles that had battered Liège and Antwerp. There were also two 15-inch naval guns, seventeen Austrian 305-mm. mortars, called Beta guns, many quick-firing 210's, some long 150's, and seven batteries of 130-mm. "whizzbangs," the greatest frayers of infantry nerves, because their shells came at a man like bullets, with no warning sound. Most of these, and the giant mine throwers, were in addition to the heavy weapons organic to the units of the Fifth Army. Each type had its particular mission in the pounding of the forts, the shelling of the fortress city, the destruction of communications, and the pinning of French infantry to its trenches. To feed the batteries, there were stockpiled close to three million shells, or enough to supply the guns all around through six days of continued fire. Five new narrow-gauge railway lines had to be built across the Fifth Army's operating zone to get weapons and ammunition to the appointed positions. At the end of January the Crown Prince reported to Falkenhayn that the artillery was emplaced.

The German buildup—six new infantry divisions and the forest of guns—somehow remained invisible to the French. Joffre and the French High Council for National Defense met in Paris on February 8. All present agreed that a German offensive in the near future was unlikely. If a surprise was to come, the stage would probably be Flanders. But that chance was so heavily discounted that the Allies would be advised to make preparation for the summer offensives their first order of business. The Historical Section of the French General Staff provided comforting words. The contending sides were now approximately equal in the count of men under arms, balanced at six million. The Allies had 132 divisions on the Western Front, thirty-one of them being in reserve. It was calculated as a safe margin, the Allied superiority offsetting the German advantage in operating on interior lines.

But there were at least two Frenchmen soldiering at Verdun who did not hold this roseate view. One was the artilleryman General Herr, who commanded the entire fortified zone. He sifted reports about intensified activity in the line opposite, and his intelligence people noted a great increase in enemy traffic on the Meuse railroads. The other was Lieutenant Colonel Emile Driant, an ex-Regular, who had retired and been elected a Deputy from the Verdun district, then had been recalled to duty as a reservist, and, by a strange irony, had been posted to a battalion holding one of the most exposed forward positions covering the fortress. Driant knew what his soldier's eyes told him: the Germans opposite were preparing something big. He tried to arouse higher authority, but his warnings were brushed off. Meanwhile, supported by General de Langle de Cary, who commanded the group, Herr kept pressing for reinforcements. He was given driblets, a few fighting detachments and too few pioneers to stay the erosions of the existing roads.

Why the French were deceived is precisely because the German buildup was staged over a very narrow front. Not only did most of it stay hidden, being echeloned in depth behind the Meuse ridges, but the French feared only a breakthrough, which couldn't be forged on such a small anvil. Had the mass deployment been organized on both sides of the Meuse, with many divisions shaping a power base behind twenty-five miles or so of trench line (which was what the Crown Prince repeatedly protested to Falkenhayn should be done), the defenders would have read the warning signs. But they couldn't fathom a design so insidious that it made sense only to the dark mind of Falkenhayn; the French were fooled, being unable to rationalize the irrational.

Verdun itself was no longer an entrenched camp. Because of its natural strength, the French counted on holding it, despite the fact that most of the guns had been sent away, the revetments were falling apart, and the garrison was victim of the sloth that settles upon troops in a quiet sector. Being the cap of a salient, the fortress was wholly unsuitable for mounting offensive operations. For that reason, fewer soldiers stood guard at Verdun during 1915 than in time of peace.

Above the trench of the Meuse, covering the face of the city, are the heights of Belrupt, La Chaume, Saint Michel, and Souville, They seat the forts of Marre and Vacherauville on the west bank, and of Douaumont, Vaux, and Tavannes on the east. Douaumont is the hub of the system. But there were many more minor works spread along the four natural lines of defense guarding the city over a radius of five to ten miles. At least twenty forts and forty strong-walled redoubts were in the reticulation. but after the shattering of Liège and Antwerp, French G.Q.G. had swung over to the new view that ring forts had become deathtraps for their inmates. So the cannon, for the most part, were trucked off, to be used in mobile battles that had everything but mobility The despoliation in midfield is described by Pétain: "Between the forts and beyond them was only desolation. Innumerable trenches, many of which had fallen in, and broken barbed wire entanglements covered with an impenetrable labyrinth the ragged wood . . . and the muddy flats."

Such was Verdun on the eve. General Chrétien, the new corps commander, soon to take over and bear the brunt, called it *"un terrain à catastrophe."* It need not have been. Soldiers were doomed because sentiment was blind and generals were dumb. In its dilapidated state, Verdun had ceased to be a major bastion, worth the spending of an army. Falkenhayn had no awareness that the French had let it decay. But he calculated rightly that they would never willingly yield it, whatever their other follies. So live legions were spent to save dead ground and reburnish stale glory. Attila had once burned the city. There the heirs of Charlemagne had signed the treaty by which they had divided Europe among them. The great Vauban, from whom all French military engineers descend, had employed his architectural genius

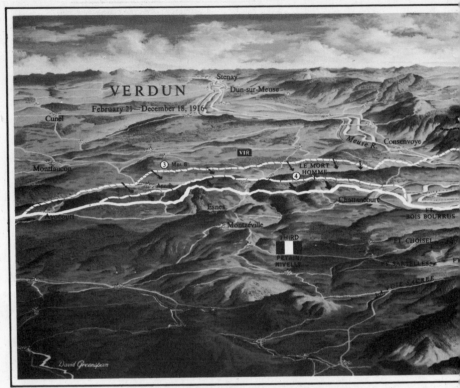

On February 21, 1916, the initial German
assault at Verdun (German advances shown as
black arrows) struck the French (1, broken
white line) east of the Meuse. Four days
later, Fort Douaumont (2) fell. On March 6
the German drive was extended west of the
Meuse (3), and by April 9 substantial gains
had been made on both sides of the river
(second broken white line). Through May
heavy fighting raged about *Le Mort Homme*

(4) and Hill 304, two miles west. Final
German victories east of the Meuse included
the capture in June of Fort Vaux (5) and
the Thiaumont Works. By August 8, the
Germans had made their deepest penetration
(solid white line). In October, the French
counterattacked (white arrows), retaking
Vaux and Douaumont and advancing two miles
(6, solid black line). By December, 1916, the
French had recovered most of the ground lost.

to convert it into the place unconquerable. There were other precious reasons, familiar only to scholars, for resolving a stand there to pale Thermopylae.

But beyond sentiment, there was no reason at all. By February, 1916, Verdun was no longer an indispensable anchor of the Allied front. It was far enough removed from Paris so that its loss would not have induced a convulsive change in any direction. Along the French-held front, in fact, there could have been a power-saving line shortening. The main rail line leading south from Verdun had already been cut by the Germans near Saint Mihiel. The north-facing forts would have been useless to the Germans. There were no great stores of matériel present to change hands. So in hard terms, the stakes for Joffre were as intangible as the stakes for Falkenhayn.

CONSCRIPTION IN BRITAIN

As Germany girded for Operation *Gericht*, Great Britain at last faced up to the universal service issue.

By January, 1916, approximately one million British males had entered war service voluntarily, and approximately 400,000 had been lost in battle. To fill the gaps, some 5,000 volunteers were needed every week. But in addition to the losses in action, there was another drain. The Armed Forces were still operating under peacetime law. Regulars had not been frozen in their jobs; when their terms of enlistment expired, they were free to return to civilian life. Right through the summer of 1916, an average of 5,000 NCO's and privates bailed out of the army in this manner each month. The figures on intake made it clear that either the nation would adopt conscription for the first time in its history or the B.E.F. would ultimately be decimated by death and wounds.

Prior to the forming of the Coalition Government in May, 1915, the Tories had spoken up somewhat half-heartedly for conscription, but had then let the question die. Lloyd George was its most vocal champion, though his Liberal Party was against it. Their ministers, believing that it was Kitchener's duty to take the lead, stayed circumspectly silent. The Field Marshal himself maintained a sphinxlike silence, reiterating that he would need seventy British divisions in the field to implement the great design for 1916, without ever suggesting how they might be raised.

Asquith's pressure on Kitchener was responsible for the latter's failure to take a stand. Kitchener was in his debt politically and Asquith knew how to stake a claim on loyalty. He abhorred conscription, mainly because Lloyd George wanted it, and also he feared that he might lose office over the issue. So Kitchener stayed aloof while Asquith went ahead with a crackbrained idea called the Derby Scheme, which was supposed to obviate the need for conscription. Its farcical results led to the draft.

Lord Derby was Director General of Recruiting. To keep voluntary service alive he proposed that on a given day all males of fighting age should register and certify their willingness to serve if called. Married men would not be called until the supply of bachelors was exhausted.

So on the appointed hour, hundreds of thousands of married men visited the booths to attest their patriotism, confident that they would not be called. But a million able-bodied bachelors remained at home; government's hot breath was too close to their necks. These not unnatural reactions ruined the Derby Scheme.

The debate on conscription in the House of Commons was unexpectedly short, and after the second reading on January 12 the measure was passed 533 to 41. The act also received widespread popular approval and press support. One feature of the bill added a new term to the English language. Alternatives to front line duty were provided for persons classed as "Conscientious Objectors." One London newspaper gave it a banner headline: "New Name for Slackers—Conscientious Objectors."

There were too many loopholes in Britain's first draft act; there had been too little honest surveillance of the manpower requirement. Asquith saw to it that the Military Service Act that passed in January exempted all married men and single men who would claim dependents. Thus, when four months later only a little more than one million additional soldiers had come under training, it was evident that the numbers would not be sufficient to power the ambitious operations already scheduled for the summer. For it had been agreed by Britain, France, and Russia that 1916 would be the year of the supreme effort to roll back the Germans and end the war. The British had already decided where they would stage their great show and knew more or less what size host would be needed to feed the battle. Haig and his generals had long been dreaming of collision on the Somme.

There was a delay in the German attack due to thick fogs along the Meuse. In the respite, G.Q.G. at last got a bit nervous about the rumors from the north and posted a couple more divisions to Verdun. On February 12 the Crown Prince talked big to his soldiers: "The iron will of the sons of Germany is still unbroken and the German Army, when it moves to attack, stops for no obstacle."

Two days of full-scale bombardment—then the shock divisions were to reap the harvest of chaos. With all guns speaking till the crews stopped from exhaustion, the Germans really expected to create a zone of death (their term) where no Frenchman drew breath. Beginning early on the morning of February 21, over a six-mile front, two million shells were thrown at the narrow triangle defined by Brabant, Ornes, and Verdun. These were ingenious fires, mixing shrapnel, high explosive, and poison gas, the block-busting projectiles being reserved for the forts. Ravines, forests, trenches, and redoubts were all worked over. The shells came down at the rate of 100,000 rounds per hour. French forward trenches were obliterated. Survivors went for the woods, to die amid the splintering trees.

Colonel Driant lived on a few hours to rally the forward survivors for a last shot at the Germans. All that was left of his 1,200-man command in the Caures Wood by the second day were seven wounded lieutenants and about one hundred Chasseurs. They had lived long enough to baffle the enemy. Just before dusk of the first day the German infantry came forward cautiously in packets of skirmishers, not so much to assault as to take over the abattoir. They expected to cross a passive field of mangled corpses and crazed derelicts. Instead, Frenchmen black as stokers, uniforms ripped off, looking more like scarecrows than soldiers, stirred amid the desolation and pumped away with their rifles. The Germans should have known that artillery by itself can never saturate and silence an entrenched resistance. Having lasted twelve hours that day, the bombardment resumed the following morning. The iron storm—not the iron will—delivered to Germany the frontal trenches on opening day. But that was all. The lines held.

It could not stay that way for long. By night of February 24, Verdun itself seemed in imminent danger, as the French saw it, though Falkenhayn, by withholding reserves from the battle, insured its continued defense on his own mad terms. That gave the Frenchmen in the trench line and the High Command at Chantilly time in which to recover from the initial shock. When the battle opened, the closest French front line was eight miles north of the city; the Germans got to within four miles of the city before the month was out. By the third day they had 10,000 French prisoners, 65 cannon, and 75 machine guns. On February 24 they stormed and took the French secondary system of trenches. Always the bombardment moved ahead of them, collapsing trenches, shattering pillboxes and redoubts, and crushing survivors to death. That night General Chrétien, who comanded the French XX Corps on the crumbling front, checked his losses and knew that he was finished. Divisions were cut to one-third strength, which meant that practically all infantrymen were dead, wounded, or taken prisoner. Artillery battalions were down to one or two guns per battery. Not one rifle company remained in reserve. That night also General Balfourier took over the sector from Chrétien. But most of the troops forming his XXX Corps were still on the road.

On the afternoon of February 25, the 24th Brandenburgers of General von Lochow's III Corps attacked and won Fort Douaumont, the keystone of the whole massive ferroconcrete arch supporting Verdun. It was not a blood-and-iron triumph. Although Douaumont had come through the iron tempest practically unhurt, the French, by monumental carelessness, had almost stripped it of defenders. In prewar days, five hundred infantrymen and twoscore artillerymen manned the fort and its outworks. When Joffre uttered the dictum that forts were useless, that quota was cut to fifty-six territorial gunners under one Sergeant Major Chenot. The intense pressures of the siege of Verdun wiped Douaumont from the minds of French higher commanders. No reinforcement was sent to it. The inept detachment waited within the walls for whatever came, unset to do anything about it. So the great prize fell to the Brandenburgers like manna.

The same day, General Pétain, then with his staff at Noailles, was ordered posthaste to Chantilly. Joffre told him Douaumont had fallen, then passed him along to General de Castelnau, with the task of organizing the Verdun defense. De Castelnau put it to him: "You must avoid errors like the one committed this day." Pétain moved fast. Just before midnight he assumed com-

To stem the German tide at Verdun, France
sent an unending column of men. Over two
million fought during the ten months of
battle there. "My heart leapt as I saw our
youths of twenty going into the furnace of
Verdun," wrote General Pétain. "But... when
they returned... their expressions... seemed
frozen by a vision of terror; their gait...
betrayed a total dejection; they sagged
beneath the weight of horrifying memories."

mand while still leagues distant from Verdun.

On the telephone he said to Balfourier: "General Pétain speaking. I am taking over. Inform your troops. Keep up your courage. I know I can depend on you."

Balfourier answered: "Very well, sir, we shall bear up. You can rely on us, as we rely on you."

The right man had at last come to his greatest scene. Verdun's defense from that hour forward was dramatically reenergized. Until the early morning hours, Pétain sat with his Chief of Staff, General de Barescut. In charcoal, on a map pasted on the Town Hall wall at Souilly, he sketched the sectors already won by the Crown Prince and the areas for which he could be expected to strike next. Then he dictated the orders that were to be delivered to all of the holding forces by sunup.

That was how he took control, still not knowing that he had sped toward the Germans at their high tide. The German offensive would go on for another four months. But while no one sensed it, the great crisis was past.

Falkenhayn was satisfied. He had "shaken the whole enemy front in the West very severely, and the effects were not lost on the peoples and Governments of the Entente." But even as the Crown Prince toasted the fall of Douaumont, he must have had his reservations about what still confronted his army. He had hazarded that he would have Verdun by the fourth day. The sixth sun was now rising and he was still far short.

The advent of General Pétain at Verdun on February 25 coincided with a logistical half-pause in the battle. Both sides were spent. German ammunition dumps had emptied and French supply of all kinds was at bottom, due no more to the excessive fire rates than to the destruction of depots and the choke in the roads. Pétain saw that his main task was to establish adequate communications. It was an engineering job; the fighting could be left to lesser generals. Serving the decisive front were only one branch line and a narrow-gauge railway—this to supply one-half million troops and 150,000 draft animals. It couldn't be done. So Pétain rebuilt the road from Bar-le-Duc, later called *La Voie Sacrée* (the Sacred Way), and introduced into warfare the supplying of a fighting front via motor convoys manned and loaded to deliver like a moving belt. There were 3,000 trucks in the system. Altogether, sixty-six French divisions were delivered into the battle. Pétain's great contribution was not a creation of genius but of applied common sense. The exhaustion interlude enabled him to take firm hold. In that interval the trucks brought forward 27,000 tons of ammunition and other matériel and 190,000 men.

The German Fifth Army again hit hard on March 6. But the line of attack had been changed. Too late, Falkenhayn deferred to the bitter protests from below. The attack was launched west of the Meuse. That was a boon to Pétain. The enemy struck where troops were freshest and best provisioned. The Germans were forced to make this shift by the flanking cannonade from across the Meuse. The more they extended on the east bank, the more deadly became the cross fire from the west.

The blood-drenched clash around *Le Mort Homme*, a hill that was the linchpin of the west bank defenses, as Douamont had been of the east, wore dismally on. The battle's ghastly terms remained inexorable: kill as many men as necessary to take or defend a little ground although it might have no importance in the last accounting. The French continued to hold *Le Mort Homme*. It was well named. Both sides spent a mountain of slain in contest for a scabrous ridge. The final full-scale German attack came on April 9, and it failed. Although the attempt did not mark the end of the battle, it was the climactic lunge of an army wearied of a plan that spelled only doom to soldiers. The Germans relapsed into nibbling tactics, taking Hill 304 at the beginning of May, *Le Mort Homme* at the end of the month, and Fort Vaux on June 2.

In mid-April, however, the French had turned to the counter-offensive. Except in German minds, that ended all doubt as to who had won the battle, and as the French gains on both banks of the Meuse extended into midsummer, the victory was recertified. The final French offensive, October 24 to December 18, was crowned with the retaking of Forts Douaumont and Vaux.

The recovery gave France a new galaxy of heroes, Pétain chief among them. Then there was a new name, General Robert Nivelle, who in late April had been given command of the French Second Army when Pétain took over the Central Army Group from Langle de Cary. Nivelle took off like a rocket, sparkling throughout the counteroffensive. From this came unlimited consequences to Father Joffre and Mother France.

The costs of Verdun are best recapitulated in cold, round figures, no exact statistics being possible, due to the battle's confusions. France lost half a million soldiers—dead, wounded, missing, prisoners. Germany lost upwards of 400,000. Approximately forty million artillery rounds were spent by the two sides during the half-year battle at Verdun. Not counting the losses from bullets, bayonets, mines, self-inflicted wounds, and all else, about two hundred artillery rounds had to be fired to take out one soldier at Verdun.

The statistic refutes the quaint notion held by General Falkenhayn and other high commanders on both sides that artillery alone can fragment an army. The earth is vast in open space and man is a very small thing upon it.

THE EASTER REBELLION

Fate played strange tricks with the life of Sir Roger Casement, an Ulster Protestant. He was a great son of liberty, who wanted freedom for everyone. Had he died in 1914, he would have been remembered as the humanitarian who had exposed the slave trade in the Congo. The war, however, led him to treason.

Traveling incognito, Sir Roger entered Germany via Norway early in the war. There he attempted to subvert Irish POW's. Many were loyal to Britain; but others were ready to cooperate and a plan was hatched to organize rebellion in Ireland.

On April 20, 1916, a German ship, loaded with arms, was taken by a British patrol craft off the Irish coast. A German U-boat put Sir Roger ashore later that same night at Kerry. What Casement didn't know was that British intelligence had had its finger on him from the time he left Germany. Stepping ashore, Sir Roger went walking to the gallows. Waiting guards pounced on him before he could make one move. It was Good Friday.

The Irish rebellion had been timed to explode when Casement landed. Sir Roger's capture upset the plans, but, nevertheless, under James O'Connell, the Citizen's Army sprang to arms in Dublin on Easter Monday, took over the Post Office, Saint Stephen's Green and Jacob's Biscuit Factory, and proclaimed the Free Irish Republic with P. H. Pearse as President. For one week there was great terror in the city. Then a British column entered Dublin and beat down the rebellion with fire.

Casement was hauled off to the Tower of London, given a formal trial under the Lord Chief Justice, and on August 3 was led to the scaffold, where he died smiling. Fifteen of his coconspirators in Dublin got short shrift—a speedy court-martial and summary execution.

Throughout America, the press raged at England for this act. That the crime was technically treason in wartime was overlooked;

Britain was blasted for "tyranny" and for "taking vengeance." From Washington the British Embassy cabled London that American sentiment for England had sunk to its wartime low.

JUTLAND

In late May the Admiralty learned through radio intercepts that a flock of German U-boats was moving to positions somewhere off the English coast. Warning messages were flashed to Admiral Sir John Jellicoe commanding the Grand Fleet at Scapa Flow and to Vice-Admiral Sir David Beatty commanding the battle cruisers at Rosyth. Both fleets put to sea on May 30 to conduct a sweep. They did not know that the German High Seas Fleet under Admiral Reinhard Scheer had risked the open seas and was steaming toward the Skagerrak, the waterway separating Norway from Denmark's Jutland Peninsula.

Under Jellicoe were twenty-eight battleships, nine battle cruisers, eight armored cruisers, twenty-six light cruisers, and seventy-eight destroyers. Scheer had twenty-two battleships, five battle cruisers, eleven light cruisers, and sixty-one destroyers and flotilla leaders.

The British first learned that they were on a collision course at 2:20 P.M. the next day, when the *Galatea* signaled that she saw two enemy vessels engaged in boarding a neutral steamer. Next came the message: "We see a large amount of smoke as from a fleet bearing E.N.E." Jellicoe then messaged Beatty to change course with his battle cruiser fleet and steam for the smoke. It was soon identified as coming from the five German battle cruisers under Admiral Hipper. The fight began at 3:48 when Beatty opened fire at 18,500 yards.

Before the hour was up the British battle cruiser *Tiger* had been hit, four shells from the *Lutzow* had crashed into Beatty's flagship *Lion*, and the *Indefatigable* had received her first wounds. She sank within thirty minutes, losing all but two crewmen. The *Queen Mary*, blown apart, went down at 4:26 P.M., with 1,266 crewmen.

All of this time Beatty was on a course designed by Scheer to lead him into the High Seas Fleet. The *Princess Royal* caught a German salvo and was mistakenly reported as blown up. But Beatty kept on going.

As the twilight thickened, Beatty pulled away, steaming north toward the Grand Fleet. The Germans followed. It became a running fight. The *Von der Tann* was knocked out of action, the

The Western Front changed little in 1916,
despite German gains (black arrows) at
Verdun and those of the Allies (white
arrows) at the Somme. Throughout the first
half of 1917, the deadlock along the front
would persist. The inset details the progress
of the Somme offensive, which spanned
four months of brutal warfare. Beginning on
July 1 (broken black line), the fighting
advanced through September 15 (thin line),
when tanks were introduced, and finally
concluded on November 19 (solid black line).

Seydlitz was set afire, and the *Lutzow* and *Derfflinger* were hard hit. At 6:16 P.M., directly across Scheer's course, capping the T of his column, the Germans saw the great array under Jellicoe. Also, Jellicoe and the fleet saw the *Lion* coming on. Rear Admiral Horace Hood raised the signal to his squadron to form single line and engage ahead of Beatty on the *Lion*. The range was about 8,600 yards. Much of the confused fight that followed is still unclear. The *Black Prince* was sunk and no witness lived to say how. The *Defence* was hit by two salvos that blew her magazines, and the ship disappeared. The *Warrior* was knocked out by shells that flooded her magazines. The *Invincible* was lost. The *Warspite* fell out with a disabled steering gear. She then drifted off in such a direction that she alone was in position to see the head of the German column turn. But the crippled ship, for some reason never revealed to the public, did not send this intelligence to Jellicoe.

Grievous wounds were also suffered by the Germans. The *Elbing* and *Frauenlob* went to the bottom, as did the *Lutzow*. The *Pommern* blew up. But by 8:00 P.M., when the British Grand Fleet at last pulled away and headed for home base on a westerly course, there was no question that Britain had taken the worst of it. That didn't wholly end the battle. The German cruisers and destroyers came on after, and the cross-water fires continued till past midnight, with further damage to both sides.

Jutland, the great naval battle of the war, gave no cheer to England. If not a defeat, it was a calamitous victory. The High Seas Fleet had struck down 117,025 tons of British warships; the Grand Fleet had sunk about 61,180 tons of German naval power. German armor had stood up better; German gunnery had shown itself more accurate. Both sides claimed a triumph. The Germans did not again venture forth. For England, that was the only entry on the bright side. It afforded little comfort.

THE DEATH OF KITCHENER

Since the beginning of the war, Lord Kitchener had maintained a steady correspondence with the Grand Duke Nicholas, a soldier he much admired. As a result of this communion there came to him in mid-May a personal invitation from the Czar to visit Russia and see the fighting fronts. Kitchener at once replied, "Nothing would give me greater pleasure," and since his cabinet colleagues were equally pleased that he planned an absence, there was nothing thereafter to reverse his decision. Even the King and the Prime Minister felt that they could get along without him. So low was his stock at this time that the House of Commons actually considered a motion to reduce his salary.

One of Kitchener's final acts before departure was to square accounts with the House of Commons, setting May 31 as a day when the members could call on him and question his conduct of affairs limitlessly. So many MP's showed up that the inquisition had to be moved from the War Office to a larger hall. Kitchener performed nobly, astonishing all hands by his straightforwardness. Proud as a peacock, he went round to the King and later to Mr. Asquith, who found him "gay, alert, elastic, sanguine." Within a few minutes of that, the celebrants were getting the news of Jutland.

Four days later Kitchener was at Scapa Flow, aboard the *Iron Duke*, getting a firsthand account of how Jutland had been fought from Admiral Sir John Jellicoe, who still didn't understand it very well. Lunch finished, Kitchener boarded the cruiser *Hampshire*, which was to take him to Archangel. The weather was impossibly foul when the *Hampshire* weighed anchor. Later in the evening as the gale increased in fury, the cruiser detached its destroyer escort, not far from the Orkneys.

One week before, the German submarine *U-75*, on its way to the rendezvous at Jutland, had laid half a dozen mines off Marwick Head in the Orkneys. The object of Commander Kurt Beitzen had been to interfere with the British concentration prior to the naval action. It was there, plowing one of the exits from Scapa Flow, one mile from shore, that at 7:40 P.M. on June 5 the *Hampshire* hit one of Beitzen's mines.

She heeled over to starboard and went down in fifteen minutes. Only twelve men aboard the *Hampshire* ever made it to shore; they landed on a bleak part of the coast where the cliffs are steep; all were so shaken that no coherent account of the tragedy immediately came forth. Kitchener was never seen again. The sea had claimed what was left of the Great Man.

By noon of the next day London got the word that Kitchener must be dead. To the benumbed masses it was unbelievable. The mission to Russia had been kept a close-guarded secret. How could Kitchener be drowned at sea when he had never gone away? Rumors arose and thickened that he was not really dead but a prisoner of the Germans, that he had been kidnaped out of Britain, that he was safe in solitude on some remote is-

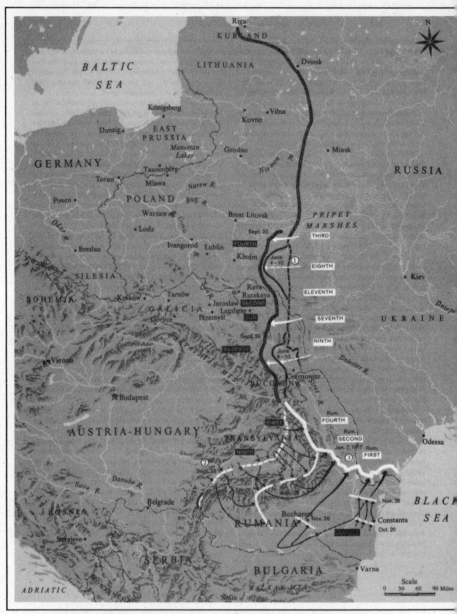

Eastern Front, 1916: Russia (1, white arrows) breaks the
Austrian lines as far as the solid black line. Rumania invades
Transylvania (2) and reaches the broken white line. Germany
(black arrows) forces Rumania back to the solid white line (3).

land, shaping his master plan to win the war.

One man not benumbed by the news of the death, though Kitchener was his friend and sponsor, was Sir Douglas Haig. He received the news while at Boulogne, waiting for a channel boat, and merely noted in his diary: "Ship struck a mine and sank. Sea very rough." Rather a cold fish, this Scotsman, soon to launch his soldiers against the Somme.

There was nothing reserved, however, in the reaction of Kitchener's fellow ministers. They shed their public tears and then started maneuvering toward the empty chair. Asquith could not forbear lamenting the ghoulishness of it in a letter to the King's Secretary, Lord Stamfordham: "All this canvassing and wire-pulling about the succession while poor K's body is still tossing about in the North Sea seems to me in the highest degree indecent." For weeks while the intriguing went on the Prime Minister held the portfolio. The winner almost inevitably was Lloyd George, who kept threatening to resign from the Government as a tactic toward taking it over. Bonar Law put his influence behind the Welshman, but General Sir "Wully" Robertson opposed him every step of the way. He didn't want a strong man in the War Ministry; having struggled to cut Kitchener's powers to the vanishing point, he couldn't see refighting a battle already won. After this duel these two figures were everlastingly at loggerheads; and, in the years that followed, divided counsel at the summit of strategy was the consequence. All too soon Lloyd George was to write: "My position in the Ministry is an anomalous one as I am completely out of sympathy with the spirit of the war direction. I feel we cannot win on these lines."

But he had been "out of sympathy" all along. Capable of atrocious blunders and misjudgments, Lloyd George at the same time was the one minister to take the blood-sweat-and-tears attitude toward the war. He objected equally to the soft approach of his political colleagues and to the toplofty arrogance of the generals. Due to his insistence, Britain had at last adopted a conscription law without escape hatches. The generals were getting what they wanted—every available able-bodied man and some not so able-bodied.

Lloyd George got the War Ministry because, in effect, there was not another suitable candidate. In a popularity contest he would have run last. Distrusted by Asquith, disliked by the King, loathed by the brass hats, rarely praised by the press, he still possessed that quality of single-mindedness essential to getting on with the terrible business at hand.

Lloyd George was one of the more contradictory figures among the earthshakers of that time. He possessed, as Churchill noted, the high attribute of being able to start each day with a clean slate, his mind refusing to dwell on the mistakes of yesterday. In the season when conscription was passed, he was also bent on reforming Britain's alcoholic ways, believing that the over-consumption of Guinness and Haig impaired the war effort. So in a moment of inspiration, he went to the King and convinced His Majesty that he should take the pledge for the remainder of the war, a noble example that, after the sacrifice became publicized, was supposed to win all of the British people to voluntary prohibition.

George V did his part. Wines, beer, and hard liquor were outlawed at Buckingham Palace and in the the other royal cottages for the duration. The great news was spread far and wide. Thereafter nothing happened. Englishmen continued to take their "usual," except as new laws somewhat restricted drinking hours. Stage by stage, throughout the war, Britain tightened toward greater sacrifices—but not this one.

Lord Derby went in as Lloyd George's Under-Secretary, and he was an odd one. He despised Sir John French and interposed to keep him off the War Selection Board, proposing instead Rudyard Kipling "because he has a very infinite knowledge of the working classes," which, if accurate, was still irrelevant. Derby also distrusted Churchill (who had returned to London after four months in the front lines), and wrote of him: "Absolutely untrustworthy, as was his father before him; as his father had to disappear from politics, so must he." A great racing name, but he couldn't pick winners.

The French, who, unlike the British, could make cabinet shifts both promptly and painlessly, now had a Government headed by Aristide Briand. Here at last was a man not afraid to fire away at Joffre.

THE BIG PUSH

History offers the explanation that the Battle of the Somme had to be fought as it was by the British to save the French Army from the crucifixion of Verdun.

It doesn't wash. In a letter to Haig on December 30, 1915,

Joffre first mentioned that a great battle would have to be staged on the Somme when the change in seasons and the manpower picture favored it.

Haig was all for mounting a great battle; but he was all against having it on the Somme front, preferring Flanders. The Somme sector had been quiet ever since First Marne, and the enemy had taken advantage of the inactivity. The German line extending both ways from the Somme River had been made impregnably strong, and the chalk hills overlooking the Allied trenches had become a catacomb. Massively timbered dugouts, rebutted with concrete and equipped with electric lighting, were serviced with an underground reticulation of laundries, aid stations, repair shops and arsenals. Life was relatively good there. The Germans didn't wish to be disturbed and felt it would be folly for the Allies to try. It was.

Haig set his jaw to oppose Joffre, then retracted to agree, and in the end, by self-hypnosis, became convinced that the Somme was an open-sesame to final victory. He would cut the German Army in two, and do it in one day. He would have the Cavalry Corps under bit and ready to charge through the shell-cratered gap and "into the blue," as proof of his intent to crush the enemy. This was big thinking. By February 11 his plan was tentatively set. By late April a great part of Europe knew that the British were organizing the Big Push and the Germans would feel it somewhere soon. But by then, also, the German pressure against Verdun had slackened and the French were counterattacking. The improvement along the Meuse only made Haig more eager for the Somme and caused Joffre to strain harder in jockeying him on. When General Fritz von Below, whose German Second Army on the Somme front had only eight divisions, reported that he sensed a great attack coming, Falkenhayn told him it was a wonderful hope. Having splintered his own army by throwing it against the immovable object, Falkenhayn couldn't imagine that the enemy would be equally stupid.

The Somme, a tranquil river, meanders northwest through Picardy to the Channel. It is shallow and marsh-bordered, spreading five hundred yards or more from shore to shore; its banks and small islets abound with rushes, osiers, and poplars, the haunt of blackbirds, herons, and other wild fowl. The river split the Anglo-French forces set for the Big Push. General Marie Emile Fayolle's French Sixth Army extended south from the right bank. From the left bank to beyond Ypres, it was all British country.

General Rawlinson's new Fourth Army was next to the French flank. Out of General Allenby's Third Army, one corps forming its right flank was also committed. Thus from flank to flank the great array measured fourteen British divisions attacking over an eighteen-mile front and five French divisions hitting on an eight-mile front. Fayolle had 850 heavy guns, so many that he could afford to lend one hundred of them to the British, who were still short of the hardware needed to crush heavy works.

Britain's army of the attack was shaped largely out of the new conscripts, half-formed soldiers who, never having seen action, eschewed the cynicism of the old sweats and truly believed that in their first go over the top they were bound for Berlin. But the more seasoned fighters present—officers and NCO's—noted that the earth-shaking bombardment that opened at dawn on June 24 still hadn't cut most of the enemy wire at month's end. There were some very shrewd soldiers eyeing preparations for the Somme, men like Majors Archibald Wavell and Bernard Montgomery. There was also a muster of poets: Robert Graves, Siegfried Sassoon, John Masefield, Edmund Blunden, and Mark Plowman. From what they heard and saw came no new songs to sing. "Trees in the battlefield," said Blunden, "are already described by Dante." "Armageddon is too immense for my solitary understanding," cried Sassoon. "I gaze down into the dark green glooms of the weedy little river, but my thoughts are powerless against unhappiness so huge." The earth churned, the landscape shriveled, the noise deafened, the fumes stifled. In that vast barrage, 1,508,652 artillery rounds were spent. And at the end of it the German works and wire were still not battered and riven into disuse.

At 7:28 A.M. on July 1 occurred, both ways from the Somme, what John Buchan, believe it or not, calls "the supreme moment without heroics and without tremor." The French and the British infantry climbed up from their trenches and jumped off into the exploding unknown. Like many British commanders a sedulous diarist, Sir Douglas Haig just thirty-two minutes later was making this entry: "Reports . . . [are] most satisfactory. Our troops had everywhere crossed the enemy's front trenches." All along the line his soldiers were falling in windrows to zeroed-in enemy machine gun and artillery fire. It was a catastrophe. By day's end more than 60,000 soldiers of the British Empire were corpses littering the field, dying men trapped in the beaten zone, burdens for the stretcher-bearers, or walking wounded. But not one

This picture captures the front-line drama
of the Somme advance on July 1, 1916. The
photographer records the progress across the
barbed wire into smoke and gunfire.
Watching from a raised observation
post, the poet Siegfried Sassoon wrote,
almost dispassionately: "I am staring at a
sunlit picture of Hell." That day alone,
Britain suffered sixty thousand casualties.

pivotal plot of ground had been won. Here and there, sections of the German forward defense zone had been shallowly penetrated, that was all. Blessed by a more systematic bombardment and a more intelligent tactical design, Fayolle's French troops fared better. But they were in too few numbers to open a decisive gap, though their lunge for the Chemin des Dames was beautifully paced.

Haig should have called off the Somme that night and cut his losses. But having failed, he was too bulldoggish to quit. In consequence, this hideous turmoil must be recorded as the most soulless battle in British annals. The Somme deteriorated into a blood purge rivaling Verdun. It was a battle not so much of attrition as of mutual destruction, and it continued until November 18.

Joffre wanted it that way. He was as demoniacal as Falkenhayn. He kept prodding Haig, insisting that the offensive be continued. At the same time, noting by the numbers (infantry were but digits to him) that his own army was fading away from the effects of Verdun and the Somme, Joffre was pressuring the War Ministry to call up the class of 1917 for training, though 1916 campaigning was hardly begun. If at this time his strategic reasoning had any end in view, it could only be that the side that could scrape up the last 100,000 men would win.

Sir Douglas was as willing as Joffre to feed more men to the fire. So more plans were drawn, the battle was reenergized, tracts of ground and rubble heaps that had once been villages were won now and then, and an army of hope-filled, promising young men perished vainly. By the end of the year, another 607,784 sprouts of the empire had been put out of action, the greater number falling on the Somme. The fact that Germany had suffered in almost equal numbers did not make less the pain and loss.

But one interesting thing happened. Britain had brought along a new weapon created to break the deadlock on the Western Front. Many minds contributed to the innovation but the main credit goes to Winston Churchill. While at the Admiralty, he had winked at regulations and made available the funds for developing a land battleship. Colonel Ernest D. Swinton had earlier urged the building of an armored fighting vehicle that could charge cross-country on caterpillar treads.

In this way was born the tank, sired by several geniuses, damned by the military hierarchy. The origin of the name is more curious.

During development, the vehicle had to be kept secret. That was a problem. A large, mysterious object shipped around the country under canvas would surely whet public curiosity. How to camouflage the secret became the question. Someone suggested that it be called a "water carrier," with the attendant explanation that it was for use in the Sinai desert. One planner said: "We call everything by initials; I will not stand for being on anything called the W.C. Committee." The word "tank" was suggested as a compromise and it stuck.

As the Somme battle carried on into autumn, the first platoon of tanks was coming out of the British plant. These weapons should have been stockpiled to at least brigade strength for the staging of a monster surprise. But Haig's desire to bull through was too great. He grabbed the first forty-two and threw them into a twelve-division attack on September 5. Considering that the tank crews had just arrived up front and that the vehicles were untried in war, the effects, if local, were sensational. The rumbling monsters seemed to scare German infantrymen out of their wits. The German High Command only dimly sensed the potential and fumblingly set about developing its own armor. Even so, a grand opportunity was frittered away.

Haig and Joffre, soldiers steeped in traditional prejudices, did not seem to comprehend such values. At just about the time of armor's debut, Lloyd George visited the two commanders on the Western Front. He mentioned that he saw little or no future use for cavalry in the struggle. These two great men-of-war told him off, reminding him that civilians did not understand military operations.

But Haig had one quality. Like the old Frenchman in the Revolution, he survived, weathering the storms that beat down his more celebrated contemporaries. Victor Hugo once said of Napoleon that he was through when God got bored with him. About Falkenhayn and Joffre it is possible to be more specific. On August 28 Falkenhayn was advised that due to Rumania's entry into the war, the Kaiser had summoned Field Marshal Hindenburg to consult on the overall military situation. The Chief of Staff knew the difference between a snub and an invitation to remove himself. He therefore submitted his resignation and H-L returned to home base to run the entire war and what was left of the empire—Hindenburg as Chief of the General Staff, Ludendorff as First Quartermaster General. Joffre was kicked upstairs in mid-December, appointed technical adviser to the Government for the duration of the war. In his place, as Commander in Chief on the Western Front, arose General Nivelle, made luminous by Verdun. A strange choice, it was determined mainly by clerical and anticlerical factionalism within the French Army and Government. Nivelle was by blood half British and spoke perfect English; while that might have been a debit, his Protestantism made him highly acceptable. Foch was also relieved of field command at the same time as Joffre and for a long time his star was behind a cloud.

Simultaneously, there was a political tempest in Britain. Asquith, who had never taken firm hold of the war's problems, became more remote after his eldest son was killed on the Somme. But he wanted to stay on as Prime Minister. A cabal was formed among Lloyd George, Sir Edward Carson, Bonar Law, and Sir William Maxwell Aitken (later Lord Beaverbrook) to force Asquith to yield war powers to a council of three men. As Lloyd George put it: "We can't conduct our affairs through a Sanhedrin." In the maneuvering that followed, Asquith was forced from office on December 4, and George V, much as he regretted it, saw no choice but to call Lloyd George to form a new Government. No one expected him to stay very long.

In France, the Government was shaken up and reformed at the same time under Briand, with General Louis Lyautey taking the War Ministry and Admiral Marie Jean Lacaze the Navy. All of these changes flowed in due course from Verdun and the Somme, which cast long shadows. What wasn't in due course was that Haig was made a Field Marshal. Joffre, the other mangler of armies, was also given a baton. These ironies were understood by the Allied peoples, who knew only what the High Commands wished them to know.

ON OTHER FRONTS

From the beginning of the war Rumania had veered like a weathercock, frowning at Germany and tightening trade relations when the Teuton armies met reverses, and easing up when the pendulum swung the other way.

Late in 1915 Falkenhayn had tired of this game. He went to King Ferdinand of Bulgaria, proposing an ultimatum to Rumania. Either she would cooperate or she would be invaded. Right about then, Rumania signed the Corn Treaty with the Teutonic powers, which made her a chief food supplier to their hungry peoples.

Rumania might have played the mean trader part longer but for the Brusilov Offensive. The last great gasp of the Russian Army was staged in June, 1916. The offensive, mounted by the general who led the southwest Army Group, Aleksei Brusilov, and named in his honor, crashed the Austrian defenses over a two-hundred-mile front, and ran westward from the Rumanian frontier. The Austrian Fourth and Seventh armies reeled and collapsed under the onslaught. The Russians got almost to the Carpathian passes before the offensive died in late June from the exhaustion of men and supply. It was almost a mortal blow to the tottering Dual Monarchy. Thoroughly alarmed, Hindenburg rushed to the fire every German division that he could spare from his overstretched front. It wasn't enough to plug the holes. Brusilov got going again in August and kept advancing into September. His fame became worldwide, for he was winning the one great Russian victory of the war. Then, in the end, motion died because men, gutted of supply, fighting with bare hands, could do no more. The figures from this campaign are appalling. The Teutonic armies lost more than 600,000 men, some 400,000 Austrians passing into captivity. But for that, Brusilov had paid an exorbitant price. One million Russians were lost, the best and most loyal soldiers in that army were now gone, and the demoralized remnants were ripe for revolution. Because of Brusilov, however, the Austrians had to ease off their offensive in main against Italy in the Trentino, and the Western Front was afforded some relief in an hour when Allied generals were squandering their own manpower at Verdun and the Somme.

Rumania, misestimating the balance of forces, because of the heavy thunder in the neighborhood, declared war on Austria on August 27. Three Rumanian armies got in motion toward the border passes. They would have been better advised to stay put and entrench. Germany had anticipated this opportunist belligerency. To the south, Mackensen had put together an army on the Danube, formed of Bulgars and Turks, with a stiffening of Germans. In Transylvania, two Teutonic armies, quickly formed under the demoted Falkenhayn, would be ready to march by the end of September. The vise was thus almost ready to close in the very hour that Rumania started and just as Brusilov was becoming spent. Nevertheless, the Rumanians decided to continue the advance into Transylvania while diverting one main column to the south to get on Mackensen's rear. For a nation configured like Rumania, this splitting of forces was the worst possible plan. Falkenhayn fell upon the Transylvania columns, broke them, and drove them into retreat homeward. Mackensen quickly captured Constanta, Rumania's main seaport, and prepared to march on Bucharest as Falkenhayn came on from the west. Within two months, it was about all over. Bucharest fell on December 6. Some of the Rumanian remnants got away and joined the Russians on the Siret River. Rumania was completely overrun except for Moldavia in the north. The campaign had cost the Germans another 60,000 casualties and had extended their front another 250 miles, logistical realities that somewhat offset the cockcrowing win over a fifth-rate opponent.

About the time Falkenhayn and Mackensen joined to gather these sprigs of laurel, Emperor Francis Joseph died at the age of eighty-six, weary of the throne, the war, and life itself. His trembling empire could hardly show grief, so heavy already was its mourning. There came to the throne the Archduke Charles Francis Joseph, his great-nephew, son of the murdered Archduke's brother Otto. The change was no boon to the Germans. Emperor Charles was determined to break their hold over his army. The Empress Zita despised them. Count Ottokar Czernin, the new Foreign Minister, far abler than his predecessors, desperately wanted peace and suspected Ludendorff of ambitions to take over Germany as dictator. More dismaying still to the Germans, General Conrad was relieved as Chief of Staff, General Artur Arz von Straussenburg taking his place, which completed the sweep of high commanders who were in on the beginning.

There had been another Russian stroke earlier in the year. Under the Grand Duke Nicholas in the Caucasus, another good general, Nikolai Yudenich, opened a campaign in January against the Turks and continued hitting them into midsummer. Plowing more than sixty miles into Turk-held country, he captured Erzurum, then Trebizond, and later Erzincan, where the high country begins. There the offensive folded for logistical reasons: too little matériel flowed from the five Russian munitions works to keep the army going. Prior to the war the overseers of these plants had all been Germans, and long since, they had been interned. Another Russian column (only 20,000 men) under General N. N. Baratov made a diversionary operation through Karind toward Baghdad in March to help the besieged British in Mesopotamia. But the Turks threw a block against it in early June and the Russians no longer threatened out of Persia.

This photograph shows a German skeleton on the
Somme battlefield. "Humanity . . . must be mad
to do what it is doing," wrote a young French
lieutenant in his Verdun diary on May 23, 1916.
"What scenes of horror and carnage! . . . Hell
cannot be so terrible." Although the fighting
dragged on for another two years, nothing in
the war ever equaled or surpassed the slaughter
at Verdun and the Somme.

British interest in Middle East oil had prompted the sending of a small expedition out of India to the Kuwait neighborhood in November, 1914, immediately after the Turks declared war. A much larger force was built up on this first exploratory but successful effort. Under General Charles Townshend, who like a singed cat was better than he looked, the small army was given an overly ambitious mission by higher command, which discounted both the military qualities of the Turks and the inordinate difficulties of the fever-ridden, obstacle-beset Tigris and Euphrates valleys. From June to November, 1915, Townshend made phenomenal progress, considering his handicaps. Then he was directed to strike for Baghdad. The army did its best, only to be lummoxed by the heat, disease, and a harassing enemy. To revive strength it went into defensive position at Kut-al-Imara in Mesopotamia. The Turks, flush with victory at Gallipoli, brought superior forces against Townshend. The wasting siege started on December 7. The garrison starved, shook from malaria, and looked to the horizon for nearly five months, but still fought on. On April 29, 1916, Townshend surrendered his force of 10,000, mostly Indians but including about 2,000 of his countrymen. One fourth of them had been wounded during the campaign; more than 2,000 had died from disease or enemy fire during the siege.

Elsewhere in the Middle East, England fared better. General Sir Archibald Murray took command in Egypt early in 1916. The garrison covering Suez had been cut to four divisions. Murray pointed them to the waterless Sinai peninsula, the land bridge between Africa and Asia, but a duneland of utmost harshness. The small spearhead toiled along, hugging the coast and building a railway, hard highway, and pipeline as it moved. The Turks gave battle at Rumani and were beaten back. By year's end, the British had taken El Arîsh and entrenched it. Ahead, one-half day's drive by motorcar, lay fortified Gaza, the outguard of Turkish-held Palestine. During the previous summer there had occured an Arab revolt against the Turks—a first sign scarcely larger than the hand of a man. The scene was thus set for the advent of two shining figures, Sir Edmund Allenby, "a very large and superior general," that being the description given him by the second, T. E. Lawrence, whose legend looms so much larger than life that today one has no choice but to go along with it. The arrival of General Allenby and his meeting with the enigmatic Lawrence were still some months off.

Of how Europe had bled and suffered during 1916, of how great armies had spent their flesh in wholly vain endeavor, claiming great victories that were all shadow without substance, America understood very little. The shore was too distant. President Wilson ran again and was reelected on his party's slogan: "He kept us out of war." But many of the more pugnacious sons of America were training in earnest in Plattsburgh and other camps for command jobs in the conflict they knew was ahead. A popular song took hold: "I Didn't Raise My Boy to Be a Soldier." It was answered by one less tuneful, less popular: "You'd Better Raise Your Boy to Be a Soldier." There was also a number for the arch isolationists: "If You Don't Like Your Uncle Sammy Then Go Back to Your Home O'er the Sea." But in that day also music had charms. A Yale student, Stoddard King, wrote a song for a college show: "There's a Long, Long Trail." It took hold over the nation, and the British infantry sang it while moving up to the trenches because it eased the pain in the hearts of men.

For soldiers who have the luck to survive, there is no one worst year in a war, nor one most wretched memory. Time seems to go out of the spinning of the world, with fear, boredom, fatigue, and filth taking its place. But from the perspective of the years, 1916 was the nadir in the ordeal of men and nations. There were no electrifying changes, either to challenge the imagination, stimulate hope, or signal an approaching climax. There was only slaughter, grim and great. The war looked so far from being won that in their misery people high and low despaired that any termination was possible.

Toward the end of the year Germany sent out peace feelers through various embassies. They came to nothing because it was apparent that Wilhelm wanted a peace on his own terms, based on the grip of his armies astride Russia, France, and Belgium. To his British cabinet colleagues, Lord Lansdowne, Minister Without Portfolio, circulated a memorandum, the sense of which was that Britain's situation was becoming catastrophic, and there was no way out of the impasse but a negotiated settlement. It was rejected by the others with words ranging from the sweetly reasonable to Sir Wully Robertson's blast at "cranks, cowards and philosophers who think we stand to gain more by losing the war than by winning it."

Still, neither Sir Wully nor the other generals had the foggiest notion of how the war could be won.

VIII

Crisis in the Allied Camp

This sign outside a New York armory promised
"no expense" to the young men who volunteered
to serve their country, and this detachment
going off to camp looks properly jaunty.

When 1917 opened, Nicholas II of Russia was afield with his crumbling armies, not commanding them, but playing soldier to the limit permitted by his abysmal lack of military aptitude and his highly effeminate nature.

The tragedy of his empire was that, amid the war's blackening crisis, it went unruled. A sovereign only by title, Nicholas could not control affairs, never being master of himself. He was not what history would call a bad man, but merely a weak and spiritually wayward person, a soft mark for every sort of oblique influence and pressure, yet obstinately resistant to advice and counsel from quarters most loyal to him. The German-born Czarina could not be counted on that side. She dominated Nicholas. But some of her associations, and many of her demands on him, were destructive of his position, his hold on the people and the confidence of the court. She gloated in his subservience and did not hesitate to write him at his field headquarters at Mogilev, frowning at some decision he had taken with the Stavka (Russian G.H.Q.): "I see that my black trousers are needed at Headquarters."

The masses turned against him because their privations grew worse and the Little Father of His People took no notice. The army soured when all ranks became aware that their defeats were due to a feeble and corrupt ministry of the Czar's choice. The Bolsheviks, who were most numerous around the industrial areas, suddenly found that they had allies on all sides in the cause of ridding Russia of Nicholas. The most patriotic elements in the national life, such as the Duma, the United Nobility, and the Council of the Empire, wanted him gone. It was simply not within the Czar's capacity as a man to restore the trust and enthusiasm of any of these groups. So he was at last supported only by his own creatures in the court and Government, including ministers who maintained a secret liaison with Germany. For a brief while in the summer of 1916, the Brusilov Offensive had applied polish to the smudged image. But when these victories burned out, bitterness against Nicholas intensified, and the camp went sullenly silent. The army first started the chant of "Bread and Peace," to which the Bolsheviks later added the revolutionary password "Land."

The Mad Monk, whose assassination is sometimes called the first act in the Russian Revolution, was the least savory character in this unholy drama. A Siberian peasant born forty-four years earlier under the name Grigori Novikh, he preferred the nickname Rasputin, which means Dirty Dog. To that extent, he was honest. Rasputin got started on his career as a horse thief, village drunk, and wasteland Casanova. Then, without taking holy orders, he posed as a religious healer, let his hair grow long, refrained from bathing in the name of holiness, and, smelling to heaven, walked barefooted to Petrograd. Beyond doubt he had great hypnotic powers; there is no other way of explaining how he so quickly became the most powerful and baneful influence next to the royal family. The little heir to the throne had hemophilia. So the Czarina came under Rasputin's spell out of belief in his mystic powers as a healer. There were other reasons why the ladies of the court swooned over him; he was also quite a beast in a bedroom. From there his influence radiated to the councils of state, and it soon became known that the one certain way to high office was to bribe Rasputin. In substance, he was the court witch doctor. Alexander Protopopov, Minister of the Interior, who was on the borderline of insanity, and Boris Stürmer, who had succeeded Sergei Sazonov as Foreign Minister, owed their offices to Rasputin. Both of these worthies plotted to come to terms with Germany. By the end of 1916, all three were hated and feared by Russians outside the royal circle.

Rasputin's finish is a tale for midnight. Two avengers, Prince Yusupov and Grand Duke Dimitri Pavlovich, might have hired professional killers for the job. They preferred to do it themselves to alleviate the shame on people of their class. Rasputin was invited to dinner. They plied him with vodka laced with cyanide. He kept on drinking. Next they emptied a pistol into him. He still breathed. So they dropped him through a hole in the ice of the Neva River. He was a long time dying, but three days later the body was found. Rasputin's executioners publicly boasted of their deed. They had directly defied the Royal Pair—and had gotten away with it. All classes of society applauded them. These things happened in Russia during the 1916 Christmas season. Nothing else was conducive to cheer over the land.

But Stürmer and Protopopov were still in business. So suspect were they by this time that the Allied Ambassadors withheld official secrets from the cabinet lest they be betrayed. Whereas Protopopov was the husk of a once dependable public servant,

Stürmer was an outright villain, bent on selling out his country to Germany. He was thwarted before he could get well started when Ludendorff dictated the creation of a royal Polish state out of Russia's slice of that country, deluding himself that a young Polish Army would spring to arms to fight under the German flag. That pulled the rug from under Stürmer; there was no room left for a deal with Germany. When Stürmer's duplicity was partly revealed, the Czar dismissed him. But Protopopov stayed on, exercising prime ministerial powers, postponing the calling of the Duma, directing the secret police, and tyrannizing Petrograd with Cossacks.

All party leaders in Russia knew of these things. All felt moved to resist them. Their opposition made more complete the Czar's isolation. The army was spared mutiny at this stage, expressing its aversion to the throne mainly by scorning the traditional forms of discipline, because it was nonengaged; the Germans were content to leave it that way so that the poison would go deeper. "Disaffection is spreading," wrote the Grand Duke Alexander, "the Government itself is preparing the revolution."

THE FALL OF THE ROMANOVS

Large-scale street rioting in Petrograd began in late February. The rioters were crying for bread. Cossack patrols sided with the rioters and intervened when the police tried to beat them back. On March 11 more than two hundred demonstrators were killed by police machine guns in the street fighting. Troops mutinied after being ordered to support the police. The Duma's President, Mikhail Rodzianko, wired the Czar: "Anarchy reigns in the capital. Government is paralyzed. It is absolutely necessary to invest someone with extraordinary powers to form a new government." The Czar did nothing. Protopopov fled, in fear of his life. The mob stormed the local bastilles, freed all political prisoners, took over the great fortress of Saint Peter and Saint Paul, and burned down the barracks of the secret police. Troops that had turned out to restore order joined the rioters and shared in the looting.

Within one week the storm had spent itself, but already the fire was spreading to other cities. What was done had the approval not only of the Council of Workmen's and Soldiers' Delegates (the Soviet) but of the armies commanded by Brusilov and

Russki. One of the first acts of the Soviet amid crisis was to publish a resolution declaring the salute abolished in the Russian armies, though not a vestige of legality attended the act. The only semblance of lawful control over antigovernment forces resided in a small steering committee named by the Duma.

It remained for the Czar to take the first step toward the final plunge. On March 14 he called in Russki, one of his better generals, and asked: "What shall I do?" It was the question of a lost child. Russki said: "You must get in touch with Rodzianko." Then immediately Russki called other high commanders to tell them of the conversation. On getting a line to Rodzianko, the Czar heard this from the Duma leader: "You must abdicate!" By then Russki was back at him. He had talked by telephone to Generals Alekseev and Brusilov and to the Grand Duke Nicholas. They all had for him the same advice: he must get out. He knew then that he had no choice. His ablest soldiers had turned their backs on him.

Two Duma members, War Minister Alexander Guchkov and Basil Shulgin, arrived the next day and met Nicholas aboard the royal train. Their monarch, haggard, unwashed, bleary-eyed, asked them the same plaintive question: "What would you have me do?" Guchkov said: "You must abdicate in favor of your son." "I can't be separated from my boy," replied Nicholas. "I will leave the throne to my brother [the Grand Duke Michael]. Give me a piece of paper." They did, and he wrote his renunciation. Otherwise he went through the scene as might an amnesiac, asking no questions, showing not a sign of emotion. Apart from loving his son nothing mattered.

However, it mattered supremely to the Petrograd Soviet that this will-less man should attempt to will their political inheritance. By March 16, the day that Guchkov returned with the precious paper, the Duma had constituted a Government composed of ten liberals of various shadings and one Social Revolutionary. Prince Georgi Lvov became Prime Minister. Pavel Milyukov became Foreign Minister. The Socialist Alexander Kerensky, tossed in as a sop to the left, was made Minister of Justice; of all the ministers, he seemed least likely to emerge as the strong man of the March Revolution. No one guessed that day that world fortune was making a pivotal turn. The majority of the Duma stood for a constitutional monarchy. But the Government, if it were to survive, had to have the backing of the Petrograd Soviet. Milyukov appeared before the Soviet that same afternoon and outlined the plan for the succession. He was shouted down. The delegates demanded a republic. Then Kerensky arose to put it to them this way: "Comrades, I am Minister of Justice. No one is a more ardent republican than I am. But we must bide our time. Nothing can come to full growth at one time." His oratory won them over. The delegates voted 1,000 to 15 to back the Government.

It was a personal triumph. Two lights dawned on Milyukov at one time: Kerensky was the man who had the power required by the touch-and-go situation; and the terms of the abdication could not stand. The Grand Duke Michael was asked to renounce the regency. He didn't resist. In this way on March 16 the Romanov Dynasty died. But even as agreement was reached on the course to be taken, War Minister Guchko, a realist, by character and training the most solid member of the Government, was writing to General Alekseev, commander of the armies: "The Provisional Government's orders are executed only so far as this is permitted by the Soviet, which holds in its hands the important elements, the troops, the railroads, the postal and telegraph services."

On the day the dynasty fell, the news of revolution in Russia at last reached Zurich, Switzerland. Nikolai Lenin (his real name was Vladimir Ilich Ulyanov) had passed most of the war in Zurich. An arch revolutionary, exiled from Russia, Lenin kept preaching to his brother revolutionaries the earth over that the supreme object of the Great War was to rid the globe of capitalism. As a volatile and prolific propagandist, he has no peer in history. The European holocaust animated, without really comforting, him. He was too far from the seat of action. But, by 1917, he had almost lost hope that the Romanovs would go down during his lifetime. "We may not live to see the battles of the revolution," Lenin had said to his wife just a few days before.

But he was no less ready to heed the call of opportunity than Kerensky, and was readier still to leap full length. In this lay a strange irony. Lenin and Kerensky had drawn inspiration from the same man. Kerensky's father had once been Lenin's schoolmaster. But the two men had learned quite different lessons.

Lenin possessed three virtues in extraordinary measure—basic courage, single-mindedness toward his life's object, and contempt for personal popularity. By letter, he was already in heavy conflict

The *New York American* announces "War with Germany" on April 7, 1917. In May, President Wilson drafted a bill requiring compulsory service for every able-bodied male between the ages of twenty-one and thirty-one. On June 9, nine and a half million enthusiastic American men lined up to register to fight.

with Leon Trotsky, based in New York. Trotsky was following the line: "True national self-defense consists in the struggle for peace." It was too ambiguous for Lenin. He believed absolutely in force.

AN END TO NEUTRALITY

As Imperial Russia tottered toward dissolution that January, Imperial Germany planted two time bombs destined to explode America out of frigid neutrality into full-scale belligerency. That was not the intention; Germany egregiously blundered. But in time sequence, the events of that fateful month are so related as to warrant the illusion that, having beaten the Eastern Colossus into submission, Wilhelm's Government was determined to provoke finally and fully the Giant of the West.

On January 9 there went from the Kaiser to all vessels of his navy a secret message saying: "I order that unrestricted submarine warfare be launched with the greatest vigor on February 1. You will immediately take the necessary steps." Then, on January 17, British Naval Intelligence in London routed an intercepted German wireless message to its Political Section because its number indicated that the subject matter was diplomatic. Cryptologists worked out the signature, "Zimmermann," the German Foreign Secretary, and toiled on, thinking it was a routine transmission.

Yet the combined impact of these two signals carried America into the war.

America got the news that the U-boats were unleashed only late on January 31, when the hour for protest had passed. Count Johann-Heinrich von Bernstorff, the German Ambassador, walked into the State Department, grim-faced, and told Secretary Robert Lansing that by imperial order unrestricted submarine warfare was begun.

Lansing favored an immediate break with Germany. Wilson equivocated morosely. The Cabinet met only to hear him argue first one way then the other. Finally Wilson made up his mind. He would break diplomatic relations with Germany. But he would do it, according to what he told his intimates, on the false assumption that the shock would force Germany to retract.

By then, in London, British code experts had broken the Zimmermann message and passed it on to their chief, Admiral Sir

William R. Hall. Although he knew it was hot as hell, Hall sat on it instead of forwarding it to the Government directly concerned, the United States. He had an acute sense of timing.

On February 3 President Wilson went before the Congress to announce that he had severed diplomatic relations with Germany. He said that he could not believe that the Germans "meant to do in fact what they have warned us they feel at liberty to do." Then he sounded his counterwarning that, if American ships were sunk and American lives were taken, he would take steps. One more overt act and we'll be proud to fight—that was the sense of it.

Zimmermann was wholly taken aback on hearing of Wilson's reaction to the news of the resumption of unrestricted submarine warfare. He had said to U.S. Ambassador James W. Gerard that same day: "America will do nothing because Wilson is for peace and nothing else." A few hours later Gerard was taking leave of him. Meanwhile, Hall was gathering even more incriminating evidence about the Zimmermann telegram, principally that the Germans had abused a diplomatic courtesy by transmitting the telegram on U.S. State Department cables. On February 23, he at last gave Ambassador Walter Hines Page the Zimmermann message, deciphered. It was addressed via Bernstorff to the German Ambassador in Mexico City. The significant passages are these:

WE INTEND TO BEGIN UNRESTRICTED SUBMARINE WARFARE. WE SHALL ENDEAVOR TO KEEP THE UNITED STATES NEUTRAL. IN THE EVENT OF THIS NOT SUCCEEDING, WE MAKE MEXICO A PROPOSAL OF ALLIANCE ON THE FOLLOWING BASIS: MAKE WAR TOGETHER, MAKE PEACE TOGETHER, GENEROUS FINANCIAL SUPPORT AND AN UNDERSTANDING ON OUR PART THAT MEXICO IS TO RECONQUER THE LOST TERRITORY IN TEXAS, NEW MEXICO, AND ARIZONA.

The other major proposal was that in the event of war the President of Mexico should be prevailed upon to invite Japan to change sides and fight as an ally of Germany against the United States. The whole idea was fantastic. Mexico had no cogent military power. Overrun by revolutionaries, she was on the verge of anarchy.

Page sped the message to Wilson, who was outraged by German duplicity. There was no chance that it might be a hoax—a check of American cable files showed that the original cipher, word for word as London reported it, had gotten through to Bernstorff. Convinced, Wilson called in the Associated Press and, on March 1, the Zimmermann telegram made headlines all over the United States. Still later, the Chancellery in Berlin clumsily admitted that the message was authentic. The chief result was to destroy the effectiveness of that small minority in the Congress that had filibustered against every measure aimed to end America's inveterate unpreparedness.

About who had baited Wilson, about who had put Germany on this oblique course, heedless of the consequences, there is no question. Forcing the decision was the hero of Liège, Ludendorff, often praised as a brilliant general, seldom damned as a grotesque meddler in the realm of higher strategy, where military and political aims are supposed to coincide. By now he dominated Germany, using the mask of Hindenburg to manipulate power with his own hand. The Field Marshal was too beholden to Ludendorff to object. Thus squeezed by the First Quartermaster General, the Government became subservient to G.H.Q. Bethmann-Hollweg fought to the end to try to keep U-boat warfare restricted; Ludendorff beat him down with the argument that victory was worth any price.

By the end of February, Ludendorff's mad policy seemed to be paying off. In that month the U-boats sank 781,500 tons of Allied shipping.

War fever heightened over the United States as the returns came in. Ex-President Theodore Roosevelt thundered: "There is no question about going to war. Germany is already at war with us." Preparedness parades had become fashionable over the country, the marchers carrying banners that read: "Kill the Kaiser!" "On to Berlin!" and "Let's Get the Hun!" But after the first wave of excitement, there was no stampede by ardent youth to the recruiting booths of Army and Navy. Americans, despite a conceit to the contrary, are not a volunteering people.

One year earlier, on March 9, 1916, the Mexican bandit Pancho Villa had unwittingly done a great service for American preparedness by his raid on Columbus, New Mexico, in which fifteen Americans were murdered and thirteen wounded. A 12,000-man U.S. Army punitive expedition had marched into Mexico to track him down and had gotten in one year of hard field service. The commander of the expedition, Brigadier General John J. Pershing,

A group of American soldiers in France learn
the techniques of a raid. High-spirited but
poorly prepared to fight, the doughboys were
immediately put through rigorous training in
trench and open warfare. "To have sent us to
the front line at that time would have been
murder, but we were all willing to go," wrote
one private. "We were woefully ignorant of
the basic principles of the soldier."

toughened by the campaign, had come into the public eye. The better part of the National Guard had been mobilized, rushed to border posts and subjected to an intense training routine. Out of an Army otherwise generally flabby and stale in the practice of arms, these were the constituent elements of the only force available and ready to go as the nation plummeted toward war in Europe in 1917. That there was no other material for the advance guard made Pershing the natural choice for the command.

Pershing was as well aware of his advantage as he was certain that soon an American Army would ship to France. By February 5, the punitive expedition—ordered home in the new war crisis with Germany—was back on American soil. On the day he returned from Mexico, Pershing called a conference of correspondents and said to them: "We have broken diplomatic relations with Germany. That means that we will send an expedition abroad. I'd like to command it. Each of you must know some way in which you can help me. Now tell me how I can help you so that you can help me."

Here was frank ambition, and nothing wrong with it. The history of America in World War I is written in Pershing's shadow because he wanted it that way. In no other war did one commander bestride the scene in the same way. Yet why this is so eludes the best of his biographers, even as it baffled many of his distinguished contemporaries and rivals. If truly great, he was not that much greater than they. He was the perfect picture of the indomitable high commander, tailor-made for monuments. The personality was frigid, if not indeed unnaturally repressed. The drive for high place was as boundless as the instinct for doing the right thing to achieve it. He inspired unlimited confidence in his political superiors. Strangely, however, almost nothing has been handed down concerning him that reflects deep military wisdom. What is real and what is legend about Pershing cannot be arbitrarily apportioned. For instance, the "Black Jack" of common report was an inexorable taskmaster, a driver of men. The picture is far overdrawn. He was never ruthless in his usage of troops, and, as a disciplinarian, he abided by the rules of fair play. The outward manner was austere, and if the inward tone was considerably better than that, Pershing still lacked those lesser graces that make a general popular with troops. Yet he had fundamental qualities that went far in the shaping of an army—patience, sobriety, emotional balance, and an unshakable fortitude.

Pershing needed these virtues even to dare the organizational task. The nation of more than seventy million had fewer than 200,000 men in its Army. Its armament from top to bottom was obsolete; the cannon and automatic weapons were hopelessly antiquated, cumbersome, and scarce. None would do for Europe. Higher commanders knew little of divisional organization; the Army had bucketed along with a regimental system. There was nothing about the old Army to attract an individual with normal ambition. A private's monthly pay was fifteen dollars, which precluded marriage. Ranks lived on "jawbone," or extended credit, from month to month. The ideal of equality of reward for service was born more than one generation later. The ration (daily food allowance) averaged about twenty-eight cents. Most of the senior NCO's coming out of Mexico were approaching the age of forty. The average man in ranks had never attended high school. The average officer was a West Pointer, more knowledgeable about cards than about Field Service Regulations and the tactical problems of the Western Front. Yet this was the most significant sector of the trained base from which an Army counting millions of men had to be fielded.

On March 16 the American ships *City of Memphis* and *Illinois* were torpedoed by U-boats. Disaster by sea, tumult by land —this was one of the great Red Letter Days in human affairs, when the power of the tide is more marked than is its direction. The Romanovs fell. Lenin decided that he must head for Russia. And Wilson sent for members of Congress to assemble in special session.

At night on April 2, armed cavalry restrained a seething multitude outside the Capitol, while in front of a subdued Congress, with a packed gallery listening, the President delivered his war message. The Supreme Court justices were present. They and most of the Congressmen wore small American flags in their lapels.

The President said: "There is one choice we cannot make, we are incapable of making; we will not choose the path of submission." The passage touched Chief Justice Edward Douglass White, a Civil War veteran. He raised his hands above his hoary thatch and collapsed in tears. Reading it now, one wonders why. These are not stirring words but rather a statement of how any free man should feel.

The President continued to a more meaningful expression of

purpose. "The world must be made safe for democracy. Its peace must be founded upon the trusted foundations of political liberty." The sentences that reflect his trial-of-soul as an individual, though oft-quoted, are of little importance. In crisis, it was the nation that counted. For the sake of that nation, he asked the Congress for a joint resolution declaring war against Germany.

On leaving the rostrum, Wilson got the greatest ovation of his life. Later, at the White House, he said to his secretary, Joseph Tumulty: "Think of what it was they were applauding. My message of today was a message of death for our young men. How strange it seems to applaud that."

At three o'clock in the morning on April 6, after an 82 to 6 vote in the Senate, the House voted 373 to 50 to support the President, and the nation was at war. The only Congresswoman of that time, Jeannette Rankin of Montana, whispered a weak "No" and almost swooned, fearful that her career as a woman's rights pathfinder was ended. Nearly twenty-five years later, on December 8, 1941, Miss Rankin, back in Congress, cast the only negative vote when the United States declared war on Japan.

As day dawned with America a belligerent, there were only nineteen officers on duty with the General Staff in Washington, the limit prescribed by law, because of the fear of militarism. Taking counsel of one another, that small group tentatively decided that one Army division should be shipped to France as promptly as possible as a token of America's determination to fight. Thereafter, if things went well, an army of approximately one million might be built up on that one division by December, 1918. There were as yet no plans for an air force. They matured out of a subsequent request from the French for 4,500 American pilots and the matériel to get them airborne and fighting. The Aviation Section of the Signal Corps undertook that program and what came forth ultimately was a vanguard of eager young pilots, but no planes.

Rear Admiral William S. Sims, in some ways a Rickover type, loquacious and nonconforming, but withal a very handsome sailor, was already on his way to London for a reconnaissance; he reported to the Admiralty three days after the United States entered the war. Admiral Jellicoe, now the First Sea Lord, showed him the figures on U-boat sinkings. The Allies had started the war with twenty-one million tons of shipping, or about six million tons more than was essential to feed Britain and kept the deployed armies supplied. The shipbuilding program had not quite stayed apace with the loss rate. Now, according to Jellicoe's figures, the U-boats had wiped out one third of the six-million margin in two months. The March losses had been 500,000 tons; April losses would pass 800,000. Said Sims: "Looks as if the Germans are winning the war." "They will unless we stop those losses," replied Jellicoe.

Sims went to work with Vice-Admiral Sir Lewis Bayly, who directed the antisubmarine patrolling out of Queenstown, Ireland. Sims was already convinced that the way to beat the U-boat menace was to run merchant ships across the Atlantic in swarms with a heavy guard of circling destroyers—the convoy system. Gradually, he convinced Bayly, and together they won over their two governments to the experiment. Within a few weeks thirty-six U.S. destroyers and an armada of auxiliary craft were operating out of Queenstown. Similar operations were established at Brest and Gibraltar. Quickly the loss rate was halved and by midsummer Washington planners knew that the U-boats could not prevent the transport of a sizable army to France.

To Pershing came the first inkling that he had not set his sights too high when a telegram arrived on May 3, from his father-in-law, Senator Francis Warren, asking if he could speak French. He replied that he could—a little bit. Four days later he was summoned to Washington. He noted in his diary: "Was informed by the Secretary of War that I was to command the American troops in France; and that I should be prepared to leave for France as soon as possible."

First he met with Major General Hugh Scott, the Chief of Staff, who asked him to pick the units to form a division for service in France. He named the 16th, 18th, 26th, and 28th infantry regiments, from which came the vanguard 1st Division, later nicknamed the Big Red One. Calling on Secretary of War Newton D. Baker, Pershing was surprised, by his own account, to find him "much younger and considerably smaller than I expected." Baker took him to meet the President for the first time. Wilson, seemingly ill at ease in military company, opened the conversation with: "General, we are giving you some very difficult tasks these days."

Later Baker handed over the orders establishing Pershing's

authority. Especially noteworthy is the fifth paragraph: "You are directed to cooperate with the other countries . . . but in so doing the underlying idea must be kept in view that the forces of the United States are a separate and distinct component of the combined forces, the identity of which must be preserved."

The genesis of that controlling principle was in a memorandum put forward to General Scott by Major General Tasker H. Bliss on May 4. Oddly enough, Pershing has been extolled for adhering to it. Yet in so doing, he was not only following orders but a national tradition and the natural inclination of every high commander. He could hardly have acted otherwise.

In much the same way, history falsely credits Marshal Joffre with initiating the prompt dispatch of the A.E.F. vanguard. By this time he had arrived in Washington and was saying to everyone who would listen that the presence of American soldiers in France would be a tonic to Allied morale in a dire season. But the recommendation that troops be sent as promptly as shipping became available was already positive in the Bliss memorandum.

However, the logistical bind finally determined how rapidly the United States could mobilize. The number of General Staff officers at the War Department had risen slowly to forty-seven by the end of May. It wasn't enough to constitute a decent subsection, considering the vast planning that was necessary. There were great cantonments to be built throughout the land and the terminal date for construction had to be estimated before determining when a national army could be called up. Weapons programs needed to be affirmed before the green light was given to arsenal and depot building. The Quartermaster General estimated that he could clothe and feed one-half million men by July 31, 1917, provided orders establishing the authority were cut at once. By year's end, he could take care of another half million, adding the same proviso. As things stood, he had only a fraction of the staff needed to deal with the contractors.

Over the objections of many in Congress, Wilson insisted that the nation adopt conscription—compulsory service for every able-bodied male between twenty-one and thirty-one. To make the law more palatable, it was called Selective Service. The initial bill called for the drafting of only 687,000 men, but only 516,212—a limiting figure set by the Quartermaster—were actually inducted in 1917. Congress swallowed hard, passed the draft law in mid-May, and on June 5, nine and one-half million American males lined up at the booths to register. To the general surprise, there was no antidraft rioting anywhere. The expected trouble in cities with a large German-American population did not materialize. The occasion went off more like a holiday than a grim mustering for war. It had been announced that none of the registrants would be called up before September; the barracks had still to be built; the fatigues, hobnails, mess gear, and packs had yet to be fabricated. The War Department was rushing production on a new rifle—the clumsy Model 1917. Volunteers who were taking the Navy route found that they also had in store a long wait around home, due to the lack of adequate training space.

There was one other thing the United States lacked—pessimism. Americans set forth on this great adventure expecting to win the war, and that confidence never flagged. The most painful brooding was among the few notables who were shut out, conspicuously Theodore Roosevelt, who had unfurled his flag, called for volunteers, and raised several divisions. Wilson didn't want Roosevelt anywhere near the action, but Pershing promised the ex-President that all of his sons would serve in the A.E.F.

Three weeks after his appointment, Pershing was at sea. His headquarters organization included only two officers from the General Staff; the rest were reservists. On May 29 the liner *Baltic* sailed from New York with the commander, fifty-nine other officers, sixty-seven enlisted men, and thirty-three field clerks. Pershing had picked as his Chief of Staff an up-from-the-ranks soldier not previously one of his intimates, Major James G. Harbord, one of the brilliant military minds of the day. Then the two together had selected their associates. During the voyage over, Pershing and Harbord discussed what size U.S. Army would be needed in Europe to assure Allied victory. But for the time being they were as puzzled as was the War Department. After they landed, they better understood the magnitude of the job, for France had been stricken afresh and for the first time was at the verge of moral collapse. Much had happened in recent weeks, all for the worse.

THE NIVELLE OFFENSIVE

From the beginning, there was nothing about General Robert Nivelle, who had taken command of the French armies in December, 1916, when Joffre was sidetracked, that suggested that he

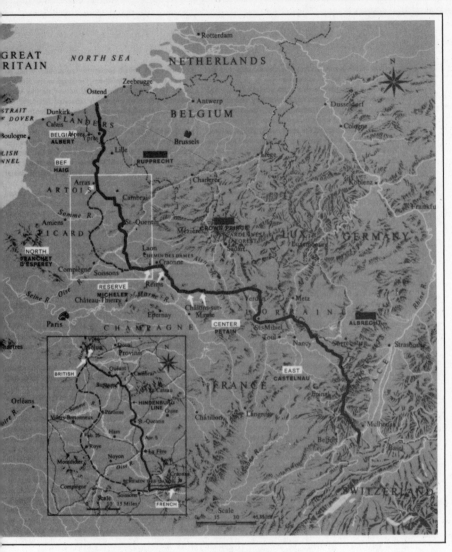

Germany's voluntary withdrawal to the
Hindenburg line, February 25–April 5 (dotted
black to solid line on both large map and
inset), was the only major change in the
Western Front trench line of early 1917. The
Allied spring offensives at Arras, the
Chemin des Dames, and in Champagne (white
arrows) failed to give them decisive gains
—territorially or strategically—and did
nothing to break the three-year-old deadlock.

was counterfeit, except that he seemed too good to be true.

Unlike Joffre, he was an outgoing man, affable, smiling, ever ready to discuss his operations and command theories, and quite capable of explaining complexities so lucidly that to the average listener he radiated power, wisdom, and confidence. Joffre himself had recommended Nivelle as his successor. There was probably more than a little guile in this. He knew that Nivelle had no experience in high command. But Nivelle was deferential to him, and Joffre expected to stay close to the scene of action. The younger man would soon start hitting the bumps, and would need the counsel of experience. Marshal Joffre would be at hand to provide it.

But if Joffre surmised even slightly that Nivelle was unprepared and therefore unfit for great undertakings, not only did he serve France badly, but his secret stayed well kept. Nivelle was highly vain, given to towering rages and preoccupation with trifles. Moreover, he disdained advice from any source, save one. Of these characteristics, his political superiors in France and the British statesmen, who came to believe that he was the answer to their prayers, got no hint until it was too late.

There existed between Nivelle and his *chef de cabinet*, Colonel d'Alenson, a relationship that bound the master to the servant. The title has no equivalent in other armies. More than a Chief of Staff, the *chef de cabinet* is a confidant, an alter ego, an assistant who knows all. D'Alenson had been with Nivelle all along. He was acute, highly intelligent, and quite capable of bending his chief to his own will. D'Alenson was dying of tuberculosis and knew that his time was nearly up. One fixed idea kept this husk of a man up and mobile. He was determined to win the war before his own sun set, and when Nivelle was made generalissimo, he believed he saw his goal in sight. But this was the wishful thinking of a man wracked with fever, though it carried armies and nations along. If ever a man needed a deeply reflective and moderating influence at his side, it was Nivelle at this stage of the war. For he was not in the strictest sense a bad general. He was overimpetuous, and his fault was that he had extrapolated too much from his local successes around Forts Vaux and Douaumont, where he had been opposed by worn-down German divisions. Out of that fortune, he had evolved what he called the "Nivelle system" and he convinced himself that what had worked in the limited French counteroffensive at Verdun could be applied to operations of the greatest magnitude. There was another thing—the Joffre inheritance. Before the politicians eased him out, Joffre had contracted with Haig for another great combined offensive in the Somme neighborhood in the spring of 1917. The plan was already in the works at Chantilly when Nivelle took over. Either he had to proceed with it or appear too timid from the start, and it was not within his nature to be other than lionlike. He took hold, saying: "Our method has been tried out. I can assure you that victory is certain. The enemy will learn this to his cost."

At least one Frenchman didn't believe him. Paul Painlevé vainly besought Premier Briand to relieve him as War Minister because he distrusted Nivelle.

With the British, it was the other way around. The cabinet at first blanched on hearing of the new plan; the sacrifices on the Somme had left the ministers sorely shaken. Lloyd George, for one, was in favor of sacking Sir Douglas Haig, and Sir Wully Robertson had to brace and fight back to save not only Haig but the Chantilly plan. Such loyalty came not out of devotion to Sir Douglas but rather out of detestation for politicians. It was an article of faith with Robertson that only soldiers understood anything about war. Lloyd George's brushes with him on the subject of spring operations eased off after the Prime Minister touched down with Nivelle. They met briefly at a French wayside station on the Prime Minister's return from an Allied conference in Rome in early January. Nivelle was invited to come to London, where he became the toast of the town. He not only brought a copy of his plan along; he had ten or more copies so that there could be general consideration of this highly secret enterprise. Further than that, he had expanded the original concept. Joffre had envisaged an attack on a 100-kilometer front; Nivelle raised it to 170 kilometers. "We will win it all," he said, "within twenty-four to forty-eight hours." Sir Wully and Sir Douglas raised questions about the weather. Nivelle replied that weather is unimportant "to an army determined to conquer." Lloyd George was enchanted. The more the War Office Staff objected to Nivelle's formula for victory, the greater became the Minister's enthusiasm. Sir Wully said rightly that Nivelle oversimplified everything, and that despite his dictum that the fight would be short and sweet, it was simply impossible to break off a great battle at will. He got nowhere. The day after Nivelle returned to France, Sir Wully was directed by the cabinet to send instructions to Haig that he was to cooperate in the letter and spirit of the undertaking. The British Government had determined to subordinate Sir Douglas to the Frenchman to better the chances of the big show. Nivelle, whatever his qualities as a soldier, had a way with politicians.

Whether it carried the day with soldiers is another question. There is a vital difference between sound operational rhetoric and sheer bombast, but Nivelle did not appreciate the dividing line. He wrote to his army group commanders in these terms: "I insist that the stamp of *violence*, of *brutality* and of *rapidity* must characterize your offensive, and . . . that the first step, which is the *rupture*, must in one blow capture the enemy positions and all the zone occupied by his artillery." No man can strain harder than that at employing words to decree miracles. The "Nivelle system," of which he made so much, had as its essence the achieving of swift concentrations, with no prolonged warning bombardment, to attain maximum surprise. But when whole armies are being staged into new sectors over many months, the secret can't be kept, and surprise is therefore unattainable. Nivelle was now commanding in a glass house and the leftward shifting of his forces was wholly obvious to the enemy. In fact, the whole design was the best-publicized "secret" of the war.

The plan itself was elementary, no worse than what had been tried, but, rather, bearing a surprising resemblance to past patterns that had dismally failed. The Somme battle had put a slight bulge in the German line next to Péronne. That accentuated the great enemy salient pointed southwestward, where the Aisne runs into the Oise. The Allies would try to close the bag, the British striking from the north around Arras with French help on their right, while another French maneuver mass concentrated on the bank of the Aisne struck north against the Craonne plateau. That one was to be the crusher. The blow would be delivered by three French armies of the new *Groupe des Armées de Rupture* (G.A.R.). One million two hundred thousand Frenchmen would attack from the Aisne.

The Germans pulled the rug from under the plan. They knew what was coming and they preferred not to risk battle on the existing line. Beginning February 9, they withdrew their forces from the Oise salient, and they got away unscotched. That was not the worst of it. The staged withdrawal, called Operation Alberich by the Germans, and taking its title from the destructive dwarf in the Nibelung saga, was one of the most fiendish affairs in modern history. Before they got out, the Germans systematically vandalized the landscape, pulling down thousands of homes, felling every orchard tree, burning forests, poisoning wells and reservoirs, demolishing bridges and rail lines, and wiping out the roadways.

The Germans dropped back to the Hindenburg Line (which they called the Siegfried Line), completing the movement by April 5. It shortened their front by twenty-seven miles, which, in effect, added about eight divisions to the defensive strength. Not yet wholly complete, this awesome tier of concrete-revetted fortifications, embracing three separate trench systems, ran from Arras south through Bapaume to the high ground overlooking the Aisne, where, taking an eastward turn, it tied into the formidable ridge known as the Chemin des Dames. Not only was the new German defensive position more menacing; the Allied offensive plan, as it stood, had been aborted. There was no longer a salient to pinch out.

Allied troops moved gradually and cautiously into the vacuum. Nivelle, when first confronted with proof of the German withdrawal, denounced it, as if outraged that the enemy should play such a dirty trick. Then, when convinced that the report was correct, he said it made no difference to his plans. That the enemy was now stronger, he waved aside. "The greater their numbers the greater my victory," he said. He deemed it inconsequential that envelopment was no longer possible. The Germans were still in reach of the British concentrations around Arras. At the other end of the buildup, the hinge in the Hindenburg Line confronted the G.A.R. massed on the Aisne. But these were now two widely separated fulcrums, and the tactical leverage was gone. Both Allied flanks would have to attack frontally against tremendously strong works, with little prospect that the blows, if they penetrated, could converge. There were many who felt that the grand design had been kicked into a cocked hat. Among them were General Alfred Micheler, who commanded the army group on the Aisne, and Painlevé, whose initial doubts had become a torment of anxiety.

So there were repeated last-moment high-level conferences, soul-searchings among generals, and sweatings at lower headquarters. Nivelle rode out every storm, head high, insistent, contemptuous of his critics, none of whom had the courage to cry: "Stop it or count me out!" At the showdown, with the political and military chiefs present, only Pétain expressed utter pessimism: "We have not the means to carry it out. Even if we were to succeed, we could not exploit it. Have we five hundred thousand fresh troops for the advance? No. Then it is impossible."

Livid, Nivelle jumped to his feet, shouting: "Since I do not have the confidence either of the Government or of my subordinates, the only course open is to resign." That did it, because not even President Poincaré was willing to call his bluff. The politicians hovered around trying to smooth his feathers, and by their appeasement they cleared the right of way for a new carnival of slaughter.

The attack unrolled on the morning of April 16, which is to say that the guns thundered, the whistles blew, and the French infantry masses picked up and tried to go forward. They got over the top but not much farther. Masses of armor had been nested to put weight into this offensive. The German artillery beat it to death, and most of the tankers were incinerated inside the hulls. The weather had turned sour and troops tried to push through a quagmire, while the heavens loosed hail, sleet, and snow. By midafternoon, German shock divisions were counterattacking out of the Hindenburg works. The French Sixth Army, under General Charles Mangin, took 3,500 prisoners, but by evening reported "infantry not capable of another great attack." The Fifth Army (General Mazel), after capturing 7,000 prisoners, began calling for reinforcements. The Chemin des Dames remained far out of reach. None of the decisive high ground was taken. The Hindenburg Line, with its main shelters hewn out of limestone, still frowned in the distance, solid, little shaken. But the battle went on because Nivelle either could not or would not call it off, despite his pledged word that if forty-eight hours proved its futility, he would desist. He persisted in the futile attacks for another ten days, and France lost another 187,000 men.

The British had attacked one week earlier around Arras, the assumption being that it would cause the Germans to divert forces northward from the French zone of impact. But the attack neither served that purpose nor accomplished anything of consequence on its own, except the taking of most of Vimy Ridge; Ludendorff had outmaneuvered Nivelle completely. In January

The main street in Bapaume, photographed on
March 17, 1917, was captured on that
day by the British Fifth Army. Ordered to
destroy everything as they retreated to the
Hindenburg Line, the Germans laid waste to
towns and farms along the way. "All through
the devastated region," wrote one British
correspondent, "one walked with an uncanny
feeling of an evil spirit left behind."

there had been but eighteen divisions manning the sectors at which the Allies aimed. By April there were 42 German divisions and 2,451 pieces of artillery to take on 46 Allied divisions and 3,810 guns.

Collapsing the French Army, the disaster scuttled its perpetrator. Having played the fool on his high ride to failure, Nivelle looked merely knavish in defeat, proving his lack of character by trying to shift the blame elsewhere. First, he picked Mangin to be the goat, and Mangin, his fair-haired boy, gave him the lie, though in the end he also was relieved. Next, he tried to unload on Micheler and the hard-bitten character lashed back in words that stripped Nivelle of all honor: "What, you try to make me responsible for the mistake, when I never ceased to warn you? Do you know what such an action is called? It is called cowardice."

The Ministry of Paris might really have endured Nivelle's follies some while longer, if only to save appearances. As it was, they packed him off to a high command job in North Africa, which was better than a decoration. But about relieving him, they had no choice. On April 29 mutiny broke out in one regiment and swept like the black plague through the French Army. The bloodbath on the Aisne had proved the last straw. Nivelle had caused the malignancy. Clearly he could not cure it. Troops rioted, threw down their rifles, set up NCO committees to replace their officers. In some cases they deserted their stations en masse and ran off rearward, stood their ground sullenly when ordered to the front, or fell in so drunk that they could not march.

Violent disease; shock remedy. Pétain, who had done his best to check Nivelle, was given the crash task of nursing the demoralized army back to health and restoring order out of chaos. He resented it, but he went ahead.

He had to set an extraordinary balance between hard punishments and an army-wide leniency and compassionate caring for troop welfare. Mutineers—some of them—had to be shot. There were many executions and the drumhead courts were not too discriminating. This was the more horrible and immediate aspect of the task. Pétain faced it and served his country nobly. The long-term and more exacting problem was to reestablish confidence in the command by giving soldiers the feeling that a new sense of fair play pervaded the army and that thereafter soldiers' lives would not be tossed away wantonly.

Pétain was just well started on his campaign of reform when Pershing landed in France. He knew nothing of the crisis; not one word about the mutinies had reached America. Whether or not the bad news proved a sobering shock, at least it added nothing festive to the welcome.

D'Alenson, the pallid and pathetic manipulator who had helped work this ruin, collapsed and died within a few months. Mangin, who was shelved for having overreached (fantastically, he had pledged that his troops would advance against fire at the rate of one hundred yards per minute), was to make a heroic comeback in the victory march of 1918.

One figure then in France who went unnoted at the time was a sergeant, Rodion Malinovsky, a Russian. Two brigades of the Czar's troops had been shipped to the Western Front in a deal by which France supplied the guns and ammunition to Russia in exchange. Even prior to the French mutinies, the Russian soldiers became subversive, fired by revolutionary propaganda circulated by Communist agents and agitated by news of the March uprisings. These activities were redoubled when the French troops went bad. The Russian influence on the French dissidents developed so alarmingly that the two brigades had to be isolated in the rear area. One of the agitators was Malinovsky, who was then starting his rise to field marshalship and minister of all Soviet armed forces in the nuclear age.

IX
Waiting for America

American troops parade proudly through
the streets of London on August 15, 1917,
while a large and hopeful crowd looks on.

Lafayette, we are here." One Colonel Charles E. Stanton, a Quartermaster officer, said it standing before the tomb, not knowing that his four words were destined for immortality and would be attributed to Pershing.

The date was July 4, 1917. One battalion of the 16th Infantry Regiment, chosen from the 1st Division because it promised a better march step than others, paraded through Paris. The French were ecstatic. Not knowing what to call the strangers—that good march number "The Yanks Are Coming" having not yet been born—they yelled from the gutters and sidewalks, "Vive les Teddies!"

What Pershing did say in that brief ceremony at Lafayette's tomb was: "I hope, and I would like to say it, that here on the soil of France and in the school of French heroes, our American soldiers may learn to battle and to vanquish for the liberty of the world." Not greatly eloquent, but modest, and the French loved it.

On the day following the parade, Colonel Charles P. Summerall was ordered to appear before Pershing and his staff at the Paris hotel serving as temporary headquarters. Summerall had been sent to France on a separate mission by Newton Baker to report on the artillery needs of the A.E.F. His tour of the front convinced him that, due to the advent of armor, the French 75-millimeter was too light a field piece, and that the United States should therefore concentrate on building a 105-mm. howitzer. (At that time the consensus was that the Allies could not win the war before the summer of 1919.)

When Summerall aired these views, he was ridiculed by the men around Pershing. But on his return to Washington he convinced Secretary of War Baker that his judgment was sound. Subsequently, by order of the White House, his report was pigeonholed and the recommendation of Pershing's staff, favoring the 75-millimeter, was substituted. It was a capital blunder. America was still waiting for the 105-mm. howitzer when a later riptide swept her into World War II.

Through his talks with Pétain, Painlevé, and others, it became clear to Pershing that in its convalescent state the French Army would require a whole summer of rest, with no great offensives during the year. The B.E.F. was still chins up, but not strong enough to bid for decision. Hence, from the outset, it was obvious that a breakthrough before 1918 was an unreasonable expectation, which meant that there was time for a decisive role by the American Army. Once these factors were grasped, Pershing and Harbord began to understand what size force was needed, and the requirements put to the War Department were accordingly scaled upward. On July 10 the headquarters forwarded to Washington a preliminary recommendation that thirty divisions be shipped to Europe during the next eighteen months. Supplementary proposals for manning the communications zone came along three months later. But the aggregate request totaled 1,372,399 men. That was far more than Washington had yet contemplated and about three times the size of the initial draft. But the under-strength General Staff took Pershing's word for it, gritted its teeth, and went ahead. The problem of transporting such a host overseas was gradually solved. The U-boat menace eased off after the convoy system was adopted. The 1st Division had made France without losing one man at sea, and the Shipping Board was making more tonnage available to the Army.

The immediate question for Pershing was where to base his advance guard so that the Army main body could build up in the same area. The provinces to rearward of the Lorraine front became the natural and almost inevitable choice. One requirement for a national force upon deploying to a war zone is to have unimpeded lines of communication that extend from its outpost line to its own home ports. The French railways and, for the most part, French port facilities were in good working condition, which greatly eased the strain on the A.E.F. command. British forces were supplied via the Channel ports. The French Army was dependent on the rail lines radiating north and east out of Paris. Pershing's Army, settling in the Toul-Dijon-Troyes region, would have clear rail communications with the ports of Saint-Nazaire and Marseille. Bordeaux and some smaller harbors would also be available, more than enough to handle the 25,000 tons of cargo daily required by an army of one million.

The trailblazing 1st Division arrived at Saint-Nazaire on June 28. The Yanks destined for combat and scheduled now for an intense training grind—with accent not on the rifle but on techniques like grenading, trench raiding, and gas discipline, about which they knew nothing—were billeted for the most part in small villages, where they moved in with French families or cleared quarters in barns. All water had to be chlorinated, which ruined the taste of coffee; it was taken for granted that all French water was polluted. Even the French didn't use it for drinking; wine was much better. Any sortie into a French orchard or berry patch was forbidden under pain of court-martial, and the rule was enforced to the letter.

It was a maladministered army by modern standards. The ration flow was irregular, as was the supply of tobacco. Chewers had to fall back on Bull Durham because cut plug didn't come through. There were weeks when no vegetables other than onions were forthcoming, and dehydrated substitutes had not yet been born. If mail delivery occurred more than once a month, it was like a gift from the gods. Months sped by, and no payday. There were no soldier shows, no soft drinks, no ice cream. Life was simpler then. Troops hardly missed what they'd never known. "All of us," wrote Pershing, "were destined to experience many discouragements before the end of the war in our efforts to improve conditions." Most discouraging of all was the effort of the average Yank to learn enough of the French tongue to get by. But gradually he came to understand that *"Sortie"* on a railway station did not identify the town.

Sometime around September 1, Pershing established his G.H.Q. at Chaumont, a provincial city near the headwaters of the Marne. Although the location was common knowledge, vast precautions were taken to keep it classified. "Somewhere in France" was the mystifying phrase attached to every bit of news put forward from the sanctum sanctorum, proving that Americans were fast learning how to operate on Olympus. Estimates of manpower and other needs continued to escalate. Pershing wrote the War Department: "Plans for the future should be based, especially in reference to the manufacture of artillery, aviation, and other matériel, on three times this force—i.e., at least 3,000,000 men." It was a new era for Leavenworth-schooled staff officers —learning to talk in seven digits. Actually, Pershing was never to get the guns, planes, and other heavy weapons from the homeland, and, fortunately, the War Department did not take his revised manpower estimate too seriously.

One early visitor to Chaumont was the Tiger, Georges Clemenceau, soon to become the Prime Minister of victory. (The Premier at this time was the octogenarian Alexandre Ribot, Briand having folded.) Yanks passed in review for him. It was no new

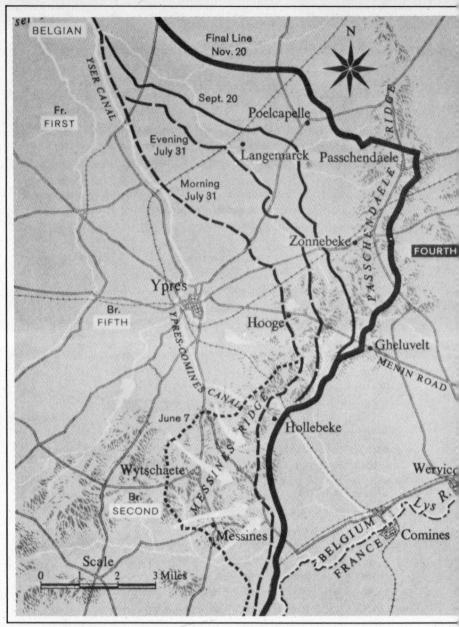

The first-day success of the British Second Army's June 7, 1917, attack at Messines (white arrows) was followed by the four-month Anglo-French struggle to gain the 150-foot heights of Passchendaele Ridge. The map shows stages of the Allied advance, July 31 to November 20, at Third Ypres, or Passchendaele.

sensation. Clemenceau, then a back-country schoolmaster, had been in Richmond in 1865 when U. S. Grant's troops marched into the city. The Tiger was but one VIP in a continuing Big Parade. Everybody wished to see the Americans. They alone gave an upbeat to an otherwise dispiriting summer.

South of the Somme there were no great battles. Both sides were winded. Trench raiding and patrolling went on, the generals deeming such activities essential "to the maintenance of the offensive spirit," a vague term that can cloak a multitude of sins. Gas clouds came over. There were big and rather aimless artillery shoots on occasion. Across the moon-cratered middle ground, the night skies glowed with fireworks. Soldiers were killed maintaining the on-guard, others were wounded and evacuated, and fed-up Frenchmen took French leave of the trenches.

For the French, the frontal fury had subsided. It was time for a break. Two and one-half million soldiers had already been killed on the Western Front; total casualties had reached an astronomical seven million. The one man not discouraged by the blood toll was Sir Douglas Haig.

THIRD YPRES

Out of habit, Haig had been planning something big since long before the disappointments of the spring at Arras and on the Aisne. He was egged on by his intelligence officer, Brigadier General John Charteris, who had the strange notion that the enemy was disintegrating. Haig now had a fresh argument with which to cudgel the reluctant ministers in London—the French Army was *hors de combat* and unless the B.E.F. put on the pressure, the Germans might smash through the ailing ally. This was a hard one to combat, though Haig had made his decision long before the French crisis in morale. The British Cabinet had no hard facts about the French mutinies, and Pétain was constrained to let them guess the worst. From several conferences, Lloyd George sensed that the French Army was abnormally depressed and that Pétain wanted only line-straightening efforts. "I suppose you think I can't fight," he said to Lloyd George. "No, General," replied the Prime Minister, "but for some reason or other you won't fight."

Small shows were not for Haig. Indomitable, he still dreamed of a crash-through into open country, with British cavalry pouring through the gap where the dust had been laid by infantry blood. His chosen scene for the new extravaganza was Flanders, that wretched bogland around Ypres. The salient was the sorriest possible ground for an offensive, both because the enemy heights overlooked the pocket and the footing was treacherous all the way. The Germans held a prominently commanding terrain feature, the Passchendaele ridge, running from Passchendaele to Messines. Provided Haig could seize and pivot on that now, the B.E.F. could break through and liberate the whole Belgian coast. Such a blow might well end the war.

For many reasons, the War Cabinet was loath to buy Haig's bill of goods. He had made too many such promises and delivered only blood-drenched plots of real estate. The ministers wanted no more great killings. Besides, Lloyd George was off on his own strategic tangent, contending that the way to win the war quickly was to deploy Allied divisions to the Italian front and knock out Austria. There were repeated disputations between ministers and generals, the tone becoming increasingly bitter. Sir Wully Robertson was in there backing his friend 'Aig, and countering Lloyd George's scathing remarks with his favorite retort: "I've 'eard different." The subject was always whether or not to have a big go at Passchendaele. The War Cabinet remained adamantine—almost. Then the ministers surrendered to the generals.

For two years that painstaking soldier, General Sir Herbert Plumer, and his Second Army had been holding the Ypres Salient and plotting a stroke against the Messines end of the ridge mass. Working like moles, British sappers had run galleries in under the German positions. By the end of May, 1917, there were nineteen tunnels, some more than one-half mile long. Five miles of gallery, the planting of one million pounds of high explosives—and it had all been done undetected. By the night of June 6 Plumer and his army were ready. Sir Herbert said in his press conference: "Gentlemen, I don't know whether we will make history tomorrow but we will certainly change geography." At 2:40 A.M., thirty minutes before zero hour, the British artillery ceased fire. So hushed was the front that waiting infantry heard nightingales singing in the nearby woods. At 3:10 the levers were pressed and nineteen great mines went off as one. Lloyd George, working in his study at 10 Downing Street, heard the rumble and felt the quake. The Germans who still remained alive after the earth fallout were shocked to a gibbering stupor. The great craters were one hundred yards across and one hundred feet deep. More than 20,000 soldiers were killed or maimed by the explosions. Plumer's divisions pressed forward into the erupted ground. By midafternoon they were in the enemy secondary positions. By dusk they reached the objective line specified by the plan and had taken 7,300 German prisoners. The fighting around Messines continued several days, as the enemy counterattacked. By the end, Plumer's army had paid for its new stand with 25,000 casualties. So, in cost, it was a standoff. Yet something definite had been planned and achieved. The south flank of the salient had been squared away, and Britons manned the high ground. The effect on Sir Douglas was like strong wine and the ministers were proportionately deflated.

But within one week Lloyd George was again throwing a block at Haig, angered because he had read in the *Frankfurter Zeitung* a glowing appreciation of German chances in the battle that the British were arranging at Ypres. More galling still, the enemy surprised and drove back Sir Henry Rawlinson's Fourth Army from the Yser River, the new position it had taken to be ready for coastal operations when the breakthrough occurred at Ypres. There were more conferences. To bulwark his resistance to Haig's proposed adventure, Lloyd George set up a new War Committee, but two of its members, Lord Curzon and General Jan Smuts, swung over to Haig. Lloyd George, in the showdown, was afraid to risk his Government by overruling Haig on a strategic issue. Haig returned to Flanders and hastened his dispositions, sweating it out now, because mid-July was at hand and torrential rains would douse the salient as promptly as August opened.

Haig had assigned the main attack to General Sir Hubert Gough and his Fifth Army. It was a weird decision. The Fifth was loosely commanded, too many of its divisions were unseasoned, and it was strange to the Ypres Salient. Due to the shift, with Plumer's army displacing to the right, Gough's supplies came up late and too many were dumped in the wrong area. About 100,000 soldiers were assigned to the assault, and they would hit over a seven-mile front. Manning the enemy ground was the German Fourth Army under General Sixt von Arnim, who had as his Chief of Staff Colonel von Lossberg, the brightest genius among the Germans in the building of defensive works. Directed by

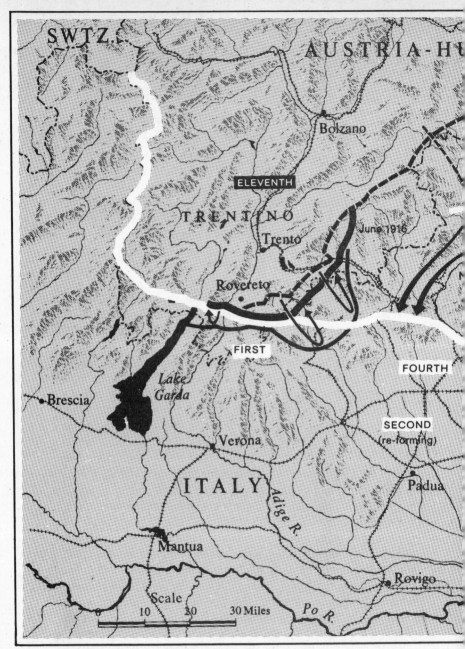

SWTZ.

AUSTRIA-HU

Bolzano

ELEVENTH

TRENTINO

June 1916

Trento

Rovereto

FIRST

FOURTH

Lake Garda

Brescia

SECOND
(re-forming)

Verona

Padua

ITALY

Adige R.

Mantua

Rovigo

Scale

10   20   30 Miles

Po R.

**Austria's spring, 1916, Trentino offensive (black arrows, left)
ended about where it started (solid black line). The October 24, 1917,**

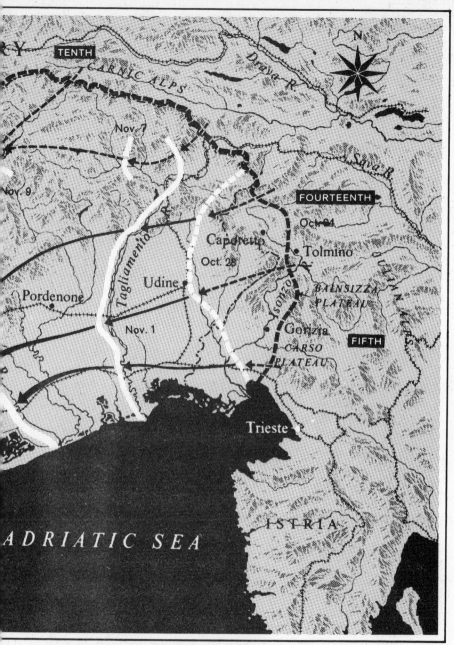

Austro-German attack at Caporetto (right) drove the Italian Third and Fourth armies to the Piave River (solid white line) by November.

Lossberg, the Fourth deepened its position until there were six successive lines of trenches and concrete-protected nested machine guns spread like a checkerboard so that they were mutually supporting. The British Tank Corps faced the unenviable task of neutralizing these crossfires. But the Ypres terrain was totally unsuited to armor and the hulls of Mark IV's were too thin to go against massed artillery. There was plenty of that on call. The German front was backed by 1,556 guns; 2,299 lights and heavies would support Gough. As to infantry, the Germans had eight divisions in line and twelve more in reserve. They were all ready.

The Third Battle of Ypres, or Passchendaele, got under way the last day of July. Preceding it were two weeks of intense artillery bombardment, another unprecedented shoot, with more than three million shells spent in the "softening up." The weather did even better. The night before the jump-off the rains came in torrents and the battlefield swiftly reverted to its natural state—a bogland. Shell craters filled and roads dissolved into ooze. The first day's objective of Gough's nine divisions in the attack was 6,000 yards inside enemy country. By nightfall, his center had lost 2,000 yards to German counterattack, the flanks were only an average of 500 yards forward from their departure line, and British casualties for the day were 31,850. The thunderstorms continued and for the next ten days the Fifth Army simply wallowed in the mire, blasted by shellfire. The weather cleared briefly in mid-August; Gough resumed the attack and his center gained five hundred yards. By that time, it was fairly clear that the Fifth Army would get nowhere. But on the first day, Sir Douglas had visited Sir Hubert to find him in high spirits and boasting about a "great success," his tired people having bagged 5,000 prisoners. So a communiqué in that mood was flashed to London. The London *Times* headlined: "Ypres Salient Widened, Two Miles' Advance." Once begun, this willful deception had to be maintained. Another dispatch read: "We have broken the German line on the whole front attacked." Haig's headquarters continued these fabrications when, a little later, Gough conceded that his army was stuck, and the task of trying to salvage something from the wrecked hope was committed to Sir Herbert Plumer and his Second Army. They did little better. The wasting effort continued through the autumn, until at last on November 20 ice sealed the battlefield. Not one thing of importance had been achieved; the campaign had cost Britain another 244,897 soldiers and airmen. The last excuse for prolonging the battle had vanished before the close of August. Instead of getting to the Channel, Haig's forces advanced 9,000 yards into the marshland.

THE SUPREME WAR COUNCIL

In the early fall of 1917, German divisions had been moved south to beef up the Austrian Army. Between October 24 and November 12, this spearhead drove into Italy and visited catastrophe on the Italian Army at Caporetto. In one battle Italy lost 305,000 soldiers, of whom 275,000 surrendered. The defenders panicked, backed away a hundred miles, and dissolved into a rabble. British and French divisions had to be rushed to Italy to keep that nation in the war. General Cadorna was sacked and General Armando Diaz took his place. Aided by General Pietro Badoglio, he began to organize a new army with more spine than the mob that had fled Caporetto. King Victor Emmanuel sounded a war cry: "Citizens and soldiers, be a single army. All cowardice is treachery, all discord is treachery." The poet D'Annunzio, and a Milan editor, Benito Mussolini, helped him rally the people.

Caporetto unnerved everybody. True, the Italian Army, having pulled far enough back, became insulated by the half-mile torrential stretch of the Piave River. There the fighting died. General Otto von Below brought his seven German divisions up to the far shore of the obstacle, along with the Austrians, where he was stopped by the weather, the thinning of his people over a wider front, and the lack of bridging material. Aware that for logistical reasons he could not bring off a decision there without further weakening the Western Front, Ludendorff gradually recalled the German formations. The French and British divisions arrived after the real crisis was past. But Italy's near collapse coincided with the fall of the Kerensky government in Russia and the take-over by the Bolsheviks. Allied statesmen were rocked by the double calamity. General Foch was dispatched to Italy to buck up the defeated army, and to advise on how the six French and five British divisions could be used to best advantage. The statesmen—Lloyd George, Painlevé, Italy's Prime Minister Vittorio E. Orlando, and Mr. Wilson's Colonel House—followed along to meet at Rapallo on November 7. In a spirit of emergency, they formed the Supreme War Council to cope with the immedi-

T. E. Lawrence poses in Arab garb. More
Arab than the Arabs in his obsessive vision
of a tribal homeland, this enigmatic
Englishman enlisted their support to rally
against the Turks. By late 1918, Lawrence
and General Allenby were operating in
tandem, pushing north through the Holy
Land on parallel routes that would lead to
Allied victory in the Middle East.

ate problems. This was the beginning of Allied unity of command, which later paid major dividends on the Western Front. Because of the bad show at Passchendaele, Lloyd George was so worried about his job that, on his return to London, he asked Colonel House for some kind of statement from the United States that would make the forming of the Supreme War Council look like a feather in his cap. House queried Wilson, who replied: "We not only accede to the plan for unified conduct of the war but we insist on it." It helped Lloyd George in a bad moment; the opposition withdrew its motion of censure.

Painlevé, who had briefly succeeded Ribot in the French premiership, was not so fortunate. Rapallo was his last contribution. He was voted down in the Chamber of Deputies on November 16. Poincaré, though he personally hated Georges Clemenceau, called him in to organize a new Government, saying: "You have made it impossible for anyone else to form a cabinet; now see what you can do." Clemenceau quickly established himself in power with such firmness that he ruled virtually as a dictator until after the war's end. At last France had a political leader who could crack the whip; and Foch had taken another step toward the overall military command.

TRAINING THE A.E.F.

By the time of Caporetto, there were three more American divisions in France: the 2nd; the 26th (National Guardsmen from New England); and the 42nd, called the Rainbow, because it was a composite from many parts of the United States. These were ponderous, bulky organizations—four infantry regiments, one artillery brigade, one engineer regiment, and various attachments, with a total strength of around 28,000. So in six months the combat A.E.F. had grown to more than 100,000 men. The more it grew, the greater became the pressure upon Pershing from Clemenceau, Pétain, Foch, and some of the Englishmen to brigade the regiments with French and British formations in the thinning Allied line. They were wasting their time; Pershing's orders and his jaw were set.

In a little more than three months the shakedown training cycle for the first arrivals was completed. Troops of France's 47th Chasseur Alpine Division (called the Blue Devils) had played professor to the green infantrymen of the 1st Division. The specialists had gone off to grenade, gas, bayonet, and demolitions schools and returned. The companies had worked daylong in dummy trench systems, learning the routines and getting the feel of Mills bombs, Livens projectors, and Stokes mortars, weapons of which they previously had known nothing. Very little time was left for going on range with the rifle.

In early October it was arranged between Pershing and Pétain that one battalion from each 1st Division regiment would go into line for ten days with the French, for the sake of experience. The chosen spot was the Toul sector, about fifteen miles northeast of that city in the rolling hills of Lorraine. It had been a quiet front for three years, and both sides appeared content to let it remain that way. On October 23 in early morning, a battery from the 6th Field Artillery fired the first U.S. Army round of the war, one Sergeant Alex Arch pulling the lanyard.

Ten days later the first set of infantry battalions finished their tour, none the worse for wear, and were rotated out. The second battalions came in. On November 2 near midnight, the Germans came over in a well-staged trench raid. They knew that the Americans had moved in and intended to humiliate them. The blow fell on the same battalion that had paraded in Paris on July 4. Helped by a box barrage, the Germans cut through the wire without being detected, slipped into the trench without being challenged, did their bloody work, and got away, all in a great hurry. They left three of their own dead. They took off eleven prisoners, the first man captured being Corporal Nick Mulhall, who was never heard from again. Three Americans were killed—Corporal James B. Gresham, Evansville, Indiana; Private Thomas F. Enright, Pittsburgh, Pennsylvania; and Private Merle D. Hay, Glidden, Iowa. By dying early, the three became national heroes.

In the hour of its battle debut the 1st Division had come under Major General Robert Lee Bullard, a nonpareil among fighting men and, unlike Pershing, one of the hearty types who have a natural way with enlisted men. Such generals wear best with American soldiers.

ON TO JERUSALEM

In much the same way that Caporetto led to Rapallo, something good had come out of Britain's sideshow at Arras in April. Haig had always disliked General Sir Edmund Allenby, commander of the Third Army, whether because he was a soldier of independent mind and considerable imagination, or because Haig, being a fellow cavalryman, regarded him as his most dangerous rival. After Arras, where Allenby's operation had started brilliantly and then drizzled off, Haig was more than willing to see him go, and Lloyd George had a major mission for him.

The situation was this: the Prime Minister had continued to eye the Middle East, where General Sir Archibald Murray—after getting his small army across the Sinai desert, so that it was based three hundred miles from Cairo—had twice been beaten back by the Turks from Gaza. He had been aiming for Jerusalem. Its capture would be a precious prize, for the Holy City is one of the great military bastions of the world, the Judean Hills forming a rampart that gives it the character of a fortress. But the expedition that had been sent against Gaza had too few troops and Murray physically was played out. Lloyd George wanted a real victory somewhere, and Jerusalem looked like the best chance. He said to Allenby: "I'd like you to take Jerusalem as a Christmas present for the nation." That was late in June. Allenby took off promptly. In that hour, the course of British operations against the Turks was already taking a turn wholly favorable to his enterprise.

A king-size army (414,000 soldiers and laborers) under Lieutenant General Sir Stanley Maude had formed in Mesopotamia to beat back the Turks from Britain's Middle East oil holdings, the task failed by General Townshend when he was compelled to surrender at Kut in April, 1916. After spending six months in working up the Tigris, the army capped its grueling march by capturing Baghdad in mid-March, 1917. It had been a fighting campaign, and quite costly, despite the fact that the opposing Turkish forces were greatly outnumbered. Total casualties were 92,501; almost as many soldiers died from disease as from wounds. Toward the end General Maude also succumbed to cholera. How many Turks died is unknown; at the end there were more than 50,000 enemy soldiers in the British cages.

T. E. Lawrence, that paladin of mystery and of history, was also getting in blows on the other flank of the great parched Arabian peninsula. The revolt of the Arab tribesmen, which he had begun fanning one year earlier, had spread for months from its base at Aqaba (next door to the modern Israeli port of Elath) and was now closing around the lower end of the Dead Sea. There is no more difficult country for military forces; the hold-

**James McBey, the official artist who
accompanied Allenby's army in Palestine,
painted the general's historic entry on foot
through the Jaffa gate to claim Jerusalem.**

ing of it revolves around possession of two great oases, one on
the eastern shore opposite Sodom and the other at Ein Gedi on
the western shore. The Turks sent an expedition to deal with
Lawrence; it was ambushed and destroyed at Tafila. These several movements put Enver Pasha, Turkey's strong man, in between
two fires. On the very day Allenby left England, Enver announced
to a high war council his decision to concentrate forces against
Maude's army around Baghdad rather than send major reinforcements to the garrison defending Gaza. It was another break for
Allenby in Palestine.

The expedition pointed at Gaza was largely composed of Australians and New Zealanders, formed in brigades, and operating
mounted, either on horses or camels. But there was one solid
British division at hand, and more were on their way from
England and India. Less important than numbers was the effect
of the arrival of Allenby, nicknamed the Bull by the army. The
landscape around Gaza is as repellent as the Mojave Desert. The
mood of the army, after months in the desert, was no less grim.
Allenby, an officer with splendid physical presence, galvanized
troops; soldiers saw him and were ready to try again.

It occurred to Allenby immediately that the key to Gaza was

the inland frontier town of Beersheba, the place of the seven walls. Without Beersheba water, his army could not continue toward Jerusalem. So he would drive on Beersheba with his right flank, while pressing Gaza with his left. His forces were large enough to undertake this stretch, where Murray's had never been so. The two-pronged movement against the dreary port and the Bedouin capital was the decisive maneuver of the campaign.

Gaza came under bombardment in late September. Falkenhayn, the German who had contrived the great slaughter at Verdun, was rushed to Palestine to mastermind the Turkish defense. Once again, he was beyond his depth. Meanwhile, the Turks were slowly organizing their counterforce to go against Maude's army at Baghdad; this body had only the advantage of a euphemistic label, *Yilderim*, meaning the Thunderbolt. With too few troops on both flanks, Falkenhayn had no magic to avert defeat. On October 31, some 40,000 British troops stormed and captured Beersheba, which was defended by 5,000 Turks. The fortress of Gaza, by then heavily invested, was abandoned by the Turks on November 7 and the British rode in.

With the enemy cut off from its base, Allenby urged on his forces in relentless pursuit. By mid-November he confronted Jerusalem. There was prolonged skirmishing in the Judean Hills. The city surrendered on December 9. Lloyd George got his Christmas present.

While the great event made no difference to operations on the Western Front, it was plain to see that Turkey was careening toward final defeat. The British Army at Baghdad was now reaching north for Mosul. Ludendorff felt compelled to send another army corps east to keep Turkey in the war. Preparing for his supreme effort in the West, he could ill afford the detachment. There remained in the field under Falkenhayn only 36,000 combatants; against them, Allenby mustered 103,000 riflemen—"A tiger fighting a sick tomcat," one British soldier wrote.

The vital statistics of the war in the Middle East are highly revealing. From January, 1915, until arms were stacked, Britain lost 51,541 men to enemy fire. But 503,377 soldiers were laid low by malaria, cholera, dysentery, various other fevers, and venereal disease. All-round immunization shots for soldiers, like plasma and blood banks, were for the distant future. Ninety per cent of the men who "died from wounds" in World War I could have been saved by the medical services available in World War II.

THE AMERICAN BUILDUP

By mid-September the new frame cantonments back in America were filled with draftees and the National Guard divisions were living mainly in tent camps. Regulars commanded most of the National Army regiments. Reserve officers usually filled the slots from battalion level on down. To stiffen the training, cadres of NCO's from the Regular Army were assigned to duty with the National Army, the average quota being about four or five to each company of approximately two hundred men.

That was enough. What the trainers quickly discovered was that the drafted men were just as willing as Guardsmen or Regulars, that they responded naturally to discipline, and that a high percentage of them were potential leaders. In consequence, getting this army fit for the field was not the formidable task that had been envisaged.

Both the training requirements and the standard of discipline were hard to the point of harshness. Leave was granted only if a dire emergency arose at home. Drill, field work, inspection, and reviews filled six days each week. First call came at 5:30 A.M. and work went on until retreat at 5:30 P.M.. After troops had become fairly hardened, twenty-mile hikes over unpaved roads were routine. One system used to qualify privates as NCO's was to test their voices when they barked orders through a two-hundred-foot thicket. If the words could be heard on the other side, the man was on his way. The Government gave troops nothing save their clothing, bedding, a toothbrush, and a safety razor. Recruits from the backwoods were prone to employ the toothbrush for rifle-cleaning, until the dental surgeon made his first inspection. When anyone came down with measles, chicken pox, or mumps, he was kept in barracks, so that every other susceptible would contract the illness and acquire immunity before going overseas. The treatment given Mr. Wilson's Army was hardly enlightened, even for that era. Yet the guardhouses did not bulge with malcontents.

The majority of recruits from German-settled areas, such as Chicago, Milwaukee, and central Texas, stayed hostile to the Great Adventure and sounded off. Their griping worried no one. It was taken for granted that when they came under fire from Germans, they would reform in a hurry. So it proved.

The nation's mobilization effort, begun in confusion, carried on with more misses than hits. Given $640,000,000 for the aviation program, the War Department set forth to build 40,000 military aircraft within one year. That did nothing to further Allied operations on the Western Front, though by war's end the much-publicized Liberty engine was a reality. A wholly new industry was established to supply aviation instruments. By the end of one year it was beginning to produce some twenty items. To fabricate planes, a certain wood was required. There came into being the Spruce Production Division, 538 officers and 17,697 enlisted men to fell and machine great trees in the Pacific Northwest. Detailed to the outfit was a draftee from the Tennessee hills, Alvin York. By rare luck, he was pulled out of the woods to become the Number One rifleman hero of the A.E.F.

One wartime discovery was that helium, a noninflammable gas, could be produced cheaply in the United States at the rate of 50,000 cubic feet per day. Its use might have saved the lives of a lot of young men doing hard duty in sausage balloons, but the idea never got off the ground and observers continued to jump fast to escape flaming death.

Two types of tanks were adopted by the U.S. Army, a light six and one-half ton and a heavy thirty-five ton. The Ford Motor Company also produced a little monstrosity—a three-ton tank for a two-man crew. Approximately $200,000,000 was appropriated for these programs. All was sheer waste. Of the 4,400 tanks put under contract, only fifteen ever reached France, getting there after the armistice in time for a meaningless testing. The United States did much better with pigeons. Lofts were raised at seventy-four training camps. After 15,000 trained carriers were sent to the A.E.F., there still remained 10,000 in the zone of the interior, for the further schooling of pigeon trainers. It is stated officially that "95 per cent of the messages carried by American pigeons in combat were delivered," including one that read: "Take it away; I'm tired of carrying this damned bird."

Yeoman work was done by the statistical bureau of the War Department, especially in its service to the Quartermaster Corps. It was learned that the average soldier in the first million was 67.49 inches tall and weighed 141.54 pounds. Compared with the Civil War figures of 67.502 inches and 136.05 pounds, it proved that Young America hadn't gotten very far in one half-century. Deflated and expanded, the ancient and new figures were identical.

Relatively few married men were taken by the draft boards; marriage was a good way to escape the war. Of 4,883,213 marrieds who registered, 3,619,477, or 74.12 per cent, were deferred.

The American Indians showed up somewhat better. Of the 6,509 tribesmen inducted from reservations, only 228 claimed deferment. Out of a total of 26,520 convicts or ex-cons in the nation, about 7,900 were taken into service; some of them proved quite expert at killing; the majority became problems for everyone else in their outfit. Before the war ended, 337,649 men were classified as deserters, and, in the final accounting, 163,738 of these had been apprehended.

There were no "conscientious objectors" in the United States; the draft law did not recognize any such classification, which is one way to skirt the problem. But a board appointed by Secretary Baker had to deal with 1,697 individuals who were, for the most part, reasonable facsimiles thereof, though 103 were judged "insincere" and seven insane.

The cost of feeding the Army throughout the war was $727,092,430.44. The Quartermaster disposed of 140,843,476 tins of corned beef, 30,961,801 cases of salmon, and 4,661,732 cases of cornmeal, to be served up as mush. These items, with black coffee, practically supplied the ration for the A.E.F., which tasted little else except Welch's grapeade, French "monkey meat" (a particularly slimy bully beef), and French hard biscuit. Sent overseas were 10,812,000 "long drawers, winter" and 3,889,000 "short drawers, summer," the long drawers usually getting there in June and the short drawers coming on in October. The A.E.F. wore out 9,136,000 pairs of hobnailed shoes. The steel helmet and the abominated wrapped puttee, which choked off circulation and was conducive to Charley horse, were provided from British stocks. Practically every American soldier in France carried a spiked ash walking stick, which eased marching. But he bought this on his own.

In the United States there was great trouble with the railroads, which mounted steadily as transatlantic cargo rose in volume. The growth of exports with no offsetting imports choked the yards in the East. New York braced for a coalless winter. Almost two hundred ships lay idle in the harbor waiting for fuel. All of the lines were undermanned, due more to the formation of railway engineering units for service in France than to the attraction of higher wages in munitions plants. The newspapers cried that something drastic had to be done. Mr. Wilson responded. Under the authority of the Army Appropriations Act, he took possession of all railroads in the nation for the duration, and named

314

Wilson delivers a campaign speech in 1916.
After seeking, throughout his first term, to
maintain an impartial neutrality, the slogan
"He Kept Us Out of War" helped return Wilson
to the White House. Ironically, he declared
war on Germany a few months later. Following
that, his speeches, elaborating on the idea
that war was necessary in order to make the
world "safe for democracy," did much to
engender American support for his policies.

his Secretary of the Treasury and son-in-law, William Gibbs McAdoo, as czar, with full authority over wage scales, rates, routings, and finance.

"It is not an army that we must shape and train for war. It is a nation," are the words with which the President put the cause to the people. It was easier said than done. But in the hope of creating a greater unity and upsetting the business-as-usual attitude, a Colorado journalist, George Creel, was brought to Washington as chief propagandist for the Government. As Wilson's mouthpiece, Creel coined most of the war slogans. His office became the oracle dispensing war news to the press corps. Working through the Department of Justice and the military services, he exercised the President's power to suppress anything of a seditious nature. Sometimes the line was drawn absurdly fine. A movie called "The Spirit of 1776" was banned because it portrayed British redcoats brutally misusing colonial patriots. Creel could attack false and hurtful rumors without seeming to tilt at windmills. But while his output was purposefully colored to glorify Wilson, he carefully avoided hate campaigning, the big lie, and exaggerations of military success.

CAMBRAI

While war was revolutionizing life in America, a change in the very nature of war was taking place in France. On several counts, the small battle of Cambrai, fought in late November, 1917, just as operations in the Third Battle of Ypres ended, remains memorable. With it dawned a new age in warfare and there was born a valid hope for breaking the deadlock on the Western Front. It was a British success. Sir Douglas Haig had very little to do with it.

After Allenby left France, the Third Army was taken over by another able British general, Sir Julian Byng. By mid-September, Byng had orders to plan and mount an attack that might draw off German strength from the Ypres front. That coincided with the search by Brigadier General Sir Hugh Elles, commander of the Tank Corps, for a sector where it might be possible to use armor en masse.

Together, Byng and Elles chose the place, and together they planned the stroke. The countryside southwest of the town of Cambrai is a chalky plain—firm ground, laced with many small streams and minor dikes. Between the Saint-Quentin and Nord canals, which bounded the flanks, was a seven-mile stretch satisfactory for armored maneuver. Elles had 324 tanks. Byng could dispose twelve divisions. Their target was one sector of the Hindenburg Line, which south of Cambrai had a fortified depth of 4,000 yards. Everything was subordinated to the principle of surprise; there would be no preliminary bombardment, and no firing to establish range. A smoke curtain would be laid down to conceal the oncoming tanks.

By the time Byng was nearly ready in early November, seven more divisions had been displaced from the Ypres front to join his army. Two thirds of the tanks were to be employed against the Hindenburg Line; the others would be held in reserve. The Germans had only two divisions on the selected front, and but 150 guns against 1,200.

The object of the attack was to crash the enemy front on a width of 13,000 yards, capture Cambrai, and seize all Germans between the two canals. There was no plan for further exploitation. So there was never any intention of making decisive penetration. For that, the tanks would have needed far more latitude than the two boundary canals permitted, so that they could move out and around, widening the breakthrough for the passage of adequate reserves. That aspect of the operation troubled Elles. He wanted to widen the front and use his armor in echelon, so that there would always be metal moving ahead of the infantry. But the Tank Corps commander and his brilliant second, Colonel J. F. C. Fuller, were overruled.

When the attack began on November 20, the Germans were taken wholly by surprise because no gunfire preceded it. They had designed their line with the intention of making it tank-proof, the frontal trenches being twelve feet wide. But when the tank brigades rolled forward that day, followed by five infantry divisions, they carried great fascines on the noses of the machines, which could be dropped in the trenches and used as roadways. This was Fuller's idea and it worked. The two German divisions were shattered, and all of their guns taken, as well as 8,000 prisoners. A penetration of 10,000 yards was achieved over a somewhat irregular line, the armor breaking through to the fourth enemy position. More ground was won at Cambrai in six hours than had been taken in Third Ypres during four months, and the cost was only 4,000 British casualties. By nightfall, 180 tanks were out of action, but only sixty-five were victims of enemy fire; the others had conked out through mechanical trouble or had been ditched. Ludendorff, getting the news, was shocked to the marrow. He ordered reinforcements rushed to the scene. But, having gained their victory, the British didn't quite know what to do with it. Dark closed over the battlefield by 5:00 P.M.. The striking forces were spread thin along a narrow salient, it was too late to get cavalry forward, and the infantry's momentum was lost when most of the tanks went out of action, as usually happens. In addition, Haig had just warned Byng that because troops had to be sent to save Italy as a result of Caporetto, he could not maintain a continuing assault around Cambrai.

So the battle virtually expired in one day of unprecedented success, and the forward divisions held in place, in the manner of a man sprawled halfway through a door. They could not remain that way indefinitely because the enemy was well set to mount a counterblow against the shoulders of the salient. Under cover of the Saint-Quentin Canal, the Germans reassembled large forces, and on November 30 launched the counterattack that regained most of the ground lost ten days earlier.

Even so, the battle was the first convincing demonstration of what tanks could accomplish when they were properly used. The Battle of Cambrai changed the climate of World War I and established a new form in military operations, one which would last for nearly half a century.

What Cambrai portended, however, was understood by only a few inspired tacticians, like Elles, Fuller, and other Tank Corps pioneers. Ludendorff dismissed the potential of the new weapon and its mass employment with the words, "They had been a nuisance but had achieved no decisive results." He took a look at some of the captured weapons but was "not impressed." At his instigation, Germany was going ahead with a tank program although his heart was not in it. Much later he pined, "Maybe I should have made greater efforts." To his mind, nothing but a superior infantry would deliver the knockout blow. That was what he had been trying to do at Caporetto. According to General Below, who commanded there, the German objective in that push was Lyon, France. Ludendorff imagined that a handful of fighting Germans could cut through the Italian Army, overrun northern Italy, skirt the Maritime Alps, and get on the French rear. No wilder dream than this befogged the war. Even less than Ludendorff did the Allies get the meaning of Cambrai. The stalemate seemed as hopeless as before. Not one prophet forecast victory within the next year. Though reeling from losses and home-front privations, which by this time were woeful in England, grave in Germany, and acute in Austria, both sides appeared to be as intransigent as ever.

In secret, however, some men were thinking of peace. Prince Sixte de Bourbon, though a brother-in-law of Emperor Charles of Austria, was serving as an officer in the Belgian Army. By blood he was French, but members of the Royal House of France were barred from serving in that army. Sixte got permission to visit Charles secretly. He found his kinsman completely fed up with the war, sympathetic to the position of the Entente, and looking for a way to end the conflict. As a consequence, there were prolonged secret discussions with the French and British ministries. It was a very hush-hush business, Charles having impressed Sixte that if the Germans got word of it, he would probably be assassinated. As the intrigues continued, there were meetings between the Allied Prime Ministers to talk over the possibilities. Following up Sixte's lead, General Smuts went incognito to Switzerland in November for talks with Count Albert Mensdorff, former Austrian Ambassador to London. All these efforts came to nothing.

Irrespective of how Charles felt, the decisive question was whether Germany would yield an inch. Count Czernin, the Austro-Hungarian Foreign Minister, undertook to stalk Ludendorff. Would Germany contemplate returning Alsace and Lorraine to the French?

Ludendorff's reply was unqualified: "Never!" And that settled that. Thus, Germany spurned the final chance for a settlement short of surrender just before 1918 opened.

X
Exit Russia

A fur-hatted general inspects a battalion of
Russian women, composed largely of war widows
determined to avenge their dead husbands; to his
left is the unit's commander, Madame Botchkareva.

Even without an assist from Ludendorff, Nikolai Lenin might well have made it to Russia anyway. The fact remains that it was Ludendorff personally who cleared the way, figuring that loosing Lenin on Russia might take her out of the war.

Looking on rather cynically from the wings was Major General Max Hoffmann, who by this time was *de facto* commander of German armies on the Eastern Front, Field Marshal Prince Leopold of Bavaria being only a figurehead. Hoffmann still had eighty divisions under his command. Although there was no truce, the Russian Army wasn't fighting, and in effect had stacked arms. Yet instead of attacking and stampeding the passive camp opposite, thereby compelling the Provisional Government to sue for terms, Hoffmann simply marked time while his soldiers deteriorated. There were two reasons for the enforced halt. The Foreign Office believed that by treating the enemy gently Germany would more likely get a bid for peace from Petrograd. Also, Ludendorff did not want Hoffmann to use up divisions that were better conserved for his supreme bid on the Western Front.

In Zurich, Lenin was on fire to get moving as soon as he heard the news of the March Revolution. (It is called the February Revolution in Russia because of a difference in the calendar.) He had already made up his mind: the Provisional Government must be overthrown. He cabled the Petrograd Soviet, which included a small minority of his Bolshevik comrades: "Our tactics—no support, complete contempt. Armed proletariat, only guarantee."

But not even Delegate Joseph Stalin, who until then had displayed no real capacity for leadership, took these fulminations very seriously. Another revolution was inconceivable. Lenin's fellow emigrees of the left in Switzerland were not less timid. They wanted to return to Russia, but they were too meek to proceed through other than orthodox channels, applying to the Swiss Government for visas.

This was too slow, too conventional for Lenin. Using the secretary of the Swiss Socialist Party, Fritz Platten, as an intermediary, he got in direct touch with the German Government. Platten's messenger boy to the German Foreign Office in Lenin's behalf was Dr. Alexander Helphand, a Russian emigree. The Foreign Office passed Helphand along to the Supreme Command. There, before Hindenburg and Ludendorff, Helphand argued that the way to get Russia out of the war was to send Lenin to spread poison against the Provisional Government.

Ludendorff fell for it, and with his approval the deal was closed, though afterward, when the baneful effect of his decision on Germany's fortunes became all too clear, he tried to shift the blame to the Chancellor. At just about this time Germany was introducing a new destructive agent along the war fronts—Yellow Cross, or mustard gas. No mask was proof against it. It burned through clothing, worked its way into the flesh, destroyed vision, and choked out life. It may have occurred to Ludendorff, when he endorsed a through ticket for Lenin, that he had let go another weapon, equally insidious, all-pervasive, and also uncontrollable.

The word from the High Command greased the wheels at the legation in Berne. Having gained his permit, Lenin stated his arbitrary terms for the transshipment. His must be a special train, with guaranteed extraterritorial rights, no inspection of baggage, or examination of passports. German officials would not board the train; members of the party would not step from it while in transit. The Germans conceded every point, and that is how the legend of the "sealed train" came to flower.

On April 9 the train left Zurich. There were thirty-two fellow travelers aboard this special. The Mensheviks, a minority group of less radical Russian emigrees, had positively refused to board with Lenin. They warned him that he would be branded as a German agent, and thereby neutralized. He had already discounted that consequence, but the attempt to discredit him was duly made. On getting news of the train, Allied propagandists broadcast the tale that Lenin had sold out to Germany and that bags of enemy gold were riding to Russia with him. The libel served better to ease his entrance than to hinder his operations thereafter. Routed via Finland, the train could have been turned back at the border by order of Kerensky and his colleagues. But they had mistakenly concluded that the stories about Lenin's sellout had spiked his guns.

Nothing of that sort happened. Lenin reached Petrograd on April 16. He was showered with bouquets of roses by the waiting comrades at a reception in the Czar's private waiting room, a detail that completes the beguiling picture. The chairman of the welcoming committee, President Nikolai S. Chkheidze of the Petrograd Soviet, said: "Comrade Lenin, in the name of the whole revolution, we greet you. But we consider that the chief task of the revolutionary democracy is to defend our revolution against every attack both from within and without." Lenin roared back: "I am happy to greet in you . . . the advance guard of the international proletarian army." So there it was, right out in the open from the beginning—a declaration of counterrevolution. With his first words he had won the crowd.

The timing of the arrival could not better have suited his purpose. The Provisional Government was reeling, due to the *faux pas* of Foreign Minister Milyukov, who in a policy statement had declared that Russia would still reach for the Dardanelles. To the Petrograd Soviet, and to a war-weary nation, this meant imperialism and a renewal of the nightmare. Lenin dashed about, haranguing the street crowds: "What do you get from war? Only wounds, starvation, and death." In an extraordinary session of the Petrograd Soviet, a vote of confidence in the Provisional Government passed by only thirty-five votes out of 2,500. Three chief ministers had resigned from the Government by May 17, the same day Leon Trotsky arrived in Petrograd from America. Kerensky went in as Minister of War and Marine, and three members of the Soviet took cabinet posts in the Provisional Government. In its first declaration the new Government rejected the idea of a separate peace for Russia while pronouncing its aim "to bring about at the earliest possible moment a general peace." At the same time it said that no land would be divided until after the ultimate calling of a constituent assembly, an error that put more water on Lenin's wheel.

During this time, the Allied Governments looked on more bewildered than aghast. Despite the growing evidence that Russia was quitting the war via the back door, and regardless of the efforts of their Ambassadors on the ground so to convince them, they refused to believe. In his first war message to the Congress, Wilson hailed the trend of events in Russia with these words: "Here is a fit partner for a league of honor." The elder statesman Elihu Root returned from a mission to Russia to urge American support for the Provisional Government. Mr. Root had seen all the foliage and missed the roots.

Kerensky was doing little better than that. In June he decided to send his motley army into one more offensive against the tired Austrians, though the Bolsheviks damned him for his folly. So

General Brusilov had to hit the road again in early July. The Russians sent forty-five divisions into the attack launched over a forty-mile front along the Dniester and in the Carpathian foothills. The Austrian Army of the South under Count Bothmer included four German divisions, three Austrian, and one Turkish. The Third Austrian Army under General Tersztyanky was even less formidable. On July 5 the Russian attack crushed his front and rolled for more than twenty miles. Then, after getting within reach of the goal—the oil fields around Drohobycz—and riding down the worst of the resistance, the Russian Army simply quit. Officers gave orders but troops would not go forward. Under Hoffmann's direction, the Teutonic forces counterattacked and made up all the lost ground. The Russians threw down their arms and many of the soldiers ran off homeward. In a diversionary effort in late July, the Rumanian divisions that had backed into Russia when their own country was overrun, and the Russian Fourth Army, staged an attack over a sixty-mile front in the lower Carpathians. This last attempt to breathe life into the Kerensky offensive was knocked back by Mackensen's army. Both sides then resumed the passive defense, the Germans having too few troops present to follow up their advantage.

The failure ruined Brusilov, who was succeeded by General Lavr Georgievich Kornilov, a brave enough soldier, popular with the ranks because he had helped unseat the Czar, but also a rattlebrain. Worse than that, the failure discredited Kerensky, and while he lingered on for a time, he was finished as a popular idol. Once again, the net effect was to help pave the road for Lenin.

Momentarily, it didn't look that way. Taking the bit in their teeth, elements in the Petrograd garrison, prodded by the Bolsheviks, had proclaimed revolt against the Provisional Government in mid-July. It was a premature, half-hearted try, quickly snuffed out. There followed a roundup and arrest of Bolshevik leaders. Lenin fled to hiding in Finland. Then in early September General Kornilov ordered his troops out to march on Petrograd to overthrow Kerensky, intending to take power himself. But though he shouted, the troops would not obey, and the march straggled into nothingness while still far short of the city. Even so, this swiftly expiring threat unnerved Kerensky. In a desperate attempt to save himself, he sought to make his peace with the Bolshevik leaders, and when the others were released from prison, Lenin came back to town. Again the Government fell apart from

The abdication of Czar Nicholas II in 1917
marked the end of the three-century-old
Romanov reign and presaged the toppling
of many other European dynasties. Fearful
of losing their giant ally in the east,
the Entente powers took heart when the
Provisional Government and its strong man,
Alexander Kerensky (shown here studying
a map), pledged to pursue the war for the
"honor of Russia."

the shock and Kerensky took over as chairman of a directorate of five.

In early October both the Petrograd and Moscow Soviets passed under control of Bolshevik majorities, with Leon Trotsky presiding in the capital. Unlike Lenin, this man looked the part of an earthshaker. Impressively tall, ramrod straight, carrying himself like a military commander, he was also majestic of face, the eyes and the jawline imparting an impression of great force combined with wisdom. When he took charge, the Bolshevik power play swiftly followed. With the object of "taking over the Government of Russia," the party summoned an All-Russian Congress of Soviets to meet in Petrograd the first week in November. Lenin, from a suburban covert, was prodding the comrades on; they must either strike now or lose out wholly. Then from the barracks came the trumpet blast that toppled the quaking wall of the March Revolution. The regiments stationed in Petrograd adopted this resolution: "We no longer recognize the Provisional Government. The Petrograd Soviet is our Government."

Spurning the thought of waiting for a vote by the Soviet Congress, crying that the hour demanded direct action, Lenin ordered revolt. The Bolsheviks' takeover of power was peculiarly unviolent and lacking in drama; they had the government after two days of practically bloodless charading. Kerensky left Petrograd on November 7, supposedly looking for troops to put down the rebellion; not finding any, he kept on going. A familiar figure in foreign capitals, blessed by longevity, in 1964 he had not yet outlived the half-century-old revolution that he had freely predicted would soon wither away.

On the following night Lenin appeared before the Soviet Congress and read his decree calling for immediate negotiations looking to a "just and democratic peace," without annexations or indemnities. The applause was deafening, the vote unanimous in support. Delegates turned to one another laughing and weeping. "The war is ended! The war is ended!" they chanted. And indeed, they believed it because Lenin had said it. Quickly, action was suited to words. On November 21 Commissar for War Nikolai Krylenko published an order to all forces that fraternization with enemy troops should be initiated and that commanders should address proposals to the headquarters opposite, seeking an end of military operations.

General N. N. Dukhonin, who had succeeded Kornilov as Commander in Chief, flatly refused to comply. He would obey "only a government sustained by the army and by the country." Thereupon Krylenko formally sacked him and tried to take over his job. But Dukhonin's soldiers would neither obey him nor wholly turn against him; while they milled around in confusion, he stayed on. Meanwhile, the Allies chased the illusion that by dealing with Russian G.H.Q. and treating it as if it were a government, they could collapse Lenin and the commissars.

On December 3 Krylenko arrived at Dukhonin's headquarters with a crowd of mutinous Bolshevik sailors. First, they demanded the General's epaulets and got them. One hour later they were back. They dragged Dukhonin from his railway car to the platform and shot him to death. It was a clinching act in the new revolution. Loyalty to the vestiges of the old order, as to the treaty that the Czar had signed with the Allies, perished with Dukhonin.

BREST LITOVSK

General Max Hoffmann still had his eighty German divisions on the Eastern Front, though he sometimes wondered why. Particularly did he wonder when Ludendorff moved against the Italians at Caporetto with only eight divisions, lamenting that he couldn't spare any more. To Hoffmann's mind that was absurd.

That Germans were not immune to the virus that had prostrated the Russian Army, he well knew. There had been some mutinies in the navy that summer, serious enough to raise inquiries in the Reichstag. To keep more of the ships' crews occupied by giving them a feeling of usefulness, he had fitted out an amphibious strike against the Russian-based islands of Dagö and Moon in the Baltic, in the late fall. There had been no resistance worth the name. The Russian defender, Admiral Vasili Altvater, told Hoffmann: "My troops melted away."

Now Hoffmann was resting on his oars and wondering what would come next. He didn't have to wait long. On November 26 Trotsky, as Foreign Commissar of the new Bolshevik Government, appealed to the German High Command for negotiations toward a settlement. "We don't want a separate peace," he said to the Allied Ambassadors, "but peace we must have, and if we can't seek it together, the blame is on you." Carrying the word was left to Krylenko; the ex-corporal, now Commander in Chief, telephoned Ludendorff, who in turn telephoned Hoffmann to ask him: "Do you think it is possible to negotiate with these people?" Hoffmann answered: "Yes, it is possible and if Your Excellency requires troops, this is the best way to get them."

Much later, Hoffmann reflected that the answer was probably one of his major blunders. By refusing to negotiate, the Germans might have toppled Lenin.

The German High Command's decision to deal with the Bolsheviks raised the curtain on one of the more bizarre dramas of the war. On December 2 the Bolshevik Armistice Delegation passed through German lines at Dvinsk and continued on to Brest Litovsk. Hoffmann was already there ahead of them and would speak for Ludendorff, though he did not believe in what the Quartermaster General was trying to do. It was not the terms of the contemplated armistice that concealed the hook: that part of it was elementary; short of a peace settlement, conquerors cannot be expected to withdraw from a territory won by force. So the High Command was prepared to advance these simple conditions: the fighting would cease and both sides would stand fast in the positions then held. As Hoffmann remarked: "There is nothing here unjust or insulting to the Russians." It was a historically correct procedure. But to the hopeful Bolsheviks "peace without annexations or indemnities" meant just what it said. Where the territory of Mother Russia was concerned, they were as imperialist as any Czarist and they came to Brest Litovsk prepared to fight for the domain as Nicholas had known it. But that was not consistent with Ludendorff's appetite. The High Command had an intricate, if vague, tentative solution for Poland, Germany taking enough of it to provide Russia with a buffer zone to the east, and the rest of it going possibly to Austria. As for Kurland and Lithuania, the House of Hohenzollern would digest what its armies had won. They would be transformed into German Grand Duchies and lieges of the Kaiser.

On a more vital issue, the far-seeing Hoffmann felt Ludendorff was going astray. They had recently met and talked over the coming decisive battle in the West. Ludendorff unloaded a new theory. He would not concentrate on one offensive, but would probe for a weak spot until at last he found it. Although this made little sense to Hoffmann, he began shifting his own divisions westward as rapidly as the trains could lift them, to further Ludendorff's design.

The century has seen no such ill-mixed cast gathered around a truce negotiation table as the group at Brest Litovsk. Heading the Bolshevik delegation was Adolf Joffe, a sufficiently presentable and intelligent individual. But in conformity with the idea that all strata of Russian society, except the aristocracy, should be represented, he had picked up on the road a peasant, one Stashkov, wholly illiterate, totally ignorant of civilized custom. There were also a sailor, a worker, and Madame Anastasia Bizenko, who had become a Bolshevik heroine by murdering a minister. On the other side were such characters as Count Czernin, Austria's polished Foreign Minister, desperately anxious for peace on almost any terms, because his country was starving. Beside Hoffmann was Baron Richard von Kuhlmann, the cooly detached new German Foreign Secretary, who wanted a peace of conciliation and was therefore at odds with the High Command. There was a general from Turkey and another from Bulgaria; Admiral Altvater was the only military figure on the Russian side, serving in the capacity of a technical adviser.

By December 12 there was tentative agreement on the terms of an armistice, approximately according to the German proposals. It was signed three days later, to run for one month. Hoffmann had foolishly agreed to the setting up of fraternization centers between the lines, which would allow the Bolsheviks to propagandize German troops. The sessions then broke off so that the delegates could report to their home governments.

There was called at Kreuznach on December 19 a meeting of the Crown Council: the Kaiser, Hindenburg, Ludendorff, Kuhlmann, and the aged Chancellor, Count Georg von Hertling. (Bethmann-Hollweg had been forced out of office in July; his successor, Dr. Georg Michaelis, had lasted only one hundred days.) Both Hindenburg and Hertling promptly fell asleep. The purpose of the council was to thresh out the vital differences between Ludendorff's and Kuhlmann's views on final terms to Russia.

Ludendorff wouldn't yield an inch on the partition of Poland and the annexation of Russia's Baltic provinces. Kuhlmann doggedly reiterated his arguments for conciliation. The Kaiser fluttered back and forth between these extremes, unable to make up his mind. Ludendorff was outraged that Kuhlmann sought to cross him. Hindenburg came awake for a few minutes when Kuhlmann asked him the blunt question: "Why do you want the Baltic territories?" He answered: "For the basing of my left wing in the next war," and again closed his eyes.

In the end no decision was made and Kuhlmann returned to Brest Litovsk uninstructed. But he knew now that he could not win his point, which made him wiser than Ludendorff, who stayed unaware that in striving to win all he would lose everything.

Three days before Christmas the delegations returned to Brest Litovsk—Joffe and his fellow Bolsheviks elated that the Germans were acting so agreeably; Hoffmann and Kuhlmann apprehensive about the approaching collision when Ludendorff's stiff terms would at last be laid bare.

It is now almost forgotten that what came of Brest Litovsk was not peace in its real sense, but war in a new form between Germany and Russia. It is forgotten, also, that German armies in 1918 were launched in a new invasion of Russia that carried them through the Crimea and beyond the Don, so that they extended beyond the limits where the hedgehogs of Hitler's armies wintered in 1941–42 after the repulse at Moscow. It is forgotten that nearly one million German soldiers wasted on the distant steppes while Ludendorff made his supreme bid for victory on the Western Front, finally to fail because he had exhausted his reserves.

By Christmas Day the two sides appeared to be in full agreement. Joffe had stated six principles to govern the peace, all glittering generalizations, including such points as self-determination, no indemnities, no forcible appropriation of territory. Kuhlmann and Czernin raised no objections because in spirit they were reconciled to such a settlement. Joffe was jubilant and telegraphed Lenin that the game was won. But the Soviets had insisted on full publicity for the proceedings and the story hit Germany. Ludendorff fired off a message to Hoffmann that he had "betrayed" the decisions made at Kreuznach, a conference about which Hoffmann knew nothing. There had been no decision at Kreuznach, but it became obvious to Hoffmann, after Kuhlmann briefed him, that he would have to follow the High Command's line.

So the dirty work was left to the soldier. Hoffmann arose and explained that the Bolsheviks were misinterpreting Germany's use of the term "no annexations," which could not preclude Poland and the Baltic States joining the German Empire of their own free will. Joffe almost fainted. Then he sobbed out: "How can you speak of no annexations when you tear eighteen provinces from us?" Next, he threatened to dissolve the conference. At that point, Czernin, who was desperate for peace with Russia, weakened and told his German partners that if the conference broke up, Austria would be prepared to negotiate with the Bolsheviks independently. Hoffmann savagely deflated the Austrian Foreign Minister by answering: "You do, and we'll recall those twenty-five German divisions now stiffening your front."

On that impasse over annexations, the early deliberations ended. In the holiday interlude, the Kaiser swung over to Kuhlmann's view that the softer approach best met the need. Back came a defiant letter from the High Command, in effect an ultimatum, which directed the All-Highest to fall in line with Ludendorff's views, or else. And of course he buckled. When the Bolshevik delegation returned to Brest Litovsk in mid-January, Trotsky was heading it and all of his great skill as a negotiator and propagandist came forward. But it could change nothing. The German High Command remained intransigent.

There now entered a new element, a delegation of young Ukrainians, who wanted independence of Bolshevik Russia, with Germany shielding the new nation. Dreaming of the Ukraine's vast granary, the Germans and Austrians quickly signed a treaty with the Ukrainians.

None of Trotsky's rhetoric could influence events because the confreres opposite were powerless to move the First Quartermaster General of Germany. Trotsky saw that soon enough, and he made his own play. All the time Hoffmann was carrying in his pocket what he thought was the high card—authority from the High Command to end the negotiations, resume the war, invade Russia, and force an unconditional surrender. Not knowing, Trotsky played his trump. Russia would not stay in the war; on the other hand, it would not make peace with Germany, though its forces would be demobilized. This said, the Bolshevik delegation walked out, leaving the Central Power delegates nonplused. "*Unerhört!*" cried Hoffmann, "*Unerhört!*" (Unheard of.) He immediately called the High Command at Kreuznach. Ludendorff flatly ordered him to resume the war. The armistice was to be denounced on February 17 and the German Eighth Army would immediately strike eastward.

Trotsky was dreaming that Imperial Germany could not make war on a land that declared itself at peace, which was a little

Still loyal to the Army, this Russian soldier
uses a rifle butt to force his comrade
to return to duty. On July 1, 1917, General
Brusilov's forces pushed some thirty miles
into Galicia, but the troops, infected
with war-weariness and a revolutionary
spirit, began to quit. Under the German
counterattack, the Kerensky offensive became
a one-hundred-mile retreat.

naïve. On February 16 he was sitting with Lenin at Petrograd. A message to Lenin came in from one of the observers left at Brest Litovsk: "Hoffmann serves notice that the armistice will be denounced and the war will be resumed tomorrow." Lenin turned to Trotsky and said: "Your test has been tried and it has failed. Now it's a question of saving the revolution. You must get back there at once and you must sign a treaty of peace."

But at dawn on February 18, the German Army in the East began the long thrust toward the Urals. It was not an attack but a march-in and most of the movement was by boxcar. There was no armed resistance. The gray columns and the rolling stock bearing the heavy matériel drove north and eastward to tie down new lands for the Crown and garner the riches of the Ukraine. But that wasn't how the operation was billed; to fool the world and enthrall upper-class Russians, Field Marshal Prince Leopold, Hoffmann's superior, proclaimed that the object was to purge Europe of Bolshevism.

The next day Hoffmann got a message from Lenin and Trotsky: Russia would sign immediately on Germany's terms. Hoffmann ignored it. With the columns cutting through to Russia's vitals, he had no intention of stopping now. In five days the spearheads advanced north and eastward two hundred miles, capturing 3,000 guns, an army of prisoners, and enough rolling stock to double their mobility. "It's the most comical war I've ever known," wrote Hoffmann. "We put a handful of men on a train with a machine gun, run them into a town, and they capture it." By February 21 German troops had landed in Finland and suppressed the Red Guards at Helsinki.

In Petrograd, some of the old Bolsheviks turned on Lenin, shouting that it was time to fight. He stood firm; there had to be a peace on whatever terms, for there was no way to resist. On February 26 the Bolshevik acceptance of the peace terms was announced to the Reichstag and greeted with wild excitement. But when an order was flashed to Hoffmann to call a halt, he replied that his armies would keep advancing until the peace was signed. As February ended, the delegations were back in Brest Litovsk and on March 3, 1918, the pact was at last completed. Under its terms Russia yielded 34 per cent of her population, 32 per cent of her farmland, 50 per cent of her industrial holdings, and 90 per cent of her coal mines. Said Trotsky: "This is a peace that Russia, grinding her teeth, is forced to accept."

But the military aggression and wild-eyed Teutonic adventuring could not end with the proclamation of peace. A million jack-booted Germans had penetrated far too deeply into the Russian interior, and there they were stuck with the problem created by overstretched lines of communication and by Ludendorff's delusions of grandeur. No people—not even the cowed Russians of that day—will suffer passively an occupation intended to grind them small. All nature is against it, and the victims started reviving in the hour when the initial shock wore off. Parties of Red Guards, fighting as guerrillas, and the freebooting Czech Legion, which had formed in Russia and would later have high adventure in Siberia, began to fight back, engaging German patrols, blowing bridges, and sabotaging military stores in the occupied territory.

Troop hardship steadily increased, while the prospect of reward from the mad adventure proportionately dwindled. The lure of the rich harvest of the Ukraine proved to be a mirage, and the attempt to establish Ukrainian independence under German tutelage failed. These reverses no more deterred Ludendorff than did the mounting appearances that the operation was failing in its objectives. The greater the frustration, the more he extended. German colonies in the Crimea were invited to request annexation by Germany. A second expedition was sent to Finland to put down a Bolshevik uprising. Another was dispatched to Baku. Yet Ludendorff withheld his armies from taking the one positive step that might have lent substance to the grand design. They did not march on Petrograd and Moscow and overthrow the Bolsheviks.

Throughout the spring and summer of 1918 Hoffmann's armies remained entoiled along these distant frontiers, during the high crisis of the war when Ludendorff struggled for decision in the West. When he was stunned belatedly into realizing the utter desperation of Germany's plight and wished to recall the lost divisions from Russia, they had become so thoroughly subverted by Communist propaganda that he dared not bring them west.

THE ALLIED ATTITUDE

From any clear view of the immediate consequence to the Allied cause, the final Bolshevik capitulation in March, 1918, should have been a near disaster.

After hearing that German cavalry had broken through the lines, Russian soldiers threw down their arms and fled.

Two facts palliated the impact on the Allied peoples. First, it was no surprise. Events had been pointing in this direction for almost a year and the military invalidism of Russia had been all too obvious for much longer than that. Second, and more important, America had been in the war for nine months and her troops were making the Atlantic passage safely and landing in France in ever-increasing numbers. If America had not become a belligerent or if the U-boat menace had not by this time markedly abated, a tide of despair might have engulfed the democracies when Russia defected. As it happened, there was relatively little shock and no marked change in the outlook. Pessimism without defeatism continued as the prevailing mood in England and France. The war had looked interminable before; nothing could make it seem longer than that. America's almost complete indifference toward Russia's withdrawal might well have been expressed in these words: "So what? We will get enough men over there and then we'll win."

French and British statesmen knew both too much and too little to remain unmoved. Their ambiguous policy was to ignore the Bolsheviks, to react as if nothing really had changed, and at the same time to seek devious paths whereby what had happened might be undone. This obscurantist approach, if understandable, was hardly wise. To the Allies, the ruling Bolsheviks had to be ostracized, not so much because they were "Dirty Reds," their menace to the existing order being but vaguely glimpsed in those days, but because they were guilty of a double cross. To the governments of the embattled alliance that was the unpardonable offense: the Russians had reneged on a solemn pledge and broken faith with the holy cause. The Allied Governments could not recognize the Bolshevik regime without endorsing what the Bolsheviks had done, at which point all of the war covenants became invalidated. The honoring of sovereignty in that hour would also have endorsed treaty arrangements Russia had already made with Germany. It was impossible; in war there are only friends, enemies, and neutrals, and Bolshevik Russia could hardly be regarded as the last, since she was openly trafficking with the archfoe on issues profoundly influencing the military outcome. So she was treated tacitly as an enemy. None of the Allied Ambassadors could deal directly with the Soviet Government. Each had to cultivate roundabout channels and depend on special agents for his reports. In consequence, the emissaries on the spot stayed less than half-informed, more propaganda than dependable news flowed out of Russia, and, for the duration, all that happened there was seen as through a drifting fog.

Quite early, the Allied statesmen, at a meeting in Paris, decided that there should be no direct military intervention aimed to overthrow the Bolshevik rule and return Russia to the belligerent fold. Yet General Foch came up with a scheme. He proposed to send an Allied expedition to Siberia, which was not yet under Bolshevik control. Lloyd George and Balfour were opposed, and so was Colonel House, for Wilson still hoped that some brands could be plucked from the burning. The motion was tabled.

The idea, though bypassed, did not die. It would have been better if it had. Later the Allies would make such attempts, dispatching forces of their own, and backing Czarist White Russians when they took the field to raise the flag of counterrevolution above meager forces. It was all done halfheartedly, too little and too late. Trotsky, when he was made War Commissar and given the unenviable task of creating a Red Army out of dissolution, surprisingly proved himself to be a quite competent soldier.

A Change of Direction

At this stage of the war, however, there was a lamentable lack of direction in Allied high councils. The vagueness about the Russian problem was characteristic. Statesmen and soldiers could agree on what should not be done; there was no such concert toward a common policy and a positive course of action. The Christmas holidays of 1917 were the Allied doldrums. The contest looked as unending as ever, the problem of how to keep on keeping on seemed too big for management. Some part of this uncertainty derived from lack of cohesion and central purpose in the military High Commands behind the Western Front. Joffre, with all his great faults, had dominated the scene, demanding and usually getting what he wanted from his Government, and forever jockeying his British collaborator. Now there was only Pétain, a negative personality, by nature an ingrained pessimist, constrained by the situation to play the waiting game, and for all these reasons inhibited from becoming a dominating military figure. Haig, both by virtue of his long tenure as senior commander and the comparatively ascending scale of Britain's war potential in contrast to that of France, should have filled the larger role, but he wasn't up to it.

The Rapallo Conference in November, 1917, had given the Allies the shadow of a supreme command without the substance. Frictions, instead of easing, were exacerbated. At a High Council meeting, General Foch, who should have known better, challenged the British on their troop strength, complaining that they could form more divisions if they tried. He was fortunate that his gross blunder did not blight his personal career. Between Allies such questions may not be raised. They are an insult to sovereignty, impugning good faith. Riding Foch's coattails to high place was General Sir Henry Wilson, Britain's perennial Ambassador to the French General Staff, who had long been a Foch devotee. This ebullient Irishman, hearty *bon vivant*, dramatic extrovert, and born conspirator is one of the most controversial figures of World War I. His enemies regarded him as a malicious meddler; his friends saw him as an inspired strategist, although he held no key position sufficiently long to be supremely tested in his abilities as a commander in the field.

There was at least one man who well understood that the British and Allied military policies were rocking at dead center. Sir

Wully Robertson believed that Armageddon Day on the Western Front was coming up fast. His papers put it to the War Cabinet that crash measures had to be taken to insure survival. About what was needed, he was perfectly clear—the diversion of more shipping to bring American divisions overseas, the call-up of every British male who might make a soldier, and the concentration of all field fighting power in France.

Pershing's staff saw clearly enough at that stage that the control of shipping and concentrating of more soldiers were the *sine qua non* of victory, but there was no corresponding grasp of that reality in Mr. Wilson's Government. The War Boards, which vitalized executive power, did not come into being until the spring of 1918. The dimensions of vast wartime operations were only vaguely glimpsed by the men next to the President. Robertson had fingered the bottleneck; the shipping allocations had to be radically altered. In the end that happened. Fifty-six per cent of American troops went to France on British ships; American vessels carried the minority.

Toward Robertson's pressures, Lloyd George remained unmoved, noncommittal, as if waiting for great events to overtake him. Passchendaele had shaken him; he wanted no more big killings. Curiously enough, however, it was not the food pinch in Britain that blocked his view of shipping, though the problem had become grimly astringent. Beef and mutton had almost disappeared from city and town markets. Butter, never displayed, was saved for wealthier patrons. Women and children queued up all day for a little sugar to sweeten their tea.

None of these griefs begot the Prime Minister's indecision. The fact was that he looked more than ever toward Allenby's crusade in Palestine as a magic deliverance from the great slaughter. He truly believed that the war might be won that way, because he could not bear to think of another year of carnage in the West. But the bottoms needed to carry great reinforcements to Allenby could not at the same time ply the Atlantic to beef up the A.E.F.

To Robertson it looked as if the Central Powers were winning the war. Provided he had taken the slightest measure of Ludendorff as a strategist, it should have been apparent to him that Ludendorff's main arena would not be Turkey. Unrestricted U-boat warfare and the heavy German troop movement from the Eastern Front signaled that the supreme trial could not be long deferred.

A self-assured Leon Trotsky (in fur hat)
arrives at Brest-Litovsk to head the Soviet
delegation seeking peace with the Central
Powers. The Treaty of Brest-Litovsk was
signed in March, 1918, after two months of
long, bitter negotiations. It was later
superseded by the armistice on the Western
Front and the Treaty of Versailles.

Around New Year's Day, 1918, the Prime Minister bucked to the CIGS a set of foolish questions, of which these are fairly representative: "Can the General Staff foresee a victorious ending to the war? If so, when and under what circumstances?"

General Robertson correctly replied that the future depended "on a variety of factors beyond the power of the General Staff to calculate." Then, to prove that it wasn't his day for handing out soporifics, he added that the British Army would grow weaker and weaker unless far more men were provided than those called for in the report of the Cabinet Committee on Manpower. Again, he got in a plug for more shipping on the Atlantic run.

To have such a military servant ever at one's elbow is gall and wormwood to the political leader who daily must tonic his own optimism. No Chief of Staff was ever more right than Robertson as 1918 opened. But he had worn out his welcome by being blunt instead of pleasing. Shortly, Sir Henry Wilson took over from him and Robertson went out on half pay. Sir Henry came in believing that the war could not possibly be won before 1919. It was one of his few claims to being farsighted. In office he was more surprised than surprising.

But where Britain muddled along with divided counsel, Ludendorff had already decided what Germany must do in 1918, and opposing opinions were brushed aside.

Ever since Falkenhayn's ghastly go at Verdun, the Kaiser's armies had eschewed major offensive undertakings on the Western Front. The defensive role had kept the cost of battle comparatively low. Even so, Germany had begun to hurt for military manpower almost as acutely as for the bare necessities of life. Starvation had set in. Even the troops were subsisting on ersatz coffee, using substitutes for grain cereals, and smoking weed. Vitamin deficiency was already destroying the tooth and bone of the young generation. White bread, butter, cheeses, meaty sausages, heating, lighting—these things were long gone. Enough meat bones to make a soup was an exceptional portion for the average family. Beardless youths and old men were being called up to flesh out the formations, and they did not mind it too much because in service they would be a little better fed than at home. The drainage resulting from large-scale assistance to the Turks and Austrians, and from pursuing Ludendorff's dreams of empire, had far overstretched Germany's human resources.

For months, this logistically precise but politically reckless autocrat had been telling himself that Germany would either win in 1918 or lose all. Through the last quarter of 1917, Ludendorff had tried to conserve and shift forces to make the supreme effort. In after years, he confessed: "I can see now that our decline began with the outbreak of the revolution in Russia." But he wholly missed the implications at the time. Preoccupied with the application of sheer force, his mind was without depth and subtlety. Although the Allies had not once indicated that they were bent on unconditional surrender by the enemy, Ludendorff could not imagine conceding space on one flank to gain time and advantage on the other. He wanted everything.

For his big try, he had already approved of a novel tactical system and was ready with both the manner of battlefield execution and the prerequisite shift in training. The method had been first proved by General Oskar von Hutier in the late autumn operations around Riga, and Hutier had already been transferred to the Western Front. Necessity fathered the invention. At Uxküll, where the Germans forced the passage of the Dvina, the Russians had been heavily entrenched and the German forces were light. So Hutier had to try something new, and what he did went almost unnoticed at the time by other tacticians, including Ludendorff, because the fight itself was so insignificant. Later the same method was used to shred the Italian Army in the Battle of Caporetto. It was called infiltration. There was nothing highly original about it. Guerrilla tactics are built around the same idea of disregarding the heavily manned and heavily weaponed high ground and strong points, while reaching for the softer spots. Troops are then sped through the openings to the enemy's rear to cut short further resistance. That was how the Japanese conducted their most dramatic campaigns during World War II. The Communist Chinese, learning more from them than from the Russians, came into Korea in 1950 against the U.S. Eighth Army, fighting the same way. But it was Ludendorff who made infiltration a big word after Hutier primed him.

Out of necessity, Ludendorff had to turn from his defensive role to become the sledgehammer of the Western Front. Out of equal necessity, Sir Douglas Haig, whose generalship so far had had all the finesse of a bulldozer, also shifted roles, this time to save himself. In the same weeks that Ludendorff was recalling troops from Italy and the Russian front with the object of break-

After the Kerenksy offensive of July 1, 1917 (broken white
arrow) buckled under a German counterattack (black arrows) and
the German Eighth Army took Riga in the north, the Bolsheviks
seized power and asked for an armistice (solid white line).
During a breakdown in the Brest-Litovsk negotiations, Germany
advanced deep into Russia and the Ukraine (dotted white line).

ing through in the West, Haig's G.H.Q. was polishing a memo-randum to all lower commands, the main point of which was that thereafter the B.E.F. would stand on the defensive. Patrol-ling and heavy trench raids would continue, and points would be awarded for prisoners taken, documents captured, and so forth—a nice touch of British gamesmanship. The memo announcing the diametric change, which all infantry officers read with a sigh of relief, did not come from Sir Douglas's reading Ludendorff's mail. Haig knew he was marked for dismissal if Lloyd George could work up the nerve. The memo, dated December 14, 1917, was written by his staff in the interest of self-preservation.

Ludendorff's change of role had been punctuated at a confer-ence in Mons on November 11, a significant date, though the conferees had to wait one year to learn why. The Kaiser, the Crown Prince, and Prince Rupprecht of Bavaria (the latter two commanding the army groups concerned) were not present. They were represented by their Chiefs of Staff. Ludendorff said: "The situation in Russia and Italy will make it possible to deliver a blow on the Western Front in the new year. The strength of the two sides will be approximately equal. About thirty-five divi-sions and one thousand heavy guns can be made available for *one* offensive. . . . Our general situation requires that we should strike at the earliest moment . . . before the Americans can throw strong forces into the scale. We must beat the British."

Why the British? It was not because Ludendorff, like Falken-hayn, saw Britain as the main enemy. Ludendorff calculated that it would take about four months to smash the armies of the Western Alliance. The B.E.F. was so placed that it had little back country in which to retreat and, if unhinged and driven toward the sea, would probably evacuate via the Channel ports; Hitler made the same calculation in 1940 and it proved correct. Then, if he could isolate the British (despite what he said to the staff officers at Mons, Ludendorff did not think of rolling back the Allied left flank in a single flow), he could turn his full attention to breaking the French Army. In the first go, he would strike where Haig's right flank joined Pétain's left. The target therefore would be General Gough's Fifth Army, which was far below authorized strength and holding more front than was prudent. Ludendorff calculated that Pétain would be dilatory about rush-ing support to Gough when the operation, code-named "Michael," sundered the line. In that, he was prescient. But Michael, which was to hit on both sides of Saint-Quentin, was in fact three separate offensives with the ultimate object of breaking the front from Vimy south to the Oise, which, as the line undulated, meant a distance of about seventy-five miles.

The Ludendorff staff preparations went far beyond Michael. Plans were drawn for Operations Archangel, Achilles, Roland, Hector, Castor, and Pollux, which, following, would batter the Allied armies from west to east. This was the shotgun approach earlier discussed by Ludendorff with Hoffmann and mistrusted by the latter. The proliferation of plans is eloquent of the doubt in Ludendorff's mind about the main blow. Far better than the high commanders opposite him, he understood how swiftly offensive energy dissipated under Western Front conditions and how soon inertia grips troops at the point of success. He would let circumstances decide how the aim should be maintained as the battle developed.

Thanks to the accommodation from the Bolsheviks, Ludendorff's manpower prospects were much better than he knew when he gave a few staff officers the word at the Mons conference. Well before the attack, the German Army on the Western Front had swelled to 136,600 officers and 3,450,000 other ranks. One hundred and ninety-two divisions had deployed into the ground between the Alps and the North Sea, and sixty-nine of them (twice the number Ludendorff had initially counted on) were concentrated along the sixty-nine-mile front facing the British. Britain, having cut basic strength from twelve to nine rifle battalions per division during recent months, still had only thirty-three divisions in France, of which twelve were either in distant reserve or in rest areas well to the rear.

There was another, graver handicap. Patterning after the Germans, Haig's armies had swung over to an elastic system of defense. The forward trenches were lightly manned and largely entrusted to automatic weapons crews. From two to three miles to the rear of the first barrier was the "battle zone," which was studded with redoubts and pillboxes. But labor troops were too few, and in Gough's army area, the battle zone remained largely in blueprint form. Some of the fire trenches had been surveyed, but digging awaited the arrival of spring.

Extraordinary precautions were taken by the Germans to keep their preparations secret. The storm battalions were brought forward by night and stayed under cover by day. At the forward railheads any appearance of congestion was scrupulously avoided after sunrise. Despite all this care, Europe knew what was afoot. Berlin radiated fresh confidence and the speeches of leading Germans became steadily more truculent. Cried one voice in the Reichstag: "Hindenburg stands in the West with the whole German manhood for the first time united, ready to strike with the strongest army that the world has ever known."

Up front, British soldiers knew. Every day or so there came from higher headquarters some new defense scheme, to be followed promptly by another paper amending it. Also, the press from home shrilled warning in terms unmistakable even to the newly arrived replacements. It was common gossip that all Germans were trooping west out of Russia with the object of exterminating the B.E.F. More positive proof was returned to the dugouts from the trench raids. German POW's can no more keep their mouths shut than any other soldiers, and what the High Command intended had sifted far down. The place, the power in attack, almost everything but the appointed hour was known. But no matter what the British said, the French would not believe. Their General Staff too greatly relished the notion that if Ludendorff was set on a prime target, he must hit the French Army. In the face of the threat, there was practically no collaboration between the two principal Allies.

XI
New Storm in the West

Sir William Orpen's embattled British
howitzer crew symbolizes Allied resistance
to Germany's brutal 1918 offensives
along the Western Front.

Woodrow Wilson made the first big war headlines of 1918 by speaking words of peace. Then General Ludendorff washed them out—the words and the headlines—by dismembering Russia at Brest Litovsk, and by staging the greatest losing battle of the century.

As of January 8, the President's convictions no doubt squared with the idealistic sentiments that on that day he pronounced as the basis for a war settlement. But even Wilson hardened under the impact of events that made his lofty phrases ring hollow. The Allies might have settled for a nonvengeful peace in the hour that he spoke. Before March ran out, Germany's rapacity in the East and fury in the West made magnanimity impossible.

Wilson had been looking for some sort of formula to end the war ever since the summer of 1917. "We have no quarrel with the German people," was a phrase that he coined early; its greatest usefulness was to provide a theme for sardonic verses by the British poet A. P. Herbert later in the days of Hitler. Colonel House was given the task of expanding Wilson's controlling idea into specific proposals. A research task force, headed by House's brother-in-law, Dr. Sidney Mezes, and including a very young Walter Lippmann, was asked to take a global view of the war issues and come up with Utopian solutions. House reported on their work during the 1917 Christmas holidays, and a speech was drafted for the launching of the celebrated Fourteen Points before Congress. Unfortunately in those days Allied leaders did not consult one another about common policy at the drop of a hat. Just as the historic paper jelled, Lloyd George talked to the British Trades Union Congress, where he said: "The settlement of the new Europe must be based on such grounds of reason and justice as will give some promise of stability. Therefore we feel that government with the consent of the governed must be the basis of any territorial settlement in this war."

Wilson felt dished. Such were his chagrin and disappointment that he proposed canceling his own speech. His advisers convinced him that Lloyd George had but scratched the surface and that he must therefore carry on for the sake of humanity. He was not only willing: rereading his own scholarly prose, he warmed to enthusiasm.

There were few people in the galleries on January 8, 1918; and, because Congress had been given only half an hour's notice of the President's appearance, many Senators and Representatives were late in arriving to hear Wilson's peace proposals. Boiled to their essence, the Fourteen Points of the famous speech were these:

1. Open covenants openly arrived at
2. Freedom of the seas
3. Removal of economic barriers
4. Reduction of armaments
5. Adjustment of colonial claims in the interests of subject peoples
6. Evacuation of Russian territory and free determination of Russian national policy
7. Evacuation and restoration of Belgium
8. Evacuation of French territory; Alsace and Lorraine to be returned to France
9. Readjustment of Italian frontiers on lines of nationality
10. People of Austria–Hungary to be accorded opportunity for autonomous development
11. Rumania, Serbia, and Montenegro to be evacuated, and Serbia given access to the sea
12. Non-Turkish nationalities in the Ottoman Empire to be assured autonomous development; the Dardanelles to be opened to ships of all nations
13. Poland to be made independent, with access to the sea
14. Formation of a general association of nations with the mission of preserving world peace.

Global reaction was profound. The German Chancellor, Count Hertling, and the Austrian Foreign Minister, Count Czernin, heartily favored the general propositions and the lofty sentiments; to the specific propositions that would deny the Teutonic powers the spoils of victory, they perforce demurred. Lenin read the Fourteen Points and became "joyous as a boy." To the practical eye of Clemenceau, it appeared that Wilson had acted to "the very best of his abilities in circumstances the origins of which had escaped him." Prime Minister Orlando of Italy grunted his dissatisfaction that Wilson "knew so little about the Austrian problem." Ludendorff merely shrugged off the package as "figments of the imagination."

In response to the Fourteen Points, there was no need for Ludendorff to intensify his preparations for the new battle in the West. They were already going full blast. Almost 6,000 German

artillery pieces had been packed into the forty-mile front stretching from the Sensée River to the Oise, so that the density was the
same as Hutier's concentration for the September, 1917, fight at
Riga, where, on a 4,600-yard front, he had had one gun for every
eight yards. Once again, as in that battle, Hutier's brilliant
artillerist, Colonel George von Bruchmüller, planned to saturate
the zone of advance with gas shells—his object being to kill enemy
soldiers, rather than to destroy wire. While sixty-two German
divisions were concentrated for Operation Michael, which in ratio
was approximately one division for each mile of front, the main
effort was to be north of Saint-Quentin, where the British and
French joined flanks. Here the guns were in greatest density, their
numbers checking precisely with the Riga formula. New schools
were established in the rear of each German army to pound home
the new tactics. As divisions moved into the buildup, their infantry regiments were winnowed, and the strongest, most aggressive soldiers were re-formed into storm groups, to carry the
assault. Besides hand weapons, they were armed with light machine guns, light trench mortars, and flame throwers. It would
be their task to do the probing for the soft spots in the British
defense and then drive on through and overrun the artillery. The
storm groups would be followed by composite "battle units" of
infantry, machine gunners, mortar teams, and engineers. Reserves
would be thrown in only where the attack was winning ground
and not where it was being held.

Confronted by this buildup was General Sir Hubert Gough's
Fifth Army. Gough's apprehension mounted, even as his problems multiplied. Allied politics had elbowed him into an intolerable position. Lloyd George had carelessly pledged the French
that British troops would take over another thirty miles of their
front, and Gough's already thin army had to do the stretching.
Haig made it clear that he could spare no support from the B.E.F.
should a battle crisis arise on Gough's expanded front; the French
would have to reinforce, and they agreed to do so. But Pétain at
this juncture took a flight into phantasmagoria. Imagining that
the Germans were preparing to outflank his line in Alsace by a
drive through Switzerland, he pushed his reserves in that direction.
At the same time, Lloyd George was holding reserves in Britain,
partly from fear of another Irish rebellion, and partly because he
was determined to check Haig's wasteful offensives.

By sheer luck, or call it coincidence, Gough learned what he was up against. On a visit to Verdun to discuss the reserve problem, he picked up a French pamphlet that described German organization and method in the battles of Riga and Caporetto. It came to him in a flash then that this would be his portion, for he already knew that Hutier was commanding the Eighteenth Army opposite him.

Although he impressed Sir Douglas with the gravity of his plight, Gough was given but three more divisions, for a total of eleven. More than riflemen, he needed labor troops, and these he could not get. The new trenches and wiring needed for his battle zone had been surveyed and staked only, and there were no dugouts. In the army area, only 165 men were left to work on defenses in January; the number was increased to 625 in February, then to 2,400 in mid-March. At the same time, more than 25,000 men were working on rails, roads, depots, and dumps to the rear. To make matters worse, February and March were unseasonably dry. Twelve miles of Gough's front, normally insulated by the flooding Oise, had become a somewhat muddy plain rather than an obstacle.

Early in February, Gough told Haig that Hutier would bring against him more than the Fifth Army could handle; his analysis of the threat was amazingly accurate. In mid-month there was a general conference at Doullens. Haig expressed his conviction that the main effort would be against the French, and that if the British were engaged, the Third and First armies would receive the main blow. Gough refused to be complacent. As the hours raced on, his raiders picked up more information from German prisoners pointing to March 21 as "*Der Tag.*" There were more conferences, and gradually Sir Douglas swung halfway to Sir Hubert's grim view of the prospect. It was agreed that the Fifth Army would probably be unable to contain the blow. Gough's people would have to do the best they could, trading ground for lives and trying to avoid rout.

Gough walked toward his supreme trial clear-eyed, doing all he could to stave off catastrophe, warning his superiors, telling it straight to his soldiers, and encouraging them to make the best of a bad job. All of these things he did gallantly, as if premonished that for him and the Fifth Army the approaching battle would be what the playwright R. C. Sherriff would in time call it, Journey's End. Just before the curtain was to rise, he summoned his division commanders so that, through them, he could tell his soldiers what he thought worth pondering.

Nominally subordinate to Hindenburg,
Ludendorff (above) was Germany's virtual
dictator—civilian as well as military—by
1918. One of the army's best masterminds,
Ludendorff repulsed a Russian invasion from
East Prussia. Credit for the victory went to
the steely-nerved, distinguished Hindenburg,
whose legendary stature in the minds of
the German people stole the laurels that
rightfully belonged to Ludendorff.

He began by quoting Lincoln: "We accepted this war for one object, a worthy object, and the war will end when that object is attained. Under God, I hope it will never end until that time." Maybe he did this because the 6th, 12th, and 14th U.S. Engineer regiments had been rushed forward to help the Fifth Army, and Gough was intensely proud of them. They had built their bridges just in time to prepare them for demolition. After that, they would fight with the shattered Fifth as infantry, the first American troops to know full-scale battle since the Civil War.

There were still a few arrangements to be completed. Tanks had never been used in defense before. Gough knew his hulls would have no opportunity to attack; so he disposed them as heavy weapons carriers in support of his infantry. Then he deployed single field guns, well concealed, within 1,500 yards of his forward infantry line, as armor-stoppers if the Germans came on with tanks. Far to the rear, along the heights affording the best fields of fire, he preset rallying points where broken formations could reassemble and fight back. These were provident arrangements, but nothing could save the Fifth Army.

On the night of March 20 all of Gough's soldiers except men on guard were ordered to turn in early and try for a night's sleep. Those who succeeded could not have guessed what was coming. The odds against them were four to one. The Fifth with eleven and one-half infantry divisions would take on Hutier's Eighteenth with twenty-one divisions, Marwitz's Second Army with sixteen divisions, and one four-division corps out of Boehn's Seventh Army. Byng's Third Army, with eight divisions, would be hit by Below's Seventeenth Army with fifteen divisions.

Ludendorff had moved his tactical G.H.Q., just four days earlier, from Spa to Avesnes, which was closer to the front, and Wilhelm arrived in his court train on the eve of the battle. Thereafter Ludendorff worried chiefly about the weather. His meteorologist, Dr. August Schmauss, told him that the wind was not too favorable for the use of gas, and that the fog would not lift. Brooding on these things, the First Quartermaster General signaled the attack.

OPERATION MICHAEL

At 4:50 A.M. on March 21 the German guns opened fire. For the next two hours their full weight was turned against the defending British batteries.

Operation Michael thus got in motion in the first light of an unpromising spring, with most of nature abetting the parents of the monster. The whole battlefield was fogbound when the bombardment began, and the shellfire cut the gloom only to poison it.

Here once again was the "greatest artillery duel in world history," a description so often repeated as to make it appear that World War I was an Olympic game, played to establish new shot-putting records. On the German side, 6,100 cannon spoke, and from the British emplacements 2,500 guns are said to have replied. If the statistics are believable, then the German counterbattery fire all misregistered. The blast-off was simply not that colossal. The Germans were depending mainly on gas shells, which go off weakly, with just enough explosive to vaporize the liquid. Two hours after the shoot began, all of the German fire was pulled back to hit the infantry positions, and at that point the trench mortars joined in.

At 9:40 A.M. the German storm troops rushed forward in an enveloping fog. Usually, fog works in favor of the defender, if he is set and confident. In Operation Michael, however, the fog not only screened the German concentrations, but further hexed the waiting British. It is much easier for soldiers to feel bold in clear sunlight; when the elements hide from view the help closest at hand, the fighting spirit swiftly withers. We can imagine how infantrymen of the Fifth Army reacted on March 21. For almost five hours the storm, begun in darkness, had been raging. Daybreak had come and the morning was well along. Yet darkness might as well have remained, for the fog, now billowing dun-and-olive-streaked from mingled smoke and gas, shrouded the foreground and eddied through the trenches. It blinded the defenders along the thinned front, for men either wore gas masks or they died, and the heat of each man's sweat befogged his goggles.

Fighters stationed forward along the lower ground, across the avenues chosen for the German advance, lost their sole chance for successful resistance, which depended on reasonable visibility and fields of fire at least one hundred yards in depth. The storm troopers were on top of them before they could take aim. But that was not the worst of it. The fog bank also made the Germans attack groups, probing the middle ground for a path through the British lines, less vulnerable to flanking fire from the defenders' strong points. Many Germans went off course from getting lost in the murk, but that was only a marginal miscarriage. The British Fifth Army had to pay the final price for four years of linear warfare in France, during which the military mind had become closed to concepts of balanced, all-round defense, the axiomatic counter to infiltration.

Until the Germans advanced, the rain of shells on the British trenches continued. Thereafter the German fire was lifted only briefly to move farther on. British officers and NCO's had to shout to be heard by men close at hand. What was said was based on surmise for the most part, because all Fifth Army communications had been severed. Where the resistance held fast, there was no sign of the German infantry, or anything else, but only fog. The few bastions on the front were already being isolated, though the garrisons hardly sensed it.

In the battle zone, brigade headquarters, battery positions, and road intersections collapsed under the shellfire. Ammunition dumps exploded, not with a roar as is usually written, but from shell pile to shell pile, with the hot rounds blistering the landscape like a Titan's pinwheel. Artillery horse-parks, aid stations, and narrow-gauge railheads were rubbed out. It was a cleverly planned, all-embracing shoot, which did its work with paralyzing directness. Almost smothered by the gas, Gough's surviving batteries continued to feed their guns, seeing nothing, but firing on known targets, according to the maps.

Noon approached, and the British commander still had only the vaguest impression of how the battle was going. By then, eight or nine of his twenty forward battalions were almost wholly a sacrifice. His defensively deployed tanks and guns in the forward zone were ciphered out by the weather; they needed 1,000 yards of visibility; they were given twenty. The front line was already gone. Its vestigial parts were now isolated islands of defense, where a few men and a few guns waited vainly for worthwhile targets to appear, while the German tide rippled on far past them, not awaiting the reserves, which would close across the rear and cut off the remaining defenders.

Ludendorff heard what was happening and was satisfied. With Hutier's army everything was going as intended. But already certain of his miscalculations were cutting his chances. He had seriously overestimated the difficulties of advancing across the Oise marshes and had directed too little force there. Also, he had mistakenly calculated that Pétain would have large reserves concentrated somewhere around Compiègne ready to counterattack the German left flank if its advance imposed a general threat.

Against Gough's Fifth Army front, where it was strongest, Ludendorff threw his heaviest masses, which meant that in the larger scale of things he was rejecting his own tactical principle of sending reserves only against weak points. Even so, the initial achievement stunned the Allies.

Around the Flesquières salient, where the Fifth and Third armies joined flanks, the Germans penetrated the battle zone while the fog held. But there and to the northward, the British were fighting from works that had been in their keeping for months and were solid enough in the beginning. Marwitz's Second Army was driving at the base of that salient from both north and south, aiming to trap the British divisions there before turning toward Péronne and Bapaume on the way to Albert. On General Byng's front, Below's storm troops broke through the center to the battle zone. Here the British had packed too many troops in the forward trenches, thereby dissipating the value of a battle zone far more stoutly constructed than Gough's. The bombardment shredded these masses; the infiltrators skirted the high ground and kept going. There was not enough strength rearward to check them.

Gough kept his nerve; there was little else to keep. When in late afternoon he got word from Byng about the pincers closing on the Flesquières salient, he realized that the Fifth Army's entire left flank would soon be dangling. That meant retreat all along the line.

When night closed down, the Germans were in possession of the forward zone on both army fronts and had dug in over most of the battle area.

Haig, faced by catastrophe, was admirably steady. Yet neither he nor the other generals appreciated that the last twenty-four hours had wholly altered the problem of Western Front operations. This is not surprising; such changes, though obvious enough in retrospect, commonly elude the keenest intelligence at the time. For almost four years, every major offensive had striven for penetration, which, it was assumed, would have decisive consequences. At last the Germans had achieved successful penetration. The result should have been final and fatal. What had been a giant siege operation would now become a war of movement. But where was the key to victory? Ludendorff's storm troops had broken through and would keep on going for a time, but unless his reserves were sufficient to round up the British and force a capitulation, he had won nothing.

That night Gough withdrew his right wing seven miles, to a

Doughboys cheer for the camera from the packed "40 and 8's," small French boxcars that could transport, if not comfortably, forty men or eight horses.

position behind the Crozat Canal. He had asked permission for his engineers to blow the railway bridges. The French had flatly refused, saying that this was their prerogative. Now in the emergency the French were not present and the bridges remained unblown. On March 22 the Germans broke loose into open country northwest of Saint-Quentin. Then came the false report that the line of the Crozat Canal had been forced. Believing it, Gough, in the early afternoon, ordered his right wing (III Corps) to retire behind the line of the Somme.

Gough's retreat further compromised Byng's army. Its left continued to hold Below in check, but Marwitz's Second Army drove through north of Péronne, widening the deadly gap between Byng's right and Gough's left. Marwitz was aiming for Amiens; if that vital communications hub fell, the French and British forces would be irreparably split. Below was to keep going toward Saint-Pol with the object of rolling back the British northern armies toward the Channel. Hutier, who was driving southwest toward Paris, would counter attempts by the French to reinforce Gough's shattered army. The French were in no hurry, though on the following day it was announced that a French army group had been made responsible for the Fifth Army zone, with Gough subordinated to it.

In the Flesquières salient, the one last linchpin of Byng's hold on the forward ground, the six battalion commanders of the Royal Naval Division decided on their own that the hour had come either to withdraw or to lose everything. So they got out on March 24, and, with that mooring gone, Byng's army hastily fell back over the cratered ground so hard won in the 1916 Somme battles. To Ludendorff's eyes it must have appeared that the game was almost over.

Haig and Pétain met that night at Dury. Morbid and withdrawn, Pétain had nothing to contribute. He told Haig that he expected momentarily to be hit by the German main blow in the Champagne. To Haig's ear it sounded as if Pétain was prepared to leave the British Army to its own fate. Pétain said to him: "Your army risks being cornered in open country while I shall be reduced to covering Paris." Haig wired his War Minister, Lord Milner, and General Sir Henry Wilson, Chief of the Imperial General Staff, to come immediately to France.

Lloyd George had anticipated him. Milner was already en route to Paris to talk with Clemenceau and Sir Henry Rawlinson, Britain's man on the Supreme War Council. But the retreat continued through the next day.

Unity of Command

On the morning of March 26 there assembled at Doullens most of the key figures in the Franco-British war camp. All of Haig's army commanders reported except Gough. Milner and Sir Henry Wilson were on hand. Clemenceau arrived, and was made acutely aware of the trembling in the camp when a French general, pointing toward Haig, whispered in his ear: "There is a man who will be obliged to capitulate in the open field within a fortnight, and we will be very lucky if we are not obliged to do the same."

Then came Foch, to cut this melancholy with his first rasping words: "You aren't fighting? I would fight without a break. I would fight in front of Amiens. I would fight in Amiens. I would fight behind Amiens. I would fight all the time. I would never surrender." A few days later, Clemenceau would take this same message, and paraphrasing it grandiloquently, electrify the Chamber of Deputies with his oratory. Winston Churchill—he was at this time Britain's Munitions Minister—well noted that speech. With little change, he echoed its words to rouse Great Britain during the darkest days of 1940.

At the Doullens meeting, President Poincaré presided. He at once asked assurance from Haig that Amiens would be held —and got it. No longer dragging his feet, Pétain announced that he had thinned out his line sufficiently to switch twenty-four divisions to the threatened front; but they could not be transported westward faster than two per day.

Then Haig spoke up, saying rather meekly: "If General Foch will consent to give me his advice, I will gladly follow it." In the greatest crisis of his military career, this canny Scot knew exactly what he was doing. That one move spiked Lloyd George's guns; thereafter the Prime Minister had to abandon all thought of removing him.

Milner and Clemenceau went into a huddle in one corner of the room. Minutes later they came up with the statement: "General Foch is appointed by the British and French governments to coordinate the action of the British and French armies around Amiens. To this end, he will come to an understanding with the two Generals in Chief, who are requested to furnish him with all necessary information."

But having gotten religion too late, Haig was like all penitent sinners. The draft was too weak to satisfy him. Foch, he said, should have the Allied armies as a whole "from the Alps to the North Sea." The draft was rewritten, the phrase "on the Western Front" being substituted for "around Amiens." It was still not enough for Haig. Both the United States and Belgium had been excluded from the conference. Playing their proxy, Haig insisted that "Allied armies" be substituted for the "British and French armies." That was how it was done and the once dour conference suddenly turned radiant.

There was one last sordid detail. Sir Henry Wilson insisted that Gough be relieved forthwith, with Rawlinson taking his command. Haig did not make a stand-up fight for his subordinate. Maybe there had to be a scapegoat. But from this move came a great myth. When Rawlinson took over Gough's people, they were redesignated the Fourth Army, and so it was assumed that the Fifth Army had been annihilated in the German offensive.

Two days later, with Rawlinson's arrival at the front, Gough ended his career as a soldier. Into retirement he carried the recollection of a last visit with General Malcolm, commanding his 66th Division. An anxious French officer asked Malcolm about the situation. "It is quite good," said Malcolm, "we have won the war." Malcolm had measured the failing energy and growing

Germany's spectacular gains (black arrows)
in three early 1918 offensives on the
Western Front—first, on the Somme,
March 21–April 5; then the Lys, April 9–29;
and finally, the Aisne, May 27–June 4—drove
deep wedges into Allied territory (broken
white to solid white lines). The successive
states of Germany's greatest advance, on
the Somme, are shown in the inset.

listlessness of the Germans on his front; he could feel that the attack was stayed. So his seemingly wild statement was a proportioned view, though the road to victory remained long.

By that time Ludendorff was having second thoughts. His original plan had to be modified. Hutier and Marwitz were forging ahead; the Eighteenth Army already had Montdidier. But Below's Seventeenth had been stopped short by Byng's Third. Resistance had tightened and at points Byng was counterattacking. The German assault was hurting for food and ammunition, while road and rail repair across the cratered ground was taking much longer than the plan had anticipated. Ludendorff determined to press on, mainly in the direction of Amiens. The Eighteenth and Second armies halted briefly to regroup and replenish. As March ended, Hutier attacked between Montdidier and Noyon. Marwitz tried again in early April at Albert, hitting south of the Somme for Amiens. Both thrusts were held. The Germans moved too fast, too far; their troops were exhausted. Ludendorff said: "The enemy's resistance is beyond our strength." The drive on Amiens was called off; the battle ended April 5.

To sum up Operation Michael, in two weeks the Germans had overrun approximately 1,250 square miles of shell-desolated French countryside, shattered one British army, sorely wounded another, and caged about 90,000 prisoners while capturing more than a thousand guns. In so doing, they had stretched their own front another fifty or so miles and lost the equivalent of one field army in dead, wounded, and missing. How these gains and losses balanced against one another toward the final accounting defied computation by the staff geniuses on both sides.

Foch had established his headquarters at Clermont. There toward the close of the battle, so legend says, Pershing appeared and spoke as follows: "I come to tell you that the American people will esteem it a great honor that our troops should take part in the present battle. I ask it in my name and theirs. There is at the present moment no other question than that of fighting. Infantry, artillery, airplanes, tanks, all that we have is yours. Dispose of us as you wish." The quote must be taken with several grains of salt. It is not Pershing's style and besides, he had no tanks, artillery, or airplanes; no doubt he did offer Foch use of his troops. General Tasker Bliss, representing the United States on the Supreme War Council, had all along espoused unified military command. At Bliss's urging, Secretary Baker, who had just arrived in Paris, fired off a strong message to President Wilson recommending blessings for Foch as generalissimo. But having pledged his forces in a tense moment, Pershing later recanted, his generosity cooling far more rapidly than the situation.

THE PARIS GUN

On March 23 at 7:20 A.M. the few Parisians abroad at such an early hour around the Quai de Seine in the northeastern section of the city were put to flight by a heavy explosion in front of house No. 6. Buildings were rocked. Windows blew in. But no one was hurt. Having regained breath, the few who experienced the phenomenon shrugged it off with a: "Mon Dieu! But what was it?"

Twenty minutes later, Paris began to understand. One and one-half miles away, near the Gare de l'Est, where the streets were teeming with people headed for the Métro, the second explosion occurred. Eight citizens were killed outright; thirteen more were wounded by steel shards. Paris, for the first time during the war, was under artillery fire, and the shells continued to burst at intervals of approximately twenty to twenty-five minutes.

These projectiles came from a gun emplaced seventy-five miles away on the eastern slope of the Mont de Joie in the Saint-Gobain wood at the Laon Corner, the German-held sector closest to Paris. There were three guns of the same design in the concealed battery. Each was a reconstruction of the navy's newest 15-inch, 45-caliber rifle tubed down to 8.26 inches. The relatively small projectiles stood about waist high. But the powder bags behind each shell were twice as tall as a man.

For firing, the piece was invariably set at fifty degrees. The theory from which the gun developed made that necessary; range was increased or lowered by the number of powder charges. Given an initial velocity of one mile per second, the projectile twelve miles up came into air so rare that it would then perform according to the law first described by Galileo for maximum range in a vacuum. Ascension would continue until the shell gradually turned over from the pull of gravity, having traveled three fourths of the horizontal distance virtually in a vacuum.

The creator of the Paris Gun was a scientist, Dr. Eberhardt, who had been born too soon to become a hero in the conquest of outer space. Early in 1916, he had asked the German Navy if it had any interest in a gun that could shoot sixty miles. The question was referred to Ludendorff; he not only said yes, he made the project urgent. Then in 1917, just before the Nivelle offensive, the Germans withdrew to the Hindenburg Line. They were no longer within a sixty-mile range of Paris. To the dismay of the project managers at Krupp there came a telegram from Ludendorff: "Make that gun shoot seventy-five miles." He was already envisaging a surprise shoot to spread panic among civilians. The first gun was already in being. Its designers had to begin anew, fashioning a shell and tubing that would meet the extraordinary new requirement. By the end of January, 1918, the guns were ready. Navy personnel went into army uniforms to run the show.

In this first bombardment the battery worked over Paris for one week, culminating in the tragedy of Good Friday, March 29. The church of Saint Gervais, opposite the Hotel de Ville, was crowded with kneeling worshipers when at 4:30 P.M. a projectile struck the roof. A stone pillar crumpled, and the stone vault that it supported cracked wide apart, dropping tons of rock on the congregation. The mass of debris blocked all exits. Rescuers worked their way through the ruins and the pools of blood to find eighty-eight dead on the floor and sixty-eight desperately injured. Clemenceau and Poincaré visited the scene of the disaster. At the other end, the Kaiser visited the Paris Gun battery to voice pride in its great work. Ludendorff heard the news about the hit on Saint Gervais; the mass funeral for the victims would be held on Tuesday afternoon. So the battery was directed to withhold fire that afternoon.

Things by then were going none too well with the Paris Gun. One big gun had blown up, killing five crewmen. French railway artillery (the emplacements were only seven miles from the French front) had found the range and 15-inch shells were crashing into Saint-Gobain wood; even some of the smaller field guns were shelling the ridge. The remaining two guns soon wore out and had to be replaced. Intermittent shelling continued to May 1, when the large guns were finally packed up and shipped out. The battery, all told, had fired some two hundred rounds.

Premier Clemenceau left the capital on April 3 for another conference, this time seated at Beauvais, though the theme remained unchanged. How much power should be given General Foch? There to deliberate the question were Lloyd George, Pétain, Sir Henry Wilson, Pershing, and Bliss. That day's deliberations are heavily dramatized by every historian who would further the impression that but for Pershing fighting a rear-guard action to keep his army from being split into picket squads, the Allies would have devoured the Americans. Beauvais clarified the main question very little. It was agreed that Foch would give "strategic direction" while the Commanders in Chief would "exercise in full the tactical conduct of their armies." Since any order to attack or to withdraw is tactical, that still left it up to Foch to play the traveling salesman and sell his policy to the other generals as best he could.

OPERATION GEORGETTE

Ludendorff's next blow, which came a week later, had been code-named "George." The Seventeenth Army was supposed to continue attacking toward Arras. The idea was to carry the heights north and east of the city; the Sixth Army would strike around Lens, with the same object—securing a base on the high ground. These things done, the offensive would push forward on both sides of the Lys River.

But in the overture, nothing went as planned. The German artillery was disappointing. Ludendorff found that he had only eleven fresh divisions on hand to throw against the armies of Sir Henry Horne and Sir Herbert Plumer in Flanders (they joined flanks at the Lys), and so G.H.Q. had to abandon the idea of attacking from both sides of the Ypres Salient to pinch it out. Instead of a thirty-mile front between Lens and Ypres, the attack would be made on a twelve-mile front between La Bassée and Armentières, as had been proposed in the first place by Crown Prince Rupprecht. Due to the contraction, one of Ludendorff's staff officers suggested that the more appropriate title for the show was "Georgette."

Beginning April 7, for two days, all British positions and villages near Armentières were mustard-gassed. The weather was hot, misty, and sticky—ideal conditions for the use of gas. For four hours on the second morning, the German artillery blasted the front with high explosives.

About 9:00 A.M. on April 9, coming on through fog, nine full-strength German divisions attacked. They drove straight for a sector manned by four Portuguese brigades serving with the British. It was no contest. The fog wafted away, and the Portuguese saw what was coming in time; these merry men—the most congenial lodgers on the Western Front—threw down their arms and fled. One battalion of British infantry, bicycle-mounted, was rushed to the gap. The retreating Portuguese soldiers outwrestled them, took the bicycles, and kept going, some making it to Le Havre, where they sat for the rest of the war.

By evening, the Germans had reached the Lys, five miles inside the British front around Neuve-Chapelle, and were well on their way to Armentières. But in the direction of Béthune and at Givenchy and Festubert along the La Bassée Canal, the attack was beaten back with heavy loss. "All of it very unsatisfactory," brooded Ludendorff. A General Staff officer returned to tell him that his infantrymen weren't grappling with the British machine guns in earnest; they were too busy searching for food.

Although the Battle of Lys is today little remembered, no less a student of war than Winston Churchill regarded it as decisive of the struggle on the Western Front and, hence, of the war. There are solid arguments favoring that judgment, if we explore the mind of the commander. Ludendorff had determined to break the B.E.F. The first great attempt had failed. The Michael tactics didn't suit Flanders: the front was too solid, the ground itself, and the distribution of defending power, too regular. This was direct assault, man against man, position by position. Here, in the deadliest form, was the no-limit contest in a squared ring, and the best man had to win. The B.E.F. could not give much ground without giving everything.

Ludendorff was trying now on his shortest line. Either he would achieve the objective, or thereafter his reserves would be fewer, and his logistical difficulties would mount, no matter how he moved. If he could not smash the B.E.F. now, it would quickly grow stronger, and his prospect of ending the war by a tactical triumph over the French would be reduced by half. Such being the possible prize and the forfeit, he saw no choice—and, indeed, he had none—but to bull ahead.

On the second day, April 10, a new assault wave by the German Fourth Army hit north of Armentières, widening the battle. The British had weakened that sector by shifting four brigades toward the fire of the first day. So five divisions fell on five brigades. Cracking under superior weight, the British line had to break. By midday the crest of Wytschaete Ridge was in German hands, as well as Ploegsteert village and most of Messines Ridge. The 34th Division barely extricated itself from envelopment at Armentières. By nightfall the enemy was in possession of the old British defensive system all the way from Givenchy to the last road juncture four miles south of Ypres. Even so, at terrible cost to the defenders, the flanks south of Givenchy and north of Hollebeke held firm. The whole battle pivoted on their so standing. Gaining ground on a twenty-mile front, Ludendorff was getting his forces more tightly enmeshed in a ten-mile-deep salient.

Through April 11, the fighting continued on these lines, more German divisions being fed into the mill, more British forces arriving, not to withdraw, not to retreat, but only gradually to yield field after field, contested to the bitter end. The rest of Messines was lost when the soldiers holding it were either shot down or ran out of ammunition.

Haig, during all this time, was pressing Foch, who was visiting him at Montreuil, to hand over the French divisions in the general reserve, for the sake of which Sir Douglas had proposed the unified command. Foch declined. Haig was furious, yet Foch had a point; there could never be a strategic reserve if with every fire call he dissipated it. In the end Foch's judgment proved to be correct.

Two major changes occurred on April 12. Sir Henry Horne was too remote from the onslaught against his own left flank. It was advisable for one army commander to handle the battle as a whole. Sir Herbert Plumer took over the sagging defensive front, which now curved like a reverse S from north of Ypres through Poelcapelle, around Passchendaele Ridge, back across the spurs of Wytschaete Ridge, and from there to Merville.

On Ludendorff's order, the Germans drove in main strength for Bailleul, just beyond the apex of their salient, a little short of the high ground of Mont des Cats, southwest of Ypres, and next door to the railhead at Hazebrouck. But in letting his eye stray to the Cats-Kemmel hill mass at this stage of operations, the First Quartermaster General was not only pushing his luck, but abandoning his role as strategist to play the minor tactician. The object of his operation was not to mount artillery against Ypres but to exhaust British infantry reserves. Already, on the local level, advantage had changed sides.

The British could get more men forward to attack the sides of the salient than the Germans could advance to renew the penetration. They came, the Australian 1st Division, the 4th Guards Brigade, pioneers, and even battalions of cyclists. Standing, they barred the path to Hazebrouck, which counted far more than the high ground. As long as it was safe, as long as Englishmen were willing to die to keep it so, Ludendorff was wasting lives in trying to fight it out on the line that he had taken.

The next day, Ludendorff changed his plan, as he increasingly did amid defeats that looked like victories. His staff argued that resistance around the Cats-Kemmel hill mass might be squeezed out more quickly if he extended the general attack and came against Ypres from the north. Ludendorff was convinced. But here was a reshifting to the original plan that had been discarded. Once again, he was going for broke, reaching for the Channel ports while trying to pulverize the B.E.F.

So mixed became the battle on April 12 that the indestructible Anzac, Bernard Freyberg, V.C., whom we last saw as a lieutenant on Gallipoli and who by now was commanding a brigade, found himself holding a three-mile front with elements of four different divisions. Haig that very morning had put the situation to his troops in an Order of the Day forever memorable: "There is no other course open to us but to fight it out. Every position must be held to the last man. There must be no retirement. With our backs to the wall and believing in the justice of our cause, each one of us must fight on to the end."

Plumer remained practical, wholly willing to comply—but within reason. His battle line was too tortuous; he was wasting men to hold ground that counted little, if this was the showdown. There had to be a line-straightening, and he ordered it within the next forty-eight hours. Back fell the tired Tommies, yielding Poelcapelle, Passchendaele, Polygon Wood, and Houthulst, to which they had clawed their way at such terrible cost in 1917. It must have been a terrible wrench for Plumer and for them. When they pulled up and faced about, they still held scrap-piled Ypres, but the profile of the old salient was gone.

The fallback came just in time to buffer Ludendorff's ramming of the salient north of Ypres. The guns were now too far back. The empty foreground, heavily cratered, deep in mud, sapped the German infantry advance of its starting energy, while the line-shortening gave Plumer's soldiers a feeling of support at hand, a tonic to confidence.

On April 25 the Germans tried to renew the offensive, but this time on a very narrow front. Mont Kemmel fell; it was too late to win any advantage from it. For a few more days the Germans persisted, but these were the erratic lungings of an animal trapped. No longer was a small local success worth the lives spent for it. On the night of April 29, Ludendorff called the whole thing off.

World War I witnessed no nobler or more decisive stand than

that of the B.E.F. in front of Ypres in April, 1918. There were no church bells to peal. Plumer's army little knew what it had achieved.

Through Michael and Georgette, the German armies had won more territory than had been gained by the Allies in all the wasting offensives mounted during three years of Western Front warfare. But the two new salients further stretched an army already hurting grievously from the shrinkage of reserves. In the two battles, 56,639 German and 21,128 Allied soldiers were killed, while 250,000 Allied and 181,338 German wounded choked the hospitals. Of the 330,000 marked missing, or presumed taken prisoner, when the accounting was made, 290,000 were Allied losses. So in the trading of bodies, Germany had won a little bit. But the Teuton reservoir was dropping fast; and the Americans were coming on.

Still, as April ended and the German fire lifted, no Allied general knew for certain whether it was respite or release. To prepare for the worst, there was a weighty conference on May 1–2 at Abbeville to tighten Allied cooperation during the crisis. A main object was to put pressure on Pershing to release his divisions at Foch's call. The Allied leaders met the immovable object.

Pershing pounded the table and shouted: "Gentlemen, I have thought this program over very carefully and will not be coerced."

Foch asked him: "Are you willing to risk the Allies being forced back to the Loire River for want of your reinforcements?"

Pershing replied that he readily accepted that risk and would not fritter away his resources on Foch's order. He would stand his ground for an integral American Army, and if Lloyd George wanted to see that army come alive quickly, he could provide the extra shipping to transport 150,000 riflemen and machine gunners to France in May and in June. Lloyd George agreed.

There is only one way of accounting for Pershing's seeming change of attitude between Clermont and Abbeville. On impulse, when catastrophe loomed, the natural man spoke. But two German attacks had been weathered and, in the interim, Pershing's staff had helped him to harden his resolve not to dissipate American troops.

XII
Enter the Yanks

Rollin Kirby's cartoon in the New York
World of a jubilant Yank brandishing
a German helmet expressed the elation
of a nation proud of its men.

In late April, 1918, General Foch had the bright idea to lift five battle-worn divisions of the British IX Corps from the smoking fields around Ypres and shift them south, to be spliced into a French field army. This was in the interest of *roulement* of French and British divisions, and Haig approved it. He was far more mellow at this stage than Pershing and willing to concede prerogatives to further the principle of command unity. So the troops went.

That was a great pity. They came under a French general who, like many French generals, suffered by his inheritance from Napoleon, arrogantly and bumptiously acting according to the assumption that what he didn't know about warfare couldn't be taught. His name was Denis Auguste Duchêne, and at age fifty-six he was commanding the French Sixth Army without leading it. No Frenchman of the time was given a better chance to strike a blow for liberty than this choleric Blimp who fought off counsel from below and above.

The center of Duchêne's sector was the Chemin des Dames ridge, an ideal rampart on which to skewer Germans, had proper use been made of it. Pétain directed Duchêne to organize an elastic defense on this strong ground to wear down the German attack, after which the main forces, echeloned in depth, would crush it. He did nothing of the sort; his infantry was massed in the front line. Duchêne, like the average infantry private, believed in the immediacy of danger only when he heard bullets whiz. He obstinately refused to hear warnings that Ludendorff would turn against his army next.

One who tried to persuade him was Major S. T. Hubbard, of Pershing's Order of Battle section, who by a process of analysis and deduction had reached the ineluctable conclusion that the next enemy blow would fall on the Chemin des Dames between May 25 and 30. Colonel de Cointet, subchief of French intelligence, was won by Hubbard's logic, but Duchêne said no. By his contempt he almost destroyed an army.

The French Sixth was formed of six *poilu* divisions and the five battered British divisions under General Sir Alexander Hamilton Gordon. The eastern end of the Chemin des Dames hogback, and the lower ground extending beyond it, was British country; the French held the other end of the fifteen-mile-long ridge, which runs east to west directly north of the Aisne. During May the British divisions relaxed and did just enough training to smarten their few replacements. Being under Duchêne, the French did nothing in particular to improve their position. During this time, fifteen German divisions, all brought up fresh, were fed into the trench system opposite; seven more deployed to the backup ground. The Germans massed 3,719 guns against the forty-mile front. And Duchêne slept.

During these days the U.S. 2nd Division was getting its first little taste of war to the southeast of Verdun in trenches well adapted to instruction in housekeeping routines, the lines having remained stable for three years. It was what the Americans called a *bon secteur*, real chairs, real tables, a stove here and there, beds with mattresses, electric lights, cupboards, and boarded floors in the dugouts and splinter-proofs. It was like playing war, with just enough of the shadow of danger to supply the fillip.

On May 27 the storm interrupted the French Sixth Army's sleep and parted the U.S. 2nd Division from its paradise. The bombardment saturating the Chemin des Dames lasted four hours and, in its intensity, was fully as destructive as the worst of Michael or Georgette. Because Duchêne's forces were massed in the forward trenches, the downpour of steel and gas gutted the Sixth Army. The slain piled high in the traverses. Men penned in the dugouts, gas-masked, unnerved by the convulsion overhead, sweating, vomiting, came through half suffocated and incapable of active response.

At 4:00 A.M. the German infantry came on behind the barrage. Less than one hour later they took over the center of the Chemin des Dames at Ailles. Already it was too late to order demolition of the bridges of the Aisne. The Germans had them and were crossing. By evening they had reached the next river south, the Vesle, and their advance parties had boxed in the village of Fismes. The tide rolled on toward the Marne, spreading to gather in the pivotal rail and road hub at Soissons. Twenty-four hours after the guns spoke, the Germans were twenty miles past their departure line and well on the road to Paris.

Off the flanks of the Chemin des Dames, the divisions on the low ground, less heavily pounded than the troops in the center, dug deeper, redeployed weapons toward the breach, and attempted to confine the penetration by strengthening the shoulders. They got away with it for a while only because the enemy was all-intent on pushing his reserves south through the opening. So the salient steadily deepened without marked broadening. Ludendorff let it go that way and rushed more troops to the fire—though in the first place he had intended this thrust as a diversion to draw off reserves from Flanders, so that he might strike there again. This was heady stuff for the First Quartermaster General—the sudden lure of possible surprise victory—and he could not resist it. The legs of his soldiers were rewriting his strategy.

The U.S. 2nd Division had been suddenly withdrawn from the Verdun vicinity. It was now in the neighborhood of Gisors, twenty miles northwest of Paris. "With the usual ostrich precautions," wrote General Harbord, "everybody in the world, except us, was told where we were going." (Harbord had begged Pershing for a line command and had been given the 2nd Division's Marine Brigade. Major General James W. McAndrew had taken his place as Pershing's Chief of Staff.) Major General Omar Bundy, who commanded the 2nd Division, had put his troops in march and left his brigadiers behind to supervise the loading, which is not the best way to run a railroad. Many of Harbord's juniors were wiser than he at this moment. On May 30, Memorial Day, one machine gun battalion commander formed his troops and said: "We're going into battle, and thank God there'll be no more quiet sectors." At daybreak on May 31 they got in motion toward the crackling fields of combat.

But these weren't the first Yanks to feel the heat. On April 20 there had been a serious affair at Seicheprey, not far from Saint-Mihiel, involving troops of the 26th (Yankee) Division. It was an isolated event, staged by the Germans to humiliate the Americans and defer the shaping of an all-U.S. Army.

The Germans were solidly based around Montsec; the sector had been relatively inactive since the first year of war. Into the area were deployed newly formed storm groups with the fixed object of wresting Seicheprey village from Yankee hands. They rehearsed the raid—about 3,200 of them—right up till the appointed hour. Then in early morning the guns from Montsec blasted the division front, and from out of the fire three columns came on, one through Remières Wood to the east, a second to the west of Seicheprey, while the third drove straight into the village. There, 470 Connecticut lads had to stand and fight because the barrage had closed all escape routes. By dawn Seicheprey was in German hands. By afternoon, a Yank major with the very German name of George A. Rau, and battalion survivors, had won it back by counterattack. Remières Wood was in enemy hands through the day. But scattered through the little forest were small packets of Yankee riflemen, who, gradually converging on one another, regained their fighting power. The next day they purged the wood of Germans.

In their withdrawal, the Germans left 160 dead behind, but they took out 136 prisoners. Total casualties in the division were 634. In the United States, Seicheprey was hailed as a first American victory and the name resounded to spur Liberty Bond sales. That was a pardonable exaggeration. The results were not flattering. They proved mainly that the Guardsmen had a plethora of fight spirit and a dearth of fight know-how.

Right after Seicheprey had come Cantigny. General Bullard's 1st Division, having been relieved by the 26th Division prior to the Seicheprey baptism, was put into the lines of the First French Army under General Debeney, three miles west of Montdidier. A little to the north, Operation Georgette was still going strong. Cantigny village lay to the fore of the 1st Division's front on a rise in German country that dominated this part of the Allied front.

So the decision was made: the Americans would wipe out this superior observation point. Before they could get to it, on the night of May 27, the front of the 2nd Brigade (26th and 28th Infantry regiments) was hit by a full-powered raid. The German infantry was beaten back, but American losses to enemy artillery were grievous.

On the following morning, the 28th Infantry Regiment assaulted Cantigny in broad day. Within thirty-five minutes the attackers had the village. That was just the beginning. There followed a daylong donnybrook, hammer-and-tongs, a seesaw of confusion as counterattack followed counterattack. Bullard's men held on.

The next day, May 29, the German infantry was at first withheld, while Cantigny became the bull's-eye for every German gun within range. Then the gray tide came on again, wave after wave, in the heaviest counterblow of all. At several points the Germans broke through and burrowed into Cantigny. One battalion of the 18th Infantry was rushed forward. The enemy was beaten back. That was his last try; Cantigny was American. The cost to the 1st Division was mournful, 1,607 men down, 13 officers and 186 enlisted men dead. But the end was sweet—the first clean-cut victory for America in France.

Cantigny like Seicheprey was a nasty, grueling fight. April 20 and May 28 both were milestones in the national history. Veterans of the two divisions would continue their argument into Valhalla. "We did it first at Seicheprey." "The hell you say! We did it first at Cantigny." Let Valhalla arbitrate it. Both were preliminaries, in that they were indeterminate of any great event. No tide or change came of them. Each had the nature of an alley brawl. The Big Parade was just getting in motion elsewhere.

Under the pressure of the bad news from the Chemin des Dames on May 27, Black Jack Pershing had again relented. He went from his visit with Haig on May 30 to dine that night with Foch at Sarcus. His earlier statement about being willing to see the French Army driven back to the Loire was now forgotten. During his talk with the Frenchman, Pershing released his first five divisions for employment in the Marne area, wherever they were most needed.

Where did this second gesture put the Pershing policy of a separate U.S. Army? It was down the drain. Not Allied pressure, but the remorseless grind of events had finished it. If Allied defeat continued, the feeding of U.S. divisions into the line piecemeal as they arrived must perforce continue. There could be no choice in this matter. But if the tide could be stemmed, with the brightening promise of a recovery, Foch could build up his margins, and as the reserve swelled, the constituting of a separate U.S. Army would be to general advantage. And that is exactly how it happened.

General Joseph T. Dickman and his 3rd Division, already three months in France, were on their way to a quiet sector in the Vosges on May 30, 1918. That same evening, they were stopped in their loading, and entrained for the area around Condé-en-Brie. The 7th Machine Gun Battalion was rushed northwest by motor. There was traffic trouble. The roads were choked with refugees heading south "as if fleeing Attila," including hundreds of *poilus* who yelled "*La guerre est finie*," as they passed. The next day at Condé, the battalion van ran into a French commander,

General Renouard, and he assumed the responsibility, saying: "Get on to Château-Thierry."

In midafternoon, the battalion pulled up at Nesle, one mile south of Château-Thierry. Half of its men were still on the road. But all of the guns were present. They were posted along the south bank of the Marne, except for one pair. Lieutenant John T. Bissell took them on to the first crossroads beyond the main bridge. More hundreds of French soldiers sifted through these lines that afternoon and the next morning. At 10:00 A.M. on June 1 the Germans came and the main bridge was blown in their faces, "destroying friend and foe alike" and stranding Bissell and his guns north of the river. The massed machine guns turned the enemy back from the north bank. Bissell and his platoon stayed under cover during the day and by night returned via the railway bridge.

Great kudos came of it. Pétain cited the battalion, "in the course of violent action . . . disputed foot by foot . . . northern outskirts of Château-Thierry . . . incomparable glory . . . its valor and skill costing the enemy sanguinary losses." Great words, but the thing was not that big. The German probe was purely exploratory, a flankwise scouting by light forces. Blowing the bridge turned out to be to the enemy's advantage, securing his left flank on the advance toward Paris, which could be reached without crossing the river. But these were the lighter hair shirts of the 3rd's first brush with fire. What its soldiers never forgot was that back home the wrong outfit got the credit. Headlines blazed: "Germans Stopped at Château-Thierry with Help of God and Few Marines."

Dickman was highly dissatisfied with his soldiers. The convoy had split on the march-up; they had gone into position carelessly. Moreover, the 7th Battalion had not played Horatius as resolutely as the papers said. Bissell, coming back that night, had passed along innocently to his comrades the false news given him by a French officer on the other side of the Marne: "Two German divisions have entered Château-Thierry over the first bridge west of here." On hearing that, the battalion commander had ordered his men back from the river to avoid capture. Before they had gotten very far, that rumor had been exploded and the gunners had returned to their posts.

Almost as quickly as the rumor, the first threat faded. For the next fortnight, 3rd Division troops were given supernumerary duties—guarding bridges, cutting trenches, repairing roads

—because the sector was no longer aboil.

In those early days of June, French morale was at dead low tide. Men training in the villages fifty miles behind the front did not sense it. The spirit of French countryfolk seemed as steady as ever. But every American up front felt the downswing. French troops shuffled along, heads low on the march, acting and talking like an army that had abandoned hope of rebounding. One could only pity them; they seemed so utterly miserable. Yet in only a few weeks—what a difference!

While the 3rd Division was plucking its little wisp of glory at Château-Thierry, Omar Bundy's 2nd Division was riding to a man's fight. Lifted by fourteen miles of French camions, driven by tight-mouthed little Annamese who could keep a truck going in convoy with their eyes closed, the division was hauled from the valley of the Marne during the night of May 30. Only the 9th Regiment marched overland, but it reached the designated area beyond Meaux ahead of the motorcade. The others closed around May-en-Multien toward sunset on May 31. General Harbord, setting up his Marine Brigade Command Post in the village of Bremoiselle, had bivouacked in a shambles. "There was every kind of vandalism which in those days we expected of our enemy," he wrote, "but the damage had been done by the retreating French."

Harbord also met an unnamed French general who replied: "*Je ne sais pas*," to every question bearing on the situation. Then Harbord asked: "May I inquire where you are going, sir?" The Frenchman replied: "*La soupe!*" which closed the interview without making anyone feel better. The 9th and 23rd regiments lay somewhere to the east in the direction of Montreuil. Harbord went that way and ran into the commander of the French XXI Corps, General Jean Marie Degoutte (soon to succeed Duchêne). Harbord told him roughly how the division was disposed. Degoutte said solemnly: "Things have been going very badly with us. The enemy [the Germans who had broken through the Chemin des Dames] has advanced over fifty kilometers in seventy-two hours. Your troops are tired. Let them rest and eat. I'll try not to call you tonight. It may be necessary. So be ready to go into line any time after eleven o'clock."

So at last Harbord had the description of the task. The 2nd had been called to dam the German flood. He hurried back to

Germany's third 1918 offensive (black
arrows) was launched against the French
Sixth Army along the Chemin des Dames
(broken white line at top). On May 27,
Boehn's Seventh Army crossed both the
Aisne and Vesle (second broken white line).

AISNE OFFENSIVE
CHATEAU-THIERRY—BELLEAU WOOD
May 27—June 4, 1918

Laon

OEHN
Ailles
CHEMIN DES DAMES
Craonne
Aisne R.
Morning May 27
FIRST
MUDRA
Evening May 27
Vesle R.
Bazoches
Fismes
Nesle
Reims
FIFTH
MICHELER
ois
Méry
Jaulgonne
June 4
Marne R.
u-Thierry
Epernay
.9. 3
Condé-en-Brie

Greenspan

Checked at Chateau-Thierry on June 1, the
Germans wheeled toward Vaux and Belleau
Wood, where the U.S. 2nd Division halted
the drive on June 4. Fierce counterattacks
by the 2nd Division (white arrows)
recaptured Belleau Wood by June 25.

alert General Bundy, passing the word to the regiments as he traversed the billeting areas.

At that same hour in Paris the Supreme War Council was gathering, as solemnly as a party of pallbearers. Foch, Bliss, and the others could hear what sounded like distant thunder—enemy artillery, yet it was no closer to Paris than it had been three days earlier. The thought that the German drive might be losing momentum cheered no one; the military members thought it possible, but couldn't be sure. But it was clear enough that once again the Germans were turning westward toward Paris; and once again the French Government was packing for Bordeaux. Thousands of terrified refugees came streaming through the city; the runaways from Duchêne's beaten Sixth Army were hardly less numerous; many had cast off not only their arms but their uniforms to hide their identity.

Foch was having his worst hours; the accusation, unspoken but palpable, was that Ludendorff had wholly misled him about the buildup against the Chemin des Dames. Clemenceau bridled at the Americans, railing that though they had three quarters of a million men in France, they were contributing only driblets to the battle; trenchant criticism, beyond answer. But the jitters were not confined to Frenchmen. Pershing cabled the War Department that "the possibility of losing Paris has become apparent," with the warning that Clemenceau might be replaced by "a Ministry favoring peace." Pétain, already beaten in his own mind, mumbled his doubt that his army would be able to hold anywhere. Not one of these men realized that Ludendorff, even as Moltke had done in 1914, was overextending.

At least Harbord was free to commit himself full-length to a simple fighting task. At dawn of June 1, his Marine Brigade, and the 3rd Brigade under Brigadier General Edward M. Lewis, a first-class soldier, began their march up the Paris-Metz road. The troops had their little jest as they unlimbered for the advance. "Here we are heading toward Metz while the French Army is moving on Paris and we're both supposed to be fighting the same war."

The countryside over which the Americans slogged forward was gently rolling farmland, graciously tended, burgeoning with the greenery of spring, and wholly unscarred by the war. Here and there were thickets and clumps of second-growth forest, neatly checkered, but heavy with duff and undergrowth. All around, the crops stood high for the season. Every vista should have been refreshing. But these were already tired troops, having spent forty-eight hours on the road.

How to relieve the French on a battle line that was everywhere wavering and in many places only a field agape between units out of contact was the first critical problem, to be solved empirically. "Just let us work this out our own way," one staff officer suggested. The relief was made more or less on that basis, the Americans taking up ground to the rear of where the fire fight went on, the French falling back through them as the pressure rose.

Harbord was with Bundy. A french liaison officer arrived, saluting as his words tumbled out: "General Degoutte's compliments. The situation is so grave that he had to send your 9th Regiment into line below the highway without waiting to put the order through Division Headquarters. He asks the Division Commander to put in another regiment at once."

Bundy turned to Colonel Preston Brown, his Chief of Staff, and gave the order: "Send the 23rd Infantry."

But the 23rd was nowhere in sight. Being last in the column, it was still on the road. So Bundy turned to Harbord and gave the order: "You must put in one of your regiments."

Harbord said: "I'd be glad to, General. But I hope you won't split my brigade in its first action. Can't you let the Paris-Metz road be the dividing line between the brigades, so that I may place my regiments now north of the road?"

It was agreed, and on that spur of the moment decision came the alignment and the tremendous consequence, to the glory of the United States Marines, to the fortunes of the two brigades, and to the future of the world.

BELLEAU WOOD

On June 1, the Germans wheeled from Château-Thierry, captured Hill 204 to the west, and occupied the village of Vaux, which lies astride the Paris-Metz road. Farther to the north, they drove into Belleau Wood.

The U.S. 9th Infantry Regiment deployed through Le Thiolet, directly facing Vaux. By evening, the Marine Brigade had established a line starting in the Clerembauts Wood just north of the road, running on through Lucy-le-Bocage and Belleau Wood to the village of Champillon. The rest of the 2nd Division was held in reserve. Occasional shellfire was now dropping into the American positions and low-flying Fokkers were strafing the troops with machine gun fire. At midnight, Degoutte called Bundy. He had just learned that a three-mile gap existed in the French line around Gandelu and the Germans were coming on. Part of the 23rd Infantry Regiment, some of the 5th Marines, and elements of the 2nd Engineers were rushed to that flank and took positions around Prémont.

From Duchêne, who was still commanding the French Sixth Army, came a message that got to Harbord: "Your men must hold the line at all hazards." Then came a second message: "Have your men prepare entrenchments some hundreds of yards to rearward in case of need." Harbord passed the two contradictory orders to his troops with his own withering rejection slip: "We dig no trenches to fall back on. The Marines will hold where they stand."

The Americans never really dug in. Bayonets and mess kit lids were their only tools. With these they cut away full-length, head-cover troughs, "our graves" they called them, in the same light way they had parodied the last line of the war's best-remembered song: "But we won't come back, we'll be buried over there." Into each grave flopped a solitary rifleman, and a space of ten to fifteen yards was all his to defend. No German ever had the chance to whistle while passing this graveyard. There was no passing. The drive that had started May 27 on the Chemin des Dames came to a standstill on June 3, just before command of the vital front was passed to Bundy.

There had still been no headlong assault by the enemy against the American resistance line. Yet the way was wide open. Degoutte had preconceived that the 2nd Division would be used largely as a backup force. His own corps had broken, then slipped away. Belleau village, Torcy, and Bussiares were abandoned. The Germans came on into Belleau Wood and made for Lucy. In relation to the problem fast developing, the catch-as-catch-can deployment of the 2nd Division could not have been bettered.

Hourly the shellfire built upward. Late on June 4, the 2nd Artillery Brigade arrived, unlimbered, and joined fire with the French batteries along the crescent of hills behind Lucy and Coupru on both sides of the Paris-Metz road. The last of the retreating

French infantry sifted through the American lines that day.

The middle ground was now clear and the Americans could fire when ready. Germans were massing beyond it, preparatory to jump-off, but the Marines sprang first.

In the early morning of June 6, the 1st Battalion of the 5th Marines (Major Julius S. Turrill) attacked from Hill 142 toward the Lucy-Torcy road and gained its objective without use of artillery. Late the same afternoon the 3rd Battalion of the 5th Marines (Major Benjamin S. Berry) and the 3rd Battalion of the 6th Marines (Major Berton W. Sibley) jumped off together, the first going at the west side of Belleau Wood, the second striking for its southern end and the near village of Bouresches. The French had told Harbord that the enemy had not taken over the wood, except for an entrenched corner in the northeast section. That was an error, and the Marines, due to greenness, had compounded it, failing to send forth scouting patrols.

Belleau Wood was an old hunting preserve, irregularly shaped, covering about one square mile. A dry ravine edged its southern face, where lay Lucy village. Bouresches was just beyond it on the east, or the enemy side. The ground covered by the forest was rough, rocky, and boulder strewn—ideal for nesting machine guns. Every forest lane in this checkered plot was also a fire lane for riflemen, and how to fight in forest was one technique wholly overlooked by U.S. manuals on tactics. Belleau Wood had become by this hour the jagged, cutting tip of the German salient projecting from the Aisne. If the Americans were determined to have it or die trying, emplaced steel, rock, and timber were all on the German side. It was the right arena for the showdown.

So back to the assault. Heads down to the fire, so that the helmet would also help cover the neck, the men of Berry's battalion went forward in line through a quarter-mile-long buckwheat field. When it is near ripening and under gentle wind, buckwheat ripples like an emerald lake. This field rippled for the Marines under the scythe of massed enemy machine gun fire. It chopped the wheat, and great gaps appeared in the Marine line as men dropped from wounds. Berry's arm was shredded by bullets but he staggered on. Two hundred, three hundred yards they made. Then the assault folded. A few hands made it to the southwestern tip of the forest. The others were pinned down in the buckwheat. Enemy fire continued to sear the field while the light lasted. When dark fell, those who could, crawled back to friendly lines.

Sibley's battalion was more fortunate. On the southern side of Belleau Wood, the ground and the shrubbery had a helpfully irregular pattern; also the ravine afforded some cover. Even so, the battalion, going forward in four waves, was singed throughout the long approach by rifle and machine gun fire. At last watchers saw it vanish into the forest, and then the real fight began.

The German guns had interlocking and mutually protecting fire bands; to attack one nest merely attracted the bullet swarm from the one beyond it. The Americans were no longer walking; they slithered on their bellies from rock to rock, then heaved their grenades, and went in with a rush. But dark came quickly in the forest and the thickening shadows signaled the need to prepare for night defense. Sibley and his men were in a thoroughly nasty position—caught in a wood with one flank absolutely open to the German Army. The enemy was bound to attempt coming around the end by night, and Sibley had no intention of withdrawing. By 9:00 P.M. he was sending back word that he had mopped up the south end of Belleau Wood and his men had dug in for the night. Two companies of the 2nd Engineers were sent in to help him hold the position.

That wasn't all for the day. As combat field intelligence flowed back to Harbord by runner, he concluded that the Germans had three lines of trenches in Belleau Wood, the first facing toward Lucy and Bouresches, the second running north to south through the center, the third about 150 yards in from the northern face. Sharpshooter pits and barbed entanglements made it a complete system. It would all have to be taken yard by yard. One company from Major Thomas Holcomb's battalion of the 6th Marines carried Bouresches village by storm. When Captain Duncan was killed leading his troops, lank Lieutenant Clifton Cates took over. So began the rise of both Holcomb and Cates to the chieftaincy of the Marine Corps.

Between what matters and what seems to matter, no true line can be drawn in combat. Belleau Wood is a prime example. As of that night, the Marines, by attacking on an order from their Army brigadier, had fixed the first wholly testing ordeal between Germans and Americans on this otherwise insignificant wood patch. Harbord's men had validated his estimate of them by embracing a completely unfamiliar task, wherein heart counted more

A French officer, arms spread, leads
doughboys in a mock tank-supported assault
in preparation for the American capture
of Cantigny on May 28, 1918.

than science. In all time before, nothing great had ever happened
in Belleau Wood. Relative to the fronts of the contending forces,
it was not a key position but a blind alley. The Germans could
not use it for the marshaling of large forces with which to resume the offensive. The Americans didn't really need it, this
springboard to nowhere, for the vital Paris-Metz road did not
run through it. Massive shelling of the wood, had there been
time, might have eliminated the block. It was not to be.

Belleau Wood was just one of those things like Lexington and
the Alamo—an accident that changed the face of history. From
the first go, both sides remained absolutely committed. And the
German Crown Prince, who commanded the army group, was a
little foolish to let it happen that way. He was hazarding the
highest possible stakes in a local dogfight; and he had picked on
the wrong people. The Marine Brigade because it was unique—a
little raft of sea soldiers in an ocean of Army—was without doubt
the most aggressive body of diehards on the Western Front.

Sibley's toehold in the wood, precarious from the beginning,
grew ever more untenable. The Marines were so close to the
Germans that the American artillery could give Sibley's line no
support. All advantage of ground, as well as of numbers, was

with the enemy. The Germans could reinforce and resupply as needed; the Americans could not. Space in which to operate was the critical factor.

On June 11 the Marines in the forward foxholes were pulled back to the southern edge of the wood. Then all the power of the Allied artillery assembled back of the Paris road was directed on the wood. That pleasant stand of greenery soon ranged like an army of gray struck dead in its tracks. Everywhere lay splintered timber, reeking of gas and the stench of the dead. The Marines drove back in again, as they ever do, while the enemy was still shocked. In that violent rebound, they captured two thirds of the wood and three hundred Germans. Then they resumed the position-by-position siege of the forest. Though thrown back, the Germans would not quit. On June 13 they mounted their main counterattack. Sixty percent of Harbord's troops were qualified marksmen. That's when the payoff came for time on the range. The attack was everywhere thrown back with heavy loss.

Due to a freak circumstance, Belleau Wood was already a famous fight, and the Marine Brigade's reputation had eclipsed the public's awareness that the A.E.F. also included a few soldiers. Floyd Gibbons, the war correspondent, had filed a skeleton dispatch with the censor in Paris, in which he identified the Marine units, shortly after the action began. Then in the attack on June 6, his left eye was shot out. But a rumor spread that he had been killed in action. The censor in Paris, who chanced to be his personal friend, heard the doleful tidings. In that moment, sentiment overrode duty; he concluded that the dispatch should go through untouched in memory of his "dead" friend. While Gibbons lay in the hospital awaiting the black patch that became his trademark, America thrilled with the revelation that the Marines were winning the war.

They didn't quite win Belleau Wood singlehandedly. On June 14 the 23rd Infantry extended its front to take over as far north as the edge of Bouresches. Then two days later the 7th Infantry of the 3rd Division moved into the wood and took over from the Marines, who needed a rest. The 7th tried, but both of its attacks were repulsed. Colonel Wendell C. Neville of the Marines had been left in command of the sector and his own people got back to him on June 23, the 7th Infantry hitting the road again.

On June 25 the 3rd Battalion of the 5th Marines, one company of the 6th Machine Gun Battalion, and two companies of the 4th Machine Gun Battalion (Army) made the last assault in the woods. When at last the line broke into the open, leaving the splintered trees cleared of Germans, it had five hundred POW's to show for the day. Marine Major Maurice E. Shearer reported to Harbord: "Wood now exclusively U.S. Marine Corps." Well, there had been just a few soldiers going along for the ride.

The 2nd Division's other brigade under Lewis had also fought through the same June. Small-scale German attacks had been beaten off; numerous raids into enemy country had been staged. But the infantry could mount nothing big because the artillery was absorbed in helping the Marines. To its front lay Hill 204, a considerable obstacle. At its foot was Vaux, a stout village of stone-walled homes, now occupied by Germans who had fire-slotted the walls and trained their machine guns on the approaches.

The brigade wanted Vaux, and its intelligence officers already had in hand the one Frenchman who knew most about how it was laid out—the village stonemason. The operations people drew up plans based on his information, whereby each squad and platoon would have a specified house or block target, and would know the route, the sortie points, and the dead space. The artillery was instructed to register fire on Vaux, but to do it in a drifting way, moving back and forth from it to other targets, so that the Germans wouldn't guess what was coming.

At dawn on July 1 the barrage was loosed. Vaux rocked. Roofs and walls were riven. One hour later the fire was lifted to the slopes beyond and the infantry charged the village. The 2nd Battalion of the 9th Infantry did that part of it; the 3rd Battalion, 23rd Infantry, took the woods around it. It wasn't a great fight; grenades and automatic fire quelled the last resistance within the houses and by noon the mop-up was complete.

The storming of Vaux completed the operation of the 2nd Division along the Paris-Metz road. That night a French regiment, supported by two platoons of the 111th Infantry of the U.S. 28th (Pennsylvania) Division tried to take Hill 204. When the smoke cleared and the dust settled, the Germans still held its crest.

The Marines had not won the war, but their brigade had stopped the Germans on the Paris road. The Crown Prince's dangerously narrow salient had afforded an opportunity to make Germans pay for reckless overextension. Yet, save for this body check by the 2nd Division, with the French Sixth Army in dissolution, the Germans would have anchored in far stronger positions before pulling up. It was Ludendorff's fatal mistake that he did not earlier compel a broadening of his front by strengthening the movement through Soissons. The two brigades under Harbord and Lewis exacted the price for that error. It is absurd to say that if the 2nd had not chosen its battlefield and then held the line, someone else would have done it farther along. Amid defeat and uncertainty there had to be one clear trumpet blast. The Americans had sounded it. The French heard it. Their hearts leaped up. They were no longer alone on the right flank.

In June the U.S. 2nd Division had taken 1,687 German prisoners, more than all the British armies had captured that month. The cost had come high. The division had suffered 9,777 casualties; 1,811 of its members had died fighting. American blood was never shed on any battlefield to better effect. The Marine Brigade had used up four enemy divisions during its month in Belleau Wood. By order of Degoutte, who had been commanding the French Sixth Army since mid-June, the skeletonized forest was renamed *Bois de la Brigade de Marine*. Enraptured, Clemenceau visited the division to add his voice to the paeans of praise for the heroes who had barred the road to Paris.

ONE MILLION YANKS

Three days after Vaux fell, American G.H.Q. at Chaumont, trying to make the most mileage from that even while at the same time exacting double duty from the Fourth of July holiday, announced loudly that more than one million Americans had arrived in France. The 26th Division had come from the Toul area to relieve the 2nd in line. The 42nd was returning from eighty-two days in line, during which it had suffered 2,014 casualties. The 4th and 5th (Regular) were finishing their on-job training, the 78th, 89th, 92nd, 37th, 29th, 90th, 79th, and 91st were all fresh off the boats. Some were superbly commanded, as in the case of the 90th under Major General Henry T. Allen; others were led by military fossils who were unduly hard on their troops.

The Americans came armed with the Model 1917 rifle, a weapon so awkward and crudely tooled that their fire would have done little execution with it, even if Pershing had put that main emphasis on sharpshooter training with which legend credits him.

They arrived in hot OD woolens with choker collars, which garb in the July heat only added another atrocity to the Western Front. When they came down the gangplank, they stood tall and appeared all-powerful, thanks partly to the campaign hat. But after the issue of that badge of the warrior, the overseas cap, they looked more big-eared than robust. Yet they radiated vigor and confidence.

There has never been a prouder, happier, more talkative army under the American flag. Their favorite expression was: "Start arguin', bastards." Amid snafus, which were frequent, some joker invariably would sound off with that pet A.E.F. phrase: "She said there'd be days like this." As they marched over the old Roman roads, they sang the bawdiest songs within memory: "Lulu," "Frankie and Johnny," and "The Fusiliers," a ditty that was later cleaned up to become the "I've Got Sixpence" of World War II. In one respect they differed from later American armies. The higher NCO's had extraordinary authority and prestige, stoutly upheld by the officer corps.

The men of the A.E.F. were not blind to their hardships or unaware that some of the load might have been lightened through more thoughtfulness on the part of others. But they saw these things as incidental. Above and beyond the turmoil, they understood that the nation was in danger, that they had been called, and that they had to do what they could. In that spirit, the 1918 soldier went forward, respecting higher authority, believing unreservedly in the sanctity of an order, heartened by his faith in the American people and his love of country. When this man fought, he and his comrades whooped it up as if the combat field were a football stadium. Training had not taught him that; he did what came naturally.

Yet neither the swarming of the Yanks, nor the proof of their mettle in the battle along the Paris road, convinced the Allies that the scale was already tipping. In the name of Foch, the three Prime Ministers—Clemenceau, Lloyd George, and Orlando—cabled Mr. Wilson their thanks, with the postscript that at least one hundred American divisions would be needed to win the war. Pershing was hardly less pessimistic. On June 18 he cabled Secretary Baker an estimate, promptly followed up by letter, that if he could be given eighty divisions by midsummer of 1919, the war might well be won by late autumn. Mr. Baker accepted Pershing's estimate, and the War Department was ordered to proceed with an eighty-division plan.

Possibly more clearly than his enemies, Ludendorff began to see the writing on the wall. His appreciation of the American fighter was revised to read: "Personnel must be called excellent. Spirit of troops is high. Moral effect of our fire does not materially check the advance of the infantry. Nerves of the Americans are still unshaken."

With Pershing's loosening of the reins, moreover, the troops already at hand were being deployed in such a way as to provide a moral bulwarking of the general front. On June 10, by G.H.Q. order, the U.S. I, II, and III corps were established with headquarters. But II Corps under Major General George W. Read was not to fight as part of an American Army. It was deployed to Haig's front, and its 27th (New York) and 30th (Tennessee) divisions, on completing training, would fight thereafter alongside British, Canadians, and Anzacs. As of that July 4, only one U.S. division of the eight occupying front line positions had thus far come under an American corps commander; it happened that very day when Major General Hunter Liggett, as chief of I Corps, took responsibility for the sector just west of Château-Thierry.

Fifteen other U.S. divisions, each approximately twice the size of any Allied division, would soon be ready for battle. It therefore behooved Pershing to urge upon Foch the immediate assignment of an American combat zone of sufficient breadth for a field army. In a talk with Foch on July 10, he renewed his earlier argument about the logistic superiority of the Nancy-Toul region, though he conceded that as operations were developing, it might be expedient to assemble the Army first around Château-Thierry. Foch agreed on both counts, saying: "Around Château-Thierry fits in better with my plans for the immediate future." However, the arrangement had to be suspended because the next German offensive came on so fast.

The 33rd (Illinois) Division had already undergone its first bath of fire with the British. It was an affair at Le Hamel. The Guardsmen had been staged into the Amiens area because that front was quiet and their training could be speeded by British instructors. But by July 1, Haig was again thinking of resuming the offensive after an eight-month lapse. Four rifle companies of the 132nd Regiment went into line attached to two different Australian brigades on July 2. It was supposed to be just a brief tour in trenches to tone up the training routine. But within a few days the British High Command decided that capturing Le Hamel village and the nearby wood would give them a purchase on the Villers-Bretonneux plateau, which would be useful in a big bust-out sometime later.

The attack started at dawn on July 4, after three hours of off-and-on bombardment by the artillery. The fireworks were heavier than the Americans ever expected to hear from British guns on that particular day. The Illini jumped off with the others, Aussies commanding them, their own officers observing. By mid-morning Le Hamel was won, and after sharp fighting with bayonet and grenade, there was a tremendous haul of prisoners for such a little show—38 officers and 1,340 men. Afterward the Australians conceded that the Americans fought beautifully, in fact, almost as well as themselves.

As Liggett's I Corps took shape that same day, the 3rd and 26th divisions already were in line at Château-Thierry. The battered 2nd was in reserve with the fresh 4th and 28th, and the 1st was coming from Cantigny.

The 42nd Division had arrived at Châlons-sur-Marne to join the French Army under General Gouraud, that lion of a man who had almost been blown apart at Gallipoli. He posted it north to go into reserve just west of Suippes. Gouraud hourly expected a German offensive in main and was almost certain it would come July 4. When it failed to develop, he took advantage of a ten-day grace period to elaborate his defense. Here was one Frenchman determined to stand and wide awake to everything Duchêne had missed.

The Gouraud plan of defense was designed to wear the Germans down before they reached his hard crust. His front line was renamed the "sacrifice line," which was harsh but realistic. Once the battle began, no troops would be left there, save a few machine gunners and observation post crews. The lookouts would steer the French counterbarrage as it rolled forward against the enemy infantry waves. The second line was a more heavily manned intermediate position, another barrier reef to help break down the surge. Well to rearward of it was what soldiers call the MLR —the main line of resistance, which had to hold. Not far behind it was arrayed the defending artillery. Set this way, Gouraud was prepared to win or lose all.

Most of the 42nd Division was fitted into the MLR. One garri-

A.E.F. artist Wallace Morgan sketched
this front-line dressing station situated
in a culvert under the road to Lucy, near
Belleau Wood. Army medics worked under
grueling and makeshift conditions in their
ceaseless struggle to treat the wounded.

son of twenty-five men was grouped around an antitank gun in the sacrifice zone. Five battalions contributed one company each to the intermediate zone. These dispositions made, they waited. The nights were starlit and cool, and regularly at midnight the infantry came to a stand-to which lasted till dawn. After a breakfast of black coffee, bacon, and French hard bread, they slept. It was just as well, for the chalk plains of Champagne glared white and dazzling under a blazing sun.

Gouraud and his Fourth Army knew what their eyes told them. This time there could be no surprise. Frenchmen manning the observation posts saw many, many enemy batteries going into positions in the open fields south of the Argonne Forest. Swarms of German infantry were seen moving up through the hills around Reims. On the night of July 13–14, French combat patrols from six points along Gouraud's front raided the enemy trenches and returned with prisoners; thereafter they knew the hour and place of the forthcoming German attack.

Based on what the earlier buildups had accomplished on the Somme and against the Chemin des Dames, Ludendorff's expectations for the new power play were not excessive. The German Seventh Army, with eleven divisions in line, four in support, and five in reserve, would advance from the eastern face of the Marne salient between Gland and Chambrecy and, attacking southeastward along both banks of the Marne, capture the crossings at Epernay and the hills southeast of Reims. Then it would push upstream to join hands with the German First Army. That army, attacking east of Reims, with eleven divisions, had Châlons as its chief objective. It was expected to crash the French front between Prunay and Auberive, wheel westward, and then advance downstream along the Marne. The battle would therefore engage the Americans in Champagne as well as those around Château-Thierry.

Erich Ludendorff was at last worrying about the fiber of his troops. Something was happening to the German Army. Where a few months previously green youngsters and men past forty were the fillers, they had become the majority. The machine-made soldier of earlier years, the goose-stepping robot, was almost gone. There is a limit beyond which discipline and training cannot go. The Kaiser's legions had reached that limit, and Ludendorff was troubled. "Many signs of disease are appearing among the German people and their army," he wrote.

At Château-Thierry, General Dickman also had a problem. The north boundary of the 3rd Division's sector was formed by the canalized Marne, there about fifty yards wide and fifteen feet deep. The hills on the enemy side of this sharply cleft valley are heavily wooded and rise to heights of 450 feet. Any number of troops might be concealed in the hill mass. South of the river, the hills do not crowd the bank, though farther back toward the Le Rocq plateau, the ridges rise to 550 feet. There are frequent bends in the river with flats on the south side more than a mile in breadth and depth. Most of these flats are farmland, with occasional patches of forest. The Le Rocq plateau would be the natural assembly point for regrouping by the Germans if they could cross the river. Next to it in importance was the embankment of the Paris-Nancy railway line near the river, to Dickman's eye an intermediate and rallying line that "could not be missed on the darkest night," and that, if gained, would subject to enfilading fire all the defensive positions on the south bank.

Still, General Degoutte wanted Dickman's regiments to defend right at the line of the Marne "with one foot in the water." Dickman, with his forces spread along seven miles of the Marne, would have none of it. He said to Degoutte: "We'll let ten thousand Germans come across to the railway unmolested, and we'll destroy them on the plain long before they can reach our main line on the crest of the plateau." But his chesty proposition was turned down.

The 4th Infantry Regiment took over the sector along the Marne directly east of Château-Thierry. From there, the division extended on eastward along the south bank. The 7th Regiment, which had been roaming about a great deal, joined flanks with the 4th, its headquarters at the Le Rocq farm. The 30th Infantry stood guard from Fossoy to Mézy. The 38th Regiment was deployed last and got the mouth of the Surmelin Valley to cover, its line extending to the eastern limits of the division, where the American flank joined the French 125th Infantry Division.

The French 125th was of dubious quality. Dickman inferred that the French High Command rated it a frail reed, not likely to stand. Accordingly, Colonel Ulysses Grant McAlexander instructed his 38th Regiment that it must be prepared to bend both ways with the blow.

Most of the U.S. 28th Division was echeloned to the rear of

the 3rd and the French 125th as further insurance for the Surmelin ingress route. But four of 28th's rifle companies were in the front line of the French division. This was a wholly unhappy situation for the Pennsylvanians. They must inevitably sustain the full shock of battle their first time out, while being divested of operating unity.

These were not happy days for the 3rd Division. The packs of the 7th Battalion's machine gunners had been looted while they were fighting for Château-Thierry one month earlier. Later, company messes had been raided and the whole dinner stolen. Dickman suddenly found his officers damning Black Jack for being so slow about organizing an independent American Army; being next to French soldiers seemed to them like being cast into a den of thieves. Official courtesies were stepped up to lubricate the friction. On July 4 General Piarron de Mondesir reviewed the 7th Battalion, and its heroes of June 1 were pinned with the Croix de Guerre and embarrassed by kisses on both cheeks. The Prefect of the Aisne, M. Chocarne, made an appropriate speech in which he said: "In the glorious hours of our defense you have helped us with supplies of all kinds."

To reciprocate for July 4, Dickman invited the French brass to a banquet on July 14, Bastille Day. They accepted heartily, then at the last moment most of the French generals canceled out. Being a stalwart trencherman, Dickman went through the meal unperturbed. But there was more bravado than appetite in the act.

For it was then that he knew something big was stirring that had kept the French generals at their duty stations. July 15 was certain to be the day of the next German attack.

XIII
Turning of the Tide

Crouched behind a rock for protection,
an American soldier fires on the enemy
at the Marne.

There are stages in life's journey when men know, more through instinct than by reason, that suddenly great blessings are preordained. Not with the persistent illusion of the optimist, but as when a searchlight beam cuts through midnight, there arises the certainty that success is at hand in some cherished enterprise. Pershing's soldiers felt that all-pervading uplift after Belleau Wood, and because it eased the suspense-filled hour, they didn't need to know the calculus of the change—that their arrival had overcome the German manpower superiority responsible for the slashing gains of the early spring. Within a few fleeting days, morally and numerically, the whole situation had been reversed, not pendulously but lastingly.

In the Champagne, General Gouraud knew beyond doubt that the German massive bombardment of his Fourth Army would begin at 12:10 A.M. on July 15, and that Below's First Army infantry would jump off at 4:15. POW's had freely divulged that vital information, an index of flagging resistance and of mounting carelessness in the High Command. For days the French had prepared to bite the biter first.

One hour before the German bombardment was scheduled to open, Gouraud's vast gunpower was loosed on the enemy front, blasting troop assembly points, battery parks, and communications trenches. French gunners had a fix on these positions, shaken from the POW's, and could take precise aim with their 768 batteries. Although the Germans had 1,656 batteries, the Allied guns offset the difference by getting in the first blow. The methodical enemy withheld fire until 12:10, while Allied shellfire ripped apart German formations.

When the enemy bombardment opened, it fell most heavily on Gouraud's "sacrifice line," first proof that Below had not divined the Fourth Army's scheme of defense. By dawn the Champagne plain was overhung with a pall of black smoke and chalk dust, which thickened as the guns kept pounding. Soon after, rockets rose from the sacrifice line, signaling that the German infantry was coming on. Having done their work, the surviving men in the outpost line pulled stakes and retired to the intermediate zone. The trap was working perfectly. The French artillery dropped on the German columns as they emerged from the hills along the north edge of the Vesle Valley, and, around noon, the advance on this part of the front was brought to a standstill.

Private Charles MacArthur, not yet a playwright but a rollicking and indifferent Rainbow (42nd Division) gunner serving under Gouraud, recorded his impressions: "Over on the left, black clouds rise from Reims Cathedral, on fire in front, a boiling bank of dirty smoke hides the flower of the Prussian Guard. In back, ammunition trains race across the fields at a dead gallop, the drivers beating their horses with steel helmets. Shells land right in front of them as they perform a brilliant right into line. . . . The guns are so hot now that they have to be swabbed after every shot. . . . A few Germans are getting through."

Another MacArthur, Douglas, the 42nd's Chief of Staff (and no relation), was winning his first Distinguished Service Medal "for serving with high credit." And too many Rainbows came out of it with Purple Hearts. The one U.S. division took just a little less than 1,600 casualties, but there were few tears; the show had been worth it. In one day Gouraud's name became hallowed with all Yanks.

Off to the left flank, between the Vesle and Marne rivers east of Château-Thierry, General Berthelot's French Fifth Army had not fared so well against a concurrent attack by General Max von Boehn's Seventh Army. The Gouraud method was not applied there. So in that area, the Allied defenders chose and heavily manned those relatively few sites on the high ground that promised some advantage forward of the main line. The garrisons were ordered to defend "to the last man," which is one of the more ambiguous phrases in the military book. No one ever chooses to be last; the group can decamp, the last man can empty his magazine, and there you have compliance, absurd but correct. The Fifth Army lost not only its line of advanced posts but its defense line. That is one of the difficulties with armies; there are not enough Gourauds.

Insofar as enemy intentions are concerned, the fight in the Champagne and the German assault east of Château-Thierry were of one piece, though they are usually treated as separate battles. From the high ground beyond the Marne's north bank, General Boehn's massed artillery opened bombardment at the same time that Below's guns first spoke in the Champagne.

So began the *Friedensturm*, or peace offensive—its object, to widen the salient begun in the May offensive, and so continue the advance on Paris. The shells rained on the U.S. 3rd Division's positions on the Marne for three hours. General Dickman had known that it was coming. He had gotten the storm warning two hours earlier from a POW. His own guns had gone into action one-half hour before the German fires dropped.

The first German boat waves began crossing the Marne just before 2:00 A.M. Riding twenty to the boat, the attackers got in under the embankment and waited. The night was ink black. From the other side, pioneers brought forward footbridges on which men could cross single file. Engineers came with pontoons, and behind them were horses, guns, and motor vehicles jamming toward the crossing. The whole Seventh Army was in motion.

Immediately it became a machine gunner's battle; boats capsized under the bullet hail, and thousands of German riflemen had to swim across the river. Aligned on the north bank, the enemy machine gunners centered their fire on the outposts next to the river and the resistance line along the railway embankment beyond.

Well to the east of Château-Thierry, the Marne makes a large loop northward, the Jaulgonne Bend. This feature made the sector of the French 125th Division a deathtrap, open to fire from all sides. The French line dissolved and the individuals faded away in panic. That left, forlorn and surrounded, the U.S. 28th Division's four unlucky rifle companies from Pennsylvania. They fought back as best they could, but most of them were killed or captured. A few kept resisting until noon, when their ammunition ran out. Their brigade was in support about four miles to the rear. Its commander got the word at 9:00 A.M. that the front had caved, which made him the blocking force. Between Jaulgonne and Dormans, the Germans were sweeping the wooded heights south of the Marne and had control of the battle east of the Surmelin. They had been in Mézy since before dawn and had mounted a fire line along the railway bank running both ways from it. That should have made untenable the U.S. 3rd Division's right flank, McAlexander's 38th Infantry, now beset from both sides.

Colonel McAlexander had anticipated just such a happening. Without yielding his hold on the Marne embankment, he refused both flanks so that his regimental front stood like a horseshoe, one battalion forward, one on either side. The man, like his outfit, was winning the nickname that they both would wear henceforth, Rock of the Marne. "The time may come when Americans have to give ground," McAlexander, moving around the besieged perimeter, told his young captains, "but right now our job is so to impress Germans with our willingness to fight that their morale will be destroyed." The 38th held.

The 30th on its left, by noontime, had been forced back to Crézancy, about two miles from the river. Here again the Germans gained the high ground overlooking the Surmelin Valley, the mouth of which was barred to them by McAlexander's stand. Farther to the left the 7th and 4th regiments had also been pushed back. Three German divisions were coming right at the 3rd Division's center. Along the Marne embankment, where the pressure was most intense, the American lines were redressed, but were not yielded. Not one regimental front broke, and by noon the German drive had lost most of its momentum. Three rifle platoons of the 7th Regiment had held out heroically in the forward ground to give the forces behind them time to re-form. They were wiped out before the action ended. Then when the main line faced about on the new ground, the Germans did not come on.

By nightfall the enemy attack across the Marne was completely defeated in the 3rd Division's sector. The 30th Regiment had recovered its lost ground, and was driving the remnants of the German 47th Infantry back across the river. More than eight hundred prisoners had fallen into division hands. The 30th and 38th had each lost about 40 per cent of their strength in one day. The German corps that had crashed the French front to the eastward was trying to organize an offensive westward into the Surmelin Valley. A young German, Kurt Hesse, adjutant of the 5th Grenadier Regiment, noted in his diary: "The result of this day—the heaviest defeat of this war."

His worm's-eye view of the battlefield did not lead him astray. Ludendorff thought the same, and realized that he was stuck; the salient couldn't be widened, he was merely wasting lives south of the Marne. At noon on July 16, G.H.Q. ordered the German First and Third Armies to abandon the offensive and reorganize for defense by pulling back certain divisions for this purpose. "To continue," said Ludendorff, "will cost us too much."

398

Although the Germans had driven a pocket nine miles long and four miles deep south of the Marne, and were at the point of capturing Epernay, the boom was about to be lowered against them. Foch had scrounged up a reserve and poised it as a hammer just beyond Château-Thierry. The commander was the up-and-down General Mangin. His counteroffensive was scheduled to blast off on July 18.

When the Germans swarmed over the Marne on July 15, Pétain canceled the attack order with a wire to Mangin: "Boche has pocket south of Marne. Suspend operation so that I can send your reserves to battle south of Marne."

Foch got this news and was furious. Immediately overriding Pétain, he directed Mangin to proceed with the attack, and he ordered Pétain to keep hands off. Within three weeks Foch was to get his marshal's baton. Without it, he was already conducting the orchestra, and if he could keep Pétain out of tailspins, there would be no downbeat. All of a sudden his two supreme gifts as a commander came to equipoise—his high heart and his extrasensory appreciation of situation. Just a few ripostes by some of Pershing's Yanks had renewed his fire. Oddly enough, Sir Douglas Haig, after three lean years, was not far behind him. The man, like the whisky, improved with age.

Foch met Haig at Mouchy right after he had overridden Pétain's order, which would have stopped Mangin. Still burning, he persuaded Sir Douglas to send four British reserve divisions to the fight in the south. But while acquiescing, Haig was still the reluctant dragoon. He vented his gripe that evening: "If the dispositions prove wrong, the blame rests on me. If right, the credit lies with Foch. With this, the Government should feel satisfied."

COUNTEROFFENSIVE

A cloudburst drenched the area around Soissons on the morning of July 18. It was the wrong beginning for the rightest day of the war. A kid sergeant in the U.S. 1st Division sounded off: "What do you know, I'm eighteen today. We can't miss. Watch the world turn upside down."

Mangin's soaked Tenth Army, thrown together like a chowline slum, was mustered to the south of the city. The mission was elementary—to advance against the German Ninth Army and cut the Soissons–Château-Thierry highway, thereby choking off arterial supply to the Germans in the Marne salient. Here was no reaching for the moon, but a quite limited object, in line with Foch's reasoning that just getting an advance started might reverse the battle tide and lead to unlimited consequence. There had been no methodical mount-up of the attack. The divisions had been marched from afar and were formed as an army in the final hours. In that way, surprise, which had eluded Ludendorff through the spring, was achieved by Foch.

Under the oaks of Compiègne forest, part of the U.S. 1st and 2nd divisions, and one Moroccan division, had been at hand for almost forty-eight hours. Although these three were to be the battering ram, they were still in a blocking position some way behind the front; the 2nd Division's Marine Brigade did not start its march-up to the forest until twilight of the night before the attack. The Marines were not beaten down; they had had time enough for recovery after the wringer in Belleau Wood. But they did not know that they had been hurriedly assembled for a relatively minor operation that was to unfold as the great turning point of the four-year struggle.

General Harbord, now commanding the 2nd Division, got his orders from the French XX Corps's Chief of Staff, Colonel Henri Giraud, later a hero of World War II. Harbord didn't like the orders; all four regiments had been ordered in line, and the boundaries permitted too little space for an American-size division. So he bucked back, as the rain continued, soaking the uncased maps.

For Harbord, it was a night to remember. "The roads were like tunnels in their gloom. The rate of movement through that dark forest could not have exceeded a mile an hour. All the arriving units told the same story of the weary night ride, the arbitrary debusment at unknown points, the lack of information and guides. They could only follow the instinct of the American soldier and march to the sound of the cannon, which they did without exception." It was good enough. No fires were allowed. The cold bully beef, served without coffee, was unpalatable. None of this seemed preliminary to a great day.

Through the cloudburst, troops of XX Corps pushed up along the national highway into the Retz Forest toward the front, cursing the storm. Yet the elements were their friends, blotting out the last chance given the Germans to detect the mass movement. Troops are never delivered fresh into battle. Every mile in an

Bayonets fixed, American soldiers storm
a German trench in this 1918 drawing by
A.E.F. artist George Harding. With the
checking of a fourth German assault on
June 9–13, 1918, the normally cautious and
pessimistic Pétain predicted, "If we can
hold on until the end of June, our situation
will be excellent. In July we can resume
the upper hand. Victory is ours."

approach march in halcyon weather still wears men down more than five when they are going away. But this march was the real cruncher. Men of the 1st Division had to splash seven miles through the ooze to get to their assembly area in that impossible slough, the Coeuvres ravine. They dropped in their tracks, too spent to unbuckle the belts to ease their shoulders; any witness would have sworn they would be unable to move at dawn.

Bullard, the new III Corps leader, was up there looking on, though tactical direction remained with the French. The 1st Division was now under Major General Charles Pelot Summerall, the hardest taskmaster in the A.E.F., who always demanded that "extra mile" from his men, sometimes when they were too beat to give it. All of the generals were stewing—no maps. Yet out of the great snafu came sufficient order before first light cracked. The darkest of all hours ran before a dawn fully glorious.

The Moroccans in the center, the 1st on the left, the 2nd on the right, they jumped at early morning into the rain-washed, ravine-split countryside, on a fair day, save for the smoke and thunder of the brief, preliminary barrage. Suddenly there were tanks out in front of them, it seemed like scores of them, and with all that metal to the fore, the doughboys picked up and sprang forward, as if refreshed by a pull of panther water.

The armor ran on toward Missy-aux-Bois, Chaudun, and Vierzy. The Germans had not had time to throw up strong fieldworks; now for the first time, their only advantage lay in their numbers, and the surprise, coupled with the smash bombardment, had cut the effectiveness thereof by half. Without loss of momentum, the Allied infantry assault carried through the German front. Prisoners streamed back. German cannoneers surrendered their guns before ever pulling a lanyard.

By 7:00 A.M. the 2nd Division had taken its first day's objective, the high ground around Vierzy, and had routed the main enemy forces from the Vierzy ravine. So broken up was this countryside that the three American regiments carrying the assault, 5th Marines and 9th and 23rd Infantry, were already scrambled. They had outpaced the Moroccan division and in consequence drew fire from undisturbed Germans on their left. The Marines mopped up Vauxcastle ravine in a dirty hand-to-hand fight.

On the far left of XX Corps in the 1st Division's zone, the 26th and 28th regiments met savage resistance around Missy-aux-

Bois. In the big ravine north of Missy, the brigade plunged through waist-deep marsh water in the face of well-placed machine gun fire and took hard losses. On the right, things went better for the 16th and 18th regiments; capturing Missy, they bounded on to cut the Paris-Soissons highway north of Chaudun. By noon, the 1st Division also had its first day's objectives, having advanced nearly four miles while bagging 1,600 prisoners and thirty cannon. By noon, the front of the German Ninth Army was ruptured.

Overhead, as the Americans swept through Vierzy and Missy, circled the German Fokkers, signaling fire direction to their own batteries and dividing to strafe the streets with machine guns ablaze. Their own bomb loads gone, they'd get off a rocket to call in more artillery on a fat target. The Allied artillery mounted up and came on. Traffic snarled and blocked under the overload, ambulances and empty ammunition trucks (now loaded with wounded) struggling to get rearward, cannons, caissons, and loaded camions banging their way forward.

The Mangin offensive continued another three days. The Americans maintained their attack unto Berzy-le-Sec and the heights southwest of Buzancy. The 2nd Division had been relieved by the French 56th, but the 1st, with some of its companies so badly shattered that enlisted men were in command, kept going. In the 26th Infantry, the senior officer was a captain with only two years' service. When the 1st was at last relieved by the 15th Scottish Division on July 22, it had driven some seven miles into the base of the German salient on the Marne. That night soldiers saw great fires brighten the skies to the south and eastward. The Germans were burning their stores before clearing away. The drive begun in the thunderstorm at Soissons had squeezed out the last great German salient.

Mangin published his thank-you to the two divisions: "American comrades! I am thankful to you for the blood so generously spilled on the soil of my country." Generous was the right word. The 2nd Division had lost five thousand in dead and wounded; the 1st had lost more. But the survivors swaggered out, saying with their legs what they told one another: "By God, we're good."

In this way began the Great Retreat of the Germans. There would be no more furious Ludendorff lunges, no carving of great salients. The forward march initiated by Foch would keep going. Great anticlimactic battles were still to be fought. At least another million men had to die or bleed to prove the point. But decision came on July 18 when the last straw broke the Teuton back. What the junior sergeant prophesied on his birthday hadn't really come true; his world was turning right side up.

But it wasn't just on the Soissons front that the pressure mounted, and not alone because of the squeeze there that the Crown Prince ordered a reconnaissance to select four rearward defensive positions for a fallback. In the French Sixth Army, which lay farther south, the U.S. 4th Division, with its brigades split, helped the French VII and II corps to drive the Germans back and establish a line well to the east of Chouy and Priez. There were rolling wheat fields beyond, well covered by enemy machine guns, and there the push was halted.

The 26th (Yankee) Division attacked from the edge of Belleau Wood and captured Torcy, Givry, and Belleau village. That emboldened the French on their right to storm and take Hill 204, the linchpin of enemy holdings between Château-Thierry and Vaux. The 26th pressed on through the Bois de Bouresches, losing 387 killed and 1,869 wounded in its first campaign. Before dawn on July 21, the U.S. 3rd Division began to cross the Marne, using among other things three footbridges with empty gasoline tins for floats. The day before, the French Fifth and Ninth armies had regained the south bank of the Marne.

That was how the recovery became energized, the Americans following the rule, "When in doubt hit out," while the French, stirred by the example close at hand, gradually regained their marvelous fighting *élan*. With Château-Thierry all but cut off, the Germans hastily evacuated it and the French moved in unopposed. By then, the U.S. 28th Division had joined the fight, and later, after the Marne was crossed, the 42nd took up the pursuit. The enemy was pulling back thirty miles, and Frenchmen of the countryside for the first time saw German soldiers running away. The Yanks followed along, singing "Old Gray Mare" and "My Castle on the River Rhine."

SIGNS OF GERMAN WEAKNESS

There was full reason for Ludendorff to reweigh the gamble, though he had become emotionally incapable of assimilating it. He had plunged on the Aisne and the Marne so that he might renew the contest in Flanders. So doing, he had stayed too long and had spent the blue chips in a different game. The ante was now with the other side.

The U.S. II Corps under Major General George W. Read had come into the B.E.F. Replacements had beefed up the British and Dominion divisions. In a three-month reprieve in which housekeeping problems could be attended to relatively unmolested, the Allied flank north from the Somme became aburst with munitions and other supplies. Tank production soared; the armor accumulated. Haig grew cannier with time, and more appreciative of ultimate values, as most Scots do. He had been broadened, not hardened, by the shock treatment of the early spring. He knew that he had done well; the resolve not to spoil what was going commendably, both for the B.E.F. and its chief, brought him to balance. Where he had been a squawk box for his staff, he became a sounding board for his army commanders, which is the better attitude.

Wherever Germany looked, there were no longer any soft spots. In Italy, the rebuilding under General Diaz permitted the return of two British and four French divisions to the Western Front, leaving only five Allied divisions south of the Alps. They were sent to the Asiago front in the mountains to prepare for an offensive there. Two Italian divisions had been shipped to France, where they participated in the recovery drive.

In Salonika, the Allied Expedition had passed from the hands of General Sarrail to General Guillaumat, then at last into the capable charge of General Franchet d'Esperey. The Supreme War Council, however, kept a check-rein on the overstrength Army of the Orient, still immobilized by its own ponderosity. But there were only three German infantry battalions and thirty-two artillery batteries to stiffen the unwilling Bulgarians. Franchet d'Esperey coiled for the knockout blow, via Lake Doiran and the Vardar Valley, planning to strike in September.

Against Turkey in Palestine, Allenby, after a prolonged sit in the Judean Hills, prepared to advance into what are now Lebanon and Syria, moving via Megiddo (Armageddon), the fortress spot covering the defile between the Mediterranean and the Sea of Galilee, where he was to fight his decisive battle. In Mesopotamia, Lieutenant General W. R. Marshall, who had succeeded Maude in the command at Baghdad, cranked up to advance on Mosul, where the best part of the Turkish Sixth Army waited.

Allenby, in the six months since Jerusalem had fallen, had operated on a more austere basis, despite Lloyd George's earlier effervescence toward the Middle East enterprise. With the cut-down forces at his disposal (all Western regiments had been returned to France), he extended his front eastward to embrace the Jordan bridgehead at Jericho and then pushed on to Amman, the capital of the present Kingdom of Jordan. Liman von Sanders, who had succeeded Falkenhayn, advised Ludendorff as August opened that he might be able to hold the Palestine coastal plain but had no troops to counter the hook into Jordan, which could prove fatal. But more and more he inclined in that direction, as Allenby feinted to draw him off balance. This army that was liberating the Holy Land was like a crosscut of Babel—Jewish battalions, Algerians, Indian Moslems, Negro units from the heart of Africa, Hindus and Bedouins, all joined in.

Marshall's army in Mesopotamia was of different complexion, the cutting edge being British. But his main forces had been kept immobilized due to some very strange British misadventures along the Russian borders, consequent to Ludendorff's grab for the oil fields around Baku. Now Allenby and Marshall were preparing to strike again, and in front of them lay a breaking enemy.

In the West, however, governments, generals, and statesmen still rejected the obvious. They viewed the series of German retreats as a phase; confronted by the long-awaited sign of a folding enemy army, they could not believe what they saw. Only Foch was sharper than the rest. Getting his baton on August 6, he responded: "This is not a wreath of flowers on my grave. If it had been, I should not have wanted it. Now we must at once exploit this great change in the military situation."

Shortly before, there had been a conference of all the great military chiefs, and General Harbord, that nonpareil fighter, for very special reasons, was also there. "Not one person suggested that the war might end in 1918," he noted. Anyway, things were looking up. There were 1,200,000 Yanks in France, and more were arriving at the rate of 10,000 per day. Secretary Baker was hitting the A.E.F. with paper rockets: "Why in Heaven's name does it take so long to unload these ships and turn them around?" Pershing reiterated his view: there must be an independent American Army and it should be set up to knock off the Saint-Mihiel salient. Foch agreed; it was time to get on with it. So at last a decision was made, not because Pershing had been right all along, but because the troops were present and events had conspired to make his design expedient. With the shortening of the German front, Foch could constitute a full-bodied strategic reserve. That canceled the last argument against having an independent U.S. field army.

Even so, Pétain was against it. *Sotto voce*, he explained why to a confidant: "The Americans are good. Their soldiers have great dash. But the higher staffs and command are not only untried; their whole organization is clumsy." It was a fairly trenchant criticism of the A.E.F.'s upper echelons. The generals were not as ready as their troops.

The U.S. First Army came into being on August 10, with its headquarters at La Ferté-sous-Jouarre. Right about then Pershing had a new job for Harbord. The War Department—in particular, the Chief of Staff, General Peyton C. March—had become increasingly annoyed at the lack of system in the A.E.F.'s communications zone. The delay in troopship turnarounds, the supply stringency, the mail failures, the foul rations, the irregular arrival of essential arms from our Allies—all of these things signaled careless management. Pershing was trying to do too much; his G.H.Q. kept looking in two directions at one time; his Services of Supply was inadequately staffed. So there arose what amounted to a conspiracy in Washington to send Major General George W. Goethals, the engineer who had completed the Panama Canal, to France to take command of all rear services. A letter from Secretary Baker to Pershing confirmed the news and one line stood out: "The plan would place Goethals in a coordinate rather than a subordinate relationship to you."

Pershing would sooner have swallowed cyanide. He recalled Harbord from the line, put him in command of the Services of Supply, but in a subordinate relationship to himself, and notified Washington of the *fait accompli*. Harbord quickly brought order out of chaos.

There ensued a big parade of Yanks from the boats to Nancy, Toul, Liverdun, Gondrecourt, Langres, Neufchâteau, and the villages around. It was not all work, no play. There was one marvelous discovery—the countryside had *real* beer. "Come quick —honest-to-God suds!" The shout dissolved many an impromptu

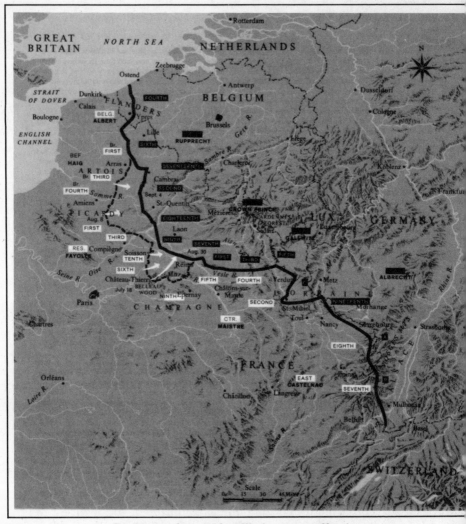

By September, 1918, Allied counteroffensives
(white arrows) had erased most of Germany's
spring gains (broken black lines). The
Franco-American offensive of July 18 in
the south pushed German troops back from
the Marne to the Vesle River. In the north, the
unsuspected Franco-British drive at Amiens,
launched on August 8, eliminated the deep
German salient on the Somme and proved to be
a decisive victory for the Allied forces.

formation. Liverdun, for example, had a monster munitions plant and the Boches knew it. Their bombers came over every night. The town's cafés and *buvettes* were perched on a hillside, with their open-air tables right at the edge of a precipice. There the troops sat guzzling beer and sippling "vin blink" in the evening. Then would come the drone of planes in the distance. From the surrounding hills searchlights caught the formation in their beams. Then the antiaircraft guns started barking; crude in those days, rarely did they tumble a target. But it was always a spectacular display, conducive to drinking.

Toul and Nancy were also bombed by night as surely as the sky was clear. There the side effects were even more felicitous for the Yank with a passing-through mission that billeted him in a hotel. The warning siren would wail. All lodgers, including the mademoiselles of the place and the more transient females, would bound out of bed in shorts or less and tear for the *abri* in the basement. Then the basement light would be turned off and the squealing would begin. Love those air raids! There was very little danger—from the bombs. The raids were more nuisance than menace; science still dawdled with the air bomb.

It was not a bad life. For selected NCO's and junior officers of the newly arrived divisions, being detailed to school duty was the best of breaks. On the whole, the British instructors were superior to the American ones, who were in the majority pedantically dull. The luckiest Yanks came under Lieutenant Colonel H. M. Hutchinson, of the Guards, who would dilate as follows:

"There will be no 'Stack Arms!' in my army. It is a thing one sees on a brewer's calendar—the Soldier's Dream—showing a brave private sleeping under a stack of rifles which it will take him a good half hour to untangle when the call comes to stand-to. No, a soldier had better carry his rifle with him to his meals, lavish his care upon it, and in short treat it more like a wife than a weapon."

His lecture on communications was another gem that his students continued to prize through the years:

"Now on the subject of messages, it might be well to say immediately that as far as I know no one has ever received a written message during a battle. They may be written, but that I think is as far as it goes. However, they are occasionally received before and after battles, and in this connection let me add it is no earthly good writing generalities of time and place. Suppose you write a message and you say, 'Report after breakfast.' To Sergeant Ramrod that might mean stand-to at three in the morning. To Captain Brighteyes it would mean, say eight. But to Colonel Bluefish it would signify some time after eleven, depending on how the old fellow is feeling. Say seven o'clock in the morning. There is only one of them."

Americans warmed to such British leaders as Hutchinson because they had insight into the nature of battle troops and knew how to nourish basic morale. The U.S. command was pretty green at this. One of its egregious blunders—line companies were compelled to bury their own battle dead. They should have been spared this, for human emotions are no less fragile on the battlefield than elsewhere. American infantrymen could endure seeing their own comrades killed; hard losses did not wither unit spirit. But when the grave-digging hour came, company morale hit bottom. Having to cut dog-tags and shovel dirt in a dead friend's face was the heartbreaker.

THE OFFENSIVE CONTINUES

There was a red harvest of young Americans through that August along the banks of the Vesle, the Aisne, and the Ourcq as the two U.S. corps under Generals Bullard and Liggett followed up the enemy reeling back from the Marne salient. As to numbers, that could as well have become the first all-American front had Pershing not already staked his claim on the Saint-Mihiel sector.

The 3rd, 28th, and 42nd divisions kept biting at the German heels after Château-Thierry as the enemy went north across the tributaries of the Seine, each one a viable defense barrier where the Germans turned and fought back savagely. It was a drive straight along the saucerlike rim of what geographers call the Paris Basin. The Germans first stood on the Ourcq, long enough to get their heavy matériel out of the area while preparing defensive positions for their next stand on the Aisne-Vesle line.

All three American divisions were badly battered in this staggered contest, wherein they tried to force a more precipitate retreat. On the Ourcq, the tired 3rd was relieved by the fresh 32nd (Michigan-Wisconsin), a powerhouse division, of which Pershing initially thought so little that he started to break it up. West of

Cierges, the 28th forced a crossing of the Ourcq. The 42nd, helped by elements of the 4th, captured Sergy. Then the 32nd, with one brigade of the 28th, stormed and took a dominant ridge. With that, the Germans lost their hold on the Ourcq.

The Allied attack northward resumed August 1. The French Tenth Army on the left made a long bound forward; the French Sixth Army on the right was stopped in its tracks. The U.S. 42nd kept ripping onward. Best of all was the 32nd, which crashed through the new German resistance line in its first stroke and held what it gained. Next day, the two French armies advanced all along the line. On August 3 the Allied front came up to the Aisne and the Vesle and occupied the high bluffs on the south side of these rivers. The French Fifth Army perched on the divide between the Vesle and the Ardre. But the Allies were hurting for food and ammunition while being flailed by artillery and machine gun fire in a volume that mocked their own supply embarrassment.

On August 4 the U.S. III Corps, under General Bullard, formally took over the zone of the French XXXVIII Corps, which brought the 3rd, 28th, and 32nd divisions under American control. In this way was begun one of the paradoxes of the war. Right afterward, Bullard was also given tactical charge of the French III Corps. On the same day, the U.S. I Corps, under General Liggett, was given tactical control of the French II Corps on its left. Thus on August 5 stood the French Sixth Army, joined in battle, with Americans in charge of its hitting forces from flank to flank. The two U.S. generals didn't rest on the honor. Next day Liggett's artillery blasted the Germans north of the Vesle, while his infantry and engineers got a bridgehead on the north bank. East of Bazoches, the 4th Division crossed the river, and the 32nd, on the right of the 4th, captured Fismes.

August 6 officially marked the end of the Allied offensive from the Marne to the Aisne. Not a great distance had been covered; in sixty days, beginning June 6 with Harbord's assault on Belleau Wood, Allied troops had advanced an average of only seventeen miles. Where there had been a deep enemy pocket there was now a straight line running from Reims west to Soissons. But every mile was a spear into the German side. The effect of this small drive was mortal. It reversed all enemy plans and policies.

The extent of U.S. participation in the great rallying is better understood when it is realized that the eight American divisions that engaged were numerically double the strength of French, British, and German divisions, which says nothing of man-for-man values. Always at the critical points, American units had spearheaded the recovery. The Allied armies and governments could not ignore that fact, nor did they wish to do so. It was this knowledge that revitalized their morale, encouraged them to re-examine their tactics, and stirred fresh hope in their war-weary troops and peoples. But it had cost more than 50,000 American casualties to go from the Marne to the Vesle.

THE BATTLE OF AMIENS

To the American taste in British generals there is a special flavor to Sir Henry Rawlinson. He is John Bull at war, solid as the Tower, but for all that somewhat elusive. While some British writers give him a hard ride, his figure towers above their criticisms. After a slow start, like General U.S. Grant, he seemed to learn some great lesson from every battle. Pressure mellowed and matured him, where it eroded and soured many of his contemporaries. He was less loved than mistrusted by others of his rank because he was suspected of harboring brains.

The little show at Le Hamel in early July in which the Illinois Guardsmen participated had been staged in Sir Henry's Fourth Army area, and from its success his ambitions expanded. In mid-July he put it to Haig that on a far larger scale his army could do the same thing at Amiens and disengage the outskirts of the city, as well as the Amiens-Paris railway, both of which were under continuing fire from the German Second and Eighteenth armies. Haig talked to Foch and both told him to get on with his plan, which he submitted to them on July 17.

The date of Sir Henry's idea needs to be noted. For he was already looking forward before the Germans had recoiled under counteroffensive in the Marne salient. That he willed it was a spur to Foch and Haig in the critical hour. By accident of timing, he was ready to hit on August 8, two days after the Marne-Aisne drive came to rest. The coincidence catalyzed Allied offensive energy.

The speed with which the British Fourth Army mounted up was truly phenomenal. Fourteen divisions of infantry, three of cavalry, more than 2,000 guns, and 450 tanks were swiftly and secretly moved into the ten-mile front. After four years of telegraphing their punches, the Allies at long last were becoming wizards at deception. Haig was gambling, putting the heavy equipment resources of the B.E.F. at one army's disposal.

All of the artillery was moved to Rawlinson's front by night (it took sixty trains), and by dawn the guns were already under camouflage. Once in position, the batteries were permitted to fire for register, under a monitoring system that permitted no overall increase of shellfire from the Fourth Army's front. They were to be directed at enemy guns to suppress fire against British tanks.

To smother the rumble of the arriving tanks as they moved to assembly in the Vaire Wood and around Le Hamel, a noise barrage was invented by the Royal Air Force squadrons with the Fourth Army. Front line forces, and troops in the buildup to rearward, were given no information about what was in store; that was reserved until twenty-four hours before the curtain rose. Normal work was carried out. There was no scheduling of dry-run exercises behind the front to keep troops in the open. There were 800 aircraft with the Fourth Army, and 1,104 with the French First Army on its right—enough to keep the sky above these preparations pretty much inviolate.

But as the outlook for smash surprise brightened, the original plan widened. Foch on July 26 directed Rawlinson to "push as far as possible in the direction of Roye." That town was approximately thirteen miles beyond the line of departure. At the same time, he placed the French First Army, which was commanded by General Marie Eugène Debeney, under Sir Douglas with instructions to use it offensively in support of Rawlinson.

At a final conference on August 5, at which Haig presided, the High Command bit off more than the troops could chew in a day. The French Third Army (General Georges Louis Humbert), to right of the First, would also go. Rawlinson was to capture the line Roye-Chaulnes, and then strike for Ham, another fifteen miles on. The French Third Army was to advance between Montdidier and Noyon. In sum, Foch and Haig proposed to retake at one gulp all of the old Somme battlefield and more. It was humanly impossible. Infantry in battle does not have that much leg push. It made no sense whatever to strike for the old Somme positions, where the Germans could regain good cover and the British armor could not maneuver because the ground was too badly cut up.

The late night of August 7 was clear starlight. Before midnight a ground mist from the river bottoms gradually thickened and spread like a comforter across the plateau in front of Amiens. Two hours later at ground level visibility had dropped to zero. Under the vapor cover the battle forces moved untouched into their final positions all along the Fourth Army's front, with the armor closing to within 1,000 yards of the infantry line. The fog disarranged the infantry deployment; men moved in bunches. It slowed the tank approach to a creep. But these difficulties were a disguised blessing. The Germans slept on. Shortly before zero hour the armor, guiding on white tape lanes, came through the infantry positions. Divisional frontages averaged but 2,500 yards; the result was an army overstrong and very condensed, where thinning it out to constitute a mobile reserve for the follow-through might have better served the end in view. But success needs no postmortems.

At 4:20 A.M. on August 8 the 2,000 guns thundered, shaking the plateau, shocking the enemy. The infantry jumped off, first moving as a wave of skirmishers, then shifting to single file to maintain contact in the fog. Cutting the vapor, shellfire danced in a line of exploding flame two hundred yards ahead of the foot troops, the creeping barrage lifting to move on one hundred yards once every three minutes. It was just the right pace. No-man's-land extended only an average of about five hundred yards. The Fourth Army crossed it, for the most part, in less than one-quarter hour—Canadians on the right, Australians in the center, and British on the left. Surprise was complete.

Except on the left, the front line Germans were swept away in rout. There the British III Corps was hit from the start by a counterbarrage of gas shells. The infantry had to don masks, which in combination with the fog blinded them. Not until daylight started to burn the fog away could these hard-tried men begin to get on their objectives.

To the British right, the French were tardy about starting. That, too, worked out advantageously. Some of the German units facing them had already shifted rightward, thinking that the show was purely British. Moreuil was captured early in the day. Then the bombardment was renewed for three hours. Mézières fell

A British soldier shares a smoke with his
German prisoner. During the battle of
Amiens, referred to as the "Black Day" by
Germans, the British took more than sixteen
thousand prisoners in less than two hours.
Few guards were needed for the German POW's;
most prisoners seemed relieved to be out of
the terror and misery of war.

later in the day, soon followed by the liberation of Fresnoy. Though the assigned objective, Le Quesnel, was not won, these were heroic strides for an army that suffered only 3,500 casualties while bagging 5,000 Germans and 161 enemy guns.

The pinching-out of Le Quesnel had been planned as the culmination of a converging movement. When the French ground to a stop at Fresnoy, that diverted the main pressure of the enemy against the Canadians on their left, giving them their first body check of the day. On the Dominion front, the three divisions in the opening assault had sailed along through the morning. By high noon, when the 4th Canadian Division pushed through to strike for the third objective line (which was won by 3:30 P.M.), most of the enemy guns had gone silent. The infantry waves were preceded by Mark V Star tanks, awkward little vehicles, armed only with machine gun crews, which in these circumstances could still lead on with impunity. The Canadian Cavalry Division came up, and meeting not enough fire to lather the horses, was ordered to trot on to Rosières. But it was a little too much. The chargers weren't jumping any German battery positions this day.

On the Australian front the 2nd and 3rd divisions gained the first objective line by 7:00 A.M.. The 4th and 5th divisions then leapfrogged them and went on to the second and third objectives, with two solid tank battalions, sixteen small Whippet tanks, and a brigade of cavalry running on ahead. Shortly after that the frontal array began to get heavy fire from the flank, resulting in severe losses. Even so, the infantry plugged along and captured its final objective line.

The day was truly extraordinary in its mixing of the sublime with the ridiculous. In its most shining strategic hour, the British High Command had brought forth a tactical monstrosity. The horse cavalry had been hitched with the armor for the go against enemy pillboxes and fire trenches, which was about as sensible as coupling a Rolls Royce to the Old Gray Mare for a breeze cross-country. It was a team effort in mutual confusion. The cavalry galloped on when the field was clear. The tanks churned on alone where resistance thickened. But the cavalry did contrive to capture a German train on the Amiens railway. When the cavalry had to retire because the steeds were thirsty, along with them went the Whippets because they had been ordered to move with the horse squadrons.

On the second morning, August 9, the British III Corps, with the help of one regiment from the U.S. 33rd Division, attacked again, captured Morlancourt on the Ancre, and the ridge beyond it. In the Fourth Army's center, the front was advanced to Méricourt and Proyart, from which ground it threatened the outflanking of Montdidier. Then help came to the British from the French on the right. Humbert's Third Army, which had not been reinforced for the battle, attacked with such forces as were present in line, gained the villages of Le Tronquoy and Le Fretoy, and thereby doomed Montdidier. The Germans stayed in place as if unaware of their danger, as the armies of Humbert and Debeney pushed on through the night. When they crossed the road to Roye next morning, that snapped the enemy line of retreat, the Montdidier garrison had no choice but surrender, and vast stores of munitions and other matériel fell into Allied hands.

Elsewhere German resistance had stiffened as the stricken Eighteenth Army reknit its units and fire bands within the works of the old Somme battlefield. Both Haig and Rawlinson realized that the Fourth Army had about spent its energy and it was time to pause. Haig asked General Sir Henry Horne to rush the planned attack of his British First Army on La Bassée and the Aubers Ridge in the Ypres neighborhood in juncture with a proposed advance by Plumer's Second Army against Kemmel, and Byng's Third Army toward Bapaume.

But Marshal Foch, who arrived at Haig's forward command post in Wiry at this moment, waved his baton like a bull whip. No, the Fourth Army must carry on and capture Ham. Couldn't Haig see that German resistance had cracked wide and that all the British had to do was stretch forth their hand and garner the prizes? Under Foch's goading, Sir Douglas weakened and ordered the offensive resumed, much to the disgust of Rawlinson, who sensed more accurately the condition of his own troops.

On August 11 the Canadian and Australian corps were thrown into battle again. Their mission: to establish bridgeheads on the right bank of the Somme between Ham and Péronne. Likewise, the French First Army was committed and directed to capture Ham. The result was grief. One hundred and ninety of the British tanks had been knocked out on the first day, and the German artillery was once again countering powerfully. In midmorning, General Sir Arthur Currie on his own canceled the Canadian attack because it was getting nowhere. The Australians, after some initial gains, by noon were stopped by heavy German counterattacks. Rawlinson knew it was time to end the battle. Haig wrote in his diary: "I spoke to Foch quite straightly and let him understand that I was responsible to my Government and fellow citizens for the handling of the British forces." Sir Douglas at last had seen the great light: battle forces are not to be used unless something positive is to be gained.

But it had been a great battle. The casualties were French, 24,232; British, 22,202; and German (estimated), 75,000. The Allies captured 29,873 prisoners and 499 guns. So as to vital statistics, Amiens was not one of the "spectaculars" among Western Front productions.

Yet many historians rate it as a turning point, worthy of a place among the decisive battles of all time. The reasons for this evaluation are nonstatistical and stem from its overpowering impact on the minds of the top Germans. Ludendorff had at last fallen apart. Here we have a man in such a state of emotional disequilibrium that on the strength of a first-day report from a limited battle, he moans to his companions that all is lost. Yet because he described August 8 as the "Black Day" for the German Army in World War I, that phrase gives undue significance to a military achievement good enough in itself.

On August 11 Wilhelm summoned a meeting of the High Council at G.H.Q. in Avesnes. Hindenburg said: "I see that we must strike a balance. We have nearly reached the limit of our power to resist. The war must be ended." Two days later the once mighty met again at Spa. Ludendorff put it this way: "It is no longer possible to make the enemy sue for peace by an offensive. The defensive alone cannot achieve that object. Termination of the war must be brought about by diplomacy." The Kaiser thereon instructed Foreign Secretary Paul von Hintze to seek peace.

The effects of the Michael failure, of Belleau Wood, the Champagne, the Marne, and the Aisne were cumulative on Allied morale, on German despondency, and on Ludendorff's peculiar personality. A moment comes when the cord parts; the once upward curve plunges downward. That it happened to the man and to one of his field armies coincidentally should scarcely occasion surprise. Neither knew when to stop: both had burned reserve energy too long. From early July onward, there was clearly marked deterioration in resistance by German infantry over much of the front. The machine gun crews in particular did not display their old tenacity, and resupply was not getting up to the fire points in the battle crisis.

The Black Day story is of a piece with the "Stab-in-the-Back" legend. Ludendorff circulated both of them in self-defense. He is hardly an unbiased witness.

Beginning August 18, the French Tenth and Third armies renewed the offensive between Soissons and Roye. Soon afterward, the British Fourth Army extended the advancing front by attacking south of the Somme. Thereafter, as the Allied line continued to shorten, battle followed battle in rapid succession.

War-weary German divisions, relieved from the front line, reviled the forces coming up to replace them with the shout: "Blacklegs, you're prolonging the war!" along with a bastardized insult: "*Streik-brechers!*"

XIV
Eleventh Hour

A sketch by J. A. Smith depicts a tranquil moment along the ravaged banks of the Meuse.

On August 10, Black Jack Pershing took command of the U.S. First Army. He was flushed with success. President Poincaré had just decorated him with the Grand Cross of the Legion of Honor and paid him a glowing tribute: "You arrived on the battlefield at the decisive hour."

After the buildup followed the letdown. A cable from the War Department advised Pershing that higher commanders would be given educational classes by selected French and British experts. That galled him and he fired back: "Recommend withdrawal all instruction from hands our Allies soon as possible." The War Department agreed in principle, but the instruction continued.

Under its chief, General Hugh A. Drum, Pershing's First Army Staff had been working up the plan for the first all-American offensive. Pershing got it on August 15; Foch saw it two days later and liked it well enough to broaden the base of attack and beef up the nineteen-division American Army with six French divisions. Pershing would have command of them all.

The plan itself was a set piece—nip off the Saint-Mihiel salient, straighten out the line, and there halt, regardless of the German reaction and the rich prizes lying beyond. But the Yanks assembling to form the First Army knew nothing of this and therefore kept circulating their pet story. First doughboy: "Pershing says he'll take Metz if it costs a million men." Second doughboy: "Ain't he the generous son-of-a-bitch."

Moreover, not one in ten thousand was aware that he was a member of the First Army, or that an offensive was being mounted. To the regiments thickening along the Puvenelle and Toul sectors the name of Saint-Mihiel meant nothing. The steep and forest-crowned hills of Lorraine hid the concentration even from those who were part of it. Most of these Americans were seeing the front for the first time and had no idea how dense an army in a quiet sector was supposed to be. What annoyed them chiefly was that the wire between the guns and the infantry line got cut every night. The romantically inclined blamed this on spies and suspected the Lorraine villagers, who were a dour lot, nasty about selling their staples and demanding from soldiers fivefold the real value. It is more likely that the Americans themselves inflicted the damage while careening about the countryside.

Like his descendant the GI, the doughboy was a careless soldier.

By the map, the Saint-Mihiel salient was a hard nut to crack. It had been there four years, but the French had not struggled valiantly to collapse it. On its western face the German line anchored on the Côtes-de-Meuse. Along the southern flank, the heights of Montsec and Loupmont gave the enemy superior observation, and around Thiaucourt the middle ground was a crater-pocked badland. Within the salient the Woëvre Plain became a swamp in wet season. The salient was laced by streams that looped from German country and back to it. No one knew how broad and deep they were. Rearward of the base of the salient were the fortress city of Metz and the railway center of Conflans, from which enemy reserves could be poured into the battle. The German fortifications were complete, the trenches heavily revetted, the shelters artillery-proof. Sausage balloons festooned both lines. Aerial dogfights occurred every day. The German airplanes seemed more numerous, their pilots more aggressive. That's always the way it looks to the ground fighter.

Yet this glowering front became almost cozy on closer acquaintance. The lines averaged about one-half mile apart—a comfortable insulation. German brass bands played concerts in the front lines of an evening. American patrols crossed no-man's-land, flattened out next to the enemy wire, and listened to the music. Occasionally they got crossed up. The nasty Germans put up flares, over the entanglement came a shower of potato mashers (hand grenades), and the uninvited guests limped home nursing their wounds. It was a circus for patrols, as was Korea in the last two years. There was more looking than fighting. Opposing patrols would meet in the middle ground, shy off from one another, and return unscathed, no one having burned to start something.

There was a nastier side to it. Big artillery duels would arise and continue for hours, for no good reason. Much of it was gas. Sweating nightlong in a mask awaiting the all clear was the little hell of this front. Sometimes the all clear didn't come because the hills and the boom-boom had cut off the relay. But the danger was real enough; the U.S. 89th Division lost the great part of one battalion in a single gas attack at Saint-Mihiel.

But as the big buildup continued, the pace of the war along the Aisne and in Flanders reduced the strategic significance of the First Army's prospective debut. There was another conference around August 30, with Pershing, Foch, and Pétain present. Foch unveiled a master plan for action all along the front. Cried the Marshal: *"Tout le monde à la bataille!"* That's it, everybody fights.

However, there was a hook in it. Foch asked Pershing to agree that as soon as the Saint-Mihiel show ended, the First Army be split in twain, one half of it to be used to attack alongside the French in the Argonne Forest, and the other half to team with the French in the Champagne. Hearing the same old argument, Black Jack at last set his jaw and meant it. The First Army under no circumstances would be broken up, though he was prepared to employ it intact anywhere Foch saw fit.

This was an embittered conversation, from which Pershing emerged with unruffled dignity, though less must be said for Foch.

Foch taunted: "Do you wish to give battle?"

Pershing: "Certainly, but as an American Army."

The Marshal then reproached him for that demand, pointing out that the U.S. divisions had no artillery pieces, tanks, or airplanes of their own, clearly implying that they were sponging on the Allies.

Pershing countered that Foch, among others, had insisted that they be rushed to France that way, with only their rifles, bayonets, and sidearms. He said: "Now you make good on your promises."

Foch said: "I insist!"

Pershing: "You may insist all you please, but I decline absolutely to agree."

Foch dropped his plan on Pershing's desk, told him to think things over, and departed.

Two days later Foch and Pétain were back with a changed tune. There would be no more cutting into U.S. forces. They could fight independently, but within the framework of Foch's grand design. Haig's armies would attack in the direction of Cambrai. The French armies would drive across the Aisne on both sides of Cambrai. The American Army could either redeploy to the Champagne or take the Argonne for its next battleground. Pershing said he preferred the Argonne because it was closer to his main depots and supply lines.

So it was arranged, more or less. But things were not quite as clean-cut as they seemed. Having yielded in principle, Foch asked that two U.S. divisions be sent to help Gouraud in the Champagne as soon as Saint-Mihiel was over, and Pershing agreed to send the 2nd and the 36th (Texas and Oklahoma National Guard). Moreover the U.S. 28th and 77th were continuing to take terrible punishment within the French Army, as was the battered 32nd, helping Mangin get from the Oise to the Aisne. The 32nd climaxed its power performance by capturing Juvigny on August 30 and by overrunning the plateau around Terny the next day. The 28th and 77th fought on under the French Sixth Army until September 8, by which time the 28th had lost 8,500 soldiers and the 77th, 4,500. Only then were they relieved to join the U.S. First Army. The record is impressive for more than one reason; the legend to the contrary, Pershing had permitted his divisions to fight under foreign command more openhandedly than had either the French or the British during four years of warfare in the West.

In the two conferences, Foch and Pétain still had not once mentioned the possibility of the war being ended in 1918. They agreed that when the Americans attacked in the Argonne, they might get as far as Montfaucon before winter set in. That makes Foch's arbitrary position all the more unreasonable; if quick victory was not in sight, if he did not envisage that his strategy of Battle Royal would end the war promptly, there was no longer any military reason for his policy of using the Americans as trouble shooters—unless he was thinking of greater laurels for France. The omission of any reference to quick victory also says clearly that Allied intelligence sensed little or nothing of the moral crack-up within Germany. Its failure was as complete as was that of SHAEF intelligence in 1944 to divine the import of the Hitler bomb plot on the control of the Third Reich's armed forces. There is no way of explaining either of these voids except by saying that in intelligence work, as elsewhere, appearances can often deceive.

Ludendorff's admission of defeat on August 13 had carried to Vienna and Sofia. Austrian Emperor Charles notified German G.H.Q. at Spa that he was coming on to discuss the debacle. The Radoslavov Cabinet fell in Bulgaria and was succeeded by the Malinov Ministry, which was notably hostile to Germany. The Bulgarian attaché, General Gantscheff, boycotted G.H.Q., while German Foreign Secretary Paul von Hintze, fearful that his manner would betray how near was the day of reckoning, stayed in Spa, instead of returning to Berlin to attempt negotiations. Yet Ludendorff's mail told him that the secret was already going the rounds.

The Kaiser, who had seemed imperturbable to Ludendorff at Spa, became the subject of belittling rumors on his return to the capital. One story had it that on passing a deputy in the street, he turned an eagle eye on him and shouted in a tragic voice: "You must protect my imperial rights!" Through an emissary, he inquired of the Spanish Embassy if he could find sanctuary in Spain. The Ambassador gave him assurances, then inquired how he expected to get to Sapin. The answer was: "By U-boat to San Sebastian." Later, he thought better of that idea, but the news spread around Berlin that Wilhelm was anxious to leave. He was haunted by what had happened to Nicholas II, who, along with all members of his family, had been murdered by the Bolsheviks in July. In fits of depression, Wilhelm imagined that Germans might act the same way.

SAINT-MIHIEL

The plan for the Saint-Mihiel concentration—and it was beautifully done—was worked out in part by Colonel George C. Marshall, the chief of operations on the First Army Staff. Sixteen American divisions were moved into the battle zone: the 1st, which had fought at Cantigny and Soissons; the 2nd, which had held the Paris road; the 3rd from the Marne; the 4th from Sergy and Bazoches; the 26th from Seicheprey and the Marne; the 28th from the Aisne; and the 42nd, hardened by the Champagne and the Ourcq. The 33rd, 78th, 80th, and 82nd were brought in from the British front. The 5th, 35th, 89th, and 90th came from quiet sectors in Lorraine or the Vosges, and the 91st (in reserve) came up fresh from the boat. They took their places in either I or IV corps on the south side of the salient or V Corps on the west. The French II Colonial Corps was at the salient's tip, operating under U.S. First Army Command.

From flank to flank, 665,000 soldiers were assembled for this one battle. Due to the augmentation of French artillery—their own batteries, or their pieces operated by Americans—3,220 guns were ready along the Army front. French and British aircraft reinforcements made up most of a fleet of nearly 1,500 planes, the greatest concentration of air power yet seen. Of tanks, there

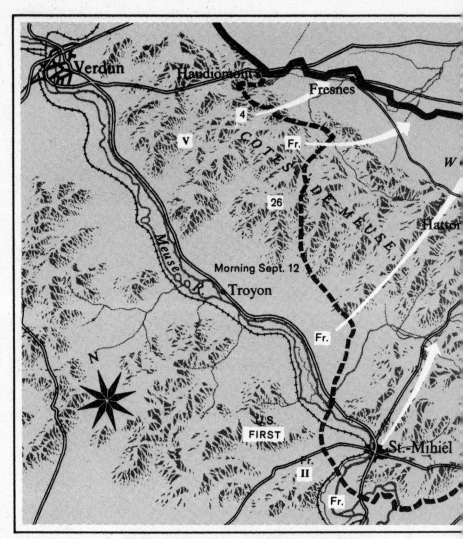

With Pershing in command, the U.S. First
Army launched its well-planned St.-Mihiel
offensive against General Fuchs's Group C
at dawn on September 12. At the same time
that the U.S. V Corps was striking east
across the Côtes-de-Meuse, the French II

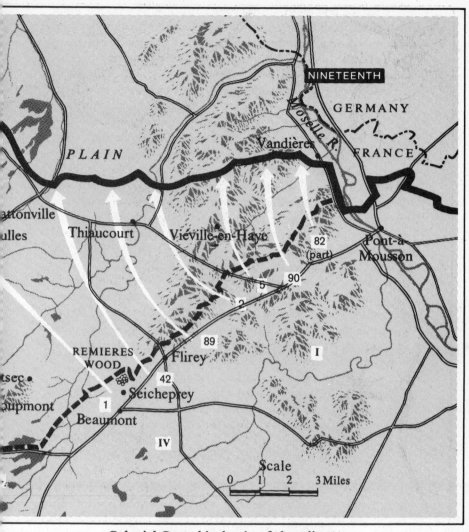

Colonial Corps hit the tip of the salient,
and the U.S. IV and I corps advanced across
the Woevre Plain northeast of Beaumont.
On September 13 the salient was eliminated,
and by September 16 the Americans had
reached the solid black line.

were far too few in proportion; the British, fully engaged along their front, could spare none of their heavies; the French could loan only a small number of their light Renaults; 267 of them started, some of them French-crewed, others handled by the infant American Tank Corps in its first bath of fire. The U.S. 304th Tank Brigade ws commanded by Colonel George S. Patton, Jr. It did not especially distinguish itself, due to the mud, mechanical failures, and lack of gasoline and fighting know-how.

The Germans in the salient, under Generals Gallwitz and Fuchs, knew that some kind of blow was coming. They figured they would let the Americans break through into the Woëvre Plain, then smash them in counterattack. Not until September 9 did the higher commanders become aware that the salient was to be hit from both sides; that meant that their own plan for a riposte must be dropped. They then set in motion a schedule for gradual withdrawal of their forces. It was done too leisurely. The heavy mobile guns went out first. Beginning September 10, the pullout of men and supplies started, which movement was supposed to have gotten the Army back to its rear defense line intact by September 18. The trouble was that the Americans intervened. From this came the belittling description of Saint-Mihiel as "the show in which the Americans relieved the Germans." Trapped at cross-purposes, the Germans could not put up a strong resistance. An army in retreat cannot about face and fight doggedly.

September 12 started as black night, foggy and drizzly, the wet being just enough to puzzle junior commanders about whether or not to order ranks to chuck their raincoats to gain greater freedom of movement. At 1:00 A.M. the American bombardment opened. It was a "buster." There was enough return fire to make the wait increasingly straining, so that the order to go over the top was heard almost as a relief. The troops jumped at 5:00 A.M., following a rolling barrage. What followed was better than any of the advancing riflemen had expected. They felt little bullet fire, they saw few live targets, and for the most part they carried their rifles slung.

The advance of the U.S. I Corps on the southern face of the salient went as rapidly as tired men can move across badly broken ground. The first waves quickly overran the enemy front line trenches, capturing Germans in swarms as they emerged hands in air from their dugouts. Before noontime, the divisions of I Corps captured Fey-en-Haye, Viéville-en-Haye, and Thiau-

Under cover of a barricade, men advance into the Argonne Forest in September, 1918. Recalled one man of this grimmest of American actions: "... I found myself... adrift in a blind world of whiteness and noise, groping over something like the surface of the moon... the ground rose into bare pinnacles... or descended into bottomless chasms, half-filled with rusty tangles of wire. We pushed on into the thickest jungle... it seemed to go on forever."

court on the Army objective line, after cleaning out a vicious complex of machine gun nests in a gas-filled blind valley called the *Stumpf Laager*. To the west, the U.S. IV Corps had harder going. The Germans were more strongly dug in; they had not yet thinned out their frontal formations. By noon the resistance was overcome and IV Corps gained its first objective line, where it stopped to regroup. The French II Colonial Corps at the tip of the salient was on its first-day objective three hours after the jump-off. The U.S. V Corps on the western face did even better, completing its day's task by 7:00 A.M. By nightfall of the first day, most of the First Army stood on the objectives assigned for the second day.

Pershing watched the battle from old Fort Gironville, perched on a height south of the salient. When information reaching him indicated that all roads leading out of the salient were clogged with German troops, artillery, and trains in flight, he directed the U.S. IV and V corps to push on through the night in an attempt to block all escape routes. The 102nd Infantry Regiment of the 26th Division moved out immediately, heading for Vigneulles. Converging on it, from the other flank, also striding through enemy country, went the 28th Infantry Regiment of the 1st Division. Both regiments got their orders around 8:00 P.M. The New Englanders of the 102nd fairly barreled over the unknown roads, rushing past villages and German barracks to close on Vigneulles at 2:15 A.M. and later capture Hattonville. The 28th Regiment joined hands with them around Vigneulles about six hours later, with the sun well up. With this juncture of the two regiments, the Saint-Mihiel salient passed into American hands. Through the next day the First Army front pushed forward to the line held by the two advance regiments.

The offensive had netted 15,000 prisoners and 257 guns, besides liberating two hundred square miles of French territory. Weighed against the effort this was no great haul. American casualties during the advance were only about 7,000; approximately the same number of soldiers were lost to the German fire during the settling-in operations along the new front. There were no trenches where the Americans came to rest, and the enemy artillery quickly returned to action.

Among the troops, no time was allowed for cheering. The men learned that they had participated in a great American victory only when that much-cherished soldier newspaper, *The Stars and Stripes*, arrived up front and told them so. They were back at trench warfare on a front boiling trouble round the clock. Troops in support took over the old German positions. They were everywhere booby trapped and lice infested. The enemy's abandoned ammunition dumps lay in no-man's-land. Still under guard by sudden-death detachments, they had to be raided and destroyed. Roads, ripped apart by the bombardment, had to be rebuilt under fire. There was no lack of material; where villages had been, there remained only rock piles.

German planes flying at treetop level machine gunned the lines daily. The Yanks blazed away at them with the stump-mounted heavy Maxims that the enemy had left behind. It was an exercise in frustration. The enemy had also left some excellent wine cellars and stores of cognac; what remained in his kitchens indicated he was subsisting on bad potatoes, black bread, ersatz coffee, and horse meat. But nothing in the aftermath dispelled the impression that the Americans had stopped short of a great victory. Pershing wrote in his final report: "Without doubt continuation of the advance would have carried us well beyond the Hindenburg line and possibly into Metz."

Foch's strategy had decreed otherwise. Only twelve days intervened between the mop-up at Saint-Mihiel and the time set for the American offensive in the Argonne. Again it became the task of George C. Marshall to manage the reconcentration. It was a 30-plus division shift, 220,000 men to be moved out, 600,000 more to take their places, making a total handle of 820,000 troops. Artillery was already moving from the Saint-Mihiel front to the Meuse before the drive ended. Divisions in reserve were also lifted at once. Convoys of French camions, driven by sleepy-eyed Annamese, moved by night without lights. There were but three main roads, all deep in mud and chuckhole pitted. Rain fell, the weather was cold (mosquitoes in this season were ubiquitous and the worst of all plagues to troops), and the cramped riders were too close-packed to sleep. Despite all difficulty, the schedule was maintained. The outgoing divisions were moved in two stages. They were hauled back to some quiet village like Lucy, there to rest for five days, stuffing themselves on the local cheeses, sausages, and beer, while watching the barefooted French vintners trample their grapes. Then it was pack up, load, and head for the front again.

Transport was strained to the utmost during the last ten days of that September. But the transplanting of the First Army was only an eddy in a mighty military current. Under Belgian command, an offensive was being readied in the Ypres-Lys region, and one American division, the 91st, would be part of it. The British were mounting their great effort on the Somme, and the American II Corps, teaming the 27th and 30th divisions, would participate. The French, hitting alongside the Aisne, were receiving the 2nd and 36th divisions to help them. But for Pershing and his Army, the Argonne was the big show. The U.S. III Corps reached its sector there on September 14; I and V corps followed on September 21.

The Meuse-Argonne

G.H.Q. prepared and executed an elaborate cover plan aimed to dupe the Germans into believing that the next thrust would be either toward Metz or in Alsace. It produced some early marginal benefits—waste motion by the enemy—but the Germans weren't easily fooled. Their wireless station east of Verdun intercepted several coded American messages, which their experts promptly deciphered. "The Americans are moving six divisions north between Saint-Mihiel and Verdun to form a new Tenth Army." On this one they bit hard, not suspecting that it was but one more extension of the cover plan. Only five German divisions were left in line between the Meuse and the Argonne, confronted by three U.S. corps. On the front that the First Army had departed, there were eighteen enemy divisions from the Moselle west, with twelve in reserve. The figures show conclusively that the Germans expected Pershing to try for Metz.

The First Army's operation west of the Meuse had as its right anchor on the river bank the French XVII Corps, which was under Pershing's command. On Pershing's left, Gouraud's French Fourth Army was poised to attack at the same time. General Paul Maistre, by agreement between Pétain and Pershing, was to act as coordinator of the two armies during their combined push.

Beyond the flat and open no-man's-land that the American divisions faced, the Germans had established four successive defensive belts, ten miles deep along the Meuse and almost double that on the Argonne end. Until they played sitting war with the Communist Chinese in Korea, it was the thickest and most elaborately ramified earthworks zone ever assaulted by U.S. troops. Far more wire, steel, and concrete bulwarked the German system. The terrain was so repellant as to suggest that nature had designed it to serve as a barrier. Twenty miles beyond the front, the watershed between the Argonne and the Meuse was a northwest-running hogback with many spurs, switchbacks, and saddles. The heights of Montfaucon, Cunel, and Romagne and the forest of Barricourt were so many rock-bound citadels along the spine of this defense. Splitting the front, the hogback perforce canalized the attack along both of its sides. On one flank, the Aire River skirted the Argonne, and the tree-covered heights of the forest dominated the valley. On the other flank, the bluffs east of the Meuse, German-held, ranged well above the valley floor. From stage center and both wings, therefore, the enemy was looking right down the American throat. It was Belleau Wood all over again, but on a much larger scale; the wonder is that Pershing, to win the argument about keeping his Army intact, accepted such an assignment from Foch with never a protest.

Under the plan, the offensive was to develop in three phases: (1) an advance of ten miles to penetrate the German third position and force evacuation of the Argonne Forest; (2) another ten-mile advance to the Stenay–Le Chesne line to outflank German positions on the Aisne; and (3) clearing of the heights east of the Meuse by changing the direction of the attack. With some modifications, the U.S. First Army got what it went after but was long, long in getting it. Its great effort and sacrifice became steadily more obscured as it slugged along. Foch had set it so that his great production flamed higher with every sun. The First Army and Gouraud's Fourth would explode on Thursday, September 26. The British First and Third on Friday the 27th would break through the Canal du Nord line and attack the Hindenburg position from the north. Plumer's Second Army, with Belgians, French, and Americans, would break from the Ypres Salient and go for the Belgian coast on Saturday, September 28. Finally, on Sunday the 29th, Rawlinson's Fourth and Debeney's Fifth would strike on both sides of the Somme River, heading for Saint-Quentin.

At 5:30 A.M. on September 26, after a three-hour bombardment by 2,700 guns, infantrymen of the First Army jumped off, following a rolling barrage. Eight hundred Allied planes gave them an early and adequate cover. Barrage and air fleet both seemed

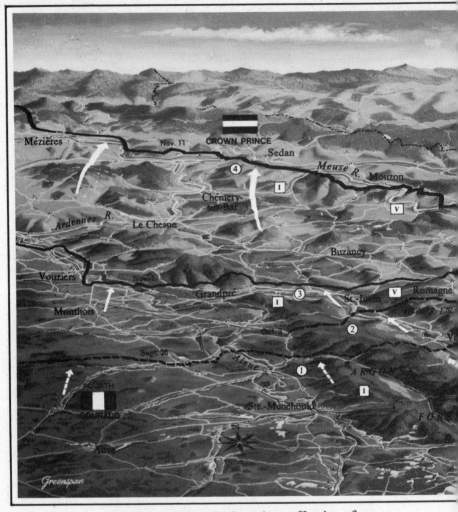

The last great Franco-American offensive of
the war (white arrows) began on September 26,
1918, with the U.S. First Army striking
between the Meuse River and the Argonne Forest,
and the French Fourth Army hitting to its
left (1, broken black line). By October 3, the

Americans had made only slight progress (2, second broken black line). In October, the Germans were cleared out of the Argonne Forest (3, thin black line). From November 1 to 11, the First Army advanced north rapidly, reaching Sedan (4) before the armistice.

overpowering in their promise; and the troops couldn't guess as they stepped out that the battle just begun would last as long as the war. "All these things," wrote Harbord, "added to nervous force, energy without limit, confidence, youth and optimism—we were substituting for experience." It was true of the First Army on that day. The nine divisions in the initial assault had not been in reserve; four had never been in battle. So they were dubbed "the thin green line."

They started with a numerical superiority of eight to one over the enemy, but the perverse terrain combined with the Germans' shrewd siting of weapons and an accurate defending artillery to cut the odds to even.

On the first day, the U.S. III Corps on the right got to the German second position; V Corps in the center was stopped in front of Montfaucon by heavy enemy fire; on the left, I Corps advanced along the Aire Valley through Varennes almost to La Forge, but its drive into the Argonne Forest bogged down after one mile. So on balance, the front was advanced only about three miles, which was a good five miles short of the day's target.

On the second day, Montfaucon was hit from both sides and pinched out; V Corps then lurched on to the Nantillois–Tronsol Farm line. But again I Corps, though it pushed on into the Aire Valley, was hard hit and stopped in the Argonne. By nightfall, the front was in a state of disorganization. Troops had lost their way; they couldn't follow the maps; the countryside was too broken. Messages went to the wrong point; supplies failed; artillery foundered in trying to get forward. There had to be a pause in the attack to get forces squared around again. While it lasted, more German divisions, and additional corps artillery, moved up to the main line position.

Among the Americans, the confusions that mounted rapidly after the first day turned to stagnation and then to paralysis as September ended. The 77th Division had taken a terrible beating in the Argonne wood, making five miles in six days. Hard-rock-bedded, slashed through by intersecting ravines, the Argonne is wrapped in perpetual gloom. Guns and heavy trucks can't traverse it. Within it, a soldier's horizon is limited to grenade range. Units found their way by guess or dead reckoning. The enemy had every trail covered and every height crowned by a machine gun nest. It was no Central Park for young men from Manhattan, though some who got lost there would find a niche in history.

The Pennsylvanians from the 28th Division were doing better, following along the Aire Valley. On the first day they captured the ruins of Varennes, where Louis XVI and Marie Antoinette had been trapped and turned back while trying to flee the French Revolution.

But the Germans garrisoning the Argonne were fleeing from no one. The American advantage in numbers was in fact working in the enemy's favor. The First Army offered too broad a target to be missed. Provided he is determined to die hard, one gunman in a thicket can stand off twenty in a posse while the search lasts. It worked the same way between armies in the Argonne.

The Americans there beat against fire and the wilderness, bravely but not very cleverly. The Germans there defended not only adroitly but determinedly, with greater savagery than is known to savages. That was the irony visited on Imperial Germany toward the end. The German soldier stayed so much more steadfast than was Ludendorff's opinion of him. How could he have had a true reckoning? He had long since departed the combat army. He was a big wheel, making imperial policy, in touch with fighting men only in that vague way peculiar to VIP's who thumb through reams of typed analyses and really think that they know what is going on.

IMPERIALISM IN A CORNER

In Flanders, Plumer's Second Army, the Belgians, and the French Sixth got off to the usual dismal start in a torrent of rain of September 28, but by the nightfall of the next day the British once more had Passchendaele Ridge.

To their south in the Somme region, the British armies of Horne, Byng, and Rawlinson also labored hard at the beginning and took hard losses. By October 6 they had smashed through the Hindenburg fortifications from flank to flank of the group front. But they were spent by the great effort it had taken.

In the Champagne, Gouraud's French Fourth Army got started late. The U.S. 2nd Division finally captured Blanc Mont Ridge October 5, and within four days the Germans started withdrawing all along the line.

The American First Army resumed its attack October 4, made progress elsewhere, but was still held in the Argonne Forest.

There was more upbeat news from the remote theatres. In Palestine, Allenby's army had broken out on September 19. At Arsuf it rode over the battlefield where Richard the Lion-Hearted had once vanquished Saladin. Beyond the Mŭsmŭs Pass, which is covered by the great battlement of Megiddo (Armageddon), and on the Plain of Jezreel within sight of Mount Gilboa, it met and destroyed two Turkish armies, then advanced swiftly to Nazareth. By the end of September, Allenby and his men were riding hard for Damascus.

Emerging from hibernation, Franchet d'Esperey's Allied army based on Salonika also struck in mid-September. In a week-long battle it broke the enemy front around Lake Doiran. By September 30 the German Eleventh Army was in retreat northeast and the Bulgarians had signed an armistice.

These were great blows to the Central Powers. But the masters of Germany had not calmly awaited their evil tidings. Retreating into depression, they invited the worst. For two months they had cringed at their own bleatings, mistaking the trembling among themselves for the crumbling of their soldiery. For what they were about to do, they blamed only an anonymous cowardice tinged with treason in their people, the ultimate in High Command ignobility. Only bathos is to be found in these scenes of Germany's decline.

One actor in the wings, thus far a supernumerary, was Prince Max of Baden, an amateur diplomat, known mainly for his liberal sentiments. Since summer, he had been writing Crown Prince Rupprecht that the Kaiser must abdicate to save Germany. For this, Prince Max was sternly reproved by Rupprecht's father, King Ludwig III of Bavaria, who was worrying just then about his own crown.

The other funeral directors forgathered at Spa, ironically in the Hotel Britannique. By way of prologue, Ludendorff fell apart in front of his staff on the evening of September 28. The act began as a routine review of the situation, phased quickly into a lachrymose self-justification, and concluded with a tirade against everyone else. He damned his military assistants for disloyalty, flayed the Kaiser for weakness, accused the German people of mass cowardice, and blasted the Imperial Navy for treacherously undercutting the U-boat campaign.

His shocked listeners watched the rage mount, the fists tighten, the neck thicken, and the face grow livid, as the words became blurred. Then the First Quartermaster General stopped, foamed at the mouth, and toppled, hitting the floor in a convulsive fit. That night, still trembling and in shock, Ludendorff called on Hindenburg. Germany was done, he said; there was no alternative but to yield all conquered territory in the West and try to negotiate a peace on the basis of President Wilson's Fourteen Points. Hindenburg, as usual, listened to his master's voice, and agreed completely.

The next morning, Foreign Secretary Hintze arrived, followed by the Kaiser and Chancellor Hertling. Hintze agonized no less than Ludendorff, but without hitting the floor. The home front was dissolving, mutiny threatened, revolution was in the offing. The Spartacists, led by Karl Liebknecht, fresh from prison, and the Nihilist Rosa Luxemburg, subverted with money supplied by Adolf Joffe, the Soviet Ambassador to Berlin, were provoking war on the state. The *Vorwärts*, organ of the majority Socialists, had just published a lead editorial: "Germany, we are resolved, will haul down her flag for all time, without having brought it home victoriously." Yes, Hintze was frightened, but he added correctly that he felt certain that the majority of German citizens remained absolutely loyal to the Government.

Shocked, stupefied, the Kaiser listened. But there was no imperial protest. Agreeing to the estimates of the two military chiefs, he suggested that something might be saved from the wreck by summoning Prince Max of Baden as Chancellor. Ludendorff replied that there was no time for this; the morale of the army was sinking too rapidly. But that counsel was waved off. Hertling arrived at the party just in time to offer his resignation, which was accepted. Hintze was instructed to make direct contact with President Wilson, express German agreement with the Fourteen Points, and suggest immediate negotiations for an armistice. A last delicate mission was confided to Hintze by the others, with Ludendorff and Hindenburg dissenting. The plea to Wilson would get nowhere unless accompanied by proof of the Kaiser's intent to make room for popular government. When Hintze broached the proposition, Wilhelm started for the door, thought better of it, and returned to sign a proclamation surrendering some of his powers.

After a talk with Ludendorff, Baron Kurt von Lersner, the Foreign Office man at G.H.Q., got off a message to Berlin: "He feels himself at the mercy of the dice. At any instant and at any point, troops may fail to do their duty."

Von Grunau, another Foreign Office observer, also sent a wire: "I have the impression that everyone here has lost his nerve." One man hit the nail on the head.

PEACE FEELERS

On October 2, Ludendorff sent a warning message to the Reichstag that defeat was close at hand, and Hindenburg followed with a more doleful forecast.

The politicians remained unconvinced, so the Kaiser and Hindenburg went to Berlin on October 3. By then the Allied attacks had subsided briefly, spent of energy. Hindenburg picked up heart and told the Reichstag: "The armies may be able to protect German soil until next spring. I do not believe there will be any general collapse."

By this time he was working both sides of the street and making every crossing too late. Prince Max had received his summons on October 1, but to the astonishment of G.H.Q. he dallied for several days, as if he hadn't heard. To prod him into line with the imperial request, on that same day, October 3, Hindenburg sent an urgent signal to the reluctant nominee: "The Supreme Command insists on its demand that a peace offer to our enemies be issued at once."

On October 4, Prince Max became Chancellor. That same day the Western Front exploded again. Twenty-four hours after settling in as chief mourner at the wake, "Badmaxe" (as the German Army called him—he had once been a cavalry general) dispatched his cable to President Wilson asking for an armistice.

Wilson sat on the message for several days, considering. He not only failed immediately to notify the Allies of the radical change in situation (all chiefs of Allied Governments were still unaware that Germany had collapsed at the top), but he withheld giving instant notice to his own military advisers. These were extraordinary lapses in judgment. Yet there was nothing in the import of the message ("To avoid further bloodshed, the German government requests the President to arrange the immediate conclusion of an armistice on land, by sea and in the air") to warrant such caution, such delay. The statesmen had their little games to play. But secrecy, much of the time, is a two-edged sword. Wilson's locked-up secret, if made public, would have crumbled the German Army. As things were, the troops had to keep on paying.

On October 8, still without confiding in his Allies, the President cabled his reply to Prince Max. It was a request for clarification. Did Germany subscribe to all Fourteen Points? Was Prince Max speaking only "for the constituted authorities of the Empire?"

Almost coincidentally, on October 7, Lloyd George, Clemenceau, and Orlando had met secretly to plan how to circumvent the idealistic Fourteen Points. There can be no quarrel with some of their sentiment. Wilson was way up in the clouds. In advocating freedom of the seas in peace and in war he closed his mind to reality. That item offended the Allies, especially Britain. She had battled through by proscribing freedom of the seas in war; and had the Grand Fleet not enforced that limitation with its armor and gunpower, the American Army would never have reached France.

But Wilson could not take the race of man as he found it, highly imperfect, ambitious for material gain, and naturally aggressive. He truly believed that if ideal peace-keeping arrangements could once be established, earth's people would turn idealistic and greet the millennial dawn. There was this vast difference between the President and the European Premiers, and when they undertook to thwart him, it was not because they were vicious children. Clemenceau had his number. He commented: "I can't understand a man who plays the Lord God one day and acts like Lloyd George the next."

Prince Max replied on October 12 that Germany accepted the Fourteen Points, that he trusted Wilson was in a position to vouch that America's Allies also accepted them (which Wilson wasn't), and that he was speaking for the majority in the Reichstag and the great body of the German people. By this time, Wilson was getting cables from Lloyd George and Clemenceau asking him to clear his main propositions with them before getting in any deeper. By sea and by land, events far more shocking conspired to chill the proceedings.

On October 8 an American platoon, attacking in the Argonne, had taken the surrender of a large German group, only to have most of their own number mowed down by machine gunners in the background. This was the start of the incident redeemed and spotlighted by the conspicuous heroism of Corporal Alvin York.

A soldier in a gunner's nest overlooks a
French village and graveyard in November,
1918, toward the end of the Meuse-Argonne
offensive. Dragging on for nearly six
weeks, it exacted a heavy toll on both
sides. Pershing called the battle a victory
for the Americans, and it was—but while
the Germans counted some one hundred
thousand casualties, the Americans suffered
seventeen thousand more.

From a kneeling position, York shot the machine gunners with his rifle. Charged by the greater part of a German platoon, he stopped them with the same weapon. Then he rounded up the survivors with his .45 Colt and marched them back. But for his performance in the recovery, the atrocious conduct of the enemy might have escaped general attention. Then on October 10, a U-boat had sunk a passenger vessel off the Irish coast, with the loss of three hundred lives. That same day, the mail boat *Leinster* had been torpedoed twice, the second tin fish exploding into her when she was already sinking, and 520 persons, many of them women and children, perished.

The wave of cold rage that resurged among the Allied peoples at last reached Woodrow Wilson. On October 14 he replied to Prince Max that the Allied military leaders would set armistice conditions for the Germans, there being no other way to deal with an enemy who resorted to such barbaric practices. (Ever since March, Ludendorff had been doing his best to scuttle the Fourteen Points, and he proposed to stay with that game to the bitter end, meanwhile whining: "Wilson gives us nothing.") Too late, Prince Max tried conciliation. His note to Wilson on October 20 advised that the unrestricted U-boat campaign had been abandoned. He also besought the President to oppose any Allied demand "that would be irreconcilable with the honor of the German people and with paving the way to a peace of justice." Ludendorff's reaction to this approach was the ultimate in hypocrisy. He damned the Government for endorsing a "cowardly note," and insensible to his own erratic behavior cried: "The cabinet has thrown in the sponge." But then, the man of blood-and-steel has to play his part, and over breakfast he may recover from the feeling at night of being consciously, irremediably defeated.

The Allies still had not been officially advised of the negotiations. They got the gist of what was going on from the press; sometimes it was leaked to them by Counselor Frazier of the U.S. Embassy in London. But the cavalier way in which the proceedings continued inevitably galled Lloyd George and Clemenceau and hardened them in union against Wilson. Even General Bliss on the Supreme War Council was getting no direct advice from the President. Acting on rumors and excluding the Americans, the council met and drafted military conditions for the proposed armistice. Later it was taken to Bliss and he refused to sign, both because he had not been consulted and because the terms drifted away from the Fourteen Points. (Colonel House didn't get to Europe to speak for President Wilson until October 26.)

Uncertain about how to checkmate Wilson, the Allied delegates were united only in their resentment of him. Another stormy meeting occurred on October 14. The consensus was that the Fourteen Points could not be the basis for an armistice. That expert in personal intrigue, Sir Henry Wilson, noted in his diary: "We considered Wilson's latest answer to the Boches. It really is a complete usurpation of the power of negotiation. He practically ignores us and the French." President Wilson was very good at ignoring, and the cost came high.

General Pershing didn't get into the act until October 28. Foch called a meeting of the military commanders at Senlis. Accompanying Pershing were four members of the General Staff. Almost from the start Pershing was at loggerheads with Foch, Haig, and Pétain. But it wasn't over the Fourteen Points; he bought none of Mr. Wilson's line. He spoke up for pursuing the offensive until the German armies laid down their arms unconditionally. But then without going into detail, he deferred to his colleagues, saying their full judgments should be expressed first, since the armistice terms were "of greater concern to France and Britain than to the United States." In the clutch, Pershing's tact was almost a rebuke to Wilson and served to lessen the sting of the President's go-it-alone actions.

Haig and Pétain saw things almost in the same way. All Allied armies were critically short of reserves. The Germans might retire to a shorter line and keep the war going for months. It was best not to demand too much. Foch cut to the heart of the situation: "Such questions are relative. The German armies are far more exhausted than our own. . . . When one hunts a wild beast and comes upon him at bay, one then faces greater danger but it is not the time to stop." Pershing went along with him: the damage done by the war, he said, forbade any leniency toward Germany. But then, when they buckled to the task of specifying what military demands were necessary to neutralize German war power, the Generals were not very far apart. Pershing's advice on the wisdom of granting an armistice had still not been sought by his own Government. It is not only at the platoon level that things often go wrong in war because the actors neglect their communications.

October had been for the A.E.F.'s Old Man the melancholy days, the saddest of the year. It was partly Black Jack's own fault, due to his lack of experience in the handling of vast forces and his determination to have all things his own way. He had bitten off more than any one commander could chew.

Pershing was commanding a theatre. He was also responsible, through Harbord, for his Services of Supply. He had ten divisions fighting with the French and British armies, which also required his administrative support. And he had a full-strength combat army engaged full-length in the most desperate kind of fighting. Yet he initially insisted on personally commanding that army, which meant making main decisions about reinforcements, reliefs, corps boundaries, changes in plan, shifts in direction, the replacement of commanders who proved unfit, the shunting of supply to the fire zone, and the clearing of administrative entanglements from its rear; and Black Jack could not be everywhere. No genius can spread himself as thin as he tried to do and come out well; his slips show and his show slips. To be quite fair to Pershing, there were no guidelines and precedents in the national experience to indicate how this many-layered command cake should be cut.

There is a passage in General T. Allen's *Rhineland Journal* about Pershing's visit to Allen's command post in the Argonne. He bared to his old friend his agony of spirit. The strain was too great; this last battle had overloaded him. The reasons why are obvious. True, he had the First Army Staff on which to lean. But the Army Staff, being ranked by the Theatre Staff, was even less inclined to make *ad hoc* emergency decisions in the absence of the commander.

The extraordinary ordeal suffered by his soldiers was not due simply to the tyranny of a harsh terrain and the frenzied last gasps of a hate-filled enemy. The weather turned bitter cold and the rains came half sleet. Taking into account these things, troops still became unduly depressed. Why? Even the greenest soldiers were aware that this battle was frightfully mismanaged. Every misery-laden adjective becomes overworked by the war historians as they try to describe how American infantrymen felt while enduring the Argonne. It is vain.

Weather and earth combined with human ineptitude to multiply the routine frictions of combat. Supplies couldn't get up.

Weapons fouled. Signals were fogged out. Contacts were repeatedly broken. Command crept in making its inspection rounds. That the Army came out of it with only one "Lost Battalion" was truly phenomenal. Major Charles W. Whittlesey's luckless outfit from the 77th Division (1st Battalion of the 308th Infantry Regiment), which is better remembered than the battle, became the chief castaway of a wretchedly coordinated battle line. It had six hundred soldiers when it lost contact on October 2, to become surrounded and besieged for five days. When at last two other divisions broke through to its rescue, only 194 men limped out.

On October 16, with the Argonne cauldron smoking hotter than ever, Pershing relinquished command of the First Army to Major General Hunter Liggett while at the same time creating the Second Army under General Bullard from the divisions in line between the Moselle River and Fresnes-en-Woëvre. Hunter Liggett was far overweight and said of it: "Fat's all right provided it's not from the neck up."

Under Liggett's direction the offensive continued. It was no less of a meat grinder than before, but supplies, energy, and lives were spent to better purpose, and the troops felt, if not happier, less disgruntled. Liggett's first act was to pause, replenish his troops and stores, repair the roads, and make some changes in his organization. While so doing, he recast Pershing's plan, shifting the First Army's weight to the center instead of battering away on the left at the Argonne and the Bois de Bourgogne beyond it, where the enemy was in greatest strength. But too much time had been lost. Though the First Army again advanced, and near the end made tremendous strides, the glittering victory that might have been won had it earlier crashed through to Sedan-Mézières receded like a mirage.

By October 5 the British to the north had gone through the final defenses of the Hindenburg Line and emerged into open country; their further progress was slowed only by the great fatigue of forces, scattered German resistance around the natural obstacles, and the devastation of the countryside. In the three weeks that followed, had the First Army been able to bound forward in the Argonne at the same time, it would have closed the escape route of a large part of the German armies. By November 5, when the First Army could move again, the prospect was gone.

Pershing's October trials, however, did not come solely of the grief laid on his soldiers. From the start of the Meuse-Argonne campaign to the end, Clemenceau was riding his back like the Old Man of the Sea, letting everyone know that in his opinion Pershing's direction of the battle "was inferior to what was permissible to expect." He wrote invidious letters to Foch belittling Black Jack's generalship, charging that his blunders were fraying the chance for victory and insisting that the Marshal should take steps to relieve the American commander.

There is no sensible explanation of Clemenceau's conduct. It was so venomous as to suggest that out of malice toward Wilson, the Tiger was venting his fury on the most imposing American target in sight. In any case, Clemenceau was far off range. How Pershing handled his troops was none of the Tiger's business. But more objectionable than his meddling, he was deliberately fomenting conflict within the Alliance when unity of purpose toward peace goals should have pervaded all councils. Not at all surprisingly, Foch fought back, defending Pershing and trying to silence Clemenceau. For that, he has been given much credit, although it is impossible to see that he had any other course. Clemenceau was not directing the armies, though he may have dreamed that he was running the war.

Wilson's blunt note to Prince Max on October 23 cut away all pretense with these words: ". . . if the United States [and he said nothing of the Alliance] must deal with the military . . . and monarchical masters of Germany, it must demand, not peace negotiations, but surrender." The implication is reasonably clear —get rid of your bad boys and maybe we'll be able to talk Fourteen Points again.

Not at all strangely, Ludendorff in his memoirs recalls that note as arriving on October 26. It was the final blow. Prince Max, on reading the threat, went straight to the Kaiser and told him that either Ludendorff would walk the plank, or he must look for another Chancellor. Thereon Wilhelm sent for the First Quartermaster General and summarily dismissed him. "I thought of Liège; there I had staked my manhood and had not changed since," wrote Ludendorff of his thoughts at the moment. His way of staking his manhood for a second time was to put on a false beard and dark glasses, and light out for Sweden via Denmark, fleeing his country lest he lose his own life. The exit of his *bête noire* did not immediately brighten the outlook for Prince Max. Having gotten by on bromide and chloral up to that point,

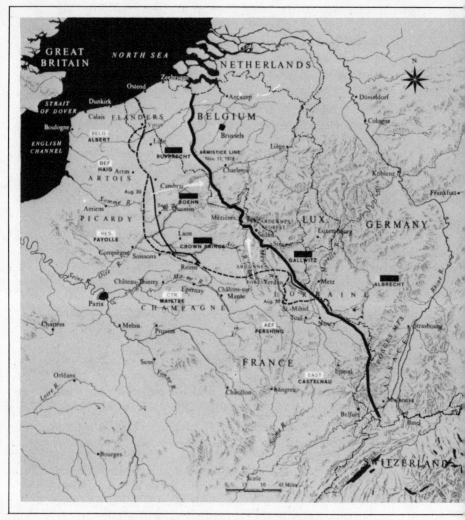

This map shows the sweeping advance of the
four Allies (white arrows) from September
to November, 1918. The elimination of the
St.-Mihiel salient and Franco-British gains
in Picardy and Flanders (dotted black
to thin black lines) were followed by the
North Sea–to–Lorraine victory drive, which
capped off the war and pushed Germany back
to the armistice line (solid black line).

he was suddenly stricken with Spanish influenza.

While he was down, the world heard the news that British General Marshall had received the surrender of the Turks in Mesopotamia. Although Bulgaria had already left the war, this was the first inkling to U.S. soldiers on the Western Front that the great crack-up was right at hand. Then the enemy ramparts tumbled like dominoes. Turkey quit the war on October 30, and Austria concluded an armistice with the Allies on November 3. To infantrymen in France, the flash from Mesopotamia was like a star shell at midnight. "Can you believe it?" they said to one another. "Maybe we'll live through this thing after all."

Upon Ludendorff's departure, the Kaiser returned posthaste to Spa, and ignoring the pleas of the Chancellery that he was needed in Berlin, thereafter clung to G.H.Q. To Hindenburg, he explained that he was filling in for Ludendorff. But to Admiral von Hintze, who was representing his Foreign Office kinsman at Spa, he spoke what was really in his mind: "Prince Max is trying to throw me out; here I am more able to oppose him in the midst of my troops." His aged Adjutant, General von Plessen, also breathed fire. "We'll shoot them down!" he said of the abdicationists, and he cautioned others in the camp: "To the Kaiser give none but good news."

But bad news was on its way. Stumped at first in his search for a messenger to go to Spa and tell Wilhelm that he must quit, Prince Max finally found one in the person of Dr. Drews, Prussian Minister of the Interior. Wilhelm refused point-blank and reviled Drews for suggesting it. Hindenburg went further—if the Kaiser was forced out, he and all officers would resign, surrendering the army and Germany to chaos. General Wilhelm Groener, who now sat at Ludendorff's desk, was one of Drews's fiercest assailants. Having squelched Drews, he left for the front to see what could be salvaged from the wreck. There the scales fell from Groener's eyes.

That day, November 4, the British broke the line between the Scheldt and the Sambre near Valenciennes, routing the German rear guard beyond recovery. Groener sped back to Spa and told Hindenburg: "We shall have to cross the lines with a white flag. Even a week will be too long. Do it Saturday [November 9]." Wilson's last note had just arrived saying that Foch would receive "properly accredited representatives." Admiral Scheer ordered the High Seas Fleet out on November 3. It was his intention to give battle and go down with colors flying. The crews mutinied, murdered a number of their officers, turned the ships around, and returned to port, with red flags flying from their gaffs. Sailors wearing red cockades and red brassards next raided the office of Albert Ballin, head of the Hamburg-America Line, and gave the venerable patriot a brutal beating. In agony, Ballin swallowed a handful of sleeping tablets, staggered into the street, and died.

On November 7 the German Armistice Commission, headed by Matthias Erzberger of the Center Party, arrived at Spa. Simultaneously, G.H.Q. received a telephone call and an ultimatum from Prince Max. Unless the abdications of the Kaiser and Crown Prince were announced by noon of the following day, the Socialists would join the Spartacists in launching a revolution. The time limit expired, with no dramatic change; violence and confusion mounted in Berlin; tension and division thickened at Spa.

FINALE AND FADE-OUT

On November 8 at 7:00 A.M. in a railway car on a siding in Compiègne forest, the spot where Hitler was to do his cockcrowing over some beaten Frenchmen twenty-two years later, Marshall Foch faced the German Armistice Commission. He enjoyed the national fondness for doing things storybook style.

He asked: "What's your purpose? What do you want of me?"

Erzberger fumbled as he replied that he had come to receive the proposals of the Allied powers toward concluding an armistice."

Foch bit it off: "I have no proposals to make." Each word weighed one ton. The Allies were quite willing to continue the war.

There was much more of this awkward word-bandying, Foch staying truculent, Erzberger backing away cap in hand. They all knew what they were there for, but attitudes had to be maintained for Clio's sake. In the end Erzberger put it straight that Germany asked for an armistice and was ready to hear the Allied terms. General Maxime Weygand, Foch's man Friday, read them out. There were gasps around the table. The Allies asked not only the immediate evacuation of all occupied territory but the stripping from Germany of all military power.

Erzberger asked that firing cease at once. That was refused, and more Allied soldiers as well as more Germans had to die in the next few days to validate a dramatic but inhumane deadline. The Allied leaders had already decided that they wanted the Great

War to end at 11:00 A.M. on Day 11 of Month 11, which, at the right time, is also a good number in dice. From Compiègne, signals were flashed to all major headquarters telling what had occurred and giving the hour for the war's termination. But troops in the line were still kept in the dark.

From Spa, other signals had gone out that day, ordering division, brigade, and regimental commanders to assemble at G.H.Q. on the morning of November 9. Hindenburg wished to question them about the loyalty of their troops to the Kaiser. He and Groener got their answers in the session at the Hotel Britannique, but what they had expected was not what they heard.

They knew then that the loathsome task of robbing their All-Highest War Lord of his last illusion must be their own and together they repaired to the Château de la Fraineuse to tell him. En route, Hindenburg lost his self-control, began sobbing, and begged Groener to take over the dirty work. Groener did, and for his pains he was skinned by a Kaiser blazing with anger.

"I will wait here in Spa for the armistice," said Wilhelm, "and then return home at the head of my army."

"Sire, you no longer have an army," said Groener. "The army will march home in peace. But it no longer stands behind Your Majesty."

The two soldiers retreated from the tirade that followed, but returned later in the day. Hindenburg had regained his composure. Glaring at Groener, Wilhelm said: "You no longer have a War Lord," and refused thereafter to speak to him. Hindenburg took over the conversation, warned the Kaiser that he could no longer be responsible for his safety at Spa, and concluded: "I must advise Your Majesty to abdicate and to proceed to Holland."

Before daylight on Sunday morning, November 10, the imperial train, its cream-and-gold décor indistinguishable in the darkness, rolled out of Spa bound toward the Dutch frontier. On the journey, the Kaiser said hardly a word; the fall had stupefied him to the point of coma. From the border he proceeded by private car to Amerongen, where he expected to find asylum in the château of Count Godard Bentinck. The silence ended as the car crossed the drawbridge into the estate. Turning to Count Godard, Wilhelm said: "And now I must have a cup of good, hot, strong English tea, yes, make it English." Without prior invitation, the ex-All-Highest adopted Bentinck as his host. They were both Knights of the Order of Saint John, and under its vows, the Knight could claim sanctuary of a Brother. The Count was willing, provided he could find room for Wilhelm's retinue. There were thirty of them and Count Godard had only four spare rooms; the overflow deployed somewhere in the near neighborhood, and as the days passed, most of them drifted back to Germany. The royal train was brought up to Amerongen on November 11 at just about that hour when other wheels in Western Europe ceased turning amid glad tidings of great joy.

For nearly fifty years writers have been trying to recapture the emotions of the ineffable moment when the Western Front went silent. Those who were there that morning and lived it would call it a useless exercise. There is only one such feeling of exquisite relief in a lifetime, though the warrior goes many times to the wars. Little Skippy, the cartoon character of Percy Crosby, gazing at a lovely landscape, cries: "Gee, it's so beautiful, I gotta give somebody a sock in the jaw." He had the words for that morning. Men stood mute, mouths wide open, as if awaiting some terrible renunciation, then broke into tears and laughter that subsided, to be followed by wild cheering as they shook hands, slapped one another on the back, and then stood straight to walk hesitantly into the open.

Around Stenay and Sedan, the day had begun in fog. The sun broke through weakly in midmorning, but as the eleventh hour approached, the mists still drifted thickly amid the dripping trees. In a few wayward outfits, led by loony commanders, pressure was continued to the last minute and lives were sacrificed on both sides with nothing to be gained. That was a fool's game and the steady majority wanted none of it. Prudent infantrymen hugged ground cover that morning and patted their rifles, knowing that before noon came, it would be all or nothing.

The A.E.F. High Command had not proved that sensible. In the last hours, it had loosed two of the divisions on a breakneck race for Sedan to euchre the French out of that great sentimental prize, though any understanding of what honor requires would have compelled G.H.Q. to order its own soldiers to stand aside. From this folly came much operational disarrangment, personal recriminations, and lasting bitterness. The details are best passed over. Let it be remembered only as an action unworthy of American arms. When in 1944, the U.S. Third Army was in position to liberate Paris and General Omar N. Bradley decided that French arms should have that honor, it atoned for the blunder at Sedan.

Some minutes after the firing ceased, Yanks and Germans got together in the middle ground. There was little handshaking or fraternization in its real sense. The Yanks went forward with weapons and kept them slung; most of the Germans had left theirs in the trenches. There was much talk in an active market. The enemy was plied with cigarettes, rations, and soap. The Yanks came back from the powwow enriched with belt buckles, Iron Crosses, bayonets, and even a few Lugers. Then in the glade where shells had been breaking just an hour before, they played duck on the rock, hopscotch, blindman's buff, and other games of childhood. It was later that the dice began rolling, and later still that liquor came along in sufficient supply to make possible a proper celebration. That morning it wasn't needed. The Army was intoxicated with life, reeling with a joy that had decided in favor of the universe.

The last shot had been fired prior to the hour when sensible Americans at home arise and shine. It was 6:00 A.M. in New York and Washington. There were no radios to spread the news. It got around slowly. Shortly after breakfast the national whoopee started along the Eastern seaboard and spread westward. Mr. Wilson got out a statement: "The Armistice was signed this morning. Everything for which America fought has been accomplished. It will now be our fortunate duty to assist by example."

So it went in Paris, London, Rome, and in every city under victory, a great tumult and exultation, crowds pouring into the streets to parade madly, flags everywhere waving, bands playing, anonymous volunteers mounting park benches to lead the singing of "Madelon," "Tipperary," "Over There," "The Yanks Are Coming," and "Pack Up Your Troubles." There has been no dizziness like it since. "And I should live a thousand years and I should never forget it." In Lavalbonne, France, which was an American officer candidates' school, the aspirants became so delirious that they bombed one another with live grenades, barracks against barracks. A dozen men got flesh wounds, which but added to the joy.

In Berlin, by order of Prince Max, placards were raised on every kiosk and street corner announcing that Wilhelm II had abdicated. Mobs of half-grown louts wearing red armbands surged through the city mugging military officers and stripping them of their decorations and epaulets. Prince Max turned the business

The news of the armistice on November 11, 1918, sent crowds of jubilant, flag-waving celebrants into the streets of New York City. Back at the Western Front, the eleventh hour brought a profound silence, followed by great relief and cheering. The war was finally over.

of the state over to the Socialist leader Friedrich Ebert, who took the title of People's Commissar and tried to restore order, while Max slunk away to Baden. King Ludwig III of Bavaria quit his throne by night. Trying to escape by motorcar, he overturned in a ditch. A peasant assisted by a cow got him rightside up and on his way again. King Frederick of Saxony took off with a little more dignity, leaving a farewell message that was memorable only for its brevity: "Make your dirt by yourselves."

Fifteen miles from the Austrian border, near the little town of Traunstein, lay a great barbed-wire compound confining thousands of Russian prisoners. News of the armistice made little difference to its garrison; the routine of guarding continued amid the deep snow. Corporal Adolf Hitler did his accustomed stand in the wooden sentry box that night. What went on in that dark mind, how he brooded, whether he already plotted and planned to avenge the defeat of Germany, is not of report.

On the morrow, the statisticians would take care of the summing up. Almost ten million men and women had been killed in the fighting. More than six million had been crippled or invalided for life. There had been a victory of sorts, but what the victors celebrated chiefly was that mass death, after four years, had taken a holiday. The illusion was that all of humanity would profit by the great lesson.

XV
Versailles

A momentous occasion, the signing of
the peace treaty in Versailles's Hall
of Mirrors on May 28, 1919, is recreated
in this painting by John Johansen.

W hen the fighting ended, the German Army stood dead in its tracks, unable to move. The men were exhausted. There was no fuel for transport. The horses were half-starved. Railway operations had broken down because of revolutionary ferment in Germany, and supplies came forward to the front only in trickles.

Foch had given the enemy army six days to clear French and Belgian soil and get beyond the Rhine. It could not be done. On November 17, selected Allied divisions marched east, bound for occupation duty in Germany, their columns taking it easy because the inert enemy still blocked the roads. There was also a technical problem: mines and demolitions had to be removed from the highways, culverts, and bridges. December had come and the year was moving toward Christmas before the occupying garrisons crossed the German frontier in strength to take over the main bridgeheads at Koblenz, Mainz, and Cologne.

Toward these confident conquerors, forcibly billeted among them, the Germans, for the most part, maintained an attitude correct but cold. Defeat imposes passivity in a people; its shock paralyzes at first; the means of collective response and action are lacking. In the Rhineland the shock passed after a time, but the sullenness and resentment did not. That is hardly remarkable. The people stayed half-starved. The Allies, including the United States, continued to maintain the blockade long after the fighting had ceased, which was worse than inhumane, for it was stupid. The governments learned nothing from the blunder. They did it again in 1945. The war ended but the suffering of old folk and children did not.

As soon as the shooting stopped, General Harbord's Services of Supply was confronted with the task of getting troops repatriated. There would be no rotation on points, a sentimental innovation that came one war later. The Americans would return as solid divisions, and, in that day, that was what most soldiers wanted—to stay with the outfit. But there were not enough ships available for a rapid exodus from France. For the fighting forces, in the long wait that ensued, Pershing ordered a resumption of hard field training. They damned him for it, but he was probably right; it kept men out of mischief. The shipping pinch lasted because the British and French had forces of their own to bring home. Even the cross-Channel packets were refitted for ocean-going transport duty. The greatest U.S. troop carrier was the *Leviathan*, which could take 12,000 soldiers at a clip. The most popular ships were the *Great Northern* and the *Northern Pacific*, because they made the round trip in nineteen days.

Overseas mail and food service, which had been understandably bad during the war, did not improve in the first months of peace. Wounded men were evacuated from base hospitals while still convalescent, herded into forwarding camps, and there forgotten. The average camp was a sea of half-frozen mud, where the troops lived in tents in the dead of winter, with no fuel and too few blankets. These hardships were not the consequence of deliberate neglect. The A.E.F. had simply grown too large too quickly. When the Allies withdrew their props at war's end, the administrative problems became too vast for the Army's leaders.

Influenza was raging in America and the last-arriving troops spread it through the A.E.F. The *Leviathan* docked on a particular day at Brest, 10,000 men aboard, 4,000 of them stricken. But the bug had beaten them to France. At Camp Pontanezen, out of 65,000 soldiers, 12,000 were down with the flu at the same time. Colonel Smedley Butler, USMC, was the commandant of the camp. He had available only nine trucks and two ambulances to haul the *Leviathan*'s sick to camp. So he marched his own regiment to the wharf and in eight hours its members carried the four thousand to camp in carts and on stretchers. At Pontanezen, Americans were dying from flu at the rate of 250 per day. Throughout the A.E.F. the epidemic was increasing at the rate of more than 10,000 cases per week. But in the Rhone Valley, one Colonel Bankhead, kinsman of the Alabama Bankheads, and later a figure in the U.S. Foreign Service, bought rum every day for his regiment, paying for it from his own pocket. There may be no connection but the bug bypassed Bankhead's outfit.

Amid hardship, however, the A.E.F. was recovering its morale through a miracle of self-help. There was no U.S.O. or its equivalent to stage for Army audiences entertainment by the stars and celebrities of the day. But such a large army could muster its own talent—singers, vaudevillians, lecturers, and professional fighters and wrestlers, and a theatre circuit was established for forces in Germany and France with none but soldiers on tour.

The A.E.F.'s four Negro regiments—the 369th, 370th, 371st, and 372nd infantry—had seen some heavy fighting in the Meuse-

Argonne and had won high praise from their officers, most of whom were white, and from the French with whom they had served. At the base ports other Negroes, serving with the Army stevedore units, had married French women. When it came time for the unit to ship out, they were given the choice of being discharged and staying with their wives or returning home alone. They couldn't understand it; they thought that the war had made all men brothers. In this they were no more naïve than the wise men of the world, who thought that the armistice would be followed by peace eternal.

WILSON GOES TO EUROPE

Eight days after the armistice, Wilson made up his mind that he would go to Europe so that his kind of peace might be settled upon it. The decision dismayed both Washington and Europe. Colonel House wired him: "Americans whose opinions are of value are practically unanimous in the belief that it would be unwise for you to sit at the Peace Conference." Clemenceau brooded that Wilson would try "to settle the destinies of nations by empiricism and idealism." But the President went.

On December 13, as French and American ships boomed their salutes, the liner *George Washington*, with Wilson aboard, steamed into Brest harbor. Pershing commented as he saw the ship approach: "He has been a good President to me but he has his hands full now." It was a great day, but already the storm was rising against Wilson in Washington, and a cloud, at first no larger than the hand of a man, appeared in the sky over Brest.

The President had already affronted the Republican opposition by appealing for the election of a Democratic majority in the Congressional elections of November 5, while the fighting was still going on. Even after the Republicans had captured control of both houses of Congress, Wilson had overlooked its most eminent members in composing his official party for the trip abroad. As members of the delegation that he would lead to the peace conference, Wilson named Colonel House; Secretary of State Lansing; General Bliss, the American representative on the Supreme War Council; and Henry White, an aging Republican diplomat with no particular political influence. Another act of carelessness soon soured American troops in Europe against their Commander in Chief. While they stayed penned to their camps at Brest for lack of shipping, the *George Washington* lay idle in the harbor waiting for the President. As the story spread, the Army's regard for Woodrow Wilson plummeted.

France was already in a bad way. Her exchange was rapidly falling in all world markets. Not only in terms of human life, but in loss of and damage to property, she had come out of the war the great loser among the Allies. The railways of France, worn out by the war years, were still overburdened by the traffic of redeployment and repatriation; her port facilities were in a like plight.

There was another thing. During the years when the hopes of Germany's militarists ran high, the fixed policy of the German Government had been to annex the northern coal fields of France and the mines of Belgium. This plan was carried to the point where German industrialists presented a memorandum to the Chancellor specifying the indemnities that, fixed on France, would cover the cost of purchasing the mines. When it became clear that Germany would be defeated, Ludendorff ordered the mines wrecked. No military object was served; the purpose was to cripple the industry of a rival. That deliberate vandalism, when coupled with the bleak prospects for French recovery, was bound to color Clemenceau's thinking and put him at cross-purposes with Wilson, while making two of his own aims incompatible. The Tiger and his colleagues, in effect, were bent on the total ruin of Germany, economically and militarily, while at the same time they were determined that the prostrate enemy should pay indemnity for war damage. That was like mining for gold in a slag pile.

Wilson would learn more about these oblique views when the peacemakers settled to their task. In the meantime, there were only parades, receptions, reviews, and parties as Wilson toured France, England, and Italy—and these went off quite felicitously.

The first thirty-six-day armistice expired about the time Wilson got to Paris, and it had to be renewed. In fact, the ceremonial rounds so preoccupied him that he found no time to visit the Meuse-Argonne battlefield, where 150,000 young Americans whom he had summoned to the colors had recently spent their lives or some of their blood. He also shunned the war-devastated areas of northern France, though Clemenceau tried repeatedly to persuade him to tour the region. He thought it would be good for the President to see with his own eyes what the Germans had done. Wilson stalled him with one excuse or another. General

Bliss got the impression that Wilson declined because the ugly sights might ruin his impartiality as the arbiter of a just peace.

Herbert Hoover, who had seen the seamy side of the war while trying to get food to the refugees and other victims, was also in France. He had no time for partying; too many things were going wrong. For one thing, the Italians were blocking food shipments to the Serbs and Croats along the Dalmatian coast; there was nothing subtle about this blockade; they expected by this means to coerce the Slavs into voting for annexation to Italy. Then, too, in Germany, food stocks were dwindling to the vanishing point while at the same time, among the masses, pro-Communist sentiment was steadily rising.

Hoover said to Bliss: "We must have some relaxation of the embargo to permit Germans to get out and sell certain commodities to other nations. German ships, crewed by Germans, must be permitted to go to sea under certain conditions. Otherwise, we face total ruin."

Bliss replied: "It was to prevent this very thing, to stop Germany from reviving trade until the Allies are well ahead in the race, that the continuance of the embargo and blockade was put into the armistice conditions."

Ambassador David Francis arrived from Russia urging a military crusade against Bolshevism. He wanted Wilson to send more American troops to Archangel, where an Allied force had been supporting a puppet Russian government since the summer of 1918. He was told no.

The armistice had to be renewed a second time before the peace conference settled to its task. Bliss called it a "criminal delay" in letters to his wife; he had become convinced that the Allied Governments were deliberately forestalling an official peace to prevent Germany from reviving. He wrote, "Bolshevism is the outcry of peoples against the idiocy of their governments; it feeds on empty stomachs."

But Bliss was not really used by Wilson at the Paris conference, and no other soldier's counsel was seriously sought by the President's European colleagues prior to the making of major decisions. This seems incredible now. The statesmen's task was to bring out of war's chaos a Europe that would have a fairer prospect for lasting peace by applying some of the principles advocated by Wilson. The reallocation of territory, however, and the determination of national boundaries are fraught with military considerations. Stability within the new system would derive in large part from the assigning of defendable frontiers. Statesmen are inclined to forget this in the moment that peace comes. So it happened in Paris in 1919: in the psychology of the conference, the generals had had their day in the sun and must now stand aside. Lloyd George, Clemenceau, and Orlando had suffered the arbitrary demands of their military leaders for too long not to relish the chance to have done with their counsels.

As for Wilson, he viewed peacemaking as his heaven-blessed mission and made it a personal crusade. Not only General Bliss, but Secretary of State Lansing and Commissioner White were retired to the sidelines. At first he listened to Colonel House, but all too soon the sage from Texas, who knew most about the Europeans, ran afoul of the President and lost all influence.

THE PEACE CONFERENCE

At last on January 18, 1919, more than one month after Wilson reached Europe, the conference of seventy delegates from twenty-seven countries assembled without getting down to business. Colonel House had almost prevailed upon the principals to do away with opening speeches to save time, but at the last moment he was stricken with influenza and the statesmen could not resist the opportunity to orate from a world platform.

Their outpourings, far from clearing the atmosphere, served only to widen the distance between them. Wilson made a temperate speech but stood firm that the League of Nations be created as an integral part of the peace treaty. Lloyd George, deliberately aiming at the President, and at the same time playing to the gallery, declared that only men who had visited the devastated regions of France were prepared for the task at hand. Clemenceau's main point was that the conference was primarily the concern of the Great Powers, though the little powers had been invited as a courtesy gesture. Belgium's Foreign Minister, Paul Hymans, asked him to explain how his reasoning squared with the repeated declarations by Allied ministers that the war had been fought to uphold the rights of small nations. Orlando, for Italy, paid a flamboyant tribute to "*la France généreuse et glorieuse*," which but confirmed the suspicion that he was courting French support for the secret Treaty of London in defiance of Wilson.

Here, indeed, was the issue that bedeviled the conference from the beginning. Very soon Orlando would threaten Wilson that the Italians would withdraw from the meeting unless he modified some of his ideas. There was no need for him to be that fast on the draw. Confronted by the challenge from the outset, Wilson wavered and equivocated. Had he immediately braced, made this the make-or-break point, and staked American participation in the conference on the outcome, there can be little doubt that world opinion would have sustained him and that the partisans of the secret treaties would have been stopped. Arthur Balfour, Britain's Foreign Secretary, for one, loathed the secret treaties, but felt bound by the position "England has signed and England must keep her word."

Doing nothing to bail Balfour out, Wilson saw the hour swiftly pass when he might have changed the climate of the conference by one bold move. He started full of good will and tried to become dictatorial too late. When, belatedly, his opposition to the Italian claims came forth, it was reduced to personal pique against one offending country.

In consequence of the tone set at the beginning, great powers, for the first time in the modern history of Europe, acted in a radical spirit. In all previous meetings on the same scale, the disposition had been to patch and conciliate in accordance with the conservative tradition. In the 1815 Congress of Vienna the main purpose had been to undo the catastrophic consequences of the Napoleonic era. Likewise the Congress of Berlin in 1878 had minimized the results of the Russo-Turkish war. But apart from their submission to the doctrine of internationalism, the architects of the new Europe at Paris were guided by no new philosophy of life or politics in creating their design for a supposedly more stable future. Their partial acceptance of Wilson's novel principle of self-determination might be considered an exception; it cannot be said that its emergence has reduced world tensions since. Fear and ambition, rather than the dynamic of new doctrine, pervaded the councils. The statesmen of 1919 were as ill-prepared to make a modern peace as were the soldiers of 1914 to wage a modern war.

The work was done at first by the Council of Ten, the political heads of government and foreign ministers of Great Britain,

France, Italy, the United States, and Japan. The small powers had a place on the sidelines, where they awaited their fringe benefits.

There was Rumania, in the person of Prime Minister Ion Brătianu, claiming the whole of the Banat region, insisting that the secret treaty signed with the Allies in 1916 pledged nothing less. Wilson asked: "Does your claim go as far as Belgrade?" Brătianu said yes. He wanted the capital of Serbia though Serbia had been an ally. To that, Dr. Ante Trumbić, Foreign Minister of newly created Yugoslavia, replied that his country considered the 1916 treaty a dead letter. The eastern part of the Banat could go to Rumania; the western part must go to his state. Clemenceau, Lloyd George, and Wilson all approved of that arrangement. Orlando objected because he had made a deal to back Rumanian claims in exchange for Rumania's support of Italy's claims under the Treaty of London.

When Clemenceau asked Brătianu: "Will you agree to get the assent of the German and Magyar inhabitants of the Banat?" the Rumanian hotly refused. The principle of self-determination didn't cut that deep. Trumbić then volunteered that Yugoslavia would accept the principle provided it applied also to peoples of the borderland north of the Adriatic, who were in pawn to the Treaty of London. At that point the Western statesmen congratulated him and the Italians withdrew in a huff. The incident typifies how the bargaining went at Paris.

Partitioning of the Austro–Hungarian Empire was a nettlesome, unavoidable labor. The Czechs and Slovaks had been pledged a country of their own in return for services rendered to the Allied cause. So had the Poles. (So had the Jews under the Balfour Declaration of November 2, 1917, though they were much longer in getting it.) Both the Poles and the Czechs claimed Teschen, the mining district in Austrian Silesia. France and Britain supported the Czech claim, and when this was announced, Polish troops overran the region and drove off the local Czechs. The danger of a new war was averted by the patience of the Czech leaders. Amid the crisis, Lloyd George, who was sitting as a referee, made his confession: "I have never heard of Teschen." The Council of Ten had to sit as a geography class to get elementary instruction on the subject. Ultimately, it was disposed to Czechoslovakia. Years later when Hitler went after the Czechs, the Poles ganged up to wrest Teschen from their stricken neighbor.

At St.-Nazaire, on Memorial Day, 1919,
American soldiers honor the war dead before
returning home to the United States. The
Yanks returned to the U.S. slowly but,
unlike the casuals who streamed home after
World War II, they came back in whole
units at a time. The men who served were
heroes. Those who survived would know the
gratitude of victorious nations.

Colonel House recovered from the flu in time to sit on the League of Nations Commission and become, along with Wilson, one of the chief draftsmen of the Covenant. The Commission was appointed on January 25 and worked with great speed. The President wanted the Covenant in final form before he returned to Washington on February 15 for the closing of Congress.

There was a hitch immediately. Clemenceau demanded the creation of an international police force subject to the League's authority. Wilson would have none of it; he objected that the Constitution of the United States forbade any such encroachment on its sovereignty. Clemenceau countered that Wilson's position made of the Covenant a philosophical treatise devoid of practical authority. The President retorted: "This is intended as a constitution of peace and not as a league for war." Secretly, House sided with Clemenceau, but could not say so out loud. These diametrically opposing views stayed unreconciled while Wilson sailed west. The unresolved argument is no less alive today. It persists in the disagreement as to whether the United Nations can ever be a practical peace-keeping body when it has no permanent military forces.

Back in Washington, instead of following House's advice by conciliating the Republican Senators and tactfully seeking their support, Wilson did the opposite. In effect, he dared them to do their worst. Just before sailing for the return to France on March 4, he spoke in New York, saying: "When that treaty comes back, gentlemen on this side will find the Covenant not only in it, but so many threads of the treaty tied to the Covenant, that they cannot dissect the Covenant from the treaty without destroying the whole vital structure." By that outright defiance he again borrowed trouble. He could not imagine the Senate daring to reject the whole package.

In the interim, at Paris there had been no real progress on the main problem—establishing a peace with Germany. Convinced that the cart was being put before the horse, House met the President on his arrival at Brest on March 13 and tried to persuade him that the order of business should be reversed. He found the President obdurate; the whole Covenant would have to be fitted into the text of the treaty before any peace could be concluded. From this fundamental divergence of view developed the chill between the President and his closest adviser, which intensified until House was practically ostracized by Wilson.

Elsewhere, things were going badly for Wilson. The British press assailed him bitterly for tying together the League Covenant and the peace treaty. But foreign criticism, like the breach with House and his withdrawal from the other American peace commissioners, by increasing his isolation, doubled his intransigency.

Not until mid-March did the conference get to the main question —what to do with Germany. For a time it considered establishing a Rhineland republic as the key move toward keeping Germany permanently demilitarized. The French wanted it done; the British beat it down with the argument that it would inevitably provoke another war aimed at reuniting Germany. But when the Council of Ten faced the question of how to give Poland an outlet to the sea, it voted unanimously to award it the port of Danzig, which meant that Poland would have an enclave of several hundred thousand East Prussian Germans. Wilson was one of the most ardent backers of the idea. No one warned, no one foresaw, that the assignment thus easily made would become one of the provocations that would ignite the Second World War.

It was agreed that the Rhine bridgeheads of Cologne, Koblenz, and Mainz should be occupied for five, ten, and fifteen years respectively, with evacuation dependent on Germany's payment of reparations. The German Army would be cut to 100,000 men with an administrative staff of approximately 1,000 officers. There would be no air force or navy. Though none of these provisions was in itself unjust or unwise, the Versailles Treaty has been almost universally condemned as iniquitously cruel to Germany, and so vengeful that it could only stir vengeance.

A deep dread of German militarism survived in Europe, animating the peacemakers as they responded to the emotions of their peoples. The terms that they imposed would have fitted the Germany of 1914—armed to the teeth, worshiping the Kaiser because of his saber-rattling, contemptuous of democracy, organized for war, strong in industry, generally prosperous. Men like Clemenceau and Foch had 1914 Germany in mind—they had known no other. But when the terms were applied to 1919 Germany—a militarily bankrupt state struggling to make democracy work under a semisocialist government, its people half starving, its industry flattened and all commerce gone —they reflected only a timidity in the Allies that discredited both their victory and their faith in one another.

Bliss, wholly disconsolate, wrote his wife: "The wars are not over." While the peacemakers worked along, heavy-hearted and heavy-handed, the Poles quarreled with the Ukrainians, the Hungarians battled with the Rumanians, Greek troops prepared to land against Turkey, and Italy threatened to fight Yugoslavia over possession of Fiume and Dalmatia. Concurrently, the tensions at the table mounted. While the castle of the new internationalism took form, the fires of the old nationalism burned as brightly as ever. Over the opposition of Britain, Wilson insisted that the Covenant be amended to affirm the validity of the Monroe Doctrine. The French demanded that their language be made official for all League business. The Japanese added to the tumult by advancing an amendment that "endorsed the principle of the equality of nations and the just treatment of individuals," a shaft clearly aimed at the American Exclusion Act.

Clemenceau and Wilson were no longer on speaking terms. "Talk to Wilson?" the old Tiger exploded, "How can I talk to a fellow who thinks himself the first man for two thousand years who has known anything about peace on earth? Wilson imagines he is the second Messiah." That outburst was provoked by the matter of the Saar Basin. Members of the British delegation had prepared a formula: France was to have the Saar under a mandate for fifteen years, at the end of which there would be a plebiscite; meanwhile it was to be demilitarized. When the formula was shown to Wilson, he flew into a rage and shouted: "I will not have it. Unless my principles are accepted integrally, I will order the *George Washington* at once and go home." But while he did order the *George Washington*, he did not go home. Gradually his principles weakened. It remained for President de Gaulle and Chancellor Adenauer to work out an amicable solution to the Saar problem many years later by negotiating out of mutual respect. There was no such possibility in Paris in 1919.

The vanquished nations were not represented while the peace terms were being hammered out. The conference was a victor's brawl over the spoils. The problem above all problems at Paris was to restore the productivity of an impoverished world as swiftly as possible. Germany, the late enemy, the sinner, was potentially the great producer of the Continent. Deprived of German industry and energy, Europe had no chance for recovery. But the Allied statesmen acted as if their main purpose was to keep Germans in destitution and despair. In effect, they continued the war by other means, though by so doing they ignored history's moral that war is mere butchery unless it gives rise to a more stable peace. To criticize them for their harshness to the Germans seems almost irrelevant; what they did to their own people in consequence became the unpardonable folly.

They should have read the lesson in the landscape during that first agonizing winter of half-peace. While Wilson, Clemenceau, and Lloyd George glowered at one another, mulling over the problems of the treaties, blockade and famine induced successful, if short-lived, Communist revolutions in Bavaria and Hungary. There were other abortive attempts by red-flaggers in several main German cities. Pogroms against Jews were reported from Russia. Food relief expeditions had to be sent to the Balkans and the Middle East. The Paris peacemakers carried on as if all this were unrelated to their problems. Their actions indicate that they truly believed that civilization is saved by redrawing maps, and could not understand that political freedom is the child of economic health. There was no surer way to make the world unsafe for democracy.

On March 25 the Council of Ten gave way to the Council of Four—Wilson, Lloyd George, Clemenceau, and Orlando. The change was inspired by Lloyd George's resentment of an attack on him in the Paris press; it was decided that too many secrets were being leaked by the larger body. The object was to tighten security, despite all the flimflam about "open covenants openly arrived at." The change neither speeded action nor improved harmony.

Immediately the Shantung question came up. Its roots lay in an 1897 incident, the murder of two German missionaries by the Chinese. In the name of God and Himself, the Kaiser had landed an expedition at the port of Tsingtao, forced the Peking Government to cede Germany Kiaochow Bay on a ninety-nine-year lease, and prepared to take over rich Shantung province as a German protectorate. In 1914 the Japanese had besieged Tsingtao and with British help had wrested it from the Germans. Although China was also an ally, the Japanese, who joined the Council of Four on questions relating to the Orient, now proposed to take over the German claim. For the sake of simple justice, General Bliss urged the President strongly to oppose the claim. Japan announced that she would not sign the treaty unless she was accommodated. Because the Japanese had been very cordial about supporting the League of Nations, Wilson compromised, though as history records, Japan much later yielded her claim to Shantung only to turn her attention northward to Manchuria.

The north Adriatic problem came aboil when a rumor spread through the conference that Orlando was about to declare on his own that Fiume was annexed to Italy. Wilson met this head on by publishing, on April 23, an *ex parte* declaration that the rights of small states had to be scrupulously safeguarded, and hence, Italy could not have Fiume and the Dalmatian lands, which were rightfully Yugoslavian. The Italians were incited to a fever pitch of nationalism by Orlando's denunciations of the American President. Orlando temporarily withdrew from the peace conference, and the Big Four became the Big Three. None of this checked Italy's headlong course. The following September a coup staged by the poet Gabriele D'Annunzio grabbed Fiume for Italy and nobody did anything about it.

The Council of Three didn't operate any more smoothly. There was a wrangle over Belgian claims to Dutch Limburg and for priority on German reparations payments. Clemenceau accused Lloyd George repeatedly of making false statements. The Welshman arose, grabbed him by the collar, and demanded an apology. Wilson broke them apart. Clemenceau offered Lloyd George satisfaction "with either pistols or swords," but refused to withdraw one word he had said. Unblessed were the peacemakers.

Clemenceau stayed the same Tiger to the end of negotiations, and his spirit, more than any or all others, directed the judgment written on Germany. Wilson's idealism could not rebuff him; Lloyd George's political adroitness could not turn him from his main purpose of making the enemy pay, irrespective of the cost to future peace.

The Italians returned to Paris on May 6. The writer Harold Nicolson, who was with the British delegation, recorded his impression of the arrival of the Italians at a meeting in Lloyd George's flat: "We are still discussing when the flabby Orlando and the sturdy Sonnino [the Italian Foreign Minister] are shown into the dining-room. They all sit around the map. The appearance of a pie about to be distributed is thus enhanced. Ll. G. shows them what he suggests. They ask for Scala Nova as well. 'Oh no,' says Lloyd George, 'you can't have that. It's full of Greeks!' He goes on to point out that there are further Greeks at Marki and a whole wedge of them along the coast towards Alexandretta. 'Oh, no' I whisper to him, 'there are not many Greeks there.' 'But, yes,' he answers, 'don't you see it's colored green?' I then realized that he mistakes my map for an ethnological map and thinks the green means Greeks instead of valleys, and the brown means Turks instead of mountains. Ll. G. takes this correction with great good humor. He is quick as a kingfisher."

THE TREATY OF VERSAILLES

In mid-April, the German plenipotentiaries had been invited to come to France and hear the bad news; they had arrived in Versailles as the month ended and were housed in a minor dwelling surrounded by barbed wire, as one might handle POW's. The sentence that they were about to receive made the treatment appropriate. The solutions for the Saar and the Rhine's left bank, with some minor changes, were as the peacemakers had discussed them weeks earlier. Also, the right bank of the Rhine was to be demilitarized along a zone thirty miles deep. German rivers would be internationalized; the Kiel Canal would be opened to all nations. Germany, by signing the treaty, would acknowledge her sole responsibility for having caused the war. She would agree to turn over the Kaiser and other national leaders for trial as war criminals. She would agree, also, to pay for all civilian damage suffered by the Allied peoples during the war. The reparations bill was still being worked out, but a five-billion-dollar down payment would be required by May 1, 1921, and by signing the treaty, the Germans would put signature to a blank check covering the ultimate Allied estimate. It came out at thirty-two billion dollars but was never collected.

The insuperable handicap put upon Germany and the strangulating effect upon her industry from these exactions are demonstrated most clearly in terms of her coal losses. The Saar and Alsace-Lorraine mines had produced fourteen million tons annually; the Upper Silesian mines, now in the hands of the Poles, had yielded yearly forty-three million tons. Besides this outright diversion, twenty-five million tons annually was required of Germany in reparations payments to France, Belgium, and Italy. To power her existing industry, she needed 110 million tons each year. There would be left to her less than half of that.

Postwar Europe had nine new nations (dark gray areas). Italy
and Rumania were enlarged at the expense of Austria and Russia,
and Alsace-Lorraine was returned to France.

POSTWAR
EUROPE

ESTONIA

LATVIA

BALTIC
SEA

LITHUANIA

EAST
PRUSSIA

POLAND

RUSSIA

UKRAINE

SLOVAKIA

HUNGARY

RUMANIA

BLACK SEA

GOSLAVIA

BULGARIA

ALBANIA

TURKEY

GREECE

Scale
100   200   300 Miles

Crete

Cyprus

N

Heading the German delegation was the new Foreign Minister, Count Ulrich von Brockdorff-Rantzau, described as a stiff-necked aristocrat. He had been privately warned that the Allied terms would strip Germany, but he continued to believe that Wilson's influence finally would moderate them. With his colleagues he was summoned to the Trianon to hear the judgment on May 7, the peacemakers having chosen that day because it was the anniversary of another great sinking—the *Lusitania*'s. Clemenceau presided. Brockdorff-Rantzau made his little speech, assailing the Allies bitterly for continuing the blockade and declaring that Wilson's Fourteen Points were binding on all nations that signed the armistice. But he sat as he spoke and Clemenceau as well as Wilson took it as the final affront, though other Germans explained later that the Count's legs were too shaky to support him, which just possibly is the true story.

The meeting ended with the delegations glaring at one another. When they filed out, one German said to Clemenceau: "What will history say of this?" The Tiger replied: "It will not say that Belgium invaded Germany."

Brockdorff-Rantzau would not sign the treaty. The German Government promptly made public its terms. French newspapers lifted the information from that source. In this roundabout way, the American people and their Congress got their first information of the proposed settlement.

A messenger awakened Herbert Hoover in a Paris hotel at 4:00 A.M. to hand him a transcript of the treaty. He was so disturbed after reading it that he arose and walked the streets. "It seemed to me the economic consequences alone would pull down all Europe and thus injure the United States," he later wrote. As he strolled through an almost deserted Paris before dawn, he ran into General Jan Smuts and the economist John Maynard Keynes, who were equally agitated. Hoover said of their talk: "We agreed that it was terrible and we would do what we could . . . to make the dangers clear."

Lloyd George was having second thoughts. He too saw the fallacy of the harsh terms, though a trifle belatedly, and he begged his colleagues to be more reasonable, cut reparations, revise the Eastern frontiers, and permit Germany to enter the League, instead of treating her as an outcast. This time it was not Clemenceau but Wilson who refused to yield an inch. The principles no longer mattered; he wished his League to remain pure in heart.

The Germans had to return to Paris. Only by signing a peace could they get the blockade lifted and better their near-starvation diet. But all over the country there were mass meetings in protest. The illusion persisted in Germany that the army had not been decisively beaten but had merely conceded on points to end the slaughter. Chancellor Philipp Scheidemann cried: "May the hand wither that signs such a peace!" His dramatics were as senseless as the public fury. The High Command said the peace had to be signed; there was no possibility of resuming the war.

So another delegation of secondary figures took the painful road to Versailles. On June 28 the papers were completed amid pomp and pageantry staged to titillate the victors. The scene was the same Hall of Mirrors where almost one-half century before, Bismarck had proclaimed the German Empire.

The last link with empire had gone to the bottom a week earlier. More tellingly than the signing, it expressed the bitterness that would last. Under the caretaking of German crews, the German High Seas Fleet had ridden captive on the waters of Britain's Scapa Flow. France expected to get most of the big ships. But while the British Navy watched dumbfounded, the Germans scuttled them on June 21, and the great prizes went down. There was a last long wail about the treachery of the enemy, which by no means dimmed the peace-signing festivities.

In Paris, bands blared, impromptu parades formed, and champagne flowed like water. At Versailles guns thundered, fountains spouted colored foam, and thousands cheered. While the Allied statesmen posed for the cameras, two Germans walked forward, poker-faced, and signed the long documents. In this way, Hermann Müller and Dr. Johannes Bell entered the pages of history, which makes no other note of them.

Frock-coated, Wilson and Lloyd George sat at the center of the horseshoe table reserved for the Allied principals. The Old Tiger again served as ringmaster. When the deed was done, he turned, his eyes brimming with tears, and murmured: "Yes, it is a beautiful day." True, the June air sparkled. But he wasn't thinking about the weather. Not everyone on his side of the table shared his emotions. Mrs. House had her moment of ecstasy when she jumped to her feet saying: "I must stand long enough to see my lamb sign." Her lamb did not share her enthusiasm. Later, House wrote of the gaudy spectacle: "It was not unlike when in olden times the conqueror dragged the conquered at his chariot wheel." Old Soldier Bliss, communing with his diary about what would come of the day's business, won a niche among the prophets: "We are in for a high period, followed by a low period. Then there will be the devil to pay all around the world." It was an inspired weather forecast, covering the next twenty years.

Following the Germans, the Austrians came to Saint-Germain-en-Laye just outside of Paris on September 10, 1919, to sign their treaty. Bulgaria got around to it on November 27 of the same year at Neuilly, which is a less ostentatious suburb of the French capital. Almost one year after the Germans signed, the Hungarians came to the Trianon Palace at Versailles and signed their contract on June 4, 1920. Turkey was last of all. Her treaty was completed at Sèvres, France, on August 20, 1920, but was later moderated by the Treaty of Lausanne, July 24, 1923. By then both the world and Woodrow Wilson had long since lost interest in the proceedings.

Consequent to the treaty signings, which were in no real sense negotiations, Rumania, after having fought so badly, emerged, relatively speaking, more heavily bloated with spoils than any other Allied nation. Hardly less gorged was Italy, whose arms, through three years of futile struggle, won almost nothing of what she ultimately dragged in. The maldistribution of loot stemmed directly from the secret treaties. In the end they triumphed over Wilsonian principles because they were more vigorously and viciously demanded. To speculate about how world fortune might have been changed had the victors seen fit to attempt continuing the Austro-Hungarian combine on a republican basis is perforce idle. The perpetuation of their union wasn't considered; split asunder, they separately became the two great losers of the war. In fact, they were treated as if the main object was to make all of Central Europe suffer into the future for Count Berchtold's sins of the summer of 1914.

Hungary under the empire had been a land of eighteen million people possessing 283,000 square kilometers of territory. It was reduced to less than eight million people with more than two thirds of the lands gone. The partitioning of the predominantly Slav-settled areas, in the process of establishing the newly independent states of Poland, Yugoslavia, and Czechoslovakia, had something to do with that. But not all. More than three million Magyars became separated from the main body of their people.

About the same number of Austro-Germans were incorporated into Czechoslovakia. Another quarter million, living in the South Tyrol, were put under the Italian flag. Truncated Austria would have preferred union with Germany for the sake of survival, having lost her ports and markets; it was forbidden. At the time, none of the peacemakers worried much about that; the grafting of the Sudeten Germans onto the body of the new Czech state caused as little concern. The trouble was that no one foresaw the rise of Hitler. He used bayonets and tanks to bring off the forbidden *Anschluss* with Austria in 1938. Afterward, the plight of the Sudeten Germans provided him with an excuse for the aggressions against Czechoslovakia.

Bulgaria lost her ports on the Aegean Sea and great stretches of her territory to Greece and Rumania. Under the secret treaty arrangement, Hungarian Transylvania went to Rumania. Then in a rash moment Rumania annexed Russian Bessarabia, for which crime the Soviets were bound to take vengeance in time. Italy grabbed Fiume and was given the South Tyrol, the Trentino, the port of Trieste, and Rhodes and the Dodecanese Islands, the latter at the expense of Turkey. She was balked in her claims for most of the islands off Dalmatia and Albania. From that came an unrighteous resentment, which smoldered past the day when Mussolini grabbed Albania in a bloodless airborne coup.

Turkey came out of the war no longer a Middle East empire but a shrunken and economically prostrate rump state. In the end, she barely retained her position on both sides of the Turkish Straits, holding onto Constantinople (Istanbul) and a strip of adjoining territory. But Palestine, oil-rich Mesopotamia, the holdings of the Arabian peninsula and Sinai, the land bridge to Suez and Africa, were forever gone. The coastline of Asia Minor and the Anatolian Plateau remained in Turkey.

Under a League of Nations mandate, the British took control of Palestine, Transjordan, and Mesopotamia; the French brought Lebanon and Syria under their not-too-protective wing. The transition for the German colonies in Africa was arranged in much the same way. Germany was stripped of all her holdings abroad. Some of the colonies were annexed by the victors. Others were administered by one or another of the powers under a League mandate, which operated not unlike a receivership. This form of government fell into disrepute during the League's existence because its thinly disguised ownership appeared to extend the colonial system. The fact remains that it was highly useful in promoting the welfare of underdeveloped areas.

Three nations—Austria-Hungary, Montenegro, and Serbia—disappeared from the map of Europe. Nine new independent states, three of which have since disappeared, came into existence. The Baltic States of Latvia, Lithuania, and Estonia established their independence of Russia in World War I only to have the Soviets reincorporate them in World War II. The other new countries were Poland, Czechoslovakia, Yugoslavia, Austria, and Hungary. Finland had won its freedom from Russia before the Bolsheviks consolidated their power. Even so, Finnish independence owes its birth to help from the German Free Corps and the leadership of a brilliant soldier, Marshal Carl von Mannerheim, though its continuation is due to the fierce feeling for liberty that burns in the hearts of several million Finns.

The peace settlement not only stripped Middle Europe of its central nervous system, the Austro-Hungarian Empire; it eliminated a common market in a large, greatly productive, and strategically decisive area. Trade barriers were raised all around. Weakening the small states economically, these walls made it impossible for them to join strength in any common cause.

With one exception—Austria—the succession states became easy victims of the Soviet march in the later years. Either they turned on their own toward communism, as happened with Yugoslavia under Marshal Tito, or they became trapped behind the Iron Curtain. Their struggle for a meaningful independence continues into the future with no terminus or improved prospect in sight.

THE SENATE AND THE LEAGUE

After signing the treaty on June 28, Wilson tarried in Europe just long enough to attend one final official dinner hosted by President Poincaré, then boarded the *George Washington* and headed for home.

What had been done merely deepened his anxiety. Unlike the other chief negotiators, his six-month sojourn in Paris had put him in tremendous political jeopardy. Clemenceau was at his own seat of government. Lloyd George was moving to and from his own capital regularly. Orlando could get to Rome overnight. If the onerous peace that these three had helped settle on Europe was not precisely what their peoples desired, it is at least of record that each won an immediate endorsement of his actions in the next elections. With Wilson, it was different. For one-half year, he had virtually isolated himself from the affairs of politics. There had been a prolonged break in his intense, highly personalized direction of government and in his evangelizing for a new world order. Over distance some of the magnetism faded. His opposition made the most of a golden opportunity.

On July 10, Wilson appeared before the Senate. The heavy, bound volume of the Treaty of Versailles was placed on the clerk's desk. When he spoke, his words in effect challenged the Senate to withhold ratification. There was the Covenant and he orated as a fiery Covenanter: "Dare we reject it and break the heart of the world? The stage is set, the destiny disclosed. It has come about by no plan of our conceiving but by the hand of God who led us into this way."

Wilson's high line was no more palatable to Republican Senator Henry Cabot Lodge of Massachusetts than it had been to Clemenceau. As Chairman of the Foreign Relations Committee, he was now in the driver's seat, and he would not be rushed, despite the President's plea for speedy ratification. He announced that public hearings would be held on the treaty beginning some time late in the month. They would be wide open to public and press.

From the beginning, the Senators heard so much adverse testimony that the President became appalled. In an effort to mend matters, on August 19, the Committee as a whole was invited by Wilson to a private conference in the White House. The resulting wrangle between the President and his Republican critics lasted three and one-half hours and by the end the President knew that the Committee would never approve the treaty as written.

Senator Hiram Johnson of California lashed out at Wilson's easy concession to Japan on the Shantung issue. Other Senators were concerned about the islands mandated to Japan and the consequence to America's strategic position in the Pacific. There was general objection to the committing of U.S. troops to the occupation of Germany, possibly for fifteen years. There were vexed questions about Article X of the Covenant, by which the United States would pledge to join its Allies "to preserve as against external aggression the territorial integrity and existing political independence" of any member of the League. Senator Johnson wanted to know what would be the consequence if the United States failed to ratify. The treaty supplied only the negative answer that it bound a nation from the time of that nation's signature.

The conference convinced Wilson that the majority of the Committee had hardened against the treaty and he decided to carry his case to the people. He started on September 3. In the early stages, for the most part, it was a bold and convincing performance, though he already suffered acutely from blinding headaches. The cheering masses turned out wherever his train stopped. Great parades were organized in support of his cause. The press gave it maximum coverage. In less than one month he toured 8,000 miles and delivered thirty-six prepared speeches and many impromptu talks from the rear platform.

But even while his health held, it was not an uninterrupted triumph. The Senate hearings were continuing. What the Committee heard was relayed to the President. The unkindest cut of all was when Wilson learned that Secretary of State Lansing disapproved of both the Shantung agreement and the League Covenant. It stunned him. He cried to his secretary, Joe Tumulty: "My God, I did not think it was possible for Lansing to act in this way."

The finish came aboard the train, en route from Pueblo to Wichita. He was hit by a light stroke and his surgeon ordered the Special to return to Washington. Three days later the diagnosis was cerebral thrombosis. For months he was desperately ill, and the vigor of mind and body never returned. While his tenure lasted, the nation was virtually without a President, and Wilson was scarcely conscious of the magnitude of his defeat.

The play continued to its predestined end, not unlike a Greek tragedy. Senator Lodge did not fit the role of the bitter intransigent in which history casts him. He tried to get to the White House with some reservations that would make the treaty acceptable. The President either would not or could not answer him. Mrs. Wilson tried to persuade her husband to moderate his attitude. She quotes him as saying: "Better a thousand times to go down fighting." But he was already down and no longer fighting.

On November 19, 1919, the treaty was beaten in the Senate. There was another try the following March with the same result. The stricken President survived by four years the death of his life's main undertaking.

A Beer Hall in Munich

While Mr. Wilson lived on in invalidism, the Great Powers, from November, 1921, to February, 1922, held a conference in Washington on the limitation of naval armaments. Their delegates agreed to scrap certain ships and withhold from building others, according to prescribed quotas. The dreamers believed that what had been wrought might well usher in the new era of lasting peace. Four years later, European statesmen got together at Locarno on Lake Maggiore. Italy and Britain agreed to guarantee Germany against any military adventuring by the French. The three Allies undertook to sponsor Germany for League membership, ending her seven-year ostracism. They further pledged to proceed with their own disarmament, which under the Versailles Treaty was to follow in due course the demilitarizing of Germany. Everywhere, the spirit of Locarno was hailed as a monument of redemption affirming European conciliation on the road to world unity. When in 1928 other statesmen met at Paris to sign a pact outlawing war, men really began to believe that these star-spangled meetings, decisions, and proclamations would determine the shape of things to come.

Compared to the attention centered on the hopeful conferences, an unpleasant incident in Munich in 1923 had gone almost unnoted. Erich Ludendorff was by then on the verge of madness. Three years earlier he had plotted, in Berlin, the violent overthrow of the Republic. When the so-called Kapp Putsch failed grotesquely, Ludendorff was permitted to retire with honor intact to Bavaria to set up another conspiratorial headquarters.

There he met the ex-corporal, Adolf Hitler. His Nazi Party, begun in 1919 with seven members, now had 70,000 men who marched, uniformed and armed. Hitler and Ludendorff teamed to plot revolution with Bavaria's political leaders. On November 8 there was a mass rally of nationalists and monarchists in the Bürgerbräu beer hall. Dr. Gustav von Kahr, State Commissioner of Bavaria, spoke, denouncing the Republic but adding that the time was not ripe for armed revolt. Midway in his speech, Hitler pushed him from the podium, drew a pistol, and fired two shots into the ceiling. Screaming that the revolution was on, he ordered his troopers to bar the exits, then drew the Bavarian leaders aside and begged them to join him and see the adventure through. While he talked, he wept with excitement, pistol in one hand, beer stein in the other. Suddenly Ludendorff appeared in

THE LEGACY OF WORLD WAR I

full uniform, all bemedaled, adding his urging to Hitler's. The Bavarians appeared to yield, but were dissembling.

There followed a night of wild disorder in Munich, the smashing of trade union halls and republican newspapers, raiding of Jewish homes, and an attempt to seize the rail station and post office. But troops and police were forming to thwart the rioters. So Hitler knew that Kahr and the other Bavarians were double-crossing him.

At dawn he ordered a parade of his followers to rouse the people and intimidate resistance. The swastika flags got only as far as the main square. There the police and soldiers were formed in strength. Then came a volley of rifle fire, badly aimed in that it missed the only two figures who counted. Hitler broke his shoulder in a dive for the pavement. Eighteen of his men were dead from the fire; many others lay wounded. The one erect figure was Ludendorff. In full regalia, he marched straight toward the troops barring the way. They opened a lane and let him pass. Such was the last significant appearance of the Robot Napoleon on history's stage. His soul kept marching with the brown-shirt army. Many of its ideas, and no small part of its mythology and vocabulary, were drawn from the ravings of this senile worshiper of Thor.

On the morning after the failure of the Beer Hall Putsch, good Germans congratulated themselves that they had been thus easily delivered from a small-time menace. Hitler, the fugitive, was expected to trouble them no more.

PICTURE CREDITS

All maps: American Heritage Picture
    Collection
Title Page, drawing by John W. Thomason,
    Jr.: Imperial War Museum
Table of Contents, drawing by Sir William
    Orpen: Collection of Mrs. J. W.
    Thompson
6:    UPI
22:   Bild-Archiv, Ost. Nationalbibliothek,
      Vienna
31:   UPI
41:   L'Illustration
49:   Musée de la Guerre
54:   Imperial War Museum
62:   Historishes Bildarchiv, Bad Burweck
77:   L'Illustration
94:   Imperial War Museum
122: American Heritage Picture Collection
126: Imperial War Museum
131: L'Illustration
145: Reuters
159: Department of the Army
162: UPI
182: L'Illustration

202: Musée de la Guerre
216: Imperial War Museum
226: Kriegsarchiv, Vienna
231: Imperial War Museum
234: Louis Raemakers, *The Great War*, 1916
246: Musée de la Guerre
259: Imperial War Museum
265: Imperial War Museum
268: UPI
274: New York Public Library
278: USSC, National Archives
291: Imperial War Museum
294: National Archives
306: Imperial War Museum
310: Imperial War Museum
315: European Picture Service
320: L'Illustration
325: L'Illustration
335: L'Illustration
339: Imperial War Museum
346: Imperial War Museum
351: Weltkriegsbücherei, Stuttgart
356: National Archives
368: National Archives
383: New York Public Library
390: Smithsonian Institute
394: U.S. Signal Corps
401: Smithsonian Institute
415: Imperial War Museum
420: Smithsonian Institute
429: U.S. Signal Corps
442: U.S. Signal Corps
454: Wide World Photos
456: National Portrait Gallery
465: State Historical Society of Wisconsin
482: UPI

INDEX

Italic page numbers refer to
illustrations.

A

and the proposed armistice
draft, 443–44
quoted on:
delay of the Paris Peace
Conference, 461
German trade after the war,
461
and the signing of the Versailles
Treaty, 476
Blockades, British/German, 165,
214
Blücher (ship), 164
Blue Devils. *See* French Army, 47th
Chasseur Alpine Division
Blunden, Edmund, quoted, 258
Boehn, General Max von, 396
Bois de la Brigade de Marine. See
Belleau Wood
Boisdeffre, General, quoted on
mobilization and war, 21
Bojna, General Borojevic von, 174
Bolimów, 161
Bolsheviks, 269
Allied attitude toward, 334–36
Kerensky and, 324, 326
negotiate with German High
Command for peace, 328
and the treaty of Brest Litovsk,
333
Boos-Waldeck, Count, 10
Bordeaux, 296
Bosnia, 8, 9
Bössau, Lake, 106
Botchkareva, Mme., *320*
Botha, General Louis, 198
campaign in German Southwest
Africa, 198, 200
Bothmer, Count, 324
Boulanger, General Georges Ernest
Jean Marie, 20
Bourbon, Prince Sixt de, 319
Bouresches, 381
Bouvet (ship), 154
Brandenburgers, 245
Brătianu, Ion, 464
Breslau (cruiser), 118–20
Brest Litovsk, Treaty of, 327–34,
339
Briand, Aristide, 256

British Expeditionary Force
(B.E.F.)
digging trenches and, 59
First Battle of Ypres and, 137
first casualties, *131*
first commander, 65–66
gas attack victims, *182*
in 1915, 208
in race to the North Sea, 129–30
recruiting poster, *216*
reserves, 230, 232
soldier shares cigarette with
German POW, *415*
status at the beginning of the
war, 53
and the U. S. II Corps, 405
First Army
in Artois, 228–29
in the Meuse-Argonne
offensive, 433
Second Army
in Flanders, 437
in the Meuse-Argonne
offensive, 433
at Messines (map), *298*
and Ypres, *298*, 300, 301,
304
Third Army
at Cambrai, 316–18
Fourth Army, 358
at Amiens, 412–19
in the Meuse-Argonne
offensive, 433
at the Somme, 258
at Ypres, 301
Fifth Army
and Operation Michael, 343,
349, 350, 352, 353–57
at Ypres, 301, 304
I Corps, 65
at Aubers Ridge, 205, 207
at Ypres, 135
II Corps, 65
in the invasion of Belgium,
70
at Le Cateau, 71
III Corps, 356
at Amiens, 414, 417
IV Corps, 134

C

Kornilov, General Lavr Georgie-
vich, 324
Kosovo Polje, 196
Kovno. *See* Grodno and Kovno
Kraków, 112
Kraut, Major, 100
Kress, Colonel von, 119
Kreuznach Conference, 329–30
Krithia, 183, 189
Krupp works, 44, 224
Krylenko, Nikolai, 326, 327–28
Kuhl, General von, 92
Kuhlmann, Baron Richard von,
329, 330
Kurland, 328
Kut-al-Imara, 266, 309
Kuwait, 266

L

Labyrinth, The, 229
Lacaze, Admiral Marie Jean, 262
Langemarck, 167
Langle de Cary, General Fernand
de, 70–71, 74, 238
Lanjus, Countess, 10
Lanrezac, General Charles, 66, 70,
83
Lansdowne, Lord, 267
Latvia, 478
Lausanne, Treaty of, 476
Lavalbonne, 453
Lawrence, T. E., 266, *306*, 309
Le Cateau, Battle of, 71
Le Fretoy, 417
Le Hamel, 389
Le Quesnel, 416
Le Rocq Plateau, 392
Le Tronquoy, 417
League of Nations Commission,
466
Lebel rifle, 17
Leinster (mail boat), torpedoing of,
443
Leipzig (cruiser), 148
Leman, General Gérard Mathieu,
61, 63
Lemberg, 113, 219

Lenin, Nikolai
calls for peace, 326
Ludendorff and, 321
and overthrow of the Russian
Provisional Government,
321–27
reaction to Wilson's Fourteen
Points, 348
and the Revolution of 1917, 273
and the Treaty of Brest Litovsk,
331–32, 333
Lens, 205–6
Leopold, Prince, 217, 321
Lersner, Baron Kurt von, 439–40
Lettow-Vorbeck, Colonel Paul
von, 200
Leviathan (troop carrier), 458
Lewis, General Edward M., 378
Liberty engine, 313
Lichnowsky, Prince Karl Max, 29,
33, 50
Liège, invasion of, 60–63
Liggett, General Hunter, 388,
411, 446
Lille, 157
Liman von Sanders, General Otto,
121, 176, 181, 183, 406
Lion (ship), 250, 252
Lippmann, Walter, 347
Lithuania, 328, 478
Little Napoleon. *See* Enver Pasha
Liverdun, bombing of, 409
Lloyd George, David
asks Pétain why his army is
not fighting, 299
attends meeting to circumvent
the Fourteen Points, 441
becomes Prime Minister, 262
and Winston Churchill, *145*
conscription and, 242
and the dismissal of Sir Douglas
Haig, 287
is appointed War Minister, 255–
56
meeting with Haig and Joffre at
the Somme, 261
and Operation Michael, 349
at the Paris Peace Conference,
470

prohibition and, 256
seizure of Passchendaele Ridge, 300
sets up a new War Committee, 301
suggests sending the British Army to the Mediterranean, 125
at the Supreme War Council in Rapallo, 305, 307
and the Versailles Treaty, 474, 475
and victory at Jerusalem, 309
visits Joffre and Haig on Western Front, *231*
Locarno Conference, 481
Lodge, Henry Cabot, 479
Lodz, 146
London, Treaty of, 172
Loos, 169, 229–30
Lorraine. *See* Alsace and Lorraine
Lossberg, Colonel von, 301, 304
Lublin, 112
Lucy, 381
Ludendorff, General Erich, *351*
  aims to smash the B.E.F., 343–45
  Alsace and Lorraine and, 319
  Amiens and, 360, 418
  at Avesnes, 418
  and the Battle of Cambrai, 318
  and the Battle of Lys, 364
  becomes First Quartermaster General, 261
  Beer Hall Putsch and, 481–83
  breaks down in front of his staff, 438
  and the Cats-Kemmel hill, 366
  and continuation of the war (1918), 340–41
  and the Eastern Front, 99–101, 141, 142, 143
  after first German drive toward Warsaw, 146
  and the Fourteen Points, 348, 443
  and the German Army, 391
  and German submarine warfare, 277

in the invasion of Belgium, 61, 63, 64
  is dismissed, 447
  Kapp Putsch and, 481
  Lenin and, 321
  meeting with Hindenburg, 100
  mines of Belgium and, 460
  offensive operations (1918), 344
  and Operation Michael, 352
  and overthrow of the Russian Provisional Government, 322
  and the Paris Gun, 362
  quoted on the American soldier, 388
  and second German drive toward Warsaw, 146
  at the strategy conference at Pless, 218
  and the tactic of infiltration, 341
  and the taking of Warsaw, 219
  and the tank, 318
  Tannenberg and, 103, 106, 108
  and the treaty of Brest Litovsk, 328–34
  Vilna plan, 221, 222
  warns of the German defeat, 440
Ludwig III, King, 455
Lusitania, sinking of, 166
Lutzow (ship), 250, 252
Luxembourg, invasion of, 51
Luxemburg, Rosa, 439
Lvov. *See* Lemberg
Lvov, Prince Georgi, 272, 273
Lyautey, General Louis, 262
Lyddite (explosive), 18
Lys, Battle of, *182, 364*

M

McAdoo, William Gibbs, 315
McAlexander, Colonel Ulysses Grant, 397
McAndrew, Major General James W., 371
MacArthur, Charles, 396
MacArthur, General Douglas, 396

and the Revolution of 1917, 272
and the Russian Duma, 224
Russian mobilization and, 38, 40
takes command of Russian
  forces, 222–23
General Tatistchev and, 39
Nicolson, Harold, quoted, 470
Niemen River, 109
Night bombing, 409
Nivelle, General Robert, 248, 261
Nivelle offensive, 284–93
Nord canal, 317
North Sea. *See also* Ypres,
  Battles of
movements toward, 129–33
Northern Pacific (troop carrier), 458
Novikh, Grigori. *See* Rasputin
Nürnberg (cruiser), 148

O

Ocean (battleship), 154
Oceania, 163
O'Connell, James, 249
Odessa, 120
Orlando, Vittorio E.
at the Supreme War Council in
  Rapallo, 305
attends meeting to circumvent
  the Fourteen Points, 441
at the Paris Peace Conference,
  462–63, 470
reaction to Wilson's Fourteen
  Points, 348
Orpen, Sir William, sketch by, *346*
Ostroda. *See* Tannenberg, Battle of
Ourcq River, 410–11

P

Paar, General Count, 12
Page, Walter Hines, 276
Painlevé, Paul, 287, 289, 305, 307
Paléologue, Maurice, 36, 37
Palestine
  General Allenby in, *310*, 405,
    406, 438

disposition after the war, 477
Paris
  French Government leaves, 82
  defense of the city, 83, 86
Paris Basin, 410
Paris Gun, 361–63
Paris Peace Conference, 462–71
  Council of Four, 469
  Council of Ten, 463–64
  Council of Three, 470
  U. S. delegation, 459
Paris-Metz Road, 378, 383, 385
Paris-Nancy Railway, 392
Pasić, Premier, 30, 32
Passchendaele Ridge, 300–305, 437
  Allied advance (map), *298*
Patton, General George S., Jr., 428
Pavlovich, Dimitri, 270
Pershing, General John J.
  at the Abbeville conference, 367
  assesses manpower require-
    ments for the war, 296
  and Georges Clemenceau, 447
  contemplates where to base his
    advance guard, 296
  estimates manpower to win the
    war, 387–88
  first all-American offensive
    and, 421
  headquarters, 297
  and an independent American
    Army, 406
  is put in charge of American
    troops in France, 282–83
  1916 expedition into Mexico,
    279
  after Operation Michael, 360–
    61
  Paris and, 378
  puts General Harbord in com-
    mand of Services of
    Supply, 407
  releases his first five divisions
    for the Marne area, 373
  relinquishes First Army com-
    mand, 446
  at Senlis meeting, 444
  sails to France, 284
  Saint-Mihiel and, 423, 431

S

Vienna, administration of Bosnia and Herzegovina, 9–10
Vierzy, 402
Vigneulles, 430
Villa, Pancho, 277
Villers-Bretonneaux Plateau, 389
Vilna, 221–22
Vimy Ridge, 157, 204
Viviani, Premier René
    French neutrality and, 41, 42
    good-will mission to Russia, 35
Voie Sacrée, La, 247
Von der Tann (ship), 250
Vorwärts, 439

W

W-Beach (Gallipoli), 179, 180
Waldersee, Count Alfred von, 20–21, 95, 97, 98
Wangenheim, Baron von, 117
    and Turkey's entrance into the war, 118
War songs, 267
Warren, Senator Francis, 282
Warrior (ship), 252
Warsaw
    fall of, 215–23
    first German drive toward, 143–44
Warspite (ship), 252
Watt, Richard M., quoted on traditional methods of warfare, 139
Wavre, 99
Wehle, Colonel von, 200
Weygand, General Maxime, 450
White, Chief Justice Edward Douglass, 280
Whittlesey, Major Charles W., 446
"Whizz-bangs," 237
Wiesner, Friedrich von, 25
Wilhelm I, Kaiser, 16
    alliance of 1879 and, 18–19
    Alliance of the Three Emperors, 18
    death of, 19
Wilhelm II, Kaiser

agrees to send out peace feelers, 439
assassination of Francis Ferdinand and, 12
Austria-Hungary's ultimatum to Serbia and, 30
becomes ruler of Germany, 20
Belgian neutrality and, 57
calls a meeting of the German High Command at Avesnes, 418
dismisses Bismarck, 20
dismisses Ludendorff, 447
early life, 19
German Navy and, 23
is told of the armistice, 451
leaves Germany, 425, 451
neutrality of France and, 51
North Sea cruise, 28
and a one-front war against Russia, 50
orders unrestricted submarine warfare, 275–76
peace and, 267
pledges Austria his loyalty, 27–28
proclaims *Kriegsgefahr Zustand*, 40
quoted on the outbreak of war, 50
Russian mobilization and, 38
Turkey and, 116
at Ypres, 135
Wilhelmina (freighter), 165
Wilson, General Sir Henry, 337
    at the Doullens meeting, 357, 358
    and the drafting of the German armistice, 444
    takes over as Chief of Staff, 339
Wilson, Woodrow
    announces the signing of the armistice, 453
    asks for a declaration of war, 280–81
    asks Germans to reconsider the Fourteen Points, 447
    attitude toward the war in 1915, 165